P9-BAW-327

The Social Work Interview

ALFRED KADUSHIN

THE
SOCIAL WORK
INTERVIEW

Second Edition

Columbia University Press
New York   1983

Library of Congress Cataloging in Publication Data
Kadushin, Alfred.
The social work interview.

Bibliography: p.
Includes index.
1. Interviewing.   2. Social service.   I. Title.
HV43.K26 1983   361.3'22   82-23670
ISBN 0-231-04762-2
ISBN 0-231-04763-0 (pbk.)

Columbia University Press
New York   Guildford, Surrey

Copyright © 1983 Columbia University Press
All rights reserved
Printed in the United States of America

Clothbound editions of Columbia University Press books are Smyth-sewn and printed
on permanent and durable acid-free paper.

361.322
K11s

To my family,
in appreciation and with love

38383

Contents

The Social Work Interview

Introduction

Many people, representing many different professions, conduct interviews. Social workers are only one such group. But for social workers, interviewing is a very important activity. They spend a great deal of time interviewing, and much of what they are responsible for doing depends on interviewing. Although social work interviews are, in many respects, like all others, they differ in some crucial ways, reflecting what is unique about social work. This book describes the general art of interviewing as adapted and enacted by social workers in a social work setting. The image of the reader that most frequently came to me in writing was of a relatively inexperienced social worker struggling on the job with all of the recurrent problems of interviewing, and seeking some specific guidelines and answers. In addition, I believe that experienced practitioners may profit from an explicit examination of their interviews and I hope this book may stimulate such self-assessment.

Because interviewing is the most consistently and frequently employed social work technique, because it is so much a part of all that social workers do, a book focused on interviewing faces a special problem. It is difficult to single out interviewing and discuss it as a separate skill, but I have aimed at a discussion of interviewing rather than of casework or integrated methods.

A major part of the book is concerned with the techniques of social work interviewing. *Technique* has a bad sound—cold, mechanical, inhuman, manipulative—applicable to things but not to people. It carries considerable negative freight. The word deserves to be rescued, its image refurbished. Techniques are devices whose application enables us to accomplish our purposes, to carry out our professional responsibilities. They are clear formulations of what we should do in a given situation to offer our service effectively and efficiently. They need not be learned by rote, mechanically or inflexibly. They are, in fact, learned best when the student understands the theoretical basis for their use. Techniques are best applied when the interviewer chooses among them with discrimination.

The interviewer should, of course, be the master of the techniques rather than their obedient servant, bound by rules. Technical skill is not antithetical to spontaneity. In fact, it permits a higher form of spontaneity. The skilled interviewer can deliberately violate the techniques as the occasion demands. Technical skill frees the interviewer in responding as a fellow human being to the interviewee. Errors in relation to technique lie with rigid, and therefore inappropriate, application. A good knowledge of techniques makes the interviewer aware of a greater variety of alternatives. Awareness and command of technical knowledge also has another advantage. To know is to be prepared; to be prepared is to experience reduced anxiety; to reduce anxiety is to increase the interviewer's freedom to be fully responsive to the interviewee.

A mastery of technology is a necessary prerequisite to competent artistry. The French say that "it is necessary to know geometry to build a cathedral; building a cathedral is, however, an act of faith"—and, I would add, an artistic creation. But neither the act of faith nor the artistic creation would have been possible without the knowledge of geometry.

But all of this is, in part, an aspect of an old controversy—the conflict between an analytical and an intuitive approach to people and their problems; between general, monothetic knowledge and unique, individual, idiographic knowledge. Technique requires generalization. It places the emphasis on the elements that are common to different interviews, making feasible a common response. An approach that rejects the emphasis on techniques focuses on what is unique about each interview encounter. While every human being is different from all others in some respects, all are alike in other respects. To the extent that each human being is like others, there are regularities that one can anticipate as one moves from one interviewee to another—regularities that legitimize techniques appropriate to all interviews.

One objection to concern with technique derives from yet another attitude prevalent among social workers, the sentiment that technique is unimportant, a poor, secondary consideration to the feeling the worker has for the client. If this feeling is right, then everything will be right; if it is wrong, then no technical expertise can rescue the interview from failure. The viewpoint is expressed well in the Chinese maxim, "When the right man uses the wrong means, the wrong means work in the right way; when the wrong man uses the right means, the right means work in the wrong way." But what then is the power of the right man using the right means in the right way? Surely he accomplishes more, more efficiently, than the right man using the wrong means even if they do work, for him, in the right way.

Many might say that if they had to choose between feeling and technique they would choose feeling as the more important prerequisite. Perhaps so, but if one has to make a choice between these qualifications, an injustice has already been done to the client. It should be possible to offer the client an interviewer who is both attitudinally correct and technically proficient. The best interviewer is one who combines the appropriate feeling and attitude with skilled interviewing techniques.

My opinion is that in balancing the requirements of attitude and technique we have exaggerated the importance of feeling and attitude and underestimated the importance of knowledge and technique. The proper attitude does not have the exclusive priority we have assumed; technique is not as secondary as we have supposed. Social work has generally given emphasis to the act of faith—our values, our philosophy, our general attitudinal stance that stresses our desire to be helpful and our confidence in our helpfulness. It is time we emphasized "geometry," the necessary technical knowledge that gives substance to our faith and enables us to implement our good will.

The greater measure of truth lies, as is so often the case, not with "either-or" but "both." If technique without feeling is ineffectual, feeling without technique is inefficient. If technical competence without compassion is sterile, compassion without competence is an exercise in futility.

A good relationship is a necessary but not sufficient condition for good interviewing. Good technique permits optimum utilization of a relationship. A good technician working in the context of a modest relationship is apt to achieve better outcomes than a technically inept interviewer in an excellent relationship. The emotional response of the interviewer may be unfailingly correct. Yet feeling does not automatically translate into effective interview behavior. And the fact of the matter is that clients are more responsive to behavior than to feelings. Only as feelings are manifested in behavior—verbal, nonverbal, open, or covert—do they have an impact on the client. Educating toward good interviewing is guiding the student to learn how to manifest, behaviorally, the appropriate feelings by applying the correct techniques, because correct techniques are the behavioral translation of the helpful attitude.

Even if it is conceded that social work interviewing techniques should be taught, can they be taught through a text? Of course not. "Knowing about" is clearly different from "knowing how." Ultimately, interviewing is learned only through doing. But even though to know is a far cry from to do, it is still an advance over not even knowing what action would be desirable. A book on interviewing is like a manual on courtship. No manual can tell the lover how to achieve his aims. But such books "can suggest some of the issues and tactics which are worth thinking about, consideration of which can make victory somewhat more likely" (Dexter 1970:24). For someone who is just learning to cook, a cookbook is an essential and welcome accessory. At the very minimum, it gives the novice a point of departure.

The perception of interviewing as a creative act as opposed to the perception of interviewing as a subject for scientific analysis research and systematic training leads to the objection that close study by interviewers of their practice would hinder rather than help them. The unhappy centipede illustrates the supposed consequence of too explicit an analysis of intuitively gifted practice.

> A centipede was happy quite until a frog, in fun,
> Said, "Which leg comes after which?"
> This worked him up to such a pitch
> He lay desolate in the ditch
> Deciding how to run.
> "The Puzzled Centipede or the Perils of Thinking," by
> Mrs. Edward Craster in *Under the Tent of the Sky*,
> John E. Bruton, ed. (New York: MacMillan, 1937).

Some people feel that competence in interviewing inevitably grows out of the repeated interaction with the client and that this is the way the skill should be acquired. It is true that if the student is forced to interview, he will interview and learn by doing. It is not true, however, that practice makes perfect. Perfect practice makes perfect, but imperfect practice merely makes imperfect interviewing habitual.

It is said of some interviewers that rather than having ten years of experience, they have one year of experience repeated ten times. There has to be some prior knowledge of what differentiates technically good interviewing from poor interviewing if experience is to result in an increase in competence.

There is no doubt that one can know all about the techniques of interviewing and yet be unable to apply them effectively. It is also true that some gifted practitioners perform brilliantly without being able to say what they do or how they do it, often achieving success while breaking all of the technical prescriptions. There is, further, some measure of truth in the contention that good interviewers are born, not made. Some intuitively gifted people seem to have a natural competence for the art of good personal relationships, of which interviewing is only a special example. But those with a natural aptitude for this sort of thing and those who interview well without knowing exactly what it is they are doing can both profit from a conscious examination of their art. Whatever the limits of our natural capacities, learning may extend them.

One must recognize in the objections the desire to protect the existential magic of the good interview. There is a fear that dispassionate, didactic analysis of what goes on in the interview will destroy the creative spontaneity of the intuitively gifted clinician in the encounter. Yet the fact that we support schools of social work and conduct in-service training courses and institutes is confirmation of our confidence that interviewing can be taught. The problems in interviewing that confuse and frustrate the student-worker have been encountered by those who preceded him on the job. Some solutions have evolved and are part of practice wisdom and the professional knowledge base. There is no reason why the beginning interviewer should not be provided with the cumulative experience of others as a basis for his own practice. What is attempted here is a description and codification of some of the helpful responses that have been developed by the field in answer to recurrent situations and difficulties encountered in social work interviewing.

All interviews have a great variety of aspects in common. They all have a purpose, use verbal and nonverbal symbols as the principal tool of communication, have differentiated roles assigned to interviewer and interviewee, involve interpersonal interaction and so on. And interviewing among the occupations classified as the human services profession have elements in common beyond these. But in each case the different responsibilities of the different groups using the interview, the different functions assigned, the different problems they address, all tend to make for a differentiation of the context in which the interview is conducted. And in each case the contextual differences require some differences in adaptation of the interview. There is an advantage then in translating general interview elements and characteristics in terms of some more specific occupational setting—in this instance the social work setting. The reader interested in and identified with social work is not burdened with the task of translating general interviewing dicta into its applicability for social work. In its selective choice of social work illustrations, the book provides the translation. This has the advantages of immediacy in recognition for the social work reader and a sense of familiarity which involves understanding of the content.

It is true that social work employs a variety of approaches in attempting to help the client. There are social workers with a psychodynamic orientation, those committed to a behavior modification approach or an existential or Rogerian or eclectic approach. However diverse the orientation to what makes for effective helping, the different approaches have considerable overlap in what needs to be done in an interview and how it is best done.

All social workers have to make the interviewee feel at ease, all have to help the interviewee talk about the difficulties with which he wants help, all have to guide the interviews so that its purposes are achieved, all have to start and end the interview in a way which maximizes helping. These suggest only some of the areas of overlap in confirmation of the contention that there is much about interviewing that is common to all social workers. There is then not only justification for a book concerned with the social work interview per se, but also one having relevance to all social workers.

What justifies a second edition of *The Social Work Interview* at this time?

During the past decade interview training in the human services, including social work, has undergone considerable change. Following from the work of the microcounseling group (Ivey and Authier 1978), the Human Relations Training research of Carkhuff (1969), and the Interpersonal-Process-Recall techniques of Kagan and Krathwhol (1967), an effort has been made to identify and operationalize quantifiable, measurable, discrete behavioral skills and components of interviewing.

Carkhuff has given more focused attention to the discrete experiential attitudinal components of interviewing—empathy, genuineness, warmth, unconditional positive regard. These "core conditions" provide the bases for establishing the therapeutic atmosphere facilitating the development of a positive interactional relationship between interview participants.

The microcounseling literature has given somewhat greater emphases to the instrumental skills in interviewing—attending behavior, minimal encouragements, question formulation, reflecting, paraphrasing, interpreting, confronting, and summarizing.

Kagan and Krathwhol have focused more directly on the attempt to synthesize both the expressive conditions and instrumental skills into a meaningful gestalt.

In addition to these training programs, additional systems of interview training have been developed which combine elements of the major programs listed above (Danish and Hauer 1973; Egan 1975; Cormier and Cormier 1979).

The approach to teaching these interpersonal-intervening skills and components is, in each case, through systematic presentation and practice. Each of the skills is clearly identified, isolated, didactically explained, demonstrated, modeled, role-played. The learner then practices the specific skill in a structured exercise or simulated interview situation. Often the exercise is videotaped or audiotaped. The exercise is played back for critical analysis, evaluation, and correction by peers, instructors, and the student himself. The student then tries again and the second exercise is similarly critiqued. There is a progression in the skills selected for teaching from fairly simple ones to those more complex. When the student reaches a satisfactory level of performance in one particular skill, the process is repeated for another. A repertoire of interpersonal skills in interviewing is built up in this way.

The microcounseling approach to interview training has been paralleled by a microanalytic approach to researching the interview. There has been an increasing number of studies concerned with identifiable specific questions regarding discrete aspects of interviewing. While it is true that most of the literature on interview training methods based on discrete units of action comes from outside social work, the literature has had a considerable impact on social work. Adopted and adapted by social work education, the literature has affected the way social work educators are now teaching social work interviewing. The approach lends itself to the possibility of teaching social work interviewing in a laboratory setting in preparation for actual interviewing in a field placement and/or in supplementation of the field experience. There are a sizable number of reports by social workers of such teaching procedures (Fischer 1975, 1978; Mayadas and O'Brien 1976; Mayadas and Duehn 1977; Hammond, Hepworth, and Smith 1977; Rose, Cayner, and Edelson 1977; Schinke et al. 1978, 1980; Katz 1979; Toseland and Speilberg 1982).

The growing wider availability of a simplified videotape technology, easy to operate and use, makes possible immediate dramatic feedback for analysis of all elements of an interview interaction. It makes possible the distribution of packaged instructional material of interview segments and vignettes as examples of good and bad interviewing and as standard stimulus situations for the training of desirable responses.

The widespread adoption of such training programs and the publication of a body of related research and practice experience is one of the reasons which justifies a second edition.

There has been a considerable growth of research since the first edition on much of the content included in a book on the social work interview—research on cross-ethnic interviewing, on male-female interviews, on nonverbal aspects of interviewing, and research on the use of a variety of technical interviewing skills. A second edition seemed necessary in bringing such content up to date.

A rigorously scholarly approach to the content would dictate an obligation to cite, in the text and bibliography, available research in support of the presentation. If conscientiously followed throughout, the result would be literally thousands of citations. Rather than smother the text in names and publication dates, I decided to cite (1) only those publications identifying a direct quotation and (2) recent relevant reviews from the literature of the content under discussion. For instance, in discussing the research regarding interracial interviewing, rather than cite the massive number of studies available, Sattler's 1977 review of some 50 relevant studies is cited.

In addition to such citations in the text, each chapter ends with a selective list of supplementary material for the reader interested in pursuing the chapter content in greater detail. I have attempted to be somewhat selective in the use of citations, balancing between the necessity of projecting a scholarly image and the sin of being unnecessarily and, perhaps, overwhelmingly pedantic. In obeisance to orthodox scholarship procedures, however, I am willing to reply to any challenge of uncited statements by mailing the reader the relevant citation. My address is School of Social Work, University of Wisconsin, 425 Henry Mall, Madison, Wisconsin 53706.

I need to include here an appeal to the reader's compassion, understanding, and common sense regarding the stylistic dilemma every author faces currently regarding the use of gender pronouns. The English language lacks an androgynous vocabulary. We have the option of a simple "he" or "she" or the more convoluted and awkward him/her, he/she, s(he), or making greater use of the sexually neutral plurals "them, they." There is almost no way of doing this without being wrong or stylistically unaesthetic at times.

I first attempted to use male or female pronouns at random throughout the text. On review, this once again proved awkward and confusing. The final decision, and the one applied throughout the general commentary, was to adopt an alternate chapter system—in odd-numbered chapters the interviewer (or worker) is "she" and the interviewee (or client) is "he"; in even-numbered chapters the interviewer is "he" and the interviewee is "she." Exceptions are made when the specific content of case examples demand that the interviewee (or interviewer) be a he or a she.

The term "client" has also developed problematic implications. Some object to the term because it emphasizes the social distance between the participants in the interview. It is seen as having connotations of inferiority and powerlessness. I see it as reflecting the reality that one person is seeking help from another who is supposedly competent to provide such help. Since no alternative term such as "customer," "consumer," etc., has achieved consensual acceptance, we decided to use the term "client" to identify the person whom the worker is interviewing while recognizing that its use may offend some readers.

Because a considerable amount of material has been added to what was in the first edition, it has been necessary to delete some first edition content to keep this edition at manageable length. For example, we decided to drop the chapter on the group interview included in the first edition. Group interviewing has its own unique theoretical supposition, its own unique problems, its special requirements. Even a full chapter would be really inadequate in presenting all the reader would need to know to do a creditable job. Adequate treatment of such content justifiably requires a book of its own. Rather than do a half-satisfactory job in the inadequate space available, we decided to delete the chapter altogether.

The book developed out of my thirty-years' experience in teaching interviewing as a unit in courses on child welfare services, casework, and integrated methods in schools of social work in the United States and abroad. I have led institutes on interviewing for staffs of voluntary and public welfare agencies and have been a consultant on social work interviewing to public agencies. The raw material for the book was provided by almost continuous engagement in social work research over three decades, much of which involved interviewing social agency clients or observing interviews. Many of these interviews were tape-recorded and transcribed. Additional recordings and transcriptions were provided by students as part of assignments for courses on child welfare services, casework, and integrated methods. As a consequence I had available literally thousands of pages of transcribed interviews from a wide variety of social work settings. Extracts from these transcriptions provide the illustrative vignettes presented here.

I am grateful to the social agency clients who participated, as interviewees, in all these interviews. But I owe a greater debt to all the students who shared the courses and institutes with me. Sometimes students, sometimes partners, sometimes colleagues, sometimes the teacher's teacher, they helped me learn what I needed to know in order to teach. And I owe them further thanks for making available the interview typescripts.

Because interviewing anywhere, conducted by professionals of all disciplines, has much to teach us that might be useful in social work, I am indebted to the general body of literature on interviewing. I have drawn freely on the insights available without always being aware of their specific sources. The references and citations, which I have tried to keep to a minimum, are a confirmation of this debt to accumulated wisdom. They also serve as bibliographical leads for the reader interested in some particular aspect of content which he would like to pursue in greater detail on his own. This resource relieves me of feeling apologetic about the need to cover so much that only a little could be said about so many different things.

In preparing this second edition we sent questionnaires to instructors who were using the text soliciting suggestions for changes. We have incorporated many of the suggestions made in revising the text. Our heartfelt and sincere thanks to those faculty members who responded to our questionnaire.

Part I

General Orientation and Some Basic Concepts

CHAPTER 1

The Interview in Social Work

Although social work involves a great deal more than interviewing, social workers spend more time in interviewing than in any other single activity. It is the most important, most frequently employed, social work skill. This observation is most clearly true for the activity of the direct-service caseworker. But the group worker, community organizer, and social actionist also frequently participate in interviewing.

Although the interview is very much a part of social work, it does not belong to social work alone. The aim of this chapter is to delineate the way in which the social work interview is different from interviews in any other discipline. It is first necessary to define the interview and to make a distinction between it and another activity with which it is frequently confused—conversation.

Distinguishing the Interview from a Conversation

The simplest definition of an interview is that it is a conversation with a deliberate purpose, a purpose mutually accepted by the participants. An interview resembles a conversation in many ways. Both involve verbal and nonverbal communication between people during which ideas, attitudes, and feelings are exchanged. Both are usually face-to-face interactions, aside from the telephone interview or conversation. As in a conversation, participants in the interview reciprocally influence each other. A good interview, like a good conversation, gives pleasure to both participants.

The crucial characteristic which distinguishes an interview from a conversation is that the interaction is designed to achieve a consciously selected purpose. The purpose may be to establish a purpose for the interview, e.g., the protective service worker, visiting a family on the agency's initiative, may be exploring with the mother how the agency can be of help. The purpose may be to resolve differences in perception of the purpose of the contact between agency and client. The adolescent on probation may see his contact with the correctional social worker as purely a formality in meeting agency requirements. The social worker perceives it as an opportunity to help the client with some specific problem. Given such disparity in expectations, the purpose of the interview may be to find some *mutually* acceptable purpose. In another interview the worker may encourage the client to define the reason for the contact. But this too is a purpose. If the interaction has no purpose, it may be conversation but it is not yet an interview.

From this critical characteristic of the interview flows a series of consequences for the way participants relate to each other in the interview, as distinguished from a conversation, and for the way the interaction is structured.

1. Since the interview has a definite purpose, *its content is chosen to facilitate achievement of the purpose.* Any content, however interesting, that will not contribute to the purpose of the interview is excluded. On the other hand, the agenda of a conversation may include unrelated and diffuse content. Where there are no boundaries, nothing is extraneous. The orientation of the conversation is associational, and there is no central theme. Because the interview has a purpose, the content is likely to have unity, a progression, and thematic continuity. It is said that the interview, unlike a conversation, is a bounded setting. There are limits to what is given attention, what is noticed, what is included.

2. If the purpose is to be achieved, *one person has to take responsibility for directing the interaction so that it moves toward the goal.* Thus there has to be a differential allocation of tasks between the interview participants. One person is designated as interviewer and charged with responsibility for the process, and someone else is designated interviewee. The role relationships are structured. There are no comparable terms to indicate status positions and selective role behavior in a conversation. In contrast participants in a conversation have mutual responsibility for the course of the conversation. Neither has a formally designated responsibility to see that anything is accomplished as a consequence of the conversational interaction.

We will discuss the task of the interviewer in great detail below. It might suffice, at this point, in making clear this distinctive aspect of the interview, to note that at the very minimum anybody who accepts the title of interviewer needs to know something about the process of interviewing to keep the interview moving toward the objective. She needs to know enough about the content to be able to recognize what is extraneous material and what is pertinent.

3. *That one participant is interviewer* and another the interviewee *implies a nonreciprocal relationship.* In an interview between a professional and a client, one person asks questions and another person answers them. This relationship is partly a result of the fact that someone has to take leadership, that one person does know how to conduct an interview and has more expert knowledge of the subject matter. But this nonreciprocal relationship also derives from the fact that the structure of the encounter is designed to serve principally the interests of the client.

The objective is primarily designed to serve the needs of one party in the relationship—the client who is the interviewee. The professional obligation of the interviewer is to perform clearly defined services for the client so that the interview is unidirectional in the purpose for which it is conducted. In an interview two people are working on the problem of one.

While both interviewer and interviewee derive some satisfactions from the interview encounter, the explicit rationale for conducting the interview is heavily weighted nonreciprocally in maximizing the pay-off for the interviewee. Interviewer satisfactions are incidental.

The interviewer acts in a manner that encourages the interviewee to reveal a great deal about himself while she herself nonreciprocally reveals little. The interviewee reveals a wide segment of his life, the interviewer only her professional self. If the interviewer asks, "How is your wife?" it is not expected that the interviewee will at some point reciprocate by asking, "And how is your husband?" Such reciprocation, the expected form in a conversation, is not helpful in resolving the client's problem in the interview. The nonreciprocal nature of interview interaction is different from a conversation where reciprocation is the expected norm.

4. Although the behavior of all parties to a conversation may be spontaneous and unplanned, *the actions of the interviewer must be planned, deliberate, and consciously selected to further the purpose of the interview;* this is part of the prescribed role behavior. Unlike a conversation an interview is a program of planned, organized communication. This pattern of behavior is predetermined by the positions people occupy in the interview, by the formal structure of reciprocal roles and expectations.

5. No one is obliged to initiate a conversation. *The professional is,* however, *obliged to accept the request of the client for an interview, whatever that professional's expectations are about how it might go.* And since the contact is initiated for the purpose of meeting the needs of the client, the interviewer has an obligation to maintain contact until the purpose is achieved or until it is clear that the purpose cannot be achieved.

Whatever her own feelings about the interview, the interviewer cannot terminate it for personal reasons without being justifiably open to a charge of dereliction of responsibility. There is less compunction or guilt associated with withdrawal from a conversation if it is not enjoyable.

Interactions defined as conversations are an end in themselves. They are engaged in because the very interaction provides satisfaction. For this reason most frequently, although not invariably, we select to converse with those with whom we have a great deal in common, who share similar backgrounds, experiences, life-style. Homophyly, "likeness," between conversational participants makes the probability of obtaining satisfaction greater. Interviews most frequently (although again not invariably) are conducted between participants who differ in terms of backgrounds, experiences, and life-styles. The young, white, upper middle-class, college-educated female may never have occasion to converse with an older, lower-class, grade-school educated, oriental male. However, interviews with such elements of disparity between participants are conducted daily. We *choose* those with whom we are likely to hold a conversation; we *are assigned* those with whom we are likely to conduct an interview. Heterogeneity of participants is a much more likely condition in an interview as contrasted with a conversation.

6. *An interview requires exclusive attention to the interaction.* The commitment on the part of the interviewer to participation in the interview is more intense. A conversation, however, can be peripheral to other activities. The commitment to participation is more lightly held. There is a greater obligation to concentrate one's listening efforts in an interview as compared with a conversation. We listen differently and with a sharper focus in an interview.

7. Because it has a purpose, *the interview is usually a formally arranged meeting.* A definite time, place, and duration are established for the interview, unlike a conversation. Unlike a conservation an interview is purposefully directed so as to accomplish its objectives within a given period of time. Unlike conversation, the formal structure and the time schedule specifically allotted to an interview seek to guarantee noninterruption of interaction. Unlike a conversation, where both participants are given entitlement to relatively equal time, time allocation is asymmetrical in the interview, the interviewee being allotted maximum time without competition from the interviewer.

8. Because an interview has a purpose other than amusement, *unpleasant facts and feelings are not avoided.* In fact there is a specific obligation to stimulate introduction of unpleasant facts and feelings if this will be of help. In a conversation the usual tacit agreement is to avoid the unpleasant. Participants in a conversation expect their partner to interact with tact and caution, to refrain from introducing anything that might be embarrassing, anxiety provoking, controversial, unduly intimate. Many of the norms

of a conversation that govern what subject matter is appropriate and permissible are suspended, modified, or mitigated in an interview.

The interview, unlike the conversation, puts a premium on making explicit what is often recognized but left unstated. Conversational rules protect the private thoughts and feelings of the participants. The interviewer deliberately needs to penetrate the private thoughts and feelings of the person interviewed. The interviewer asks questions that are not ordinarily asked, makes comments not frequently made.

Unlike a conversation, the interaction itself may become a matter for discussion in the interview. The interviewer might say in an interview going haltingly, "You seem reluctant to talk about this," an intervention rarely employed in a conversation. Not only are the norms of conversational reciprocity modified in the interview as noted above, but the etiquette of appropriate content as well. Because this is the case, the interview needs to be protected with guarantees of confidentiality and anonymity to the interviewee, safeguards ordinarily unnecessary in a conversation.

These characteristics define the interview and distinguish it from a conversation. An interview can, and does, take place on the street if a client, in a crisis, unexpectedly meets his caseworker. Interviews take place in tenement hallways, in supermarkets, and on buses as a worker accompanies a client to the hospital, employment office, or day-care center. What starts as a conversation may suddenly turn into an interview.

In summary, then, the interview differs from a conversation in that it involves interpersonal interaction for a conscious, mutually accepted purpose. Following from this premise, the interview, as contrasted with a conversation, involves a more formal structure, a clearly defined allocation of roles, and a different set of norms regulating the process of interaction.

The interview may involve more than two people as in a family interview or a co-therapy interview. In every instance, however, it involves only two clearly defined *parties*—one or more persons interviewing one or more persons being interviewed.

The characteristics which distinguish an interview from a conversation are characteristic of all interviews. And interviews are conducted for a wide variety of purposes by a wide variety of people—social workers, journalists, public opinion pollsters, doctors, lawyers, nurses, teachers, clergymen, counselors, etc. What distinguishes the social work interview from all other kinds of interviews?

The Social Work Interview

Social work interviews are concerned with social work content, are scheduled to achieve social work purposes, and take place in social work settings.

To say this is to recognize immediately the difficulty in making such distinctions. If social work as a profession were designated by society as having clear and exclusive concern with definable, unique areas of activity, the statement would have unambiguous meaning. As it is, one must concede that the content area of social work concern overlaps those of psychiatry, psychology, educational and vocational counseling, the ministry, and others. Despite the overlap, despite the blurred boundaries between related disciplines, social work does have an area of principal concern which is distinctive—its concern with people in the enactment of their social roles and in their relation to social institutions. All of the attempts at defining social work point to the relationship between people and their social environment as the focus of the worker's activity.

Social service is defined by the United Nations as an "organized activity that aims at helping to achieve a mutual adjustment of *individuals and their social environment*" (U.N. 1963:105; italics added in this group of quotations). A comprehensive study of the social work curriculum defines the focus of social workers' activity as "that aspect of man's functioning only which lies in the realm of *social* relationships and *social* role performance" (Boehm 1959:54). A federal task force defines social welfare as "the organized system of functions and services that support and enhance individual and *social* well being and that promote community conditions essential to the harmonious interaction of persons and their *social* environment" (U.S. HEW 1965:7). The Model Statute Social Workers Licensing Act defines social work as "the professional activity of helping individuals, groups, or communities enhance or restore their capacity for *social functioning* and creating societal conditions favorable to this goal" (NASW 1967:7).

Two special issues of *Social Work* (September 1977 and January 1981), the principal journal of the National Association of Social Workers, report the proceedings of two national conferences explicitly concerned with defining the nature of social work. Although there are differences in details in the various presentations, there is the repeated emphasis on the distinctive and differentiating concern of social work with "social functioning," "social problems," "social needs," "social roles," "social policy," "social institutions," "social well being." The inclusion of the word *social* in the professional title reflects social workers' primary concern with social problems and the interaction between clients and the social institutions.

More specifically, however, different agencies perform different functions relating to different social problems. The psychiatric social work agencies are concerned with the social antecedents, concomitants, and consequences of mental disabilities; the medical social worker is concerned with the social antecedents, concomitants, and consequences of physical illness; the family and child welfare agencies are concerned with the social aspects of marital disruption and parent-child relationship difficulties; the correctional social worker is concerned with the social aspects of a disordered relationship to the legal institutions of society; the income-maintenance agencies are concerned with the social aspects of a disordered relationship to the economic institutions of society.

Each agency, then, by focusing on some particular aspect of social functioning, some recurrent significant social problem area, defines for itself the content most relevant for interviews.

At whatever level in the process the social worker intervenes, whether at the community level in trying to effect change in the social system or at the casework level in trying to effect change in the individual situation, the concern is, again, primarily with *social* phenomena. The function and focus of the profession thus determine, in a general way, the distinctive contents of social work interviews, distinguishing them from all other interviews. Distinctive *purpose* and *content* of the interview follow from the distinctive responsibilities of the social agency and the profession.

A mother of four young children injured in an auto accident might be interviewed while in the hospital by three different people—a doctor, a lawyer, and a social worker. All three might employ the same general principles and procedures to ensure an effective interview. In each instance the interview would have a purpose, but the purpose would be different. Consequently the content of the medical interview might be to uncover significant details of the women's physical functioning so as to plan appropriate treatment. The lawyer's purpose might be to find out more about the nature of the accident in preparation for a lawsuit. The social worker's purpose would be to find out about the disruptive effects on the woman's significant social role relationships—as wife, as mother—and determine what can be done to ensure adequate care for the dependent children.

Because the nature of the problems brought to the social worker are often diffuse and ambiguously defined, the social worker cannot very efficiently focus sharply as might a doctor or a lawyer. Listening to social work interviews as contrasted with the interview of a doctor, for instance, shows that social work interviews tend to be longer and more discursive (Baldock and Prior 1981).

Some further characteristic aspects of social work interviews should be noted. The concern of the social work interview is with the unique entity— the unique individual, the unique group, the unique community. Casework means "the individual instance" and is not a term indigenous to social work. The use of the term "case book" in law or in business management illustrates the generality of the word "case." But the concern with the unique instance gives the social work interview a character that distinguishes it from the public opinion interview, for instance. The public opinion interviewer's approach to the respondent is as one of a number of comparable entities. The interest is not in the response of this particular person per se but in the particular person as a member of an aggregate. Hence the effort to standardize the public opinion interview, to see that one is as much like another as possible, and to do everything possible to discourage the development of anything unusual, or special, in any particular interview. Participation is controlled and is confined as far as possible to the set series of questions raised by the interviewer.

The antithesis is true of most social work interviews. Effort is made to maximize clients' participation, to encourage the development of the interview so that it follows the clients' preferences, to minimize standardization and maximize individualization of content. The social worker has no set interview schedule and attempts to keep her control of the interview at the lowest possible level. This statement must be qualified, for some social work interviews do require the worker to cover some uniform content, even though this requirement might not be spelled out on a specific form. A mental hospital social study requires coverage of psychosocial development, school history, marital history, work history, symptoms of developmental difficulties, etc. An adoptive interview typically requires coverage of motivation, reaction to infertility, child preference, experience with children, and marital interaction. A public assistance eligibility interview has to cover family composition, need, resources, and the situation precipitating the application.

The social work interview generally takes place with troubled people or people in trouble. What is discussed is private and highly emotional. Social work interviews are characterized by a great concern with personal interaction, with considerable emphasis on feelings and attitudes and with less concern for objective factual data.

Social work interviews are also apt to be diffuse and concerned with a wide segment of the client's life. Although there is some demarcation between the areas covered by different agencies, agency functions tend to be rather broadly stated. The tendency is for the worker to feel that she needs to know much about the client that, in a strict sense, might be regarded as extraneous to agency function. The more the worker explores the client's personal world with him, the greater the likelihood of affective interaction and of emotional involvement.

The diffuseness of conceivably relevant content derives also from the imprecision of technical procedures for helping. The more precise a profession's technology, the more definite its solutions, the more likely that it will be limited and circumscribed in its area for exploration and its area of intervention. If we could specify what we needed to know to do precise things for and with the client in effecting change, our interview would be less diffuse.

In recapitulation, the social work interview, wherever it is conducted, whatever the agency auspices, differs from other kinds of interviews in that it is concerned with problems relating to the interface between clients and their social environment. Compared with many other kinds of interviews the social work interview is apt to be diffuse, unstandardized, nonscheduled, interviewee-controlled, focused on affective material, and concerned with interpersonal interaction of participants. As a consequence the social work interviewer has a difficult assignment. Much of what she generally has to do in the interview cannot be determined in advance but must be a response to the situation as it develops. The interviewer has to have considerable discretion to do almost anything she thinks might be advisable, under highly individualized circumstances, to achieve the purpose of the interview. The content, the sequence in which it is introduced and how it is introduced, the interpersonal context in which it is explored—all these matters of strategy and tactics in interview management need to be the prerogative and responsibility of the interviewer.

Purposes of Social Work Interviews

The purposes of the social work interview follow from the functions of social work. The general purposes of most social work interviews can be described as informational (to make a social study), diagnostic (to arrive at an appraisal), and therapeutic (to effect change). These are discrete categories only for the purpose of analysis; the same interview can, and often does, serve more than one purpose.

The psychiatric social worker in a child guidance clinic may interview a father to obtain more detailed information about a child referred for service and, at the same time, seek therapeutically to support the father in the disturbed parent-child relationship. The child welfare worker in an adoptive-application interview may have, as one objective, to obtain the information necessary for a reliable and valid decision and, as a secondary therapeutic purpose, to help the applicants adjust to the idea of adoption as a way of completing a family. The delinquent explaining to the probation officer for a court report what precipitated his illegal actions is, at the same time, also clarifying the situation for himself.

Consideration of questions raised to obtain information forces many clients to review those questions more explicitly than they have previously, making them more aware of their own feelings about these aspects of their lives. The reverse can also be true, of course. An interview whose primary purpose is therapeutic may bring the revelation of information previously withheld. Instead of achieving clarification as a result of an interview whose purpose is social study, you sometimes receive social study information from an interview whose primary purpose is the therapeutic one of clarification.

Differences in primary purposes of interviews are reflected in the ways they are structured and conducted. An interview focused on social study is distinguishable from an interview conducted for assessment, both being further distinguishable from an interview whose purpose is primarily therapeutic. Consequently, despite overlap, there is value in reviewing separately the major purposes of social work interviews.

INFORMATION GATHERING OR SOCIAL STUDY INTERVIEWS

The purpose of information gathering interviews is to obtain a focused account of the individual, or group, or community, in terms of social functioning. The point of departure and the center of interest for such exploration is the socially stressful situation for which agency help is or might be requested.

The information gathering social study interview is a selective gathering of life history material related to social functioning. The information enables the worker to understand the client in relation to the social problem situation. *Knowledge* about the client and her situation is a necessary prerequisite to an *understanding* of the client in her situation. And understanding is a necessary prerequisite for effectively intervening to bring about change. Hence the parameters of selectivity in information gathering include both information relevant to understanding and information relevant to the kind of help the agency can provide. We do not seek to learn all there is to know about the client but only what we need to know to understand so that we can help effectively. The information we seek includes both objective facts and subjective feelings and attitudes.

In a series of contacts with the client such information gathering is cumulative; in every interview some new, previously unshared information is obtained. Early interviews are likely to be devoted more exclusively and explicitly to obtaining information, for social study is often their principal purpose. In later interviews, social study information is typically incidental to the achievement of some other purpose.

In some instances, a social study interview is the specific charge to the interviewer. The probation parole office is asked to do a social study of offenders to guide the court in dealing with the delinquent. The psychiatric social worker in a guidance clinic or mental hospital is sometimes asked to do a social study for presentation at a staff conference to determine the next step for the patient. A worker in a neighborhood service center may be asked to interview people in the community to determine what social problems cause them the most concern.

DIAGNOSTIC DECISION-MAKING INTERVIEWS

Another type of interview is geared toward appraisal and determination of eligibility for a service. These interviews facilitate definite administrative decisions. The child welfare worker, for example, interviews the foster care or adoptive applicant to determine if the agency should place a child with her. The public assistance worker interviews the applicant to determine his eligibility for a grant. The protective service worker interviews a family to determine whether a petition of neglect should be filed. Although such interviews are highly individualized, they are conducted so as to permit the worker to assess some particular characteristics of the interviewee. The characteristics are those deemed essential for eligibility for a particular service. Some capacity to establish a relationship and some ability to verbalize are required for acceptance of a child to a child guidance clinic; some willingness to work with the agency is required of foster parent applicants; some motivation to change is necessary for marital counseling in a family service agency; some ability to observe group norms and contribute to group interaction is required of a client at group meetings. The adoptive applicants need to have resolved their marital problems if a child is to be placed in their home; an abusive parent must be assessed as very likely to repeat the assault to justify removing his child from the home.

Whatever the social policy criteria that affect the decision—whether the agency offers services at a preventive rather than a rehabilitative level, whether it works with the very disabled who can make limited use of help but who need it most or with those slightly disabled who need it less but make most effective use of service, whether it plans to focus on changing the system in social institutions or changing symptoms in individual clients— whatever the orientation of the agency with regard to these and other central policy issues—an assessment interview of some kind will be necessary for the agency to make decisions regarding applicants. Because requirements for eligibility have been defined prior to the interview, an outline of the kinds of content that might be covered in such interviews is generally available to the interviewer.

The purpose of the appraisal interview is to obtain selective information needed to make some necessary decision. The decision itself involves a diagnostic process in the mind of the worker—a process of applying theoretical generalization to the data obtained and organizing and interpreting the data for valid inferences. The assessment process leads to an evaluative product—a decision on what the agency will do.

Studies of social work decision making suggest that social workers do look for definite, limited kinds of information in assessment interviews and that the decisions made are frequently associated with such information (Golan 1969).

THERAPEUTIC INTERVIEWS

The purpose of the therapeutic interview is to effect change in the client, in her social situation, or in both. The goal is more effective social functioning on the part of the client as a consequence of the therapeutic changes. Such interviews involve the use of special remedial measures to effect changes in feelings, attitudes, and behavior on the part of the client in response to the social situation. They can also involve efforts to change the social situation so as to reduce or ameliorate social pressures impinging on the client. Because therapeutic interviews are the most highly individualized and idiosyncratic, it is more difficult to develop outlines for them in advance.

The interview might itself be the instrument through which change is effected. The interviewee then is the person with, and for whom, the change in feeling, attitude, and behavior is attempted. The interview is psychotherapeutic, that is, the interviewer employs psychological principles and procedures in an effort to exercise a deliberate, controlled influence on the psychic functioning of the interviewee, with his consent and on his behalf, for the purpose of effecting changes in his feelings, attitudes, and behavior. The purpose of such interviews is helping and healing through communication in a therapeutic relationship.

The school social worker interviews a child to help him adjust to the classroom setting. The family service worker interviews a wife to help her deal with some of the inevitable dissatisfactions in marriage. The medical social worker interviews a convalescent mother to improve her attitude toward the homemaker assigned to the family. The gerontological social worker interviews an aged client to intensify his motivation to use golden-age club facilities in the community.

Interviews may have a therapeutic purpose but the person for whom the therapeutic change is sought may not be present. These include interviews with persons important in the client's life, where the social worker acts as a broker or advocate in the client's behalf. The social worker engaged in brokerage or advocacy may interview people in strategic positions in an attempt to influence them on behalf of the client. The purpose of the interview is to change the balance of forces in the social environment in the client's favor. The school social worker may interview a teacher in order to influence her to show more accepting understanding of a child. The social worker at the neighborhood service center may interview a worker at the housing authority or at the local department of public welfare to obtain for his client full entitlement to housing rights or to assistance. Or a social worker may accompany an inarticulate client to an employment interview in an effort to influence the decision in the client's favor. In each instance the scheduled interview has a definite, and in these cases, therapeutic purpose in behalf of the client.

In this book the primary focus is on social work interviews conducted with agency clients as the interviewees. However, social workers often engage in supervisory and consultative interviews where another professional is the interviewee. And they conduct interviews with clients and non-clients for specialized purposes of their own, as in research interviews. Yet even in these interviews the primary purposes can sensibly be subsumed under the headings used above. The interviewer as supervisor or consultant or researcher is trying to find out about something (informational, social study), make some decision (diagnosis, data assessment), or effect change in some situation (treatment).

The ultimate objective of the different kinds of interviews is to help clients deal more effectively, less dysfunctionally, with a problematic social situation. Each of the different kinds of purposes of the different kinds of interviews is part of the overall process. The sequential steps taken to achieve the objective of helping the social work client involves treatment (specific remedial interventions having therapeutic intent) based on understanding (diagnosis, data assessment) derived from the facts (social study data gathering).

There are, then, many different kinds of interviews for many different purposes. The diversity of interview types is compounded by the fact that each kind can be conducted in different ways—as a dyad (interviewer–interviewee), as a group interview (one interviewer–multiple interviewees), as a board interview (multiple interviewers–one interviewee). And further, interviews for the same purpose may be conducted in different ways according to the theoretical preference of the interviewer. The social worker oriented toward ego psychology as an explanatory framework for guiding her intervention will emphasize different content than will a behavioral-modification oriented social worker or a transactional analyses or existential social worker.

Social work interviews are distinguished from other kinds of interviews but within the profession of social work interviews in one kind of agency are distinguished from interviews in another kind of agency.

Alternatives and Limitations

The interview is the principal technique through which social work purposes are achieved. It is not, however, the sole technique for achieving them. As a participant observer in the activities of a street-corner gang, the group worker obtains a great deal of social study data. A family therapist poses a problem for family decision, such as having to decide on a family vacation, and learns much about the family from watching its members in action. Information for understanding the client might also be obtained from documents, from records of previous agency contacts, or from medical examinations and psychological tests.

Although the interview is the most frequently employed social work procedure for learning about, understanding, and helping the client, it has limitations. A series of studies has compared information on family functioning obtained through interviews with information obtained through direct observation (Weller and Luchterhand 1968). Other studies have compared information about child development obtained retrospectively, through interviews, with the records compiled on the same child while he was actually growing up (Yarrow, Campbell, and Burton 1964). In each instance there were discrepancies between the interview data and the observed or documentary material. There was typically less discrepancy regarding factual data and more discrepancy regarding attitudinal data. The studies establish some of the general limitations of the interview as a technique for obtaining information of concern to social work on child development and family functioning. Other studies in related fields have established the limitations of the interview as a source of valid and reliable data (Mayfield 1964).

The interview is nevertheless the most versatile procedure for access to a wide variety of insights about the client in his social situation. Unlike a questionnaire or participant observation or test instrument of one kind or another, the interviewer can flexibly adapt her approach and attention to any kind of lead offered by the interviewee. It can thus individualize interview interaction.

Through words, which are vicarious actions, the worker can experience with the client various situations in the past, present, and future. The interview is bound by neither time nor space. Furthermore, through the interview the worker has access to the client's feelings and attitudes, the subjective meaning of the objective situation.

Observation presents the worker with a sample of behavior; she still has to infer its meaning. The worker observes a mother, for example, who has come to the day care center at the end of the day to pick up her child. She shouts at her child for his slowness in putting on his boots and overcoat. Is her action displaced hostility toward her boss, with whom she has had an argument earlier in the day? Is it anxiety at the possibility of getting home late and risking another argument with her husband in a shaky marriage? Is it shame that her child is not as capable as other children? Is it an expression of generalized hostility toward the child, who is seen as a sibling rival for her husband's affection? Is it impatience because of physical fatigue? Does the child's slowness reactivate anxiety that as a working mother she is failing her child? The same unit of observed behavior—many possible meanings. An interview with the mother can help the worker understand which of the possible interpretations best explains her outbursts. Observation without interviewing yields doubtful inferences. That the same can be said about inferences derived from interviews alone indicates that, despite advantages, interviewing has its definite shortcomings and deficiencies which have been discussed at length in the literature and supported by empirical research and which need to be recognized. Nevertheless the advantages, versatility, and flexibility of interviewing have made the interview the procedure of choice for social work interaction with the client. It is very likely to continue being widely used.

SUGGESTED READINGS

SOCIAL WORK TEXTS

A number of other books published within the last ten years are concerned in whole or in part with the social work interview.

Alfred Benjamin. *The Helping Interview.* Boston: Houghton Mifflin, 1969, 1974, 1981 (177 pp.).
> A warmly written account of the details of the helping interview—the spirit as well as the specifics of practice. While concerned with the helping interview generally, the book includes the social work interview, and a good deal of the content is applicable.

Robert Bessell. *Interviewing and Counseling.* London: B. T. Batesford, 1971 (263 pp.).
> A British publication written by a former lecturer in social work. Following a presentation of a conceptual framework of the social work interview, the author discusses, in separate chapters, the one-to-one interview, the group interview, the marital interview, and the family interview.

Cristen P. Cross, editor. *Interviewing and Communication in Social Work.* London: Routledge & Kegan Paul, 1974 (166 pp.).
> One of the British Library of Social Work publications—a series designed to meet the needs of British social work training course students. The editor of this collection of articles is a sociologist who has taught courses for social workers. The orientation of the book is to treat the interview as an event requiring an understanding of the social-cultural implications of the act of communication.

Golda M. Edinburg, Norman Zinberg, and Wendy Kelman. *Clinical Interviewing and Counseling: Principles and Techniques.* New York: Appleton Century Crofts, 1975 (121 pp.).

Two of the authors, Edinburg and Kelman, are practicing medical social workers. Consequently there is some emphasis on the social work context in the brief review of the therapeutic process in counseling and the associated typical problems that the counselor encounters in the counseling interview.

Annette Garrett. *Interviewing: Its Principles and Methods.* 3d ed. New York: Family Service Association of America, 1982 (186 pp.).

First published in 1942, a classic in social work. The author, Annette Garrett, was associate director of Smith College School for Social Work from 1934 until her death in 1957. The book was revised by Elinor Zaki and Margaret Margold, a second edition was published in 1972, and a third in 1982. It contains a clear statement of the attitudes and understandings required for a good interview with an exposition of some of the basic interviewing techniques. This is followed by some illustrative excerpts from social work interviews.

Margaret Schubert. *Interviewing in Social Work Practice: An Introduction.* 2d ed. New York: Council on Social Work Education, 1982 (82 pp.).

By a professor of social work, an 82-page tightly written account of some of the essentials of the social work interview, the recurrent problems encountered, and the solutions developed through practice wisdom.

FROM COUNSELING AND PSYCHOLOGY

A number of books have the counselor or psychologist as the target audience. However, much of the content is very useful to the social work interviewer.

William Cormier and L. Sherilyn Cormier. *Interviewing Strategies for Helpers: A Guide to Assessment, Treatment, and Evaluation.* Monterey, Calif.: Brooks/Cole, 1979 (557 pp.).

Organized around three major foci—assessment, treatment, and evaluation—in personal helping, the book details the interview interventions necessary in implementing these processes. The layout is interesting with boxed summaries of key points and exercises designed to involve the reader.

David R. Evans, Margaret Hearn, Mat R. Uhleman, and Allen E. Ivey. *Essential Interviewing: A Programmed Approach to Effective Communication.* Monterey, Calif.: Brooks/Cole, 1979 (271 pp.).

A programmed text addressed to the broad spectrum of professionals who have responsibility for helping, through the interview, people with personal problems. Following micro-counseling principles, selective interviewing skills are introduced and explained, and are then practiced by the reader in completing the assigned program.

Benjamin Pope. *The Mental Health Interview: Research and Application.* New York: Pergamon Press, 1979 (540 pp.).

Written by a professor of psychology and part of a General Psychology Text series. The book presents a very comprehensive and thorough view of the research relating to the interview and then systematically translates the implications of the research into suggestions for the practicing psychologist engaging in an interview.

Evaline D. Schulman. *Intervention in Human Services.* 2d ed. St. Louis: C. V. Mosby, 1978 (250 pp.).
Written by a professor of community mental health and directed to a broad range of human service personnel at the community college level. Despite the title, most of the book is concerned with the human services interview. It is graphically written to convey simply and effectively the essentials of interviewing that a beginning interviewer needs to know.

PUBLIC OPINION INTERVIEWING

A number of books which describe, discuss, and analyze the interview address primarily non-social work, non-human service professionals as their audience. They are, nevertheless, potentially helpful and useful to the social worker interested in learning more about interviewing.

The following two books are written by authors whose area of concern is the public opinion interview.

Raymond L. Gordon. *Interviewing: Strategy, Techniques, and Tactics.* Rev. 2d ed. Homewood, Ill.: Dorsey Press, 1975 (587 pp.).
The second edition of this text is once again directed to the public opinion interviewer, but the strategy and tactics discussed will strike a chord of familiarity in the social work interviewer. The general overview of interviewing and communication provide a perceptive orientation to interviewing.

Robert L. Kahn and Charles F. Cannell. *The Dynamics of Interviewing: Theory, Technique, and Cases.* New York: Wiley, 1957 (368 pp.).
Published over twenty-five years ago and unfortunately not subsequently updated, but one of the better books on the interview. It is a sophisticated treatment of the subject, clearly written and aptly illustrated with appropriate case material.

FROM THE MEDICAL PROFESSION

Since doctors and nurses are regularly involved in interviewing patients, it is not surprising that there are a number of books on interviewing directed toward that audience. Once again, the social work practitioner, particularly those involved in health settings, may want to take a look.

Lewis Bernstein, Rosalyn Bernstein, and Richard Dana. *Interviewing the Patient: A Guide for Health Professionals.* 2d ed. New York: Appleton-Century-Crofts, 1974 (194 pp.).

George L. Engle and William L. Morgan. *Interviewing the Patient.* Philadelphia: W. B. Saunders, 1973 (129 pp.).

Allen J. Enlow and Scott N. Swisher. *Intervieiwng and Patient Care.* New York: Oxford University Press, 1972 (229 pp.).

Robert E. Froelich and F. Marion Bishop. *Medical Interviewing: A Programmed Manual.* 2d ed. St. Louis: C. V. Mosby, 1972 (130 pp.).

CHAPTER 2

The Interview As Communication

An interview is a specialized form of communication. A communication interchange in the interview involves two people, each of whom possesses a receiving system, a processing system, and a transmitting system. The receiving system consists of the five senses, the receptors. Communication in the interview involves primarily the use of two sense receptors—the eyes and the ears. Having received the incoming signal, one processes it; this involves making sense of the received message, giving it meaning. The processing activity consists of recalling stored information, relating relevant information to the message, thinking about the message, evaluating the message, translating it so that the message is coherent with the receiver's frame of reference. As receivers, we select certain items from the incoming message, ignore others, and rearrange what we hear into interpretable patterns. We then formulate a message in response. Selected words and nonverbal gestures are transmitted by "effector organs"—the voice, the mouth, the hands, the eyes, etc.—so that they can be received by the other participant in the interview who, in turn, processes the message as a basis for formulating his response.

While receiving, processing, and responding to messages which originate externally, the participant in the interview is also receiving, processing, and responding to messages which originate internally. We are constantly engaged in checking how we feel inside, physically and emotionally. The brain acts as a communication center processing all the messages, interpreting them, and formulating an appropriate response.

Let us follow the details of the process of communication, noting the more frequent problems encountered at significant points in the process.

The Process of Communication

ENCODING THE MESSAGE

The message to be communicated originates as a thought in the mind of one of the participants in an interview. Events and experiences cannot be communicated as such. They have to be translated into words which "carry" a symbolic representation of the experience. When received, the experience has to be reconstructed from the words.

The message, as transmitted, is the thought or idea encoded into the overt behavior of words and gestures. (There are multiple channels available for communication, but for the sake of simplicity I shall, at this point, discuss primarily only the verbal channel of communication, leaving for another chapter a discussion of nonverbal communication.)

Even before the thought is put into words for transmission, it must pass through a series of internal screens. A thought which, if encoded and transmitted, is likely to lead to our being rejected or derogated by the person receiving the message will not be spoken. A thought which, if spoken, would make us more aware of that which we are ashamed of, leading to a risk of self-rejection, will not be encoded. These screens of psychological resistance and psychic repression block communication of emotionally unutterable, anxiety-provoking thoughts. Resistance is conscious suppression of thoughts that seek expression. Repression indicates that barriers to the expression of some thoughts exist below the level of conscious awareness. The thoughts themselves are screened out without the person's recognizing that they exist or are being censored.

The client may be willing and ready but unable to communicate some of the necessary information, attitudes, and feelings about his situation. Some facts and feelings have been forgotten and are difficult to recall for retelling; some have been repressed so that they are beyond recall. Freudian slips are, of course, examples of thoughts that have eluded the screens and filters and achieved expression.

Other filters inhibit the encoding of thoughts that violate the etiquette of the communication situation. Four-letter scatological or curse words and openly hostile remarks get blocked out at this point. Interviewing regarding behavior and attitudes about which there are strong and unambiguous social expectations encounters the screen of social desirability. Self-censorship—suppression of socially and personally unacceptable comments—is illustrated from a postinterview interview with a client.

A woman, 46, white, has discussed a problem of residential care for her mother with a medical social worker.

When I first came, I thought I would say how I felt my mother was very difficult to live with, and I want an old-age home for her for my own comfort as well as because it might be good for her. But how can you say that, that you really don't like your mother when she is old? How can you tell that and not think people will feel you're lousy? Even when I say it to myself—that my mother annoys me, that she can be a pain—I think, "What kind of a daughter am I?"

Readiness to share and the location of the boundaries between public and private information vary among individuals and among groups. Individuals are more or less reticent; different groups in the community regard sexual life, financial situation, and marital interaction as more or less private.

Readiness to share, willingness to communicate, is a function of hope and confidence that such involvement will result in some benefit for us. We accept the doctor's request to undress because we feel some assurance that if we do so he can help us with our pain. But if we lacked such motivation, would we be willing to undress? Why should we share our secrets if nothing useful for us will be achieved in exchange for such self-disclosure? We only entitle the interviewer to access to as much of ourselves as he needs to know in order to help, and do so only because we feel some assurance that, as a result, he is willing, ready, and able to assist us.

A barrier arises from a feeling of social distance between client and worker. Clients have sometimes felt it hopeless to expect the worker to understand them. In the clients' perception, the parties to the interview live in two different worlds. Rather than attempt to communicate what is felt to be uncommunicable, the client screens out the message.

Male, 18, white, probation interview.
So then they sent me to the school counselor, but he never took speed or acid—he never even tried pot—so I figured how can you talk to him? He wouldn't know how it was, and I didn't know how to tell him. I couldn't rap with him.

Discretion in the face of power is a barrier to free communication. Frequently the interviewer controls access to some service or resource which the client wants and needs—medical care, adoptive children, money, or institutional placement. Frequently the interviewer also can apply punishing legal sanctions—in probation and parole, in protective service, in public assistance. The client has to censor his communication so that he increases the possibility of getting what he wants and needs and prevents the application of negative sanctions.

There are filters that determine what is appropriate in a given context. What is appropriate in a conversation may be inappropriate in an interview, and a comment that is appropriate in an interview in a child guidance clinic may not be appropriate in a public assistance district office.

Generally any thought or feeling that is considered for expression is part of a series of interchanges. The decision as to whether the thought is advisable, permissible, and appropriate for transmission is conditioned to a very considerable extent by the communications received from the other participant(s) in the interview. Thus communication is not only the product of what each person brings to the interview but also a consequence of what he experiences during it.

A thought which succeeds in satisfying the demands of the various criteria still needs to be encoded for understandable transmission. Having decided that a thought is permissible and appropriate to the situation and to the role in which he is engaged at the moment, the interviewer still must find the words to express the message for undistorted reception. The worker needs a vocabulary rich enough to convey the meaning of his thought, and varied enough to adapt to the vocabulary of different clients.

Worker and client may nominally speak the same language but actually not understand one another. The language community of the worker is not necessarily the language community of the client. There is no equivalence of meaning to many of the words they use in common. "Eligibility" sounds one way and has one meaning to the worker; it sounds quite different to and evokes a different set of responses in the client. We say "home study" and "court record" and "therapy" without knowing how these unfamiliar words sound to the client.

Middle-class language is different from lower-class language; black vocabulary and syntax are different from white vocabulary and syntax; professional language is different from lay language. Komarovsky notes differences in word connotation between blue-collar respondents and college-educated interviewers in a study of blue-collar marriages.

> The word "quarrel" carried the connotations of such a major and violent conflict that we had to use "spat," "disagreement," and other terms to convey a variety of marital clashes. To "confide" often meant to seek advice rather than share for its own sake. "Talk" to a few implied a long discussion (telling each other news isn't talking). "Intelligent" and "smart" were the terms used, not "bright"; "unfair," not "unjust." What kinds of things make you pleased or satisfied with yourself, we asked. "When I get my work done," "When I get a bargain," and similar responses were given by some. But to a large proportion of the men and women the phrase "pleased with yourself" implied the unfavorable connotations of being "stuck on yourself." These tended to answer the question in the manner of one confessing moral defects. (1967:19–20)

As Kinsey points out, the lower socioeconomic interviewee "is never 'ill' or 'injured,' though he may be 'sick' or 'hurt.' He does not 'wish' to do a

thing, though he 'wants' to do it. He does not 'perceive,' though he 'sees.'
He is not 'acquainted with a person,' though he may 'know him' " (1948:52).
Social workers rarely tell people anything—they "share information"; they
do not explain agency service but "interpret" it; they may not make friends
although they do "establish relationships."

A middle-aged man referred to a family service agency for marital counseling is talking about a problem he has in being on time for appointments.
The worker tries to determine whether tardiness is a general problem:

WORKER: Do you have other kinds of difficulties in this area?
CLIENT: No, not in this area, but I did have the same trouble when I lived
   in Cincinnati.

To ensure good reception of the communication, not only does the worker
have to select the appropriate matching vocabulary, but he needs to consider the client's frame of reference as well. The communication will not
be received unless the client can perceive it as relevant to his situation.
The following indicates a failure in both choice of vocabulary and selection
of content for effective communication:

Worker: male, 23, white.
Client: female, 67, black, Supplemental Security Income application.
WORKER: People can be eligible for both Social Security and Supplemental
   Security Income. If the budgeted amount is in excess of Social Security
   benefits, a supplemental assistance grant can be authorized for the dif-
   ference.

Instead the worker might have said:

For instance, let's take your situation. You get 122 dollars a month from
Social Security. We have figured it out, and we know that is not enough
to live on for a person like yourself. We figure that you need at least 170 a
month. So we might be able to give you the difference between what you
get from Social Security—the 122 dollars—and what we have figured somebody like yourself needs. If you are eligible, you would get 48 dollars a
month from us in addition to the 122 dollars from Social Security.

Not only is word selection more appropriate, but the message is apt to be
perceived by the client as more relevant and applicable to her situation.
The client does not want a discussion on agency policy and services in
general. She wants to know only of those services appropriate to her situation and those policies relevant to her problems, communicated in a way
which translates services and policies in terms of these particular concerns.

The words themselves, the symbols transmitted, are only part of the message communicated. Nonverbal images, smiles, hand gestures, etc., accompanying the sounds uttered are communicated simultaneously and modify, cancel, mitigate, or reinforce the meanings being given to the words. Vocalizations—pauses, inflections, amplitude, tone accompaning the words themselves—are additional significant components of the message that shape the meanings intended by the sender. These word accompaniments instruct us as to how the words are intended to be interpreted. These instructions accompanying the message telling us how the message is to be interpreted are known as meta-communications.

Depending on the meta-communication, the message explaining the message, the same words can be a question, a paraphrase, an order, a request, a neutral descriptive statement. "So you went with them to have a drink," said one way, is a paraphrase, said another way is a reprimand, said another way is a question, and another way is an accusation. Effective communication requires that we attend not just to what the words mean but what the speaker means.

TRANSMITTING THE MESSAGE AND WAITING FOR FEEDBACK

Having encoded the desired message in words that are most likely to ensure its undistorted reception, we still face the mechanical problem of transmission and reception. The setting for the interview might be very noisy. The message to be transmitted may have to compete with the rumble of traffic, cross-talk from other interviews, the hum from fans and air-conditioning motors, the sounds of radio or television. If the client has a speech defect or talks very rapidly or without sufficient volume, there is likely to be some failure in communication. The ear, fortunately, is highly selective and tries to screen out extraneous noises, but it does this at a cost of effort and loss of accuracy. It is surprising how few people articulate clearly with sufficient volume and how many talk through pipes clenched in their teeth, through cigarettes drooping from one side of the mouth, or from behind a hand. Clear transmission of a message in a quiet context, adequately protected from competing noises, is apt to be more the exception than the rule.

Once the message is encoded and sent, the sender loses control over it. What is done to it, how it is received or ignored or misinterpreted or distorted, is beyond his power to change. Just as the receiver never knows what the message actually was as formulated by the sender for sending, the sender never knows how his message was actually received. The receiver only hears the words and sees the nonverbal cues which stand for the message sent; the sender only sees and hears the behavioral and verbal responses which stand for the message received. He may try again, in response to feedback on how the message is received, if he recognizes that he has been unsuccessful. We are often tempted to say, "I know that you believe you understand what you think I said, but I am not sure you realize that what you heard is not what I said."

Illustrating that you do not really know what you have communicated until you get the feedback, someone said, "I never know what I said until I hear the response to it." The meaning expressed is not always the meaning communicated. The interviewee has to be encouraged and given the freedom to offer feedback. Lacking either the courage or the entitlement to offer feedback leads to misunderstandings on the part of the interviewee.

A worker asks a client about whether any "repercussions" followed after she stayed home from work to care for a sick child. The client looks puzzled and asks, "you mean?" The worker then translates "repercussions" and comments: "Fortunately, the client was willing to display her ignorance. Had she wanted to impress me, or had she been an adult embarrassed because she didn't understand the terminology used, she may have given an inaccurate and/or very general response."

We not only get feedback from others—in their nod of recognition, in their happy smiles or puzzled grimaces, in their responses which indicate we have hit the desired target—but we also get feedback from ourselves. We listen to the way we say what we mean to say and evaluate the success with which we have said it. If it sounds unclear to us, or muddled, or ambiguous, we pat it into shape with an explanatory phrase here or a clarifying sentence there. And since language is inexact, we make ourselves understood by a series of repetitive statements, a series of successive approximations to our meaning.

DECODING THE MESSAGE

Just as there are difficulties in speech transmission, there are possible problems in speech reception. The person to whom the message is directed may fail to hear it because he has a hearing loss, because of the high noise level, or because he is inattentive at the moment and has his receiver tuned to another internal or external message. The message receiver may have failed to pay attention and thus did not listen. Listening is a significant, distinct component in the communication circle of particular significance for interviewing. It is discussed at some greater length in chapter 12.

But let us suppose that his ears hear exactly what the speaker has said. Communication has not yet taken place. The message itself as sent is only one variable determining the message as received. The person to whom the message is directed has his own set of mental barriers, screens, and filters that guard against the reception of messages which make him feel anxious or uncomfortable or which threaten his favorable perception of himself, his psychic peace and quiet. He may hear what was said with his ears but never permit the message to reach his mind.

The process of selective perception permits us to hear only what we allow ourselves to hear, in the way we allow ourselves to hear it. It has been noted that there is no "immaculate perception." What is filtered in is converted so that it relates with minimum conflict to our experience, our values, our ideas and preconceptions.

Each defense mechanism is a different kind of distortion of the message heard. In projection we hear the message not in terms of what was said but in terms of what we would have said in this situation; in displacement we attribute to one person the message from another; in repression we are deaf to the message being sent and block its reception; in reaction formation we hear the opposite of the message transmitted. These mental processes protect us from hearing what would be inconvenient, or hurtful, or frightening.

Our expectations increase the possibility that we will distort the communication we receive. Thus we hear not only what we choose to attend to but what we expect to hear—whether the person said it or not. Studies by Rosenthal (1966) have established that the expectations of scientists in rigorous experimental situations often tend to determine their observations of experimental results. If expectations are a contaminating factor in sharply controlled situations, one would expect them to operate more markedly in the more informal social work interview situations.

The interviewer's belief system comprises expectations that predispose him to "hear" certain responses. If the interviewer hears the interviewee say that she likes things neat and orderly, the psychoanalytically oriented interviewer, associating certain personality traits with the anal character, is all set to expect the interviewee to say things which suggest that she is also frugal and stubborn. We think in categories and expect a person to behave in some consistent manner, according to the pigeonhole to which we have assigned him. As a result we think we know more about the interviewee than we actually do. If a man is a policeman, we expect that he will behave as a policeman. We attribute to individuals the attributes of the groups with which we perceive them to be affiliated and we tend to hear what we expect them to say rather than what they did say.

Communication once initiated is a circular reciprocally interacting process. The receiver-decoder of the message becomes the encoder of the next message. Participants in the communicative act are both senders and receivers of messages. They each respond to stimuli received, and generate a stimulus which evolves a response. Each affects and is affected by the other. Each seeks to influence the other and risks being influenced by the other. This is why communication is a threatening undertaking and why people erect so many defensive barriers to open communication. As Barnuld says:

> No one can leave the safety and comfort of his own assumptive world and enter that of another without viewing the risk of having his own commitments questioned, not only questioned, but perhaps altered. To communicate fully with another human being since it entails the risk of being changed oneself is to perform what may be the most courageous of all human acts. (1974:163)

But even if the person to whom the message is directed is psychologically free to receive it undistorted, communication has not yet taken place. The ear having received the message, psychological sentries having passed it, the mind now faces the responsibility of decoding it. As Whitehead once said, "Spoken language is merely a series of squeaks." The mind has to translate the squeaks so that they make sense. If the message is to be received with the same meaning that was intended when it was encoded, the words received have to be decoded by shared definitions. Few aspire to the extreme individualism of Humpty Dumpty, who said to Alice, "When I use a word, it means what I choose it to mean—no more, no less." But shades of meanings we give to words differ for all of us because our experiences have been different. The word "ghetto" evokes very different images in the mind of a black militant in Chicago, a white matron in Greenwich, and a Hasidic Jew in Brooklyn. We need to be reminded often that there are about six hundred thousand words in the English language and that the five hundred most commonly used words have fourteen thousand dictionary definitions.

Words, Words, Words

Because of the nuances of difference in meaning evoked by different linguistic symbols (words), essentially the same experience and behavior can be given different connotations, as illustrated in a cartoon by Jules Feiffer. One of his drawings shows an old gentleman sitting in a straightbacked chair and musing: "I used to think I was *poor*. Then they told me I wasn't poor, I was *needy*. Then they told me it was self-defeating to think of myself as needy, I was *deprived*. Then they told me deprived was a bad image, I was *underprivileged*. Then they told me underprivileged was over-used, I was *disadvantaged*." In the final panel of the sketch, the old man says, "I still don't have a dime."

The popular game of conjugating adjectives describing the same situation further makes this point: "I am firm, you are obstinate, he is pigheaded"; "I am fastidious, you are fussy, he is obsessed"; "I am stocky, you are plump, he is fat"; "I am reserved, you are haughty, he is a snob."

Words that seem obvious to the interviewer may not be so obvious to the interviewee.

Following a discussion of an unmarried mother's reaction to the recent birth of her child and that of her parents who were pressing for adoption, the social worker summarizes:

WORKER: "You seem to be really happy about being a new mother, but there still seems to be some residuals of unresolved conflict between yourself and your parents."

CLIENT: (after a short pause) "I don't get you."

Out of habit we toss off acronyms which are old friends to us but baffling strangers to the interviewee—AFDC, OASDI, SSI, DVR, CETA, WIN, etc. We use terms such as: "support network," "generic approach," "self-actualization," "treatment milieu," "systems intervention," which make sense to us but are likely to bewilder the interviewee.

While it is expected that the social work interviewer and interviewee might give different meanings to technical terms, this can also be true for the use of everyday phrases. For instance, Wile et al. (1979) noted that doctors and patients interpreted the phrase "going home from the hospital soon" quite differently. The doctors interpreted "soon" to mean two to four days. Many patients interpreted it as meaning "tomorrow."

No two people belong to the same psychological, experiential community because no two people have had identical experiences. Consequently the same word, defined in essentially the same way, will evoke different images and meanings in the two participants in the interview. Living in private worlds the meanings we give to words are systematically personalized, bearing an individualized thought-print.

The message "It must have been hard for you" will be very differently received by people with different developmental histories and different reference groups. "It must have been hard for you" may reduce to tears a young girl who feels lonely, rejected, and misunderstood. It will be received with anger by a 25-year-old male who prides himself on his masculinity and his ability to cope with difficulties. The message is the same; the reaction is different because the perception of the meaning of the message is different.

Consequently even under the very best communicative conditions there will always be some disjoints in meaning between the message as understood by the sender and the message decoded by the receiver. We use our imagination and any analogous experiences to bridge the gaps between the message received and the message as sent. While we may never have experienced starvation we have been very hungry at times; we may never have experienced divorce, but we have experienced deeply moving separations.

Meaning is not automatically transferred in interchange of symbols, the words and nonverbal gestures which are the actual substance of communications. Only symbols are transmitted and the symbols activate meaning, evoke meanings. But the meanings evoked are dependent on the subjective perception of the symbols by the person receiving the symbols.

The verbal symbols, the impulses, that are encoded and transmitted, received, and decoded have no intrinsic meaning. Meaning is given to the symbols by the participants in the communication interaction. "Speech is produced by the human voice received by the human ear and interpreted by the human brain" (Pei 1965). Meaning lies in people not in the words, the linguistic symbols, themselves. The act of communication is an effort to make our meanings appear in other people's minds through the transmission of our meanings as encoded in verbal symbols.

Cantril (1956) illustrates the precept that communication is not complete until the receiver has translated the message in recounting the discussion of three baseball umpires. The first umpire says, in calling the pitch, "some are balls and some are strikes and I call them as they is." The second umpire says that "some are balls and some are strikes and I call them as I see them." The third umpire says, however, that "some are balls, some are strikes and they ain't nothing 'til I call them."

Because the interests, needs, and previous experiences of the listener are crucial in determining the message that is actually received, no matter how it is sent, the interviewer must give active consideration to the listener's background and situation. This requirement is the source of one of the most frequently repeated aphorisms of social work practice wisdom, "Start where the client is." To ignore this precept is to risk ineffective communication.

All messages are received through intervening, mediating variables provided by the communication-processing center. The dictum "no communication without interpretation" implies that the message we ultimately receive is not the same as the message that was sent. We classify, catalog, and interpret the incoming messages by relating them to past experiences and learning. The material selectively received is organized in a search for meaning. We need to orient ourselves to whatever situation we find ourselves in and to do so we try to make sense out of any communication we receive. In imposing meaning on the communication, we bring to the communication itself the explanatory schemes we have learned through our education and life experiences. These include not only cognitive belief systems, but also affective schemes—our feelings about our relationship to the world and to people.

During an interview, the worker invests a considerable amount of energy in the processing of communications received. After the worker decodes what he has heard, but before he responds, he attempts to make sense out of the communication. This is the diagnostic process in microcosm. How does this particular item of communication fit into the series of messages previously received? What does the client mean? How am I to understand this? The process is illustrated in the following introspective comment by a worker in a public assistance agency:

Up until now we were discussing how hard it is to feed the kids adequately on the AFDC budget. The last remark was about the fact that she hadn't gotten a new dress in two years. What is she trying to tell me? That she, too, is deprived? That I should have some pity for her? That she is trying hard to be a good mother, putting the kids' needs first? That I ought to try to do something to help her and not only be concerned about the kids? That she missed, and wanted, some guy hanging around? What makes her say this at this point in the interview? I also tried to decide at this point how concerned she was with this, because I was not sure whether to shift the interview to focus directly at this point on her concern about a new dress or table it and bring it up later while I continued to focus on the problem of feeding the kids on the budget. I decided that she was upset, but not all that upset about it that it couldn't hold and, although I didn't clearly understand what prompted the remark at this point, I decided to acknowledge the remark, indicate we would come back to it later, but continue, for the time, to discuss the problem of feeding the kids.

The following interview and worker's introspective comments demonstrate the problem faced by the interviewer as he processes what he hears:

Client: female, 54, white, protective service.
MRS. L.: Yes he is, I'm telling you. He's very hard to understand. If I knew to this day . . . that he was mean to his first wife in ———— here, he lived here . . . I'd've never married the man. (Pause.) His folks are . . . oh, *wonderful* people, they're . . . they love me, and they love the kids, but I never hear from them. Because they're real old. They're uh. . . .

They uhm. . . . They stopped sending Christmas cards after uh . . . I was divorced from him. . . . They didn't send no more Christmas cards. . . . They, uh, ask about me, they ask about my stepson—they ask, they all ask *about* me, and that's all right. They ask about us, and I ask about *them*. We get, I get along with the two sons that I kept in touch with, even Sid came and seen me, and he was jealous of his own son come and visit me. His son come and stayed . . . when he was goin' away to Chicago, he came and visited me. . . . And just 'cause he stayed here till noon . . . to have dinner with me, he was very jealous. He thought I had intercourse with his own son. (Pause.) His imagination, you know, I mean sort of. . . . And then when I visited, we used to be down to his own father. . . . He thought I'd have intercourse with his own dad, imagine. . . . His imagination, that was all in his head. . . . Because he, that's all what *he* always wanted all the time I lived with him. Constantly. And that's what he wanted.

The worker comments:

This is the type of response which confused me most. I just did not and do not understand this "free association" of topics and lines of thought. Similarly, I do not understand what function this seemingly aimless talk played for Mrs. L. Was it to ward off questions or comments which she feared? Was it preferable to any silence? Was the tension of the interview bringing it about or does she always speak in such a manner? Was it a desperate attempt to show she was "good" and worthy of my care, that it was everyone else who did "bad" things? Was she not even perceiving me or was she checking out my reactions while she talked? All these various alternatives were going through my mind and suggesting alternative modes of action. I did not know whether she was crying out for some external ordering from me or whether she feared that as of yet and needed to be accepted in her wandering, dissociated ways before she would be able to accept direction or direct herself.

We noted above the encoder's need for feedback in checking whether or not the communication he was sending was, in fact, being correctly received. Similarly the receiver of the message, the decoder, has the responsibility of seeking feedback in checking that the message she received is the message which was sent. The fact that communication goes on at so many different levels, through so many different channels, and is so easily subject to distortion and misunderstanding argues for the necessity of such feedback. Often we do not realize that we do not understand. As Whyte says, "The great enemy of communication is the illusion of it." Achievement of good communication requires, then, a presumption of ignorance, the frequent acceptance of the fact that although we think we know what the interviewee said, we may, in fact, not really know. The corrective for presumptive ignorance is feedback. We check our understanding of the message by asking for confirmation.

Good communication exists when the thought is encoded and transmitted freely and with fidelity and where the message finally decoded in the mind of the hearer is a faithful reproduction of the message originally encoded; when there is exact correspondence between meanings intended by the symbols transmitted and the meanings ascribed to the symbols when received; when the meaning of the decoded symbols received is congruent with the meaning intended by the sender of the message. Communication then has high fidelity. When this happens we come closest to approximating the derivation of the word communication, namely "communis"—common, establishing a shared commonness.

The difficulty of receiving the message exactly as transmitted is repeatedly confirmed by the parlor game of sending a whispered message around a circle of participants, each repeating to the next person the message he thinks he received. The message as stated by the last person in the chain invariably is substantially different from the message as sent on its way by the first person. That communication is a serial process makes it a hazardous undertaking. Each cycle of interaction—encoding, sending, receiving, processing, decoding—follows from the previous cycle of interaction so that difficulty encountered in any one cycle adversely affects communication in the subsequent cycles. Each step follows the preceding step in sequence, so that a difficulty at any point along the line of the process results in a fault in all subsequent steps in the series.

Communication has the additional difficulty of being an irreversible process. What has been said cannot be unsaid. Unlike the written word which can be erased or edited, the spoken word is irretrievable. If your foot slips you can regain your balance; if your tongue slips you cannot recall your words.

Messages achieve part of their meaning from the context in which they are sent. The same question in different settings will evoke different aspects of the client's life situation. The question "How are things going?" in a public assistance setting relates to budget and finances; in a child guidance clinic setting, to the relationship with the child referred for service. In an interview in a medical social work setting, the question relates to an illness or disability; in the marital counseling agency, to the marriage.

Communication is contextual. The same statement appropriate and acceptable in one context—the locker room—may be inappropriate and unacceptable in another situation—the classroom. But even more important the interpersonal context, the nature of the relationship between sender and receiver, determine the meaning given to the message.

The communication event is structured and patterned in accordance with a set of rules and regulations established by the culture. Patterned interaction follows rules of language on taking turns in speaking, length of talk time, the nature of attention manifested, as well as rules regarding the etiquette of language and behavior.

Communication involves not only an external dialogue between worker and client, but also a series of internal monologues—client with herself, worker with herself. They are talking and listening to themselves while talking and listening to each other. Both the external dialogue and the internal monologues go on at different levels of more or less explicit communications. There is the overt, manifest content and the latent, covert content. There are the words directly spoken and the less obvious, indirect meanings of what is said.

The following is a section of a social work interview with both manifest and latent content presented, the material having been obtained from the participants after the interview.

Interviewer: male, 32, white, social worker.
Interviewee: female, 30, black, lower middle class, family services-home-maker unit.
(Manifest comment is in open roman, latent comment in parentheses and italics.)

Manifest Content	Latent Content
WORKER: Could you tell me something about what brings you to the agency?	*(Black. Hope she won't think we're racist if we turn down her request, whatever it is. Hope it's something simple we can handle.)*
CLIENT: The social worker at the hospital. . . . I have to go for an operation, and there is not going to be anybody to care for the kids because my husband works all day, and the kids have to have somebody look after them, and she said I might have a homemaker to look after the kids while I am away.	*(Honky, always a honky. Can't I ever get to talk to a black worker? Is he going to think I really need this or is he going to give me all that "uh" "uh" and get my black ass out of here? What will the kids do then? I really got to sell this.)*
WORKER: What kind of an operation is it you're scheduled for? How long will you be in the hospital?	*(How necessary is this and for how long? We only have a few homemakers, and if we tie up one for a long time we will be in a bind.)*
CLIENT: I have this trouble with my gall bladder all the time, all the time. It gets worse, and the doctor said I need this operation. It will	*(Does he believe me? Does he think I am making it worse than it really is? How the hell do I know how long it's going to take?)*

be worse for me and the kids the longer I put it off.

WORKER: Could you tell me who your doctor is and when we can contact him to discuss your situation?

(You can't expect the patient to know the medical details. If we have to plan for this, we should find out the situation from the person who knows it best—the doctor.)

CLIENT: Sure, sure. Dr. —— is the one I see when I go to the clinic. He knows all about it. Why do you have to talk to him?

(What does he want to know this for? Is he going to check what I tell him? I wonder if Dr. —— will back me up on this. He gets sore if a lot of people ask him questions.)

WORKER: That's a good question. It's not that we don't believe you or that we want to check up on you, but we find that the person asked to have the operation, in this case yourself, doesn't often know the medical details we need for planning. For instance, if we were going to put a homemaker in the home—and at this point we are just talking about it—we would have to know for how long and what you could do after you came home from the hospital on convalescence and how much the homemaker would have to do.

(Suspicious? Worried about our talking to the doctor? Afraid he might tell us something she would not want us to know? Or is it that she really doesn't know what purpose would be served in contacting the doctor? Have to be careful about making it clear what we have in mind.)

CLIENT: Well, I really need a homemaker if I am going for the operation. The kids can't care for themselves. They are too young.

(Why do they always have to make it so complicated? He hasn't even asked me about how old the kids are and how many of them there are. Right away they want to speak to someone else. Speak to me. I know more about this than anybody else does.)

In recapitulation, communication is an interactional cycle of coding, sending, receiving, processing, and decoding verbal and nonverbal symbols which have no intrinsic meaning in themselves. Maximum communication is achieved when the message is decoded in exactly the same way as it was encoded. However, physical, social, and psychological barriers, both in encoding and decoding messages, make fidelity in communication difficult.

SUGGESTED READINGS

There are whole libraries of books directed to interpersonal communication. The following are highly selective limited examples of this literature. The books cover the essential concepts that help in understanding interpersonal communication and offer leads on additional reading.

Bobby R. Patton and Kim Giffin. *Interpersonal Communication: Basic Text and Readings*. New York: Harper & Row, 1974 (495 pp.).

A good, solid, readable basic text in interpersonal communication. Selected from among dozens of such texts because it seems to provide the essentials briefly and clearly.

William W. Wilmot. *Dyadic Communication*. 2d ed. Reading, Mass.: Addison-Wesley, 1975 (234 pp.).

Because the interview is primarily an example of dyadic communication, this adaptation of principles and concepts of communication to the dyadic context is especially useful.

CHAPTER 3

The Interview and
Interpersonal Relationships

In chapter 2 I discussed some general problems in communication that are of concern to the interviewer. A further, and very significant, problem follows from the fact that all communication is interactive and interrelational. Each person in the communications network affects the other person and is, in turn, affected by him. The nature of the interpersonal relationship between participants in a communication system is, then, of considerable importance. Communication involves not only what is said and heard—the message encoded, transmitted, received, processed, and decoded—but also the interpersonal context in which the process takes place. The emotional interaction between parties in the communication transaction affects, positively or adversely, the pattern of communication. The emotional interaction between people is what we mean by the term "relationship" as used in social work.

If the relationship is positive, if there is good feeling—a relaxed, comfortable, trustful, respectful, harmonious, warm, psychologically safe feeling—between worker and client, each is more likely to be receptive to messages being sent. Perlman (1979) talks of relationship as the emotional bond, a connection of some emotional intensity. It is the connecting bond of feeling between interviewer and interviewee which gives a sense of alliance and solidarity. If the relationship is negative, if there is bad feeling—hostile, defensive, uneasy, mistrustful, disrespectful, discordant, psychologically threatening feeling—between worker and client, there is less desire and readiness to hear what is being said.

The relationship is the communication bridge between people. Messages pass over the bridge with greater or lesser difficulty, depending on the nature of the emotional interaction between people. Social and emotional screens and barriers are lowered or become more permeable in the context of a good relationship. The readiness to return to the agency and the willingness to participate in the interviews are heightened. It is easier to be an open person in such a facilitative, benign emotional climate of mutuality and nonpossessive warmth. A positive relationship acts as an anodyne, an anesthetic, to the sharing of painful material on the part of the client; it heightens the salience and credibility of the communication coming from the worker. It frees the client to reveal himself without defensiveness or distortion because a good relationship promises acceptance and understanding and freedom from punishing criticism, rejection, or reprisal. Such a relationship reduces the possibility that the interview will become a competitive struggle and increases the likelihood that it will become a collaborative endeavor. If the relationship is a positive one, the client perceives the interviewer as trustworthy, attractive, and competent.

Components of a Good Relationship

In the interview the protective functions of the ego, which counsel concealment, are in conflict with the adaptive functions of the ego, which counsel revelation to obtain help. The conditions making for a good relationship favor those components of the ambivalence which favor revelation.

A good relationship intensifies and amplifies the consequences of any interaction in the interview. It makes the worker's influence greater, her suggestions more appealing, any of her techniques more effective. The good relationship provides a favorable context for effective learning, for it predisposes the interviewee to accept the teaching communicated by the interviewer. Since the relationship mobilizes feelings and makes for a more emotionally fluid situation, it increases the possibility of effecting change. A good relationship makes the interviewer a more potent, more influential source of imitative behavior in accordance with which the interviewee can learn to model himself.

The interviewer, acting as a warm, accepting person, establishes an atmosphere which reduces anxiety and threat. As a consequence the relationship itself acts as a counterconditioning context. The interviewee may talk about problems and situations which normally provoke anxiety. However, in the context of a relationship which counters anxiety, the same material now evokes less anxiety. A positive relationship does the same work of counterconditioning as the behavioral-modification relaxation procedure which prepares the client for engagement in desensitization. When such a relationship has been achieved, there is a feeling of rapport between inter-

50   ORIENTATION AND BASIC CONCEPTS

viewer and interviewee. The word "rap," meaning "to get together, to talk
in an atmosphere of warm friendliness," derives from the word "rapport."

The most consistent finding in studies of effectiveness of casework, counseling and psychotherapy generally is the importance of the relationship
between the helping person and the person seeking help. A nationwide
study of the results of family service contacts notes that "one of the most
striking findings of the present study is the marked association of outcomes
with the counselor-client relationships." This association was highly significant statistically (Beck and Jones 1973:129). Analyzing a variety of service
factors thought to be related to outcome, the researchers found that "the
overpowering influence of the counselor-client relationship was startling. It
had more than doubled the predictive power of the second highest factor"
(p. 146).

In a study of the effects of intensive service in keeping children in their
own homes and out of foster care, the researchers found that the "overall
quality of the worker-client relationship was by far the most potent factor"
in accounting for results achieved (Jones, Neuman, and Shyne 1976:116).
Other research studies of how clients view their experience with social
agencies confirm a clear recognition of the crucial importance of the worker-
client relationship as the basis for effective helping (Maluccio 1979; Sainsbury 1975:116, 125).

A detailed research study of the outcomes of psychotherapy by behavior
therapists and psychoanalytically oriented psychotherapists found that the
"patient-therapist relationship appears to be a critical factor in the success
of psychotherapy and important in behavior therapy as well" (Sloan
1975:225). Reviewing different relevant studies of therapy outcomes Gurman (1977) found that 23 of 26 studies reviewed found positive outcomes
were associated with the quality of the interviewer–interviewee relationship as perceived by the interviewee. A review of some 100 different psychotherapy research reports concluded that "the different forms of psychotherapeutic treatment have a major common element—a helping
relationship is present in all of them" (Luborsky, Singer, and Luborsky
1976:17). Orlinsky and Howard, in a detailed review of research regarding
the process of psychotherapy, concluded that "the studies done thus far
suggest that the positive quality of the relational bond, as exemplified in
the reciprocal interpersonal behaviors of the participants is more clearly
related to patient improvement than are any of the particular treatment
techniques used by therapists" (1978:296).

While much of the discussion of "relationship" as a potent factor in enabling the interviewer to do the work of the interview comes from Rogerian
and psychoanalytically oriented therapists, behavior therapy also recognizes its importance. In *Social Casework: A Behavioral Approach* the au-

thors note that "relationship factors play a critical part" in the behavioral interventions (Schwartz and Goldiamond 1975:270). Even in such routine procedures as systematic desensitization there is acknowledgment on the part of behavior modification interviewers that relationship is an important factor (Morris and Suckerman 1974).

Despite the fact that many social agency clients come for, and receive, concrete help, hard services, the relationship between client and worker, the nonmaterial aspects of the service delivery, is of considerable importance and significance to clients. On the basis of detailed interviews with 305 clients McKay, Goldberg, and Irvin report that "in describing the good social worker—respondents laid the greatest stress on personality characteristics such as understanding and sympathy, a pleasing personality and social ability to put one at one's ease" (1973:488).

Because the relationship—the context in which communication takes place—is such a crucial determinant of the success or failure of communication, there has been considerable concern with attempts to define the attributes of a good relationship and the behavior of the worker-interviewer associated with the nurturing of such a relationship.

Relationship is a global, nonspecific term. It encompasses a variety of different behaviors and feelings which pass between interviewer and interviewee. Efforts have been made to break open the term and define the discrete, molecular elements which go to make up a good relationship.

Social work has been struggling with this for some time. The literature of social work has, historically, identified and discussed such elements as acceptance, individualization, self-determination, nonjudgmental attitude, confidentiality (Biestek 1957). More recently the social work literature has modified some of the terms employed in discussing "relationship." Borrowing from the research conducted by Rogerian oriented psychotherapists such as Truax and Carkhuff on the essential facilitative conditions that characterize an effective relationship, there is currently more talk in social work of empathic understanding, unconditional positive regard or nonpossessive warmth, congruence, genuineness, and authenticity (Fisher 1978).

These attitudes and interpersonal orientations have been identified as necessary core conditions for developing a helping relationship and, inferentially, as necessary for effective interviewing. There is still considerable debate, however, about the specific components of a good relationship, their definition, and how they are manifested (Lambert and Dejulio 1977; Krauft et al. 1977; Perloff, Waskow, and Wolfe 1978).

But despite the continuing debate about specifics, there is a general consensus that the nature of the interpersonal relationship between interviewer and interviewee is of crucial importance in determining how the interview will go, and there is a general consensus that development of the kind of relationship which makes for most effective interviewing is characterized by elements of warmth, acceptance, trust, understanding, respect. After studying the extensive research literature, a complete review of which I have spared the reader, I am reminded of Aldous Huxley's remark that after a lifetime of study of what makes for an effective relationship he was chagrined to find that it all boiled down to "being a little nicer."

It is at this point that a book is the least successful device for teaching what needs to be taught. In talking about relationships we are talking about emotional interaction. The nature of the technically correct feeling which the worker-interviewer needs to manifest might be described and, perhaps, clinically illustrated. One can exhort the worker to feel what she should feel in order to develop a desirable relationship in the interview. But it is not possible to teach anybody how to feel the necessary feelings through description or exhortation. For those who have achieved these attitudes, the reminder is unnecessary; for those who have not, the reminder is ineffective.

Recognizing the deficiencies of a book as an instructional medium for teaching certain kinds of content, and recognizing the futility of exhorting the worker-interviewer to be respectful and compassionate, accepting and understanding, gentle and noncritical, we will only briefly and didactically review some of the essential attributes generally recognized as components of a good relationship.

CLIENT SELF-DETERMINATION

In adhering to and encouraging clients' self-determination, the worker-interviewer establishes an atmosphere of mutuality, encourages clients' participation in problem-solving efforts, and respects clients' initiative. Her behavior implements her belief that the client has the right, and the capacity, to direct his own life; she works *with* the client in problem solving; she communicates confidence in the client's ability to achieve his own solutions and actively helps the client to achieve his own solution in his own way. Self-determination guarantees the interviewer's help without domination.

The effort to actualize client self-directive decision making implies a recognition of, and confidence in, the client's capacity for constructive self-determination. It indicates a respect for the interviewee's autonomy.

Some argue that "self-direction" might be a more accurate term to apply to this. What is involved is a recognition and an implementation of the fact that the interviewee has a clear prerogative, an entitlement and a right, to make his own decisions, that he should not be coerced or controlled either overtly or subtly to do or feel as the interviewer prefers him to do or to feel.

There is wisdom in the adage that "a man convinced against his will is of the same opinion still." The clients see this in terms of the worker's behavior in the interview: "She acted as though we were co-workers on a common problem." "She made me feel that I didn't have to agree with her if I felt differently about something." "She tried to get me to make my own decisions." "She encouraged me to work on my problems in my own way." "She didn't seem to think it was necessary for me to accept her idea, opinions, advice, if I wanted her to like me."*

The case vignettes below are followed by a series of possible interviewer responses, some illustrating an attitude respecting self-determination and some illustrating an inappropriate violation of this approach.

Client: female, 27, white, lower class, public assistance.
CLIENT: So I don't know. I think I should try to put the kids in a day center or maybe even in a foster home and get a job and make some money so we can get back on our feet again—but that might not be so good for the kids.
APPROPRIATE RESPONSES:
1. You're puzzled about what to do.
2. It's hard to know what would be best.
3. "Not so good for the kids"?
INAPPROPRIATE RESPONSES:
1. Well, if you got a job you would be off relief.
2. My own feeling is that it would be better to stay home.
3. It wouldn't be so bad for the kids.
Client: female, 55, middle class, medical social work agency.
CLIENT: I know I have to have this operation, but I would rather not talk about it.
APPROPRIATE RESPONSES:
1. It's hard to talk about.
2. Thinking about it makes you anxious.
3. Okay, perhaps there is something else you would rather talk about.
INAPPROPRIATE RESPONSES:
1. But I was supposed to discuss this with you.
2. Not talking about it won't make the problem disappear.
3. Well, it has to be discussed sooner or later, so why not now?

Problems and limitations around adherence to and encouragement of client self-determination have been discussed extensively in social work literature (Biestek 1951; Biestek and Gehrig 1978; Kassel and Kane 1980).

Adherence to the entitlement of client autonomy and self-determination

*Some of the phrasing is adapted from G. T. Barrett-Lennard, "Dimensions of Therapist Response as Causal Factors in Therapeutic Change," *Psychological Monographs* 76, no. 562 (1962).

requires a presumption of reasonable decision-making competence on the part of the interviewee. We do not grant infants the right to self-determination. We limit the autonomy of people who are clearly psychotic and we do not accept a person's decision to commit suicide.

There may be, and often is, a conflict between client preference and the worker's responsibility to the agency and to the community, as illustrated in Hardman's (1975) amusingly perceptive article "Not With My Daughter You Don't."

There is conflict between the desire to grant the client his own decision and a conviction about which decision is the more desirable one for the client to choose. The conflict is between honoring the promise of freedom for the client and meeting responsibility for client needs.

A medical social worker talks to a 32-year-old mother who is reluctant to schedule a needed operation because of concern about care for her three young children during the period of hospitalization. The worker has offered homemaker service, but the mother is rejecting the idea. The worker comments:

I could understand her objections, but I also realized that unless she accepted the service she might delay scheduling the needed medical care. Frankly I wanted to throw the weight of my influence in favor of inducing her to accept homemaker service, but I was deterred by the dislike for manipulating and denying her maximum freedom in determining her own decision. Despite everything, my bias in favor of getting her the necessary medical attention without undue delay got past my professional safeguards. The questions I asked in discussing this with Mrs. R. were formulated in a way to suggest answers in favor of homemaker service. Instead of neutral questions starting "What do you think . . . ," I tended to ask questions starting with "Don't you think that. . . ." My verbal skirts weren't long enough to keep my bias from showing.

Recognizing the variety of considerations—biological, practical, philosophical—which limit the client's freedom and independence in identifying and implementing his preference, one can still cite adherence to client self-determination or self-direction as an important attitudinal component in developing a positive relationship. A worker who approaches the client with a conviction of the desirability of maximizing client self-direction tries to push against the limits restricting client choices. She seeks to determine the preferences of the client, even if these preferences cannot always be accepted; she seeks to get the client's reaction to any inevitable restrictions on the client's choice; she seeks to increase feasible opportunities for client choice-making; she makes a decided effort to be aware of her own preferences and any tendency of hers to impose these on the client; she respects the client's preferences even though, for a variety of reasons, it may be necessary to modify them; she exercises the absolute minimum of control and interference necessary to balance conflicting responsibilities to the client and the community. This attitude is in contrast to the worker who is convinced that only she knows what is right for the client, who seeks to manipulate the client both overtly and covertly to accept her choices, and who has little interest in and/or respect for the client's choice or preference.

The end result may be the same. The client may be required or induced or influenced to do some things different from his own first best preference. But the process by which this is achieved can either make the client feel esteemed, respected, individualized or, on the contrary, dehumanized, stereotyped, denigrated. An attitude and orientation that communicate sincere consideration for the client's entitlement to self-determination results in a positive feeling-interaction between interviewer and interviewee, even if the entitlement may sometimes have to be modified, curtailed, or even denied.

Although social work has identified self-determination as a vital ingredient for developing a positive relationship, other groups involved in the helping interview have not dealt with it as a separate consideration. Self-determination is, however, subsumed for these other groups as a component of empathy and positive regard. If the client is to be understood and respected, then his choices and preferences need to be understood and seriously considered. Preferences and choices are regarded as an expression of the interviewee's individuality and uniqueness over which he has control and jurisdiction.

INTEREST, WARMTH, TRUST

Genuine *interest* is a great help in establishing and maintaining a positive relationship. A worker expresses interest by showing concern about a client's needs, indicating readiness and willingness to help, communicating the feeling that she really cares what happens to the client, over and beyond her formal responsibility to the job.

Clients have testified to a high level of interest by the worker in such statements as the following: "She did everything she could to help me." "She could be trusted to do what she said she would do." "She was ready to do things to help me even if it meant some bother for her." "She cared about what happened to me." "She didn't rush to finish the interview." "She seemed to *want* to hear what I had to say."

We demonstrate interest by asking the interviewee for his story, his feelings, his reactions, his responses, by making replies that indicate how well we have been listening, how much we have remembered of the interviewee's statement, how carefully and attentively we have heard him. Examples below exhibit both appropriate and inappropriate worker responses.

Client: male, 22, black, lower class, probation agency.
CLIENT: I am not sure if I can explain how I got into this jam.
APPROPRIATE RESPONSES:
1. Take your time.
2. Tell it your own way and perhaps I can help if you get stuck.
3. Uh-huh (expectant silence).
INAPPROPRIATE RESPONSES:
1. Well, we have very limited time. . . .
2. Well then, perhaps we can go on to something else.
3. Well, it may not be so important.

The appropriate response indicates an interest in hearing what the client has to say, a receptiveness to and encouragement of communication. The inappropriate response indicates lack of interest and impatience to hasten the end of the interview.

Client: female, 26, black, lower class, public assistance.
CLIENT: All those things you asked me to bring—some of them I have, some of them I can't find. I don't know how I can get them, where to go. I have the rent receipts and gasoline bills and for the electricity, but like the marriage certificate, and the birth certificates of the two boys—these I don't know about.
APPROPRIATE RESPONSES:
1. I'll be glad to show you how to get what you need.
2. Let's go over this and see what can be done.
3. Try again to find them. We'll help you get duplicates if you can't.
INAPPROPIATE RESPONSES:
1. Well, I am afraid that until you bring these things we cannot make out a check for you.
2. Well, you'll just have to find them.
3. I thought it was clear that we needed this for your eligibility.

There is a thin line between interest and curiosity. Curiosity implies seeking access to information to which the interviewer is not entitled because it does not further the purpose of the interview. The focus of legitimate interest is selective and discriminating. Principled adherence to confidentiality would then suggest that we need to encourage and help the interviewee to be silent about anything that is none of our business.

Warmth suggests a commitment to the needs of the interviewee. It involves a caring for and about; it involves a sincere interest in the client and his predicament and a willingness to extend oneself to help.

Warmth is communicated by a positive response actively displayed in eye contact, a forward lean, smiling, frequent short encouraging verbal responses, positive statements about the interviewee. Speech is calm and has a friendly overtone.

Respect is displayed by adherence to the appropriate social amenities, the common human courtesies—but not effusive, overdemonstrative friendliness. Affirming the client's worth and uniqueness by understanding and acceptance is an indication of respect.

The interviewees who felt that the interviewer communicated warmth and respect for them said: "He was friendly and polite and he seemed to have a regard for my feelings"; "She really seemed to care what happened to me"; "He not only was interested in trying to help me with my problem, he was interested in me as a person"; "She treated me like the adult I am"; "He didn't try to act smug and superior as though he were trying to outsmart me."

Trust is more likely to develop when the interviewee perceives the interviewer is favorably disposed toward him, has good intentions toward him, wants to be helpful, demonstrates competence and expertise in being helpful, and can be relied upon.

Trust and warmth and respect are hard to separate from each other and from the other components that go to comprise the orientation that makes for a positive relationship. There is a considerable overlap between warmth and liking and respect and acceptance and positive regard.

RESPECT FOR CLIENT'S INDIVIDUALITY

Demonstration of respect for the client-interviewee's individuality helps to establish and maintain a positive relationship. This involves an attitude and behavior that support or enhance the client's self-esteem. The atmosphere between interviewer and interviewee is one which suggests that, as people, they have equal value. The worker responds to the client as a unique individual rather than as one of a whole class of persons. The orientation toward the interviewee is not "as *a* human being but as *this* human being with his personal differences" (Biestek 1957:25). It involves the personalization of any generalization and suspension of its application until there is clear evidence that it is applicable to this particular individual.

The client-interviewee perceives respect for individuality demonstrated by the worker-interviewer who behaves in the following manner during the interview: "She was friendly and had great regard for my feeling." "She was interested in my individuality." "She didn't talk down to me." "She never made me feel I was just another client." The vignette below is followed by appropriate and inappropriate worker responses.

Client: female, 19, white, lower middle class, child care agency.
CLIENT: Well, Catholics are against abortion, and here I am pregnant and all.
APPROPRIATE RESPONSES:
How do you yourself feel about abortion?
What are your ideas about what you want to do with the baby?
And you, what do you think?
INAPPROPRIATE RESPONSES:
Well I guess, as a Catholic, abortion is not a possibility for you.
Okay, so abortion is out then.
What is your thinking about adoption?

Stereotyping is the reverse of individualizing the client. On the basis of a limited amount of information we assign a client to a group and then attribute to him the attitudes, feelings, behavior generally attributed to members of the group. Having classified and labeled we then tend to perceive the interviewee not as he is in all his own special individuality but in terms of the expected pattern drawn from the stereotype. Stereotyping reduces our sensitivity to differentiate this interviewee from others and to make precise discriminations.

The persistence of the tendency of interviewers to stereotype presents a problem because, to some extent, it is functional. It would be impossibly difficult to meet every interviewee without some generalization in mind which enable us to organize the complex data we have to process. While we are opposed to stereotyping we recognize the utility of generalizations, scientifically derived, which professionals apply in the use of all sorts of diagnostic labels. Stereotypes are lay generalizations derived from empirical lay experience. As such they have an element of validity. Members of a particular age, sex, race, ethnic group do have some elements in common. At the same time each member of the group is different from every other member of the group. The stereotype or scientifically derived generalizations emphasizes group characteristics and are useful in that it tells us something about the interviewee that is likely to be true. Individualization emphasizes the unique aspects of the interviewee.

Because it is functionally useful and necessary in organizing the world around us it is likely that, despite all our exhortations, stereotyping will continue to be a problem.

The best we can hope for is that the interviewer will be explicitly aware of the stereotypes and generalizations she holds and that she will hold them lightly and flexibly, applying them only when it is clear that there is sufficient data to warrant their use. Such an interviewer gives the client the "space" and the freedom to communicate data which contradicts the generalizations she holds and is open enough to receive such data.

The "halo or horns" syndrome also leads to denying some aspect of the client's individuality. The "halo" effect suggests that if the interviewee is considerate in one situation he will be considerate in all situations and conversely for the "horns" effect, i.e., if the client is selfish in one situation he is likely to be selfish in others. This denies people their tendency to be wonderfully inconsistent and to act differently in different situations. Like a stereotype or a scientific generalization "halo or horns" effects makes our job easier because we presume to know more about the individual client than we, in fact, do.

Consistent application of the principle of individualization implies a contradiction to everything that is said in this book regarding principles of interviewing. Every suggested principle of interviewing is a generalization. While the suggested principles are likely to work for most of the interviewees most of the time, the principle of individualization cautions the worker to be sensitive to the exceptions, to look for, and monitor, feedback carefully and adjust the application of the principles to the individual instance.

ACCEPTANCE

An accepting, nonjudgmental attitude helps in establishing and maintaining a positive relationship.* The worker manifests acceptance by behaving so as to indicate her respect and concern for the client, regardless of behavior which the worker may reject; she is compassionate, gentle, sympathetic. The client is given the freedom to be himself, to express himself freely, in all his unlovely as well as lovely aspects. The worker is not moralistic, cold, aloof, derogatory, or disapproving. She should be mindful of Samuel Johnson's statement that "God Himself does not presume to judge a man till the end of his days." The nonjudgmental attitude is one which suggests that the interviewer is not concerned with praise or blame but solely with understanding. The accepting worker seeks to determine what explains the individual's behavior rather than to determine the worth of such behavior. The "object of acceptance is not the good or the bad but the real; the individual as he actually is, not as we wish him to be or think he should be" (Biestek 1957:70).

Although acceptance does not necessarily mean agreeing with or condoning the client's frame of reference, his point of view, and his concept of

*We have phrased the conditions for a good relationship in terms that reflect social work usage. Other groups also vitally concerned with relationships have used somewhat different terms to designate essentially the same attitudes. Perhaps the best known comparable term for "acceptance" is the Rogerian "unconditional positive regard."

reality, it involves granting their validity. It implies interpreting others in terms of themselves. Perhaps it means being "human enough not to be alienated by some of the unpleasant manifestations of being human."

The following poem expresses a client's conception of an accepting worker:

> This woman
> talks to me
> in a warm language
> between her feelings
> and mine.
> She has no whip
> in her talk,
> no snarling teeth;
> She does not need to
> see the color of my blood
> to know me.
> This woman,
> seeing the gap
> in my fence,
> walks through it
> knowingly; and I,
> I let her stand in my
> field,
> unharmed.   C. ANATOPOLSKY*

The client feels accepted when the worker evokes the following kinds of responses in the client-interviewee: "She made me feel free to say whatever I was thinking." "I could be very critical of her or very appreciative of her without it changing her good feeling toward me." "I could talk about most anything in my interview without feeling embarrassed or ashamed." "I had the feeling that here is one person I can really trust." "I could talk about anything without being afraid she would think less of me as a person."

The feeling of acceptance is described by an interviewee when he says that the interviewer "let me say what I felt," "didn't accuse, criticize or condemn me," "didn't hold anything against me," "I could trust her, I could say anything," "didn't put me down" (Maluccio 1979:124). "She didn't seem to make judgments about me—to fit me into a certain pigeonhole," "I feel I could get angry with him or criticize him and he wouldn't resent it or reject me."

*Reprinted, with permission, from the *AAPSW Newsletter* (Winter 1937).

Client: male, 46, white, middle class, family service.
CLIENT: It's just that I can't keep my hands off the stuff. I run into the slightest trouble and I reach for the bottle.
APPROPRIATE RESPONSES:
There is trouble and you feel you need a drink.
You reach for the bottle.
How does reaching for the bottle help?
INAPPROPRIATE RESPONSES:
Well, drinking doesn't solve the problem, does it?
That's not so smart, is it?
You ought to have more will power than that.

Client: male, 75, lower class, Old Age Assistance.
CLIENT: All you social workers are alike, one God-damn question after the other. Why do I have to tell you so much just to get the help! You could see I need it if you only used your eyes more and your mouth less.
APPROPRIATE RESPONSES:
You think I talk too much?
We make it hard for you to get help you feel you need.
You're sore because you feel much of this is none of my business.
INAPPROPRIATE RESPONSES:
I don't like having to ask them any more than you feel like answering them.
You're making my job harder to do.
Well, I am afraid you'll just have to let me get this information if you expect us to help you.

Being accepting and being nonjudgmental are different aspects of the same basic attitude—acceptance is an act of commission, being nonjudgmental an act of omission. The difficulties of implementing an accepting, nonjudgmental attitude are discussed extensively in social work literature.

Perlman suggests that the attitude which the term *acceptance* identifies might be better named "nonblaming," "noncensorous" (1979:56). Since the interviewer is supposed to make "judgments" about what changes the interviewer hopes to achieve with the client her work cannot be "nonjudgmental." But the "judgments," the assessment of the client in his situation which needs changing is without blame. A truly "nonjudgmental" attitude would express a neutral indifference to the client's behavior—it really doesn't matter. To the interviewer who cares about the client it really does matter that the client may be acting in a way that is dysfunctional or destructive for himself and others in his family.

Acceptance implies granting the right to be different. Unconditional acceptance and indiscriminate approval, however, may reflect indifference and noninvolvement. If I am not concerned about the consequences for you of your behavior, I find it easy to accept anything you plan to do.

The interviewer's acceptance and support of behaviors which differ to some marked degree from usual social norms may leave the interviewee with suspicions about either the sincerity or the competence of the interviewer. It might also lead to a feeling that the interviewer is being ingratiating or manipulative. The interviewee is generally keenly aware of community attitudes toward dysfunctional behavior. Rather than being helpful, the interviewer may be creating additional difficulty for the client by condoning and sanctioning behavior which is problematic for the client. It is clear then that a distinction needs to be made between accepting the person, his thoughts, and his feelings and responding with some concern to behaviors which create and maintain social problems for the client.

Admittedly and parenthetically (since an adequate discussion of acceptance would require a book in itself), this does not settle the matter. Questions can be raised about behaviors, labeled dysfunctional by the community, which derive from a pathological society in need of reform, or about behaviors such as homosexuality, which may have considerable community disapproval but which may not be dysfunctional for the individual. In general, social work has been ready to accept a wider range of behaviors than has the lay community (Pilsecker 1978). Broader acceptance does not imply an absence of limits of acceptable behavior. Reactions to rape, incest, child and spouse battering are testimonials to this.

EMPATHIC UNDERSTANDING

In empathic understanding the worker is demonstrating response to the latent as well as the manifest content of a client's communication. She understands, sensitively and accurately, the nature of the client's experience and the meaning this has for him, and understands the client's world cognitively and empathically from the client's point of view. She understands with, as well as about, the client, and has the capacity to communicate her understanding to the client in words attuned to the client's feeling; she really hears what the client is saying, so her responses have an "I am with you" quality, fitting in with the client's meaning and mood. If she does not always understand, she is always sincerely striving to understand, to reach out and receive the client's communication.

The interviewer feels *with* the client rather than for him. Feeling *for* the client would be a sympathetic rather than an empathic response. Somebody once said that if you have a capacity for empathy you feel squat when you see a squat vase and feel tall when you look at a tall vase. Empathy is entering imaginatively into the inner life of someone else. It is not enough simply to be empathically understanding; one needs to communicate to the client the fact that one accurately perceives and feels his situation.

The client perceives the worker acting in response to empathic understanding when, in the client's words, "She was able to see and feel things in exactly the same way I do." "Many of the things she said just seemed to hit the nail on the head." "She understood my words but also how I felt." "When I did not say what I meant at all clearly, she still understood me."

Client: female, 37, white, upper lower class, child guidance clinic.
CLIENT: I know I am supposed to love him, but how much can you put love in a kid without getting some back? You can't just go on feeling love without his showing you some love, too, in return.
APPROPRIATE RESPONSES:
1. It's very disappointing for you.
2. It must be hard to do what you have to do under such circumstances.
3. That must hurt.
INAPPROPRIATE RESPONSES:
1. Well, he is only a kid and he doesn't understand.
2. Still and all, you are his mother.
3. Many kids don't show their love for parents.

Empathy is the conscious awareness of another's feelings by the act of transposition. In sympathy we recognize the other person's feelings but feel differently ourselves about what is taking place. In empathy the feeling we have about what is taking place is like that felt by the other person with whom we empathize.

The term *empathy* has not as yet achieved a consensually accepted clear definition (Macarov 1978). Many writers use it to mean the interviewer's ability to understand the interviewee from his frame of reference, from his point of view. The interviewer's response is "on target," "in line with," "tuned into" the meaning and significance the experience has for the interviewee. She is on the same "wave length" of the interviewee and "knows where he is coming from." The interviewer enters into the client's world of perception "as if" it were the interviewer's own; she puts herself in the "other person's shoes."

This suggests that the interviewer demonstrates accurate interpersonal perception. The meaning of empathy in this sense is that it is a cognitive process. Through empathy we share the "state of mind" of the interviewee. What is supposedly involved in this kind of empathy is a relatively conscious control which permits us to become absorbed in another person's thinking—a kind of "listening with the third ear."

Others use the term "empathy" to point to a process which has stronger affective elements. Not only does the interviewer understand the interviewee on his own terms, but she also is feeling as the interviewee feels. There is, beyond cognitive understanding, a "matching of feelings." Empathy here involves not only accurate perception of the other person's feelings and attitudes, an imaginative transformation of thinking by the interviewer so that she understands the situation as the interviewee understands it, but it involves, further, the mobilization of feeling in the interviewer corresponding to the feelings being felt by the interviewee. This suggests a more affective process of understanding; not only to "see with the eyes of another," "hear with the ears of another" but also to "feel with the heart of another." It is understanding through analogous experiencing.

Empathy involves feeling oneself into the experience through self-arousal. In empathizing we categorize the client's experience and evolve an analogous personal experience. Foster care placement is an experience of separation and loss for the parent. Categorizing this as a general experience of separation and loss, the interviewer, who has never experienced foster placement, evokes the feeling associated with going off to college, empathizing with the client. The client's pain and fright of learning about a need for an operation may involve self-arousal of analogous feelings by the interviewer of pain and fright at having to take an important exam.

Empathy is implied when the interviewee says of the interviewer that "She appreciates what my experience feels like to *me.*" "She understands both my words and the way I feel."

There is the danger that projection may be mistaken for empathy—"this is the way I would feel in this situation, so this must be the way he is feeling." The interviewer has to discriminate between her own feelings and the feelings which originate in the interviewee. It requires the ability to oscillate between subjective enmeshment with the interviewee and affectual detachments, sensing the client's inner world of private, personal meanings as if it were the interviewer's own, while recognizing the separation implied by the "as if." An excess of empathy would imply overidentification with the interviewee and a loss of objectivity necessary for effecting interviewing. As Mattinson notes: The interviewer's "psychological skin needs to be sensitive enough to pick up some of the psychic difficulties of his client but it needs to be firm enough around his own being to be able to distinguish between what belongs to him and what is, in fact, some feeling he has introjected from the client" (1975:31).

GENUINENESS AND AUTHENTICITY

The Rogerians, existential therapists, and others concerned with the interview, particularly the therapeutic interview, have identified genuineness, or authenticity, as an essential condition for a good relationship.

Though this condition has received limited explicit consideration in the social work literature, Bradmiller (1978) found that honesty, straightforwardness, and sincerity by the interviewer—all elements of genuineness and authenticity—were seen by social workers as of almost equal importance to "respect," "warmth," "empathy and understanding" as "necessary elements of a helping relationship."

Authenticity on the part of the interviewer requires that she be real and human in the interview. It implies responsiveness and spontaneity, the willingness and readiness to share with the interviewee one's own feelings and reactions about what is going on in the interview. Genuineness means that there is a striving toward congruence between the worker's feelings and her behavior.

Interviewees talk of genuineness in the interview when they say "She does not put on a front with me," "She doesn't put on her social worker role when she talks to me," "She seems willing to express whatever is actually on her mind with me, including any feelings about herself," "She is not full of pretensions and is not a phony," "He is not artificial or pompous but natural and spontaneous."

The interviewer perceived as genuine has no need to share her feelings if such sharing is not important to the conduct of the interview. Where sharing her feelings is helpful to achieving the objectives of the interview, the genuine interviewer shares openly without resistance, defensiveness, or self-protective apology. She does not deny her feelings. The interviewer perceived as genuine is able to openly admit mistakes that she made and to admit ignorance when she does not know the answer to a question.

As with empathy and respect, scales have been developed to measure levels of authenticity (Carkhuff 1969; Kiesler 1967; Carkhuff and Truax 1967).

Low authenticity, genuineness, and congruence are at one end of the scale. The interviewer is guarded, defensive, and reticent about making any disclosures about herself. She seems detached, depersonalized, anonymous. In answering any question raised she either fails to answer or answers briefly and ambiguously without communicating any information except the most superficial and obvious. The interviewer's answers appear evasive, closed, enigmatic. The atmosphere generated is formal and professional; social and psychological distance is maximized.

At the high end of the scale the interviewer openly provides information requested and when appropriate initiates the sharing of information. She answers spontaneously, candidly, openly, and fully, sharing information that might be helpful to the client. The affect with which self-disclosure is communicated is spontaneous rather than sounding habitual, artificial, or canned so that what is said rings true rather than sounding phony.

Authenticity is related to, but separated from, the problem of interviewer self-disclosure in the interview. One can be authentic, that is, without pretense, unaffected, true to oneself, not falsely assuming a role, while not sharing too much about oneself with the interviewee. The supposition is, however, that if one is authentic and genuine there will be a greater predisposition, willingness, and readiness to be "open" and sharing with the interviewee. The subject of interviewer disclosure is discussed more fully below in chapter 11.

CONFIDENTIALITY

A strong assurance for the client-interviewee that, in revealing himself to the worker-interviewer, he is not making such information available to a wider public, reduces the level of ego threat and facilitates communication. Threat to self-esteem resulting from disclosure of unflattering material is limited if only the interviewer will know this potentially damaging material. Information about one's person is a private possession. In sharing it with the worker, the client is not giving permission that it be broadcast and used indiscriminately.

Adherence to confidentiality is, in effect, a corollary to acceptance of the interviewee. It demonstrates that the interviewer does respect the interviewee's rights and entitlements as an individual and that she can be trusted.

The pragmatic basis for adherence to confidentiality is that if the social work interviewer is to perform her functions effectively, she needs to know a great deal about the personal intimate life of the interviewee. The assurance of confidentiality facilitates inducing the client to disclose such information and entrust it to the worker. The work of the agency generally is facilitated by assurances of confidentiality. Without such assurance some people who might need, and be able to use, agency service would be discouraged. Knowledge about a person, particularly personal intimate knowledge, gives others power over that person—for potential damage, to hurt and embarrass, as well as for potential assistance.

The ethical basis for adherence to confidentiality is that personal information is a possession of the client, analogous to his hat and coat. In disclosing information about himself the client lends this to the worker in exchange for being helped. But despite the fact the interviewee is induced to "lend" information to get what help he wants, such information still belongs to the client and cannot be "lent" by the interviewer to others without his permission.

Confidentiality guarantees that private affairs will not become public property. It might be advisable if, early in the interview, in establishing the ground rules for participant interaction, the interviewer says something about the confidential nature of the encounter.

It is clear that the worker has an obligation to guard confidential information very carefully and discreetly, that it is shared with others, after obtaining client's permission, only when it is necessary to help the client more effectively. Obtaining client permission is not a simple procedure but currently involves great emphasis on "informed consent"—which means the client clearly understands what information is shared, with whom, for what purpose. The client is informed that such information, while disclosed to the interviewer in privacy, may be shared with supervisors, typists, colleagues who might, at some point, be involved with the case. The greater use of the team approach in offering services increases the need for inter- and intra-agency sharing of information.

In rare instances there might be a need to tell the interviewee that the assurance of confidentiality is not absolute, that information disclosed which indicates that the client may be planning to hurt others or hurt himself may, protectively, need to be shared with others without the client's consent.

Finally, despite assurances of confidentiality agency records may be opened by court order. Social workers do not generally have the protection of privileged communication. Privileged communication is a special legal concept in support of agency confidentiality. It provides legal protection to the professionals' refusal to share information obtained in the confidential worker-client interview and/or agency records. Such privileges have been granted to clergymen, lawyers, and doctors in the statutes of many states. Extension of this privilege to social workers has been granted by very few states and then only with considerable extenuating provisions. This trend may be accelerated with the spread of social work licensing and certification.

The limits of any realistic promise of confidentiality lies then in saying that you will not willfully or carelessly share a client's information with anyone who, in your best judgment, does not need to know it or can possibly hurt the client.

The Practicalities of a Good Relationship

These then are some of the necessary conditions of worker attitude, as reflected in appropriate worker behavior, which are prerequisites for establishing and maintaining a positive relationship. Relationship is interactive however, and interaction implies that more is required than the input of the worker-interviewer. The client-interviewee is an equally important factor in developing and maintaining a relationship. The worker may offer the necessary conditions for optimum relationship, but it may fail to develop because the client lacks the capacity or the desire to interact.

The worker's actions may not be the sole determinant of the client's response to her efforts. Interaction may be the result of transference as well as objective elements in the interaction. Transference means that the client reacts to the worker as though she were another person out of the past.

The interviewer has control only over the attitudes she communicates. She has no control over how her communication is perceived. Interviewer-offered conditions may not be the same as interviewee-received conditions. There is evidence to indicate that there can be a discrepancy between objectively rated therapeutic conditions and client rating of them (Gurman 1977). Generally one can count on some congruity between the two. But the true test of the effect of the facilitative conditions is ultimately not what the interviewer does but what the interviewee perceives her as doing.

The more frequent situation, however, is that, having been met with interest, respect, understanding, and acceptance on the part of the interviewer, the client responds with reciprocal warm feelings of liking for the interviewer. The interaction then spirals in a positive direction, toward increased mutual attractiveness of the participants.

The principle of reciprocal affect suggests it is easier to like people who like us and contrariwise easier to find ourselves disliking people who dislike us.

The importance of the interviewer-interviewee relationship is a factor common to all interviews conducted by social workers, whatever their approach to the client-interviewee. Both a worker employing behavioral-modification techniques and one who is psychoanalytically oriented need to give active consideration to the relationship. Indeed, one may argue that these conditions are just a somewhat exaggerated delineation of what is required in any good human relationship. As Oldfield notes, "interviewing is a special branch of the general art of conducting human relations" (1951:139).

In and of itself, however, a good relationship accomplishes nothing. It offers the potential for use in communication, but it needs to be used toward this end. Rapport can be high, both participants may talk easily, spontaneously, and comfortably, but if there is no agreement on purpose and/or no one who takes responsibility for holding the participants to the accomplishment of the purpose, then there will be no productive interview. Both the interviewer and interviewee may share in a conspiracy to evade the painful work that may be required for a productive interview.

A good relationship is like the heat which makes bending of iron possible. But while the iron is hot, somebody has to make the horseshoe. Heating alone will not accomplish this. A good relationship is not invariably pleasant. What helps is not a relationship that is always nice, but one that is actively utilized to further the purpose of the interview, even if to do so is to risk challenge, conflict, and unpleasantness. The worker strives to be consistently useful rather than consistently popular.

This might require, on occasion, the use of confrontation in which the interviewer presents the interviewee with contradictions between his words and his behavior; it might require the use of authority, for example, to protect a child from abuse; it might require an unequivocal statement of the expectation the worker has that the client will implement whatever responsibilities he agreed he would accept. However painful for the client such necessary approaches may be, they meet with less resistance if they are advanced in the context of a good relationship.

The ultimate purpose of developing a relationship is for more effective interviewing. It is not for the purpose of making the interviewee love the interviewer or feel grateful to and appreciative of the interviewer. One interviewer said in talking about this: "I just wanted people to like me . . . so I nodded like mad, murmured encouraging sounds, looked terribly interested, laughed at all jokes, patted all dogs, said hello to all dullness, etc., because this seemed like a good way to get people to like me" (Converse and Suchman 1974:11).

Developing a relationship is not for the purpose of ingratiation or an ego trip on the part of the interviewer. It is not for the purpose of making things nice and comfortable. While all of these may happen, the rationale for working to establish a relationship lies in the fact that it is necesssary for effective achievement of the purpose of the interview.

EXPRESSIVE-INSTRUMENTAL SATISFACTIONS

While delineating the desirable characteristics of the interview relationship I do not want to ignore the instrumental aspects of interviewing. It might be well at this point to discuss the balance between the client's expressive satisfactions and his instrumental satisfactions in the interview. The expressive satisfactions are derived from the relationship established, the context in which help is offered. Instrumental satisfactions are derived from what the worker actually does to help the client deal with the problems he brings. Polansky (1956), in postinterview interviews with social agency clients, confirmed the hypothesis that they received these two different kinds of satisfactions from the interview.

One important reward which motivates people to communicate in the interview situation is that, as a result of such communication, the pain, discomfort, and inconvenience stemming from a dysfunctional psychosocial situation will be reduced. The hope is that the interviewer will say or do something that helps solve the problem to some degree. This is the instrumental consequence of interview participation for the interviewee.

Another important reward is the pleasure, the ego gratification, which comes from contact with an interested, understanding, accepting person who appears willing to listen to your story with empathy, sympathy, and emotional support. This is the expressive consequence of participation for the interviewee. Such expressive rewards are most fully achieved as a result of the kind of relationship described in the preceding section.

The Vizier Ptah-Hotep, sometime between 2700 and 2200 B.C., gave advice to his son in recognition of these considerations.

> If thou art one to whom petition is made, be calm as thou listenest to what the petitioner has to say. Do not rebuff him before he has swept out his body or before he has said that for which he came. The petitioner likes attention to his words better than the fulfilling of that for which he came. . . . It is not necessary that everything about which he has petitioned should come to pass, but a good hearing is soothing to the heart.

Some four thousand years later this statement is equally true, although social workers need to be more concerned with "the fulfilling of that for which he came" than was a grand vizier.

For many kinds of social work interview situations, the instrumental consequences are of overwhelming importance to the client. Without the public welfare grant, the client cannot pay the rent or clothe the children. The deserted mother about to be hospitalized needs to find foster homes for her children. The wife of the marginal-income worker needs to have her preschool child accepted at some low-cost day-care center if she is to accept the job she has just found.

While the clients, like all people everywhere, would like to be, and without question should be, interviewed with courtesy and respect, with concern for their autonomy and uniqueness, these expressive considerations are of secondary, or even tertiary, importance to some clients in situations of pressing need. Above all, they are concerned with what the interview can do to help them get money, find a suitable foster home, obtain admittance to a day-care center. What the interviewer does or can do is then of far more importance and significance to the client than the way he does it.

A study of the reactions of mothers to interviews with pediatricians, based on tape recordings of the interviews and postinterview interviews with the mothers, found that most of them expected technical competence and were not disappointed. The instrumental purposes of the interviews were, by and large, satisfactorily achieved (Korsch 1968). However, many mothers had expectations which transcended technical competence. They wanted the doctor to be friendly, concerned, and sympathetic. It was with these aspects of the interview, the expressive aspects, that most mothers were disappointed.

A similar careful study of social work interviews might find the opposite to be true—considerable satisfaction with the worker's handling of the expressive aspects of the interview, less satisfaction with the instrumental problem-solving consequences of the interview. As a perceptive caseworker once said, "I feel like a Good Humor man with an empty cart." We need to give greater consideration to our "utility value" to the client-interviewee, to what we do as well as how we do it, to the instrumental purposes for which the relationship is established, as well as to the nature of the relationship we establish.

Inner Attitudes and Outer Behavior

One more important consideration needs to be discussed regarding the relationship we have attempted to describe above. The portrait painted here of the ideal worker-interviewer may strike one as a picture of God's perfect creature, impossible to emulate. It is, therefore, reassuring to note that the interviewer's behavior rather than her attitude tends to be of more critical importance. The client-interviewee reacts to the overt behavior the worker-interviewer manifests, rather than to her underlying attitudes. It is, of course, most desirable for the overt behavior and underlying attitude to be congruent. This would eliminate the possibility that the overt behavioral message might be contradicted by the covert attitudinal message. It would also reduce psychic stress on the worker who feels one way but is constrained by her professional role to act in another way. But if the two messages are contradictory, the message of behavior seems to have clear priority, according to results of studies where both worker and client were interviewed about their experiences after their interview together (Hyman 1954). In some instances the worker confessed that, although she tried to act in an accepting manner, she did not feel accepting, that although she acted as though she liked the interviewee, she did not really like him. The interviewee's perception of the same interview rarely indicated any recognition that the worker's underlying attitude was negative. He perceived and reacted to the worker's positive verbal and nonverbal behavior toward him.

As Hyman notes, in reporting this study, "Feelings are one thing, overt conduct [is] another. It is purely an assumption based on little fact to conceive of the interviewer's feelings spewing forth in all directions" (1954:40).

"Perhaps we have gone too far in thinking that the danger from the interviewer's negative feelings is that they might be *communicated* to the respondent and affect his replies" (1954:43).

A similar conclusion results from another careful study of interviewee-interviewer interaction in a health interview survey, based on reports of the same interview obtained independently from interviewer and interviewee. "The study started with the assumption that the attitude and feeling variables were the most important and significant factors determining interview interaction. The results of the study contradicted the hypothesis and indicated that the actual behavior of both interviewer and interviewee were the variables of greatest importance in determining the course of the interview" (Cannell 1968:5)

Some research on empathy points to additional confirmation of this. Hogan notes in discussing this research that "whether or not a counselor is in fact empathic is irrelevant. What counts is whether the counselor *acts as if* he or she understands client's expectations and cares about the client's welfare" (1975:17).

This result should not surprise anybody who has engaged in interviewing, despite the fact that it contradicts a cherished social work myth—that the client (particularly a child) always "knows" what the worker is feeling. If the practiced professional finds it acutely difficult to know what the client is feeling, as is often the case, why should it be easy for the client to be invariably so intuitively gifted?

The important implication of these findings for the student interviewer is that success in establishing good relationships is possible without being godlike. Although admittedly desirable it is not necessary to feel invariably respectful and accepting. It is enough to *act* respectful and accepting. All one can ask of the interviewer is that she be capable of a disciplined subjectivity, not that she resolve all her prejudices, her human dislikes and antipathies. She is asked to control negative feelings in the interview so that they are not obvious. If the research has validity, this control is likely to be sufficient for the establishment and maintenance of a good relationship that facilitates communication.

In truth, many clients are so preoccupied with their own problems that they have little free psychic energy to devote to psyching out the interviewer. We often say exactly this about the interviewer, that concern with her own problem in the interview reduces her ability to empathize.

There is a further implication. It is true that if we truly feel the correct attitude we are likely to say the correct word. However, oddly enough, the reverse also can be true. If we keep saying the correct word, we are likely to begin to feel the correct attitude. Cognitive dissonance is a strain which is resolved by bringing behavior and attitude into congruence, this time by bringing the attitude closer to the word (Halmos 1966:55–56).*

The prescription does not require that the interviewer invariably achieve an accepting, respectful, empathic feeling of positive regard for every interviewee. It is contrary to the human condition to expect that an interviewer will be able to like and feel concern for all of the different kinds of people who come to her social agency. It is naturally to be expected that an interviewer will like and care for some clients more than others and be turned off by some (hopefully limited) number of clients. Interviewees are, at times, demanding, dependent, irresponsible, nasty, frustrating, boring, not particularly lovable, as is true for all of us. To deny this is to suggest that interviewees are more than human.

Some clients may be so different in their life experience and the values by which they order their lives that the workers might find little basis for empathy, despite the best efforts to feel empathic. But while recognizing that it is difficult, the interviewer has a professional obligation to make the effort to understand, to remain open to understanding, to study the literature available which helps to explain the problem the client brings.

That some amount of failure is likely to be inevitable does not absolve the worker from making the effort. But, then, making the effort is the requirement that needs to be met, rather than actually achieving acceptance in every instance.

Apparent Contradictions

Can there be a relationship that is too comfortable? There is some suggestion that such might be the case if we follow the question by asking another: "Too comfortable for what?" There is work to be done in achieving the purpose of the interview. If the relationship is too comfortable, if it is too relaxed and warm, it may interfere with getting the work done. The satisfactions in the relationship may discourage taking any risks which might threaten such a desirable state of affairs.

The fact that too much of even a seemingly good thing can have consequences that are not entirely desirable may help explain some of the contradictory findings, for example, about therapist "warmth." Warmth would seem to be unreservedly desirable, yet a review of the relevant research

---

* Dissonance theory posits a tendency toward psychological consistency. Inconsistency between behavior and feelings creates a psychological tension which is resolved by efforts to reduce the inconsistency. James Lange's theory of emotion also supports this; it suggests that although we act in response to our feelings, we also feel in response to our actions.

by Papel (1979) shows that in some circumstances with some interviewees the consequences are not uniformly positive.

There are other seemingly contradictory, antithical attitudes that are elements of the good relationship configuration. There is, as has been noted, the difficulty in separating the person from his behavior so that we accept the client as a person while not condoning his behavior. There is the difficulty of accepting a person "as he is" and working toward helping him change, which implies a rejection of him "as he is."

Accepting the client as he is and leaving him there does not achieve the purpose of helping. Accepting the client as he is while assisting him in achieving what he can and wants to be is what the social work interviewer is being asked to do.

Schulman (1977) notes that the interview is a demanding interaction requiring a good deal of concentrated work and effort. It is the interviewer who shoulders the responsibility for holding the interviewee to the tasks of the interview by holding to focus, by making demands and communicating expectations. But demands and expectations are made more effectively in the context of a positive relationship; "a worker who is demanding but not empathic will be experienced by the client as rejecting. On the other hand, the worker who is empathic but makes no demands will be experienced by the client as easy to put off. It is the critical syntheses of these two behaviors that will lead to effective work" (Schulman 1971:48).

Thus the worker is faced with antithetical responsibilities in the interview—accepting the client while communicating expectations for change.

One additional consideration of prime importance needs to be recognized and explicitly stated. Establishing a relationship as described requires considerable emotional energy. Such a commitment is enervating and psychologically depleting. One cannot expect workers with large case loads, facing frequent emergencies and dealing with frustrating, intractable situations of considerable environmental stress, to establish such relationships with any frequency. Although knowing what is desirable, many workers, despite their commitment and dedication, may have to settle for less.

SUGGESTED READINGS

Felix P. Biestak. *The Casework Relationship.* Chicago: Loyola University Press, 1957 (149 pp.).
First published in 1957, but still one of the clearest statements of the components of the effective interviewer-interviewee relationship.
Lawrence M. Brammer. *The Helping Relationship: Process and Skills.* 2d ed. Englewood Cliffs, N.J.: Prentice-Hall, 1979 (180 pp.).

Written for the counseling psychologist by a counseling psychologist. In describing the helping process, it presents a clarification of the nature of the helping relationship and the skills employed in using the relationship to help people.

F. E. McDermott, editor. *Self-Determination in Social Work: A Collection of Essays on Self-Determination.* London: Routledge & Kegan Paul, 1975 (245 pp.).

A sophisticated and critical analysis by a group of social work philosophers and theoreticians of a key component of the helping relationship.

H. H. Perlman. *Relationship: The Heart of Helping People.* Chicago: University of Chicago Press, 1979 (236 pp.).

Written with warmth and wit by an eminent social worker, the book clearly details the importance of relationship for social work.

CHAPTER 4

The Participants: Interviewee
and Interviewer

This chapter is concerned with some further general material pertinent to all social work interviews. It will consider what each participant brings to the interview, attributes that are characteristic of the competent interviewer and cooperative interviewee and the general tasks each needs to accomplish in the interview. We are concerned with these considerations as related to the interviewee separately, to the interviewer separately, and to the interaction between these two.

Background of Interviewee

The interviewee brings reference group affiliations, primary group affiliations, and biopsychosocial history and current functioning to the interview.* The client is a member of a sex grouping, and age, racial, occupational, class, religious, and ethnic groups. He is identified, for example, as male, young adult, white, bricklayer, lower middle class. Catholic, of Italian origin. Or as female, 45 years old, black, homemaker, lower class, Baptist, of American birth. Each of the identifying labels tells us something, within limits, of the likely behavior, feelings, and attitudes of the client. Affiliation with each of these different significant reference groups affects some aspect of the client's behavior in the interview. But the client is more

---

*The reference group is that large identifiable social aggregate with whom the person identifies and is identified. The person's behavior is patterned in accord with its norms and perspectives. The primary group is the face-to-face group.

intimately a member of several primary groups—a family, a particular peer group on the job, a particular congregation, a friendship group.

All the primary group contacts modify in some way the behavior, feelings, and attitudes dictated by membership in a particular reference group. It may be that lower-class adolescent males are struggling for emancipation from the family. But, it happens that the peer group of adolescents with whom client John is most intimately associated are not as yet manifesting this kind of rebellion and alienation and seem comfortable in their dependent ties to their families.

John further has a particular body, a particular physiology. He is tall or short, fat or thin, active or lethargic, invariably healthy or somewhat ill. And he has had a particular psychosocial history. He grew up at a particular time, in a particular place, in a particular family, with a particular set of parents, and his life in growing up with these circumstances was unique and idiosyncratic—never before experienced in just this way by anybody, never again to be experienced in just this way by anybody else.

All of this background accompanies the client into the interview situation, shaping the way she will think and feel and behave. Not every role, not every group membership, has potency and relevance for determining the interviewee's reaction in the interview. Attitudes, beliefs, and behaviors associated with those roles which relate to the purpose of the interview will be of greatest influence. The middle-aged woman talking to the medical social worker will introduce into the interview those group and individual attitudes which are related to illness, to medical treatment, to temporary institutional living. The relevant social role is that of a patient in a hospital, and all the beliefs and feelings of her reference groups about being a patient, as well as those which derive from her own personal history, will be activated in the interview. Beliefs and feelings about her other significant social roles, as wife, mother, daughter, employee, etc., are less relevant to this interview situation.

Background of Interviewer

The worker also brings to the interview a configuration of determinants. The worker also has reference group affiliations—male or female, young or old, of some color, ethnicity, and religion. But having been educated in graduate school, undergraduate school, or an in-service training program to enact a professional role, the social work interviewer does not allow these identities to determine his interview behavior. The whole point of such training is to replace the behavior generally anticipated from, let us say, a white, young, middle-class Protestant by the professional behavior expected of a social worker. If the interviewer consistently succeeds in doing this, we say he is acting professionally in the interview. He has developed a professional identity which reflects the ways of the occupational subculture. The principal reference group affiliation which he brings to the interview is that of the profession. The picture he has of what is expected of a social work interviewer is the configuration to which he feels constrained to conform.

Professional affiliation determines what areas will be explored in the interview and how the information obtained will be processed by the interviewer. It provides a particular orientation for the interviewer which guides his perception. A study of the response to the same social study data by interviewers who held different orientations toward human behavior concluded that they paid attention to different aspects of the situation. Each had a set of perceptions which determined what data he would unconsciously, or consciously, accept. The interviewers organized material presented to them in terms of these sets. The way the profession teaches us to explain a situation determines the way we perceive the situation.

Although the profession generally dictates particular forms of behavior in the interview, these, too, are modified by primary group pressures. Here the principal primary group dictating the adaptation of professional behavior is the peer group of fellow social workers in an agency. For instance, the profession has declared allegiance to certain theoretical explanatory configurations. In general the concepts of ego psychology, with generous sociological modifications, were, until comparatively recently, the theoretical framework most consistently taught in schools of social work and through the professional literature. More recently, learning theory, behavior modification techniques, and an ecological systems perspective are contesting the primacy of this orientation. Each of these explanatory frameworks explains not only how social problems originate and develop, but also what can be done in the interview, or through it, to help people deal with such problems.

Some agencies emphasize deficiencies in the social situation as the primary contributing factors in the client's problems; other agencies emphasize the client's personal deficiencies as contributing factors. The social workers in these agencies will therefore focus on different content in an interview and direct their interviews toward different solutions. Billingsly (1964) found clear differences in the orientation of social workers in a family service agency as compared with a child protective agency. Both groups regarded themselves as social workers. But in both instances the agency, dealing with different groups of clients, dictated a different adaptation of the professional way of serving the client. Billingsly concluded that "the

agencies exert a major and differential influence" (1964:187) on workers'
role orientation and role performance.

Identification with the profession as a reference group not only implies
adherence to certain interview techniques and utilization of a certain explanatory cosmology, but also calls for behavior in accordance with certain
professional values and ethics. These values also undergo some modification in each particular agency. In any conflict between agency policy and
standards of the profession, the worker tends to act in accordance with
agency policy.

The profession is a remote and ambiguous entity; the pressure and sanction of the agency are immediate and visible. The interviewer solicits agency
peer group acceptance and the agency supervisor's approbation, and these
needs determine his choices in interviewing behavior.

The agency may be only one of the primary groups to which the individual interviewer is responsive, particularly in a large social agency. The additional primary groups may be the unit to which he is assigned within the
agency, or a friendship clique of fellow workers.

Within the same agency, social workers seek out colleagues whose orientation to the work is similar to their own. They support each other and
reinforce their tendencies to handle their interviews in a particular manner. For many professionals the judgment of colleagues is the one of greatest concern. The reputation a worker has in the agency is more frequently
the result of how he relates to his colleagues, how he is perceived by them,
than of the way he relates to and is perceived by the clients. The worker
is under great pressure, therefore, to conform to the ways of the agency.
Preserving an acceptable relationship with agency colleagues is likely to
take precedence not only in any conflict between agency and profession
but also in any conflict between the agency and the needs of the client.

The framework provided by the profession, as modified by the agency,
is further adapted by the individual interviewer in terms of his idiosyncratic biopsychosocial preferences. The particular items within the framework that are emphasized, the particular interviewee responses that have
high visibility, differ from interviewer to interviewer within a single agency.
But again the professional requirement is that the worker make every effort
to ensure that these considerations are excluded from the interview. Ideally the worker is aware of those needs which derive from his own psychosocial history and controls their manifestations.

The aim and hope of professional education and in-service training is to
reduce the idiosyncratic component in the interviewer's behavior. Instead
of responding as a middle-aged, middle-class, white female with a unique
developmental history, the worker will respond as a professional in terms

of some standardized, presumably technically correct, precepts. All social work interviewers following a uniform theory should, then, respond to the same interview situation in a similar manner.

That aim is only partially achieved. A study of tape-recorded interviews made by experienced, professional social workers indicated that although there was some uniformity in their interview behavior, there was also considerable diversity (Mullen 1969). This result is to be expected even where a uniform theory, a set of clear explicit generalizations, is available to guide the worker in most situations encountered. The problem for the social worker is compounded by the fact that for many significant situations recurrently encountered in the interview, the field does not have an applicable generalization. The worker then has to fall back on responding in terms of his nonprofessional background and makeup.

Despite these qualifications, however, the process of socialization of the recruit has the goal of developing some uniformities in interviewer thinking, feeling, and behavior that reflect the profession's expectations for anyone occupying the status of social worker in a particular agency.

Both interviewer and interviewee bring to the interview the conversational habits developed over the course of a lifetime as well as the learned adherence to the rules of normative conversational interaction. The interview is a small special social system set in the context of the encompassing general community. The rules of interpersonal conduct which govern relationships in the larger social system of the community continue to operate within the social system of the interview.

Through experience in conversation we have learned a complicated set of formal and ceremonial rules that govern acceptable verbal interaction between people. The expectation by others that we will observe these rules reinforces our habituation to their use.

Expectations are the result of recurrent experience in interaction in which patterned regularities of behavior have been followed. These expectations of conventional behavior are brought into the interview. Such learned, familiar, routine patterns in verbal interaction take precedence in determining our behavior in the interview situation which tends to be perceived, at least initially, as analogous to other social-conversational situations.

Certain communications are regarded as rude, inappropriate, impolite, disrespectful. Others are embarrassing, or threatening. There are recognized and consistently adhered to forms of communication when a younger person addresses an older person, a man addresses a woman, a woman addresses a man. They are illustrative of the patterns of conversational behavior to which we have been socialized and by which we tend to determine our conduct in the interview.

We move from being regulated in our interaction by the social norms of interpersonal communication, which we bring into the interview, to professional norms.

Professional norms are imposed on or modify social norms in dictating perceptive and proscriptive behavior of the interviewer—what he should do and what he should not do. The conflict between social norms, the rules of etiquette and the requirements of the interviewers' professional role is sometimes made explicit.

After interviewing a voluble, articulate client who takes charge of the interview and talks nonstop, the worker commented: "I didn't know how to politely break into her talking. Is there any polite way of doing this? Perhaps one has to learn to be impolite if the task of the interview demands it. Over the years I had learned the opposite—being polite. I paid for it here in having to listen, it seemed endlessly, to a lot of irrelevant detail. I guess I deserved it if I was too weak to interrupt."

But another interviewer in a school social work setting interviewing an equally talkative interviewee says: "Let me interrupt, okay? I just want to see if I'm getting this straight, 'cause you told me a lot of different things, and I'm trying to understand how they all fit together."

The interviewer who, qua interviewer, has to ask and obtain considerable personal information which transcends the etiquette barrier may feel a sense of discomfort at the breech of etiquette. This is suggested by the interviewer who says:

> The interviewer is required to be *two* things to all people. First he must be a *diplomat:* warm, sympathetic, sensitive to the respondent—just the sort of person who in ordinary social life does not go about asking embarrassing questions because, through sensitivity and tact, he knows how to avoid them. But at the same time, he must be something of a *boor:* no sympathetic understanding of the respondent will prevent him from elbowing his way right in with questions that might embarrass or discomfort the other person. (Converse and Schuman 1974:31)

What happens in any one interview is the result of what the interviewee brings to the encounter, what the interviewer brings, and the interaction between the particular pair of participants at this point in time in the history of their contact with each other. The interaction is "reciprocally contingent," each person responding to the other's behavior, each a partial cause of the other's behavior. The interview is a system in which each participant is seeking, accepting, or resisting the other's efforts to influence him.

All of this suggests a reevaluation of the relative importance of the various factors that feed into the interview. Despite the initial importance of background factors, reference and primary group affiliation, life history of

ual participants, professional training and theoretical orientation that
ants bring to the interview; once the interview begins, the most
potent factors determining the behavior of one participant is the behavior
of the other. With the start of the interview a new set of variables is activated that is specific to this particular encounter.

Power Struggles and Manipulation

Although interview interaction is one of reciprocal, mutual efforts by both
participants to influence each other, the influence potential of the interviewer is greater than that of the interviewee because he has more power
and greater varieties of power. The interviewer has "reward" power in his
control of access to special services the agency can make available. He has
control of access to the "therapy" he dispenses, a therapy which the client
very much wants if she has any confidence in its ability to make her feel
less anxious, lessen her conflict, or help her to grow. The worker has "expert" power in the special knowledge he supposedly has available to help
the client solve the problems which cause her anguish. He has "coercive"
power in agencies which operate with legal sanctions, as in corrections or
protective services. Once a relationship is established, he has "referent"
power in the meaningfulness, to the client, of his expressions of approval
or disapproval. Because the client wants his approval as a person of meaning in his life, the worker does exercise a measure of control over the
client's behavior.

The interviewee has few sources of power at her command to give potency to her efforts to influence. She may, as in the case of the involuntary
client, have the power that derives from her indifference. This is the power
of the party of "least interest" in any transaction. The interviewee can refuse to cooperate with the interviewer; she can frustrate the accomplishment of the purpose of the interview; she can deny the interviewer the
gratification of conducting a good interview; she can deny the interviewer
the psychic compensations of expressions of appreciation and gratitude; she
may refuse to make this an easy interview, offering limited or unproductive
responses. The interviewee may deny the interviewer the satisfactions which
come from a confirmation of his competence, or she may offer them selectively, in return for the interviewer's giving her what she wants.

Interviewees attempt to control interviews by being uninterruptible
"super talkers," by reversing roles and asking the interviewers questions,
by responding to questions with very spare, ambiguous answers, by talking
so that it is difficult to hear, by frequently changing the subject so as to
destroy interview coherence, by nonverbal signals which indicate hostility,

resistance, unwillingness to cooperate. Interviewees attempt to control interviewers by making deliberate conscious efforts to influence the reactions of the interviewer.

Social agency clients have some idea of what is expected of them in playing the role of a client. Accordingly some may manipulate their self-presentation so as to make themselves more acceptable to interviews (Jenkins and Norman 1975:96–101, 114–15).

The social work interviewee often has an important stake in the outcome of an interview and consequently might deliberately attempt to influence the worker's discretionary decisions. For instance, social workers make discretionary decisions to grant assistance, to increase a grant, to support a request for a job or housing, to accept an applicant for adoption. A study of outcomes of interviews in a public welfare agency showed that clients were most successful in getting what they wanted, "if their interview self-presentation included an apparent understanding of the worker, the mention of employment" as an interest, a self-assertive manner, and an orientation of friendliness toward the worker (Street 1979:81–83).

Despite the differential of power in the interviewer's favor, the interviewee, is then, not without influence. While it is clear, and expected, that the behavior of the interviewer exerts an effect on the behavior of the interviewee, available research indicates that the opposite is also the case (Van der Veen 1965). Detailed studies of interviewer behavior indicate that although there is a core of reliability in the behavior of the same interviewer as he moves from interview to interview, there is some modification in response to the individuality of different interviewees. One study showed that the interviewers tried to compensate for lower interviewee activity by increasing their own activity but that they decreased their own activity in contact with active interviewees (Lennard and Bernstein 1960). Dependency in the interviewee evokes dominance and reassurance in the interviewer. Hostility or friendliness in the interviewee evokes a parallel response.

Although both interviewee and interviewer modify their characteristic patterns of interaction in response to each other's behavior, studies show that the interviewer tends to make a greater effort to accommodate than does the interviewee. This finding is to be expected since the interviewer has a professional responsibility to ensure the success of the encounter.

Nonetheless, the greater power of the interviewer gives him greater potential for influencing the content and direction of the interview.

By responding with interest every time the interviewee mentions her mother, the interviewer can "condition" her to talk at greater length about her mother. By responding with interest whenever the interviewee talks about her mother's overprotectiveness, but never when she talks about her mother's efforts to support her steps toward independence, the interviewer can condition the client to focus on the overprotective component of her mother's ambivalence and hear less about her concern for her daughter's autonomy.

In verbal conditioning, the interviewer conditions the interviewee by a deliberate, controlled use of words and vocalization. The rewards are words of praise, approval, and the sounds that indicate that the interviewer is paying close and interested attention. The punishments are the withholding of words of praise and vocal evidence of attention, or words actually used to discourage some statements: "No, that's not important." "Let's not discuss that now." Every interviewer, no matter how determinedly nondirective, conditions the client by some selective responses to what the client says or does.

The Competent Interviewer

Research which attempts to factor out the personality characteristics associated with competence in interviewing yields a rather confused picture. The confusion may result because interviews conducted for different purposes may, ideally, require different kinds of interviewing personalities.

The warm, accepting qualities necessary for interviews whose primary purpose is therapeutic are not those required for the interview whose primary purpose is assessment. The "therapeutic" interviewer in an assessment interview may fail to probe inconsistencies or may make compassionate allowance for interviewee reluctance to discuss essential but difficult areas. The interview whose primary purpose is reliable judgment, diagnostic assessment, may require a reserved, extraceptively oriented person; the therapeutic interview may require a warmer, more spontaneous, intraceptively oriented person. The interviewer engaged in advocacy may need a more aggressive, directive, dominant approach to the interview.

Different interviewers may be more or less competent with different kinds of interviewees. For instance, some interviewers are uncomfortable unless the relative status vis-à-vis the interviewee is in their favor. Consequently, while they may be comfortable and competent in interviews with lower-class clients seeking agency help, they would be uncomfortable in interviews with the director of an agency whose influence they are trying to enlist in their clients' behalf. In general, however, those interviewers who manifest the personal qualities associated with establishing a good relationship—warmth, patience, compassion, tolerance, sincerity—are likely to be among the more successful. These are the kinds of interviewers preferred by clients. The less anxious, less maladjusted the interviewer is, the greater the likelihood of competence. Greater interview competence is associated with open-mindedness and low dogmatism in response to such instruments as the Rokeach dogmatism scale.

Other studies of the characteristics of competent interviewers suggest that they have a rather reserved, controlled, low-level social orientation and retain a certain amount of objective, detached sensitivity to the interviewee. They are serious, persistent, reflective, and interested in observing and understanding their own behavior as well as the behavior of others, and they are tolerant and understanding of other people and human weakness. One recurrent finding is that a high degree of extraversion and sociability is not related to high interview competence. Greater interview competence tends to be associated with an interest in people that is scientific and objective rather than highly emotional or personal.

Studies show an association between intelligence and good interview performance, although intelligence is not a guarantee of good performance. It is generally agreed that it is desirable for the interviewer to have a variety of interests and a wide range of experiences. He then has the capacity to empathize with a greater range of people, since his own experience may parallel theirs. He also has a broader base for communication.

Some studies have attempted to determine the characteristics of the competent interviewer by more indirect methods. The assumption is that interviewers who establish the facilitative conditions for relationships that we have discussed must be competent. The research then seeks to find out what kind of people establish these conditions. Tape-recorded interviews are played to a panel of judges who then decide the level at which the interviewer has established the facilitative conditions. After sorting out those who have done very well, the study then goes on to sift out their personality characteristics. As might be expected, the results tend to show that such interviewers are independent, self-actualizing, sensitive, and psychologically open.

If the trait analysis of the competent interviewer still leads to ambiguous answers, the results of studying the behavior of experienced interviewers seem somewhat clearer. The supposition is that the more experienced interviewer is the more competent. Experienced interviewers are apt to be less controlling, to be less active, and to be less inclined to offer advice and suggestion than are inexperienced interviewers. Inexperienced interviewers are apt to talk more and to take more responsibility for the conduct of the interview. The difference may reflect the greater anxiety and insecurity of the beginning interviewer rather than his technical inexperience. The experienced interviewer is not passive, however. He tends to be more discriminating and modulates his activity. He says only what needs to be said, at the moment it needs to be said, so that he is more efficient, making every comment count.

Changes which result from training for psychotherapeutic interviewing may also suggest differences between experienced and inexperienced interviewers. As a result of such training, interviewers become more reluctant to initiate interaction, giving the interviewee greater opportunity for this, and become less inclined to assert themselves during the interview by interrupting the client.

In one study, interviewers were shown a film of an actual interview. The interview was stopped at various points and the interviewers participating in the research were asked what their response might have been at this time if they had been conducting the interview. Inexperienced interviewers tended to ask questions; experienced interviewers tended to make statements. Inexperienced interviewers tended to respond to discrete ideas, to specific words or phrases; experienced interviewers tended to respond to the gestalt of the client's presentation.

Experienced interviewers tend to make fewer directly manipulative responses and more communicative responses conveying a thought or feeling. For example, a client begins to pace the floor in an interview. The inexperienced therapist is more likely to make a statement designed to elicit a certain desired response (manipulative) such as: "If you don't sit down, I am afraid I won't be able to help you." A communicative response of the more experienced interviewer might be: "I have the feeling that you are trying to impress me with how upset you are" (Ornstein et al. 1970:10). A more detailed recapitulation of differences between experienced and inexperienced interviewers is included in the appendix.

The most judicious conclusion to be drawn from the variety of studies available is that no clear pattern of personality traits clearly distinguishes the good from the poor interviewer. Good interviewing is the result of the complex interplay of the interviewer, the interviewee, the purpose of the interview, and the setting in which it is conducted. The general direction of the research findings suggests that the more successful interviewer is likely to be warm, accepting, psychologically open, but in flexible control of himself and the interview situation.

NEED FOR KNOWLEDGE

A thorough knowledge of the subject matter of the interview is a mark of the competent interviewer. The medical social work interviewer must have at his command a detailed, specialized knowledge of the social antecedents, concomitants, and consequences of physical illness; the psychiatric social worker, of mental and emotional illness; the gerontological social worker, of old age.

Such a knowledge base enables the worker to make sense out of what he is hearing, of seeing relationships between different items of information that would escape someone ignorant of the subject matter. Knowledge alerts the interviewer to areas of significance the client might not have discussed that could lead to the formulation of appropriate questions. Knowledge provides the basis for evaluating the validity of the information obtained, for the critical analysis of such material. It helps the interviewer to remember what has gone on in the interview because knowledge provides more interpretive associations.

Unless the worker has detailed knowledge on the social problem area for which he is offering service, he will not know what questions to raise, what information is most significant, what items need to be pursued in greater detail. He needs to know the generalizations which the social and behavioral sciences have made regarding, for instance, delinquency, child placement, or school phobia, so that he has some concepts available to make sense out of what the interviewee is telling him. He needs to have sufficient grasp of the relevant generalizations regarding the particular social problem so that he can translate these into appropriate questions, comments, and probes during the interview. Chance favors a prepared mind. Some statements by the interviewee which have no meaning for an interviewer with scant knowledge will suggest a series of fruitful questions to the interviewer who knows what the remark implies.

Assessment interviews require a knowledge of normative expectations. If the child is toilet trained at 20 months, is it late or early? If he first started talking at 15 months, is this indicative of developmental lag or normal development? What parental behavior suggests "overprotection," and what kinds of separation behavior are normal for a hospitalized, school-age child? To know what is unusual, unexpected, or atypical, one needs to know the usual and typical.

The interviewer whose purpose is advocacy, and whose interview orientation is to persuade and convince, needs to have considerable knowledge about the rights and entitlements of his client; he needs to have a good command of the regulations and procedure of the agency. Without such knowledge he cannot challenge, with assurance, any decision denying aid or service. He must understand the agency's structure so that he can appeal, or threaten to appeal, an adverse decision made at a lower level in the agency's administrative structure to somebody farther up the line.

Furthermore, knowledge about possible solutions, about available resources and therapeutic procedures, is also necessary, since that guides the interviewer in determining which aspect of the client's situation might be most productively explored.

Knowledge increases security and lessens anxiety. If the worker goes into the interview with an expert knowledge of what the literature and practice wisdom of the field make available, not only with regard to the etiology of the problems but also regarding how he might help, he is more apt to feel confident in his own ability to conduct the interview successfully. This, in itself, increases the probability that he will conduct a successful interview. Lack of precise knowledge makes the interviewer uncomfortable and unsure of himself in handling the interview.

An applicant for becoming a Big Brother asks the interviewing social worker if the agency covers insurance for the Big Brother if there is an accident while on a trip or during swimming. The worker, not really knowing the policy, says:

This is something the YMCA is looking into right now. I know that our insurance covers group activities that are a function of the Y, and as far as we know we are checking into ones specifically if it goes as far as Big Brother and Little Brother pair activities. It seems like it should cover but, ah, to tell you the truth, I don't know.

Commenting on his response, the interviewer said:

Mr. M. asked a good question which I was not prepared to answer. Because I felt on the spot I hedged, feeling uncomfortable. The more I fumbled the more Mr. M. seemed to be turning off. That's when I decided to level with him and admit I didn't know. I should have said at this point that I would try to find out. I didn't say this till later in the interview.

There are, then, two different clusters of expertness required and expected of the interviewer. One is expert knowledge regarding the conduct of the interview. The second is knowledge about the social problem subject-matter—its nature, its origin, the approaches to its possible amelioration. The social work interviewer is both a specialist in interviewing and a specialist in the social aspects of mental deficiency or old age or child neglect or marital conflict, the stresses encountered by people facing such problems and the variety of ways people cope with such stresses.

The client is not competent to assess the knowledgeability of the interviewer regarding interviewing, although a client knows in a general way when an interview is competently or poorly conducted. The client is, however, very competent to assess the social worker's knowledge about the subject matter since she is living the problem. Senseless, irrelevant questions, or comments that clearly betray that the social worker knows little about the situation, encourage disrespect for the worker and erode client confidence. A thorough understanding of the subject area enhances the client's confidence in the interviewer as someone who knows his job and can therefore be counted on to help. A detailed knowledge of the problem area reduces social distance. It indicates that both the interviewer and interviewee share some familiarity with the problem. If she perceives the interviewer as knowledgeable and realizes that any fanciful, deceptive responses are likely to be received with skepticism, the interviewee is more likely to be honest and straightforward with the interviewer.

Kinsey found knowledge of the subject matter to be an important component in rapport. "The background of knowledge which the interviewer has is of great importance in establishing rapport with his subjects. The importance of this cannot be over-emphasized. An [interviewee] is inevitably hesitant to discuss things which seem to be both outside of the experience of the interviewer and beyond his knowledge" (1948:60).

It is necessary to emphasize the imperative significance of knowledge, since among social workers an anti-intellectual derogation of the importance of knowledge is prevalent. The profession has emphasized "feeling and doing" rather than "knowing and thinking." Good interviewing is impossible, however, without a considerable amount of knowing and thinking. In public opinion interviewing or in research interviewing, the public opinion staff or the research staff has thoroughly analyzed the relevant knowledge and has formulated a series of relevant questions and probes to be used by the interviewer who, consequently, does not need to be a subject matter expert. The social work interviewer, however, has to be his own staff person, formulating his own appropriate, relevant questions and responses as he experiences the interview unfolding. He translates his hypothesis into an interview outline and into specific questions. Knowledge provides each interviewer with his own interview guide, a cognitive map of the area to be covered.

As I read typescripts of interviews, listen to tapes, and observe interviews, both role-played and real, I am impressed by the frequency with which an interviewer fails for lack of knowledge rather than lack of proper attitude. The proper attitude is frequently manifested—a basic decency, compassion, acceptance, respect. But the interviewer does not know enough about the particular subject matter which is the concern of the interview to ask the perceptive questions, to make sense of what he is hearing, to know what facets of the problem should be explored, to know the normative stresses the problem situation creates for people and the recurrent adaptations people have developed in responding to such stresses. Not only is there a lack of knowledge to permit helping the client productively explore her situation, but there is a lack of knowledge for feedback. The interviewer often does not know enough to answer the client's implicit or explicit request for helpful information or advice.

INTERVIEWEE'S PERCEPTION

Studies indicate that client-interviewees have their own image of the ideal interviewer: he does not engage in behavior that indicates a lack of respect for clients, such as being "aloof, insincere, in a hurry, interrupting, yawning, lacking warmth, being late for the interview; [clients] said they would not like the [interviewer] to do most of the talking but stated significantly more annoyance at the idea of her doing little of it" (Pohlman 1960:550). Clients show a preference for interviewers whose "actions suggest that they can help them *do* something about their problems" (Pfouts 1962:552). The interviewer's "warmth" was perceived as self-assurance, sensitivity, and competence.

The interviewees' concern may be focused primarily on the interviewer's capacity and willingness to help them. Yet they are gratified when he acts in a manner that indicates personal interest and respect and when he takes the trouble to personalize even interviews that have a restricted, instrumental purpose.

A client discussing her experiences with welfare interviewers:
She's supposed to ask, "How are you doing? What do you need? What can I do for you?" My investigator she is always in a rush. There's only two things she ever asks—"Where is your light bill?" and "Where is your rent receipt?" Then she rushes out.

An investigator like that has no appearance. There are a few good ones. Like a friend of mine, she has an investigator when he sees her on the street he stops and says "Hello!" He says "How are you? When did you see your mother last? How is your sister?" Now that's mighty fine of him. An investigator like that makes you feel good. It can't help making you feel good when someone talks to you like that.

Like, I had an investigator once—a man. If he came in and there were people around, he'd say, "Is there someplace where we can talk?" And then he'd go into another room with you and ask you how you were doing. But most of them they come in and tell you what to do. They treat you like a child; no, worse than that, they treat you like a doll, like a nothing. You have to beg and whine and it makes you feel—well, terrible.

Another client describes his picture of the "good" social worker:

[One] who in your first acquaintance lets you know by his or her expression that he's in your home to be of service to you if possible; and to show trust because most people are trustworthy if one shows trust in them; to be able to understand reasonably well problems concerning the family as a whole; not to criticize but to analyze why a person or a family is in unfavorable circumstances; to give helpful advice in a way that isn't demanding but that lets a person feel that it's his own idea; one who has a sincere desire to help people, feeling that it might have been her as well as they but for the grace of God; one who encourages you to go above the capabilities that you thought you possess; one who guides you and makes the way possible but insists that you do for yourself what you're capable of doing. (Overton 1959:12)

Repeated interview reports from a group of clients in psychotherapy indicated that they experienced the most satisfactory interview when the interviewer was "actively collaborative, genuinely warm, affectively expressive," and humanly involved, rather than when she displayed an impassive, detached, studied neutrality (Orlinsky 1967; see also Strupp 1969). There is a preference for interviewers who share their own experiences when these are pertinent. It makes the interviewer less distant, more human, easier to identify with. Personal examples suggest that the worker can understand since he himself encountered similar experiences.

As might be expected, client preferences for interviewer characteristics tend to vary with the kinds of problems they bring. Grater (1964) found that interviewees with personal-social problems regarded the interviewer's affective characteristics (warmth, friendliness, kindness) as more important than cognitive skills (logic, knowledge, efficiency). Interviewees with primarily educational-vocational problems were more likely to prefer interviewers who demonstrated cognitive skills. It is likely, although there is no research available on this, that clients whose problems are primarily related to a deprived social environment would show initial preference for interviewers with strong political power who command access to jobs, housing, an increase in income.

Preference is also related to personality characteristics of the interviewee. Egalitarian interviewees prefer a client-centered, nondirective interviewer; the more authoritarian interviewees prefer a more directive, more structured interview approach.

One important factor determining the interviewee's behavior is the need to communicate a favorable image and to maintain self-esteem. A good relationship that offers acceptance and immunity from rejection tends to mitigate the need, but it still exists. Social work interviewees may feel they need to project an expedient as well as a favorable image. A welfare recipient expresses this feeling during a discussion at a community action center:

Mrs. C. abruptly interrupted, "Who says being on welfare is not work! You've got to learn how to act just right when you go down for an interview for wel-

fare." She stood up, unbuttoned her coat and rebuttoned it, skipping one button-
hole so that the material bunched up and the hem hung unevenly. She hunched
over, lowered her head and raised her eyes to make eye contact with the rest
of the group and with a dramatically forlorn expression explained, "You've got
to make sure to keep your head down and look sad and not speak up and all
that." The group laughed and Mrs. C. began to laugh with them. She added:
"It takes real training to be on welfare. I don't mean to fake, that's not what I
mean. I mean when you need welfare you still can't go in there and look too
proud because you're liable to get a bad time. You know the people who have
you fill out the forms expect you to look a certain way. Well sometimes it takes
work to look that way." (Zurcher 1970:213)

The Interviewer's Tasks

The task dimension of interviewer behavior relates to what the worker must
do if the interview is to accomplish its purpose. At this point we are concerned with outlining the general tasks required of the interviewer. In
chapters 8 through 10 we will cover the detailed behavior associated with
implementing these general tasks.

KEEPING IT GOING

In general the interviewer has to keep the interview moving productively in the direction of its purpose and keep the interview system operating smoothly.

In accomplishing the first task, the interviewer has to do several things.
He has to work collaboratively with the interviewee to establish a definition
of the situation, a purpose for the interview, that is mutually understood
and accepted. He must be skillful in the use of a variety of methods of
intervention to keep the interview moving or get it started again. The interviewer acts as a dynamic force and catalyst. The interviewer helps the
client select and articulate the information, feelings, and attitudes that have
greatest salience for accomplishing the purpose of the interview.

In facilitating client communication, the interviewer (1) encourages the
interviewee to talk, (2) gives her ample opportunity to talk, (3) helps her
to know what she should be talking about, (4) rewards her when she does
talk about things which further the purpose of the interview, and (5) helps
her in her talking as in the following:

A client is discussing her resentment of her pregnancy because it means
temporarily giving up a career. She says of her husband:

INTERVIEWEE: [he] tries to understand what that means and how that makes me feel. I really think he does. But at the same time it's still hard for him because he has his job and his career. He knows how much it means to me, but it's still not the same. It's still me that is going through this and he can share as much as he can, but he still is, still is. . . .
INTERVIEWER: Still outside of the problem.
INTERVIEWEE: Yeah, still outside of the problem, and I am inside of it.

The interviewer later comments that "the client paused and fumbled for words so I helped her complete her statement. It seemed that what I suggested was what she wanted to say."

INDUCTING THE INTERVIEWEE

Another task for the interviewer is to induct the client into her role of interviewee. Because there is less actual as well as vicarious exposure to the role of social work interviewee as compared with, let us say, medical patient interviewee or legal client interviewee, many people come to the social work interview with ambiguous or erroneous expectations. Relatively few people have ever participated in a social work interview and few have seen or heard a social worker doing social work in a movie or on the radio or TV. In inducting the interviewee into what is for many an unfamiliar social role the interviewer reinforces some responses, refrains from reinforcing others. When the client talks about feeling, the interviewer becomes active verbally and nonverbally—leans forward and says "yes," "good," "that's it." When the client is talking about some irrelevant inconsequential matter the interviewer is passive and unreceptive.

Explicit instructions can be used in helping the client be a "good" interviewee: "During our meeting together it would be most helpful if you talked about _____"; "I will be asking you questions about _____ and hope that you will feel free to share with me what you think and what you feel about it." "In such interviews people who have come here with concerns similar to yours have talked about _____." The interviewer inducts the interviewee into her role by modeling effective interview procedures and by signaling the order in which participants speak, how much, about what, and when. This process of socialization to the role of interviewee is illustrated in the following extracts:

Client: male, 27, white, lower middle class, family service-marital counseling.
WORKER: Just a little while ago you were telling me about this argument you had with your wife about the way she spends the money and the trouble you two have in budgeting. How does it make you feel the way she spends the money?

MR. R.: You want me to tell you how I feel?

WORKER: Well, yeah. What happened is important, but how you feel about what happened is important too.

MR. R.: So I am supposed to say how I feel.

WORKER: Well, it would help to understand the situation.

Client: female, black, upper lower class; child guidance clinic.

MRS. E.: Well, I have been talking since I came in here but you haven't said hardly anything at all.

WORKER: [Laughs.] What did you want me to say?

MRS. E.: At least more than you have been saying. Am I supposed to do all the talking? Doesn't anything come back from you?

WORKER: Like what?

MRS. E.: Well, like if we are doing anything wrong and advice about what to do.

WORKER: I am not sure that advice would be much of a help.

MRS. E.: You don't give advice?

WORKER: Not in the way you mean it, no.

Client: female, 58, white, lower middle class, ward interview (client has been talking about results of recent blood tests).

MRS. P.: I never talked to a social worker before. Are these the kinds of things you want me to talk about, the kinds of things you talk with a social worker about?

WORKER: Yeah, sort of, any kinds of troubles, difficulties you have because, you know, because of the diabetes.

As part of the process of induction, or socialization, the worker encourages the development of some aspects of the client's role behavior as appropriate and discourages others as inappropriate. Social chit-chat and overtures directed toward personalizing the relationship are discouraged, and a focus on the problems and expression of feelings is emphasized. The interviewee thus learns what content is relevant to the interview. The interviewee also learns some of the presuppositions of social work—that feelings are facts, that the past is structured in the present, that it is better to express feelings than to deny them, that behavior is purposive, that the interviewee generally makes some contribution to her problem situation, that ambivalence is ubiquitous.

PUTTING IT ALL TOGETHER

The interviewer has a great deal of mental work to do during the interview. The interviewer has to receive and process complex data, make complex decisions about how to respond, make the selected responses, and evaluate their effect.

The client's story is generally presented as pieces of a jigsaw puzzle, disconnected, with significant items embedded in much irrelevant "noise." The interviewer has the task of assembling the items, organizing them in his mind, putting the pieces of the puzzle together so that they make a comprehensive picture. The interviewer has to listen actively as a data processor, not passively as a receptacle.

In implementing the task of keeping the system operating, the worker has to establish and maintain a good relationship with the interviewee, and stimulate the interviewee's motivation to participate productively in the interview.

In implementing the expressive tasks, the interviewer acts to reduce the interviewee's anxiety, embarrassment, irritation, and suspicion. He puts the interviewee at ease and gives her psychological support at difficult points in the interview. To do this, the interviewer has to be sensitive to the changing emotional climate of the system. His responses offer gratification to the interviewee for participation and reassure her of her adequacy as a person and in the role of interviewee. Attention to expressive needs helps keep the interviewee involved in the interview. If the interviewee is present physically but has withdrawn psychologically and emotionally from the interview, nothing can be accomplished. However, if sole attention is devoted to expressive needs and little attention is paid to the instrumental reasons that brought interviewee and interviewer together, there can be an interview system which operates smoothly and satisfyingly but produces nothing of consequence to anybody.

Instrumental task considerations, however, may take precedence over expressive needs to the detriment of the interview. A worker describing one of his interviewees says: "Mike had a cold and his nose was running. I should have offered him a tissue at this point, but I was so concerned about getting the most from the interview that I wasn't thinking of his need to blow his nose. My agenda comes out as more important than his feelings."

At each moment the social worker intervenes to guide and influence the natural development of the interactional process to ensure that the purposes of the interview are achieved. Every response the interviewer makes should be deliberately selected to further the purposes of the interview. Thus one might justly accuse the interviewer of being manipulative. However, the entire process is manipulative, that is, it is designed to achieve certain results through selective interviewer inputs. The very attitudinal set manifested by the interviewer—respect for and interest in the client, the concern with self-determination and acceptance, etc.—is manipulative. The attitudes are deliberately selected and communicated for the purposes of encouraging client communication, reducing anxiety, removing barriers to a confessional. The interviewee is presented with a particular stimulus configuration to increase the probability of responses regarded by the interviewer as helpful. We tend not to use the word "manipulation" to describe this behavior. But in the most accurate, most neutral, least pejorative sense, everything the skilled interviewer does is manipulative.

The Interviewee's Tasks

The interviewer is only one half of the dyad and only partially determines the success or failure of the interview. The willingness and capacity of the interviewee to perform her role competently is also an important determinant. Although the interviewer takes responsibility for providing the psychological atmosphere in which a good relationship can be initiated, the interviewee has to have the capacity to engage in a relationship.

The role of interviewee does make some minimal demands. The person occupying the position has to have some capacity for communicating, some ability to translate feeling and thinking into words, and some ability to organize her communication. She has to be able to understand and respond to the intervention of the interviewer and to follow his leadership. The capable interviewee derives satisfaction from successfully implementing the role.

In addition to motivation and capacity, the interviewee's perception of the situation is important. She acts in response to her perception rather than the "true" and objective situation. The worker can, in fact, be accepting, interested, understanding, and noncoercive. However, he may not be perceived in this way, much to his disappointment and chagrin. The interviewee's ability to accurately perceive the interviewer's communication of the essential conditions of a relationship may be as important in the success of an interview as is the interviewer's ability to actually provide these conditions.

CHAPTER 5

Interviewer Preferences, Problems, and Style

The interview encounter evokes many kinds of feelings in the interviewer, some of which create problems. It is useful and important to call attention to such feelings.

Preferences

Every interviewer tends to dislike some kinds of interviewees. Sometimes the dislike is based on countertransference. Negative feelings are activated because the interviewer associates the client with some significant person in her own past. The interviewer may be aware that she experiences antagonism or anxiety in the presence of the client, but she may not be aware of the source of these feelings.

Sometimes the dislike is based on prejudice and suggests a denial of the client's individuality. It involves a preconceived judgment about a group and attribution of the judgment to every member of the group. We are careful not to manifest the blatant, socially reprehensible prejudices. It is the small prejudices that create difficulty. We may be convinced, for instance, that a receding chin denotes a weak character or that failure to maintain eye contact implies shiftiness.

Sometimes the dislike is based on more objective considerations. Anyone tends to dislike the person who makes satisfactory completion of his or her job more difficult. Some interviewees assist the interviewer in her work and make her job easier; some impede the interviewer and make her job more difficult. The preferred interviewee helps the interviewer feel competent and adequate.

Interviewers have a clear idea of the kinds of people they prefer to interview. Ideal interviewees generally possess those attributes which make the interviewer's job easier and enhance her pleasure in a job well done. They tend to be people who are persistent, intelligent, articulate, nondefensive, psychologically open, anxiously introspective, and willing to accept blame. On the contrary, interviewees who are erratic, inarticulate, passive, defensive, dogmatic, dependent, demanding, and who project blame are generally disliked. People with limited pathology who feel maximum discomfort about their difficulty are preferred. "Good" interviewees are healthy enough to be able to use the interview productively and uncomfortable enough to be highly motivated to cooperate. Here, liking is based on objective interviewee characteristics that make life less difficult for the interviewer, that pose less threat to the interviewer's self-esteem. Interviewers respond positively to interviewees who cooperate with them to implement their role fantasies.

The interviewer needs to be aware of how she perceives her role. In our dramatic reveries we might see ourselves as a compassionate father/mother confessor, a friend of the oppressed sharing their burdens, an expert problem solver who will put things to right, a system changer stimulating clients to organize for their rights, a junior Sigmund/Sieglinde Freud. While all of these are, of course, stereotyped exaggerations they nevertheless make the point that different interviewers enter the interview with different conceptions of the part they are playing which, in subtle ways, determines their choices in the interaction and the kinds of interviewees they prefer.

The interviewer's favorite interviewee is manageable, treatable, and likable. He is conforming and deferential, willing and competent to assume the role of interviewee. He is receptive of the interviewer's efforts to be helpful and can make effective use of the interviewer's interventions in helping. He is agreeable, friendly, and warm. Such an interviewee has been termed a YAVIS—young, attractive, verbal, intelligent, successful. In addition, an interviewer prefers the client whose problems enable her to use the skills she has learned, who presents problems of sufficient flexibility and limited intractability so that they might be changed, in some measure, as a result of the worker's activity. She prefers the client who is likely to actively involve himself in the change process and who is not likely to become a long-time dependent on the agency.

In contrast, the interviewee who is apt to evoke rejecting responses in the interviewer is assertive, uncooperative, manipulative, demanding, and controlling. He is resistive to involvement, is inarticulate, apathetic, and uninterested in being helped. He is poorly organized and defensive and cold. The social work interviewer tends "to dislike people who [give] the impression of seeking help in inappropriately assertive ways and behaving as though the main responsibility for effecting change [is] not their own" (Rees 1978:51).

The interviewee who evokes worker feelings of self-doubt or frustration is apt to be responded to negatively, e.g., the interviewer may respond indifferently or actively avoid material introduced by the interviewee about which the interviewer feels powerless.

Thus the interviewee who acts in a manner to make the interviewer's job more difficult and less satisfying so that it is anything but an ego-enhancing experience for the interviewer may find that his interview time has been shortened and that he is not encouraged to return.

In studying the response of social workers to prospective clients, Rees found workers "avoiding situations of greatest uncertainty in which steps to follow were not well known, which they felt powerless to help, in which continued association held out little prospect of change." They responded positively on the other hand to clients "in contexts of less uncertainty, in which there were known procedures, or there seemed some prospect of change as when clients reciprocated a social worker's interest by evidence of being willing and able to help themselves" (1978:37–38).

SEEKING GRATIFICATION OR AVOIDING A PUT-DOWN

The interview encounter offers various satisfactions for the interviewer that do not contribute to the purpose of the interview. The interviewer can use her power and control of the interview to impress the client with her wide knowledge about, and experience with, the subject matter of the interview. This is a simple narcissistic pleasure. The power granted the interviewer, by virtue of her position, to ask questions about the client's life is generally used legitimately. However it might be used voyeuristically or to embarrass the interviewee or dominate him. The worker needs to be aware that she may be tempted to exploit her position for these kinds of gratification.

The interviewee's explicit acknowledgment that an interview has been gratifying and helpful is a satisfying psychic reward for the interviewer, especially since objective evidence of interviewing competence is difficult to obtain. As expected, interviewers solicit such testimonials in many subtle ways. Beginning interviewers, particularly, need such reassurance to allay their own doubts about their performance. The interviewer may create a situation of reciprocal flattery or try to induce the client to like her by allying herself with the client against the agency, especially against those agency requirements about which she herself has doubts.

The interviewer responds positively to the client who offers professional satisfactions. A hospitalized 56-year-old male, recuperating from a serious operation, repeated to the worker something she said before the operation which had been very helpful in diminishing his anxiety. The worker notes her reaction as follows:

> His bringing this up surprised and touched me, that he had put this much stock in what I had said and that it was that close to him. It triggered in me feelings of tenderness, humility, and gratitude, and I suddenly felt much warmer toward him and closer to him.

Naturally, challenges to the interviewer's adequacy stimulate defensive responses, as illustrated by the worker's introspective comments on the following interview:

Social worker in an institution for dependent and neglected children talking with a 15-year-old boy about his contact with the shop teacher, Mr. S.
CHARLES: Mr. S. is one of the best guys to go to with your problems. If you tell Mr. S. your problems, he works them out the best he can.
WORKER: He has many years of experience. [I am feeling with him and showing that I share the same respect for Mr. S. I must admit that I felt a little envious of Mr. S.'s influence with the boy.]
CHARLES: I think it's twenty-five years he's been a teacher. He puts himself in your position and, well, he thinks if he was in that situation what would he do and he gives you his advice.
WORKER: A lot of times what you'd want is not advice, though, but really to look into your situation so that you can make your own decisions. [My envy shows through in my response here. I wanted to show him that there were limits to what Mr. S. was capable of.]

This extract suggests that the interviewer also has her needs in the interview, satisfaction of which depends on the interviewee. A worker's conception of the ideal client and the tendency to seek and encourage continued contacts with such clients is an aspect of the worker's attempt to ensure that such satisfactions will be available.

Problematic Factors Affecting Interviewer Behavior

SELF-DOUBTS AND HOLDING BACK

Obtaining intimate information regarding the client's life may be necessary in order to help him, and therefore the interviewer is entitled to inquire about such matters. However if the interviewer doubts her ability to help, she is robbed of her assurance that she is entitled to the information. Consequently, doubt about her capacity to help makes her hesitant about intruding into the client's personal life.

The same is true for particular items of information the agency asks the worker to obtain, but about which the worker herself has no conviction. It is hard to ask the client to discuss material which the interviewer thinks unnecessary. For example, adoption workers in a denominational agency who are themselves agnostics may find it difficult to explore seriously the religious practices of adoptive applicants. They lack conviction that such information is significant.

The introspective comments of a 26-year-old, white, female social worker assigned to a terminal cancer ward of a large city hospital provide another illustration.

As I review the tape of the interview, I am struck by how frequently I introduced a question or a comment with an essentially apologetic preface. At one point I said, "You probably don't see much sense in this question." Another time I said, "You might not want to answer this question," and again I said, "Would you mind if I asked you. . . ." I even went so far as to say at another point, "I am supposed to ask you. . . ."

I think it's because I am new to the agency and I have a feeling that there is nothing we can do. The fact that these people are dying is the overwhelming consideration, and I am not sure talking to them and getting them to talk to us serves any useful purpose.

Some interviewers are highly sensitive about the pain occasioned for the interviewee in asking about his failures and personal tragedies. "Inexperienced doctors or nurses sometimes give an injection so slowly and gently that instead of avoiding pain they cause it. Student social workers, too, are sometimes too gentle to probe into (or even allow the client to probe into) sensitive areas and they offer reassurance or change the topic. The more honest of them will admit that, in truth, it was pain to themselves that they were anxious to avoid" (Foran and Bailey 1968:45).

When under pressure of making decisions on many cases, the social work interviewer may fail to ask questions or to hear answers that are likely to make it more difficult to expedite the case decision. Jacobs (1969) details this tendency among social workers in a public welfare department. Although information on relatives available to help was needed, workers recognized that relatives were rarely able or willing to help. If legally responsible relatives were acknowledged, they must be contacted; meanwhile the case decision must remain open. Expediting the work load became simpler if the worker failed to ask questions about relatives or did not listen to the answers, noting on the record there were no such relatives. The pressure of work can make a quick decision, rather than what's best for the client, the overriding influence upon interviewer behavior, as an AFDC worker's comments show:

I had a feeling of apprehension about asking how things had gone with Mrs. G. during the past week. I knew I had to ask, yet I was afraid of the answer. Aware that the situation had been precarious, I was afraid to find out that everything had fallen through. If she were having all sorts of problems, which I dimly suspected, I did not really want to know. Once I found out I would have to start working all over again putting Humpty Dumpty back together again. Just for once I wanted things to be nice and uncomplicated. As long as I did not ask and give Mrs. G. a chance to tell me, that's the way they were as far as I knew.

While one can confidently count on the interviewee's repeated efforts to present his concerns, if the interviewer consistently fails to listen, the interviewee gives up. A tape-recorded study of mothers' interviews with pediatricians showed that "if the doctor fails repeatedly to heed her statements of some basic worry or of her main hopes and expectations from him, she may cease to try, as evidenced by the fact that she either becomes completely mute or reduces her answers to toneless 'hmms' and 'yeses' (Korsch 1968:864).

TOO-CLOSE-TO-HOME SUBJECT MATTER

Social work interviews are concerned with the problems of everyday living—marital interaction, parent-child problems, earning a living, managing a budget, and facing illness and death. Consequently, there is a great deal of interpenetration between the problems the interviewer encounters in her own life and those she deals with on the job. What is discussed in the interview may remind the interviewer of unresolved, or partially resolved, problems in her own personal life. If she feels discomfort about a certain problem, an interviewer may be reluctant to pursue it even when the interviewee himself initiates discussion. She may also project onto the interviewee her own discomfort about a discussion.

A 24-year-old disabled client, talking about his family's reaction to his disability while he was growing up.
MR. D.: They did not want the responsibility of a disabled person in the house. There were always arguments over who was going to put my shoes and socks on, which I couldn't do myself. Things like that you know. It really hurt.
WORKER: How many brothers and sisters do you have?

The worker comments:

I was aware that I did not follow his lead about his strong feeling reaction to his experience. I demonstrated fright for what was for me a painful subject. I heard echoes of my own family's arguments about who was going to take turns in pushing the wheelchair of a paralyzed grandmother.

As Sullivan says, when interviewers communicate a reluctance to discuss some particular feeling or problem, "the records of their interviews are conspicuous for the fact that the people they see do not seem to have lived in the particular area contaminated by that distaste" (1954:69). For instance, the interviewer who has some personal difficulty regarding expression of hostility is less likely to permit, or encourage, such expression on the part of the interviewee. Bandura obtained independent ratings from peers on interviewers' level of anxiety about hostility. Interviews were analyzed to determine how interviewers with high anxiety about hostility dealt with it. The results indicated that interviewers "who typically expressed their own hostility in direct forms and who displayed low need for approval were more likely to permit, and encourage, their patients' hostility than were therapists who expressed little direct hostility and who showed high approval seeking behavior" (1960:8). When the interviewer, out of his need to avoid this material, indicated disapproval or discouragement of expressions of hostility, the interviewee was likely to drop or change the topic. Interviewer deflection was accomplished in a number of ways:

Disapproval:
CLIENT: So I blew my top.
WORKER: Just for that you hit her?
Topical transition:
CLIENT: My mother annoys me.
WORKER: How old is your mother?
Silence:
CLIENT: I just dislike it at home so much at times.
WORKER: [Silence.]
CLIENT: So I just don't know what to do.
Ignoring hostility:
CLIENT: I lose my temper over his tardiness.
WORKER: What are the results of the tardiness?
Mislabeling hostile feelings as nonhostile:
CLIENT: When are you going to give me the results of those tests? I think I am entitled to know.
WORKER: You seem almost afraid to find out.

PERSONAL BIASES

Conflict for the worker involves more than evocation of her own personal biases. Many social work situations call attention to a worker's unresolved position on moral or ethical questions. For instance, a young student in a public assistance agency is struggling to define her attitude toward a client's entitlement to a full public assistance budget when a live-in boyfriend is contributing some support. She feels that the client is sufficiently deprived and should, in any case, get more than the official budget allows. She knows, however, that what is happening is in some respects illegal, and she further fears that another client, or prospective client, may be thereby denied some assistance because available public funds are limited. Ergo, a bothersome ethical conflict. The problem manifests itself in the interview by the interviewer's reluctance to ask significant questions about the client's primary group affiliations. She and the client become involved in a tacit conspiracy to avoid any mention of the boyfriend or the use of the grant, since an honest discussion of these topics would break open the question of the additional support and would require some response to an unsettled ethical question. The interview, then, is full of strange gaps and abrupt transitions as both participants detour around "unthinkable" areas. The worker is not aware of the pattern until later when, listening to a tape of the interview, she says:

Mrs. M. gave a nervous laugh because the subject of Frank [the live-in boyfriend] is a rather touchy one and we both kind of shy away from it.

I suddenly started asking about John [client's 7-year-old son]. Why did I start talking about John when I was thinking about Frank? I wanted to avoid Frank because of the bad vibes I got every time the interview headed in his direction.

A worker is counseling with a teen-age, single pregnant woman about educational planning. The client is in the first trimester of pregnancy and as far as she is aware, nobody at her school knows that she is pregnant. The worker says, "And that's your preference, I am assuming." In commenting on her own response, the worker says:

I think my own personal attitude about unmarried pregnant girls comes through in this remark. I think I see it as a stigma and a source of shame and I myself would prefer to keep it hidden. It turned out that Jane really didn't care whether or not the school knew. It's just that at this point the pregnancy had not made for any change in her activities and it had never come up at the school.

The problems of keeping one's feelings and biases from intruding into the interview is expressed by a social worker in a planned parenthood clinic who has strong feminist convictions:

One of the hardest parts about my role at Planned Parenthood is that we are supposed to be nonjudgmental and not to show feelings. That is often hard to do. Vicky had expressed to me several times that she was very concerned about losing Don (the putative father) and consequently this fear was the basis of her motivation in many circumstances. I personally was having some problems with this and was questioning whether losing Don would be that much of a loss. From Vicky's description, I perceived him as selfish, self-centered, and inconsistent. But as angry as I was with him, I was also very disturbed with her for the fact that she allowed him to manipulate her and pressure her. I was also disturbed that she did not protest his ideas as well as the fact that even though she knew better, she continued to have unprotected intercourse because this is the way he wanted it, rather than to assert herself.

It is difficult, however necessary it may be, to keep one's personal likes and dislikes, personal preferences and predispositions, from affecting interview interaction. For instance, an interviewer introspectively examines her impatient negative reaction to a difficult and frustrating attempt to set so simple a thing as a mutually satisfactory time for scheduling a next interview. The client has rejected several suggestions for an appointment early in the day because of her need to sleep late and for appointments at later times by boasting of her busy social life. The worker says:

Why was I feeling so impatient? The client was threatening me on several levels. First, I value intelligence and am dealing with a woman who is lacking in this quality. Feeling guilty, I admit that I am struggling with equating being intelligent with being human. Second, I am threatened by the client's need to feel important and her quest for recognition, qualities which I am trying to overcome in myself. Finally, resenting conversations with my brothers and my husband about their respective needs for sleep, I cannot exhibit empathy for the same complaint in a total stranger. How can I accept in this woman a quality which annoys me in those I love?

Interviewers may falter, avoid controversial areas, and fail to follow up many worrisome, debatable questions. The worker may be convinced about the desirability of some woman's working but also worry about the negative consequences for the children. Torn between supporting the right of women to work and a feeling of responsibility to the children, the worker would rather not find out too clearly that in this instance the children may, in fact, be reacting negatively to the experience. In the interview this area is quickly glossed over with platitudes and solicitation of confirmation that things are going well through the use of questions that answer themselves.

Your children seem to enjoy the day-care center, don't they?
You haven't had any trouble with Gordy's going to the center, have you?
Stanley seems to be all right since you're working, doesn't he?

FEAR OF HOSTILITY

Questions may remain unanswered and certain content unexplored because of fear that any attempt to introduce the material will evoke hostility toward the interviewer. The interviewer may be reluctant to confront an interviewee with inconsistencies in the material he has shared, avoiding a possibly hostile reaction. But beyond this there is a hesitancy to challenge even when the interviewee is obviously lying, because it suggests mistrust and disrespect. For many interviewers such a challenge seems like checking up, demeaning to both interviewer and interviewee.

LYING

Lying and fabrication by the interviewee present a difficult problem for the social work interviewer. The whole attitudinal stance of the profession suggests that we should accept, with respect, everything the interviewee says and that to question the interviewee's truthfulness is derogatory. Yet it is no tribute to a client's membership in the human family to act as though clients are angelic and never stoop to conning us. We feel stupid and imposed upon if we suspect lying but continue to act as though everything the client says is gospel. And we appear stupid and gullible and weak to a client if she is lying, knows she is lying, and seems able to put things over on us.

Social workers have conflicting feelings about doubting the client. They feel guilty and unhappy because skepticism seems to violate the professionally dictated need to be "accepting" and to treat the client with respect. Yet they live in a real world with clients who often do lie and they live with agency regulations that require objectively accurate data. These conflicting feelings are reflected by a correctional social worker, listening to a tape of his interview with a recently released, 24-year-old rapist. At this point in the interview the social worker was asking questions about the kinds of drinking sessions the parolee had been involved in during the previous week. The worker's response to hearing his line of questioning follows:

It bothers me to listen to this—it reminds me of the welfare snoopers who I deplore. All those damn questions. But then I felt if he wasn't being honest with me, we wouldn't get anywhere. Also pride came into it. One hates to be conned. But pride does have a positive side to it in that if one lets oneself be conned, the relationship and ability to help is damaged. So I don't know. It's a compromise that requires your doing the things you don't really feel comfortable about doing.

We tend to suppose that we have to choose between maintaining a working relationship and questioning the lie and threatening the relationship. This is hardly correct. Not to question the lie means maintaining an ineffectual relationship built on duplicity. A relationship built on lies and maintained through lies, one lie leading to others, involves a complex mixture of feelings, none of which can lead to good, easy, comfortable communication. The interviewee may feel guilt toward the worker, contempt of the worker, shame in lying, anxiety about the possibility of being found out, disappointment in, and resentment of, the worker for not being strong enough, or capable enough, to call a halt. Furthermore, lying robs the relationship of its reason for being. The relationship exists to enable the worker to help the client. But lies make it difficult, if not impossible, for the worker to help effectively, since he is denied the opportunity of knowing the client's actual situation. Consequently, one does not risk the relationship in calling for the truth when one suspects lying. A good relationship obviously has not existed and therefore cannot be lost.

In many instances the social worker does not know what is objectively true about the client's situation. One tests for plausibility and internal consistency. Is it likely, from the social worker's knowledge of similar situations, that something like this could have happened in this way? It is helpful to ask for details, which can come easily if the story is true but are difficult to think up if it is a fabrication. Is the material consistent? Is one element congruent with others? The social worker can appeal to the interviewee to help her understand since the story doesn't seem to hang together and she wants to be sure she has correctly heard what the client has been telling her.

If you suspect lying, ask yourself what prompts this behavior—what purpose does it serve for the client, how can you understand it and, through understanding, discourage its continuance or reduce it?

One of the best defenses against lying is prevention. The client lies for a purpose. Our effort is to act in a manner which would deny him all reason for lying. Clients lie because they want to be accorded respect and acceptance; they want to present a socially desirable facade, hiding their imperfections. One effect of the nonjudgmental, respectful approach is to communicate to the client that he need not lie to be accepted, that we are ready to offer him acceptance and respect even though we know about the imperfections he hesitates to share with us. In reducing threats to the ego, we reduce the motivation for defensiveness and lying. Similarly, the boast of accomplishments never really achieved is made unnecessary by an accepting attitude.

We prevent lying by indicating the acceptability of even the least "socially desirable" responses. We make some lies unnecessary by sharing, with neutral affect, information we may already know. We say matter of factly.

I know from the school that John has been expelled for taking drugs. . . .

We know that you have had two previous convictions on charges of breaking and entering. . . .

Yet often the interviewee has significant, realistic motives for falsification, involving possible punishments for not lying or rewards for lying. In corrections, in protective services, in public assistance programs, the interviewee is concerned with important, real consequences of what he says. We might anticipate that, being human, the interviewee will surely be tempted to lie.

The impact of "vested interest" on interviewee response was experimentally demonstrated by Braginsky and Braginsky (1967) in a study of hospitalized schizophrenics. Patients in one group were told that the purpose of the interview was to see whether they might be ready for discharge; another group, that it was for deciding admission to an open or closed ward; a third group, that it was aimed at evaluation of their feelings and their progress in the hospital. The interviewees responded in a manner designed to accomplish their aims. Patients anxious to leave the hospital or get into the open ward presented themselves as "healthy"; those who wanted to remain in the hospital presented themselves as "sick."

Because the vested interest can be such a strong force favoring lying, confrontation may on occasion be necessary and justifiable.

Gee, help me out here. I am not sure I get it. The whole thing just doesn't hang together. A little while ago you were saying that your husband is indifferent to the kids, never helps you with them, couldn't care less for them, and now you're telling me that he brings John to the day-care center and picks him up at night. I don't get it.

You know, I am sitting here thinking you are trying to give me a snow job, that you're kidding me. What you're saying doesn't seem plausible. Here, let me show you what makes it difficult for me to swallow.

The admittedly very difficult, yet necessary, saving aspect of effective confrontation is to reject the falsification without rejecting the falsifier. It would be a mistake for the interviewer to react to the client's false statements as though it were a personal affront.

Nothing said here is meant to suggest the abrogation of common sense. If there is doubt about whether the interviewee is lying, it is best to let the matter rest. If the content of the suspected fabrication seems relatively insignificant for the central purpose of the interview, it might be casually overlooked and not raised as an issue.

The interviewer has to feel confident in her ability to call for honesty and responsibility without being punitive, however tempting this may be. Even more difficult to achieve is the requirement that the interviewer herself set a scrupulous example of honesty. Her honesty robs the interviewee of a powerful justification for lying and sets a positive example of behavior for interviewee emulation. Interviewer honesty implies never falsely reassuring, never making a promise without fulfillment, openly sharing one's position and responsibility as a community representative and as an agent of social control, sharing the limitations of one's helpfulness and responding with genuineness, when appropriate, in terms of the feeling evoked by the client.

The task of the interviewer is to obtain accurate information so as to enable her to be as helpful to the client as possible. It is not the interviewer's responsibility to improve the client's ethics and morality by her response to the interviewee's lying.

BOREDOM

Experienced interviewers face some special hazards. Spontaneity is bound to wilt after repeated interviews with different clients on the same general problem, while boredom increases. It is understandably hard to maintain the same level of attentiveness and interest after five years and a thousand interviews with as many unmarried mothers about their plans for the unborn child. There is also a feeling of *déjà vu*, of having heard it all before, which makes it difficult to separate each interviewee clearly in all his individuality. Clients tend to merge. The hopeful optimism of the enthusiastic beginner is likely to be gradually modified to a cautious pessimism as the interviewer develops a realistic assessment of the limits of her influence and skill.

More recently worker "burn out" has become the subject of considerable investigation and discussion. Constant interaction with clients around problems which evoke strong feelings leave the worker emotionally depleted. They become bored and somewhat calloused having listened repeatedly to a long series of difficult problems which often have many similar elements. Repetition increases the danger of stereotyping the client. Frequent experience with failure of the proposed intervention to effect the desired change results in increased impatience with clients, in disillusionment and cynicism about one's work. In self-protection workers distance themselves psychologically from clients and become indifferent. This configuration of feelings is antithetical to the attitude most desirable for the interviewer to communicate to the interviewee for effective interviewing.

Interviewer Style

Each interviewer has his or her own preferred general style of interacting with the interviewee. If that preferred style meshes or harmonizes with the client's expectations, an effective interview interaction results. If it does not mesh or harmonize, dissonance is the result. And often such dissonance is not immediately evident or easily recognized.

Studying worker–client relationships Maluccio gives an example of this lack of harmony in a family service agency.

> Mrs. Bates equated professional competence with formality and structure. She was assigned to a worker with an informal and spontaneous style. She was critical of the worker's overly casual approach and did not feel sufficiently confident in the worker's ability to help her. After a few sessions Mrs. Bates withdrew. (1979:63)

There are a number of special dimensions to the interview, and an interviewer's decisions about them tend to determine his or her characteristic style. Among the dimensions are:
1. Balance of control between interviewer and interviewee.
2. Balance between maximum and minimum structure.
3. Balance between activity and passivity.
4. Balance between bureaucratic and service orientations.

INTERVIEW CONTROL

Control does not imply coercion. Skillful control of the interview involves giving direction without restriction; it implies stimulation and guidance without bias or pressure. It involves a confident flexibility that permits granting the interviewee temporary complete control if this expedites a more efficient accomplishment of purpose. In general, "control" has negative connotations that are really not applicable here. In this context it more aptly means "Who is in charge here?"

Many different aspects of the interview are subject to control. They include the topics to be discussed, the sequence in which they are discussed, the focus within each topic, the level of emotionality with which the material is discussed, the person initiating the transition from one topic area to another.

The degree of interview control involves not only a technical decision but also a philosophical one. Those who feel that the needs and desires of the client have priority, that the client should have the right to determine the content and conduct of the interview, will opt for granting the interviewee the greatest measure of control. This group of interviewers believes that only the client knows where he wants to go and how to get there. Those who believe that the interviewer must serve the best interests of the client rather than the desires of the client, that acceding to the wishes of the interviewee in every instance is professionally irresponsible, would opt for greater control of the interview by the interviewer. This group of interviewers believes that the client knows where he wants to go but is not clear on how to proceed; the worker, once she knows where the client wants to go, can help him get there.

Control also implies a nonegalitarian relationship, which is antithetical to some interviewers' conception of the most desirable client-social worker relationship. In actuality, however, all professional relations are nonegalitarian. This does not suggest that the participants are unequal as people but only in terms of the specialized knowledge that brings them together. If the patient knew as much as the doctor, the student as much as the teacher, the client as much as the lawyer, there would be little need for the professional contact.

Even yielding control to the interviewee is a contravention of the interview as an egalitarian enterprise. The interviewer, in effect, asserts her dominant position, since only those who have control can grant it to another. A truly egalitarian relationship might well produce anxiety for the client. He looks to the worker to help him find some answers, to make available greater knowledge. He may feel he is denied support if the worker communicates the feeling that he is equally powerless. At the very least, the relationship is unequal because the worker has skills to help the client find the answers he cannot find by himself. In the most egalitarian professional relationship the worker remains first among equals, based on his superior knowledge of interview content and process.

The ultimate purpose for which control is exerted is important. If the interviewer is acting in accordance with professional dictates, she exerts control for the purpose of meeting the interviewee's needs. It is an action taken with an intent to be helpful and in response to the interviewer's best professional judgment as to what will be optimally helpful to the interviewee.

Following the client's lead is a defensible procedure if it derives from the interviewer's conscious recognition of how, and in what way, this lead might contribute to a productive interview. If the interviewer follows the client's lead because she herself has no real direction for the interview or in abrogation of her responsibility, the results are not as likely to be helpful.

The philosophical question which affects the decision on the balance of control accorded the participants in the interview can be discussed interminably, like all philosophical and value questions. However, from a technical point of view, one might note that conducting an interview is a complex procedure. The interviewer presumably has greater expertise in this matter than the interviewee. To ensure successful attainment of the interview's purpose, it may be necessary to permit the interviewer some degree of control of the process.

Control must be exercised lightly and flexibly if it is to ensure a productive interview. The following excerpt and worker's comments illustrate the shortcomings of too rigid an exercise of control:

A social worker in a home for the aged, interviewing an 82-year-old white woman.
MRS. A.: I fell on the bathroom floor on my back.
WORKER: Um-hum.
MRS. A.: And I hurt the end of my spine, and it's just gotten well this week.
WORKER: Well, I see. One of the purposes of this interview is to find out if the names of your correspondents or the people who visit you, if the names and addresses are the same or if they have changed. Do you have visitors often?

In retrospect the worker comments:

Listening to the tape, it was clear that my concern with the interview guide had been given overriding importance. I failed completely to respond to the poor woman, became extremely direct, and made an abrupt change of topic. I should have taken into consideration here Hamilton's suggestion that the essence of the interviewer's skill is to ask questions responsive to what the client is already saying. I would have said, "You have gone through a great deal. I hope you are feeling better now," or "It must have been pretty painful, and I am glad you are feeling better now." Something, anything to show I had been listening and had some feeling for her. I then could have gently gotten back to the principal purpose of the interview.

By virtue of her coming to the agency for help, the client has conceded some leadership responsibility to the interviewer. The interviewer must not only accept this responsibility, she is in fact held accountable for implementing it. If the interview is a failure, the fault is attributed to her. It is manifestly unfair to the interviewer to hold her responsible, and accountable, for interview outcome and at the same time deny her significant opportunity to determine the interaction. Furthermore, it appears that the interviewee herself appreciates skillful control of the interview by the interviewer. It is an indication of the interviewer's competence and increases the interviewee's confidence that the encounter will be productive rather than wasteful.

INTERVIEW STRUCTURE

The interviewer must decide what degree of interview structure she prefers. The degree of structuring indicates how explicit the interviewer is in explaining what is expected of each of the participants. A greater degree of structuring implies that the interviewer will state the ground rules for interaction, explaining to the interviewee what to expect during the course of the interviews. A lesser degree of structure suggests that the interviewer will say nothing about these matters but passively permit whatever is said to develop freely; here structure grows out of the interactional experience. The degree of structuring is related to the dimension of control, more explicit structuring being associated with greater interviewer control of the interaction.

The following is an example of minimal structure:

PATIENT: Where shall we begin?
THERAPIST: Wherever you feel like.
PATIENT: Is there anything in particular that you'd like me to talk about?
THERAPIST: No, I just want you to talk about anything.

The excerpt below is from an interview offering a moderate degree of structure. It is followed by the same interview as it might have been conducted by a worker who performed minimal structure.

Interviewee: male, 23, white, lower class. Veterans Administration psychiatric outpatient clinic.

MR. K.: Well, I'm not sure. I have this leg pain, and they gave me all the examinations they could give me, but they don't find anything wrong. So I don't know. They said maybe it's just nerves and they sent me here. What am I supposed to do here?

WORKER: Well you can talk about anything that's bothering you. You know any troubles you are having?

MR. K: Well, I'm not much of a talker.

WORKER: I'll be glad to listen to anything you care to bring up.

MR. K.: Well, I don't know.

WORKER: For instance, since you came to the Veterans Administration about your leg trouble, we can talk about that.

MR. K.: And what happens then—you just listen?

WORKER: Well, I listen, but I also try to help you get a clearer idea of the things that are bothering you. For instance, you said they thought it was nerves. What do you think?

The same interview, conducted by an interviewer who feels that structure should evolve primarily on the initiative of the client, might have gone something like the following:

MR. K.: Well, I'm not sure. I have this leg pain, and they gave me all the examinations they could give me, but they don't find anything wrong. So I don't know. They said maybe it's just nerves and they sent me here. What am I supposed to do here?

WORKER: What would you like to do here?

MR. K.: I'm not sure.

WORKER: What ideas do you have?

MR. K.: I don't have any ideas, but I sure would like to get rid of the pain in the leg.

WORKER: How do you think we can help with that?

MR. K.: Well, they said it's nerves [pause].

WORKER: [Expectant silence.]

Preference for degree of structure is related to the interviewer's perception of herself vis-à-vis the interviewee in the interview situation. Here, as with the control dimension, some feel that structuring violates the client's integrity and falsely presupposes that the interviewer knows best not only what needs to be done but how it should be done. However, the whole process of structuring the interview on the nature of reciprocal role responsibilities and behavior has the effect of increasing the interviewee's confidence in the interviewer. It is a demonstration of competence.

Control and structure reduce the ambiguity of the interview situation for the client. As a result of clear leadership from the interviewer and a clear sense of the ground rules, the client is less anxious. He knows better how he needs to act in fulfilling the role responsibilities of interviewee. Research relating levels of interviewee satisfaction with structure has shown that there is more satisfaction with interviews in "which the therapists' verbal activity is highly structured" (Lennard and Bernstein 1960:185). When the interviewer did not make clear to the interviewee what was expected, the situation provoked anxiety and uncertainty for the interviewee. The client's response was to talk more but to be hesitant and cautious in his speech. The client talked more because he needed to search more widely for feedback from the interviewer to indicate that he was doing the right thing.

One of the principal conclusions from discussions with forty former AFDC clients about their experiences was their frequent confusion because of caseworkers' failure to structure explicitly the purpose of the interviews (McIsaac 1965). When there was little structuring by the interviewer, clients expressed uncertainty about the purpose of the interview and about what they were supposed to do in the interview.

Schmidt (1969) studied clients' responses to social workers' differences in communicating an interview structure. One structural element was selected for examination, namely, the purpose of the interview. Some workers clearly and explicitly structured the purpose of the interview and shared the statement of purpose with the client for her to accept or reject. Other workers made no mention of purpose. The workers who refrained from structuring confused their clients; the clients did not perceive what the workers had in mind. The expectation that the client would select a purpose was not fulfilled. As Schmidt notes:

> One thing is clear. . . . A worker's silence on the subject of the interview's purpose in no case conveyed his actual intent to the client, namely that the focus and content of the interview should be shaped by what was then most important to the client. . . . It is sometimes assumed that when workers inject no direction, or make no attempt to formulate their own objectives then clients are free to choose (or in some way indicate) how the sessions will be used. There appears to be some basis for questioning the validity of this assumption. Unless a client knows clearly how his worker views their respective roles in determining interview content and direction, he is not free to make a choice. (1969:80–81)

An interview with very little structure is not likely to be anxiety provoking, however, if minimal structure is what the interviewee expects. Clemes had interviewers deliberately vary the degree of structure with which they conducted interviews. The interviewees were asked beforehand about the kind of interview they expected and then were tested for level of anxiety experienced during the interview. Interviewees who expected little structure experienced low anxiety when that was what they encountered. Interviewees who expected considerable structure were not made anxious when they experienced it. The interviewees were most anxious when they encountered an interview that was contrary to their expectations.

ACTIVITY-PASSIVITY DIMENSION

Control and structure are related to a third important variable, the relative balance between activity and passivity of the interviewer. Preference for low control and limited structure suggests lower levels of activity by the social worker. The relationship between greater interviewer activity and greater interviewing directivity or control is confirmed in Mullen's (1969) study of social work interviewers.

Greater directiveness involves more frequent initiation of topic change by the interviewer as compared with interviewee initiations, more frequent leading rather than following the client, more interventions that employ the interviewer's frame of reference rather than the interviewee's frame of reference.

The following is an example of an interviewer with low activity level:

PATIENT: [Clearing throat.] Do you think we are getting anywhere, doctor?
THERAPIST: What do you think?
PATIENT: First of all, today I'd like to ask, uh, if you have any evaluation to make of myself as a patient. Is, uh, there anything wrong with my, uh, attitude, conscious or unconscious, that I can possibly do something about? Uh, is, uh, has anything I said worked anytime as far as you know, uh, or have I been trying to get at the right thing so far?
THERAPIST: Well, uh, may I ask how you feel about this?
PATIENT: [Laughs.] That's what I expected.

Low levels of worker activity increase ambiguity felt by the interviewee, which increases uncertainty and anxiety. This effect may help explain the results of Lennard and Bernstein's study of tape-recorded interviews. Low therapist activity was associated with patient dissatisfaction with communication (1960:107). "Dyads in which the therapists were most active showed the least signs of strain" (1960:114).

Heller and his associates had interviewers vary their behavior in some specific way. Interviewees' reaction to the variations were studied. Active-friendly interviewers were liked best and passive-hostile interviewers were liked least. Interviewer passivity, resulting in lack of communication and lack of orientation cues, was felt by the interviewee to be a punishing situation. In general, when measured by such factors as volume of interviewee verbalization, level of interviewee satisfaction, consistency of meeting interview appointments, and continuance in treatment, the more active therapists had a better showing than less active therapists.

As with other factors, the effects are not linear—more is not always better. Control, structure, and activity appear to have more favorable effects on the interview than abrogation of control, lack of structure, and passivity, but only up to a point. If the interviewer goes so far that the result is authoritarian domination and inflexibility, the interview is adversely affected. When the interviewer limits the freedom of the interviewee to introduce material, when she restricts the interviewee by asking specific questions requiring specific answers, when she forces the introduction of content without regard for the interviewee's preference, when she specifically excludes content of interest to the interviewee and specifically limits the range of the interviewee's response to any question she carries control and structure beyond the point where it yields positive returns.

Optimally, choice of emphasis toward either end of these dimensions—control, structure, and activity level—should be determined by the content of the interview and by the needs of the particular interviewee at one or another point in the interview. Some interviewees need more or less control, more or less structure, more or less interviewer activity. And the same interviewee may need more or less control, structure or activity at different points in the interview. In general, most interviewees might need more structure at the beginning of an interview, when they have not yet learned what is expected of them. When they are concerned with content that is familiar, when they are ready, willing, and able to discuss topics, they may need minimum interviewer control and activity. When the interview is concerned with highly subjective areas of content, maximum initiative might be transferred to the interviewee. Greater interviewer activity may be desirable at those points in the interview when the client is ambivalent about discussing significant material and needs encouragement to do so.

The interviewer thus needs to have considerable flexibility and a willingness and capacity to modulate these dimensions in terms of the client's needs and interview requirements. This is a heavy burden, since the interviewer has her own needs and works more (or less) comfortably with greater or lesser structure, control, and activity. In addition, the interviewer is anxious to conduct a good interview so as to receive the approval of the colleagues and superiors who, in her thoughts, share the interview room with her. When an interviewer feels most anxious about an interview, when it seems to be going nowhere, she is likely to become more active, extend a greater measure of control, and enforce a tighter structure in response to these pressures.

The need for control, structure, and activity varies with the interviewee's age, intelligence, and experience in the role. Children, mentally deficient clients, and clients who are seeing a social worker for the very first time may all warrant more structure, more control, and more activity on the part of the worker.

The purpose of the interview also influences the level of structure and control. The social study interview and the assessment interview require that certain content be covered. Consequently, such interviews may need to be directive. Situational factors may be determining. At times of crisis, when some emergency action needs to be taken, or when the interviewee is very upset, there may be need for more worker control and activity.

We have, then, a complex relationship between the needs of the two participants, individually and in interaction, in a particular situational context. An interviewer who finds high control and firm structure congenial to her mode of operation is likely to be successful in interviews with clients with similar predispositions. With a client who needs less control and a flexible structure, the skill of this interviewer may be shown by her ability to modify her approach to meet the client's needs. Recognizing that both parties bring preferences, the hallmark of the good interviewer is the extent to which she can relinquish her own preferences in favor of the client's. The axiom might be that the interviewer should provide the least amount of structure and exert the least amount of control and activity necessary to achieve the purpose of the interview.

In general, the research available suggests that social work clients respond to, and appreciate, clear structuring on the part of the worker and a moderate level of control and activity.

BUREAUCRACY VS. SERVICE

Yet another dimension, of a somewhat different nature, requires a decision from the interviewer and further determines her interview behavior. Most social workers conduct interviews as agency representatives in the course of implementing agency functions. The interviewers must take some stand along the continuum between total concern for the agency's administrative needs and concern for the client's needs. This is true particularly for the public welfare agencies, where case loads are high and the pressure of work is great. In such an agency, an extreme bureaucratic orientation in the intake interview would dictate an approach that was concerned with answering, as efficiently as possible, the question of client eligibility. Only content that contributed directly to the answer would be explored. Anything else would be discouraged as irrelevant. The agency requires rapid disposition of an application, one way or another, so that it can go on to additional pending applications and to the other applications that will be made tomorrow and the day after tomorrow. Unless the interviewer sticks to the necessary business, the system risks being overwhelmed. Content is therefore sharply focused, and worker control of the interview is high.

The bureaucratically oriented worker is concerned with procedures, is inclined toward a strict interpretation of agency regulations, and is sharply task focused. By contrast, the strongly client-oriented approach gives primacy to client-initiated content, whether it is directly related to the task of determining eligibility or not. Rules are liberally interpreted, and greater client control of the interview is granted.

The difference is between a task orientation and a person orientation, between giving priority to meeting the needs of the system or meeting the needs of the client. The following worker in a public assistance agency expresses a client-oriented approach to the intake interview:

I always try to avoid [placing a strong emphasis on eligibility] unless somebody really begins to give me a hard time. You have to point out to them that we have only so much time to work on this; this is what must be done. But I never throw it at them the first time. I know persons in this office who have a very small case load because they are so cold and abrupt to people that they make them withdraw. . . . In the first interview I have the feeling that this seems awfully cold and abrupt, just to get names and addresses and information and never listen to the real reason they have come in. I have heard workers on the phone say, "Now Mrs. Smith, just a minute. You listen to me. I want you to get this. One, two, three," and this is no exaggeration of their tone of voice. [She had affected a severe, sharp tone of voice.] To me that isn't the way to treat people, but it is more efficient.

A second worker expresses the bureaucratic orientation:

If someone wants to go into "My mother comes over and we fight," and "My husband I think is going out with this person," and "I think my child had this problem in school," they are not really pertinent to the intake. Many workers will sit two and a half, three hours in an intake [interview] and just listen to that crap. (Zimmerman 1969:256)

Although such pressure for completing assigned work tasks is perhaps obvious and pressing in a public agency offering assistance to meet emergent needs, every social agency faces similar demands. Foster home and adoptive applicants are made anxious by long delays in processing their applications. Court calendars set time limits for probation studies. Scheduled diagnostic conferences impose constraints on social studies in mental hospitals and clinics.

Agency scheduling and demands for completion of clearly defined tasks within time limits tend to determine workers' behavior in the interview. If the worker is applicant-service oriented, she will tend to take the time to explore each of the client's problems to the point where she is confident that she understands the client's needs. However, such an orientation lengthens the time she must allot to interviewing a client. If she persists in trying to implement such an orientation, she finds herself falling further and further behind in completing eligibility studies or social studies or intake interviews. She risks censure from the agency administration. A worker is thus under pressure to modify the applicant-service orientation to the interview in the direction of a case load-management orientation. This means that the worker approaches the interview with the idea of directing the interaction so as to permit her to make the necessary decisions in the most expeditious manner.

Cold and businesslike as this approach may sound, it often is in line with the client's own preference. The public assistance applicant wants to know as quickly as possible if he can get a check, the adoptive applicant wants to know as quickly as possible if he will be granted a child. The more precise and efficient the interview leading to a disposition of the request, the greater the satisfaction of many interviewees.

In sum, then, both interviewer and interviewee bring their reference group, primary group, and biopsychosocial backgrounds to the interview. The influence of any specific variable brought to the interview is modified in the interaction. The interviewer's own feelings, preferences, and needs pose problems for effective interviewing. In addition, the interviewer has to make decisions regarding interview control, interview structure, level of activity, and the balance between bureaucratic and service needs. The interviewee, in turn, has his own tasks, preferences, and problematic needs in implementing his role.

SUGGESTED READING

LYING

Sissela Bok. *Lying: Moral Choice in Public and Private Life.* New York: Vintage Books, 1978 (354 pp.).
    While not concerned in any way with the interview situation, the book is such a clearly stated exposition of lying behaviors generally that it easily translates to problems of lying in the interview.

Part II

The Interview Process

CHAPTER 6

Introductory Phase

Each interview in a sequence of interviews, is part of a process, a series of steps that, over time, implement the goal of the contact between agency and client. Each interview, however, viewed as a discrete unit in the series, itself embodies a process with a beginning, a middle, and an end. The interview process is the consciously implemented, dynamic movement through successive stages in accomplishing the purposes of the interview.

The sequential steps in the social work, problem-solving process—study, diagnosis, and treatment (or data collection, data assessment, and intervention)—are not clearly demarcated. Similarly, in a given interview the introductory phase activities are not sharply differentiated from those of the middle or development phase which in turn are not clearly demarcated from those of the closing or termination phase. Process is somewhat like a symphony. Although at any particular time, one phase, one theme, may be dominant, the other steps in the process can be heard, muted, in the background. For the purpose of more explicit analysis, we will artificially separate the steps in the process and discuss each in turn.

Paths to the Interview

The interview begins before it starts. It begins before the two participants meet, in their thoughts and feelings as they move toward the actual encounter. The client's decision to contact the agency for an interview is often the result of a series of complex, interrelated subdecisions. The residuals of these subdecisions may affect the client's initial behavior in the interview.

The prospective client first has to recognize that she has a problem, one that she cannot resolve on her own. She may choose an informal, non-professional source of help, such as a friend or relative or the local bartender. Some people have neither friends nor relatives in whom they can or would like to confide, or find that their friends and relatives have neither the competence nor the resources to help them. At this point the prospective client has to make another decision. Having decided she has a problem which she cannot resolve alone and having decided that the informal sources of help are either not available or not effective, she must turn to the more formal, professional channels for the help she needs and wants. She now must choose among the numerous professional resources that are available. The kinds of social, interpersonal problems that are brought to social agencies are brought, with even greater frequency, to family doctors, local clergy, etc. The prospective client who contacts the agency to schedule an interview has then made a decision which is the end result of a series of prior decisions, namely that she has a problem with which she wants the help of some professional person and has further identified the social agency as the source of such help.

For many social agency clients there are few options available, and consequently the decision-making chain is relatively simple and direct. Social agencies have a monopoly over important social resources needed and wanted by the client, and the need for contact with the agency is apparent. This situation is particularly true for the client needing financial assistance, but it is also somewhat true for the prospective client needing foster care, homemaker services, a child for adoption, or a maternity shelter.

The route to the agency is not mandatory, however. People borrow money from friends, relatives, and loan companies. They make informal arrangements for child care when they are working or hospitalized. They adopt children through independent channels and find jobs and housing on their own. Although situational imperatives may not make coming to an agency the only alternative, they limit free choice, that is, if the client wants to eat or meet other strong needs.

For another group of clients, coming to an agency is more clearly an imposed, involuntary action. Abusive or neglectful parents may be ordered by the court to obtain agency service; delinquents may be required to maintain such a contact. They have been sent on ahead to the agency or pushed ahead to the agency by others in the community rather than having freely made the decision to come.

The source of referral is a determinant of how the worker might orient himself to the interviewee. If the client is referred by a psychiatrist or a prestigious organization the worker might feel induced to do a better job than if the client is self-referred and there is no feedback responsibility to another professional or agency. Clients identified or affiliated with groups that have an active advocacy organization such as the Welfare Rights Organization or the Black Panthers may affect the interviewer's orientation to the interview.

In some instances the interviewee does not take the initiative to make the first contact. Rather, the agency represented by the interviewer makes contact with the client. "Outreach" programs and "aggressive" casework programs are examples of such agency efforts to initiate contact.

An interview scheduled after the prospective client has made the sequential decisions listed above is apt to be different from the interview which begins after only some, or none, of these decisions have been reached. The correctional client may appear for the interview as requested, but if she has not decided that she has a problem and wants the interviewer's help, it will be difficult to establish an understandable, mutually acceptable purpose for the interview.

The prospective client whose decision to come to the agency was forced by limited options is apt to be more resentful, initially, than the client who felt she made a voluntary choice.

In each instance, then, the interview is affected in some measure by the events preceding it. The start of each interview in a series of interviews is affected by what took place during the last interview and by the intervening experiences encountered by the client.

It is undoubtedly true that interviews with clients who voluntarily come for service, who are motivated to participate in the interaction, who are there because they want to be, are easier than interviews with those who are there because others have pushed them or outright ordered them to go. The reality is that many social agency clients come with varying degrees of ambivalence as a consequence of external pressure from others as well as in response to their own true preferences. It is a reality to which the interviewer needs to accommodate.

There may be a need to overtly recognize that the client is not happy with having to come to the interview and this feeling is then acknowledged in open discussion. "I know you wouldn't be here if it wasn't required and you might rather be somewhere else. Let's talk about it for a while." Acknowledging such feelings may enable us to understand the basis for the client's opposition to coming. The interviewer does not question or challenge the interviewee's entitlement to her feelings or their legitimacy. He would like, however, to understand them better and perhaps respond to them in terms which might make the interview more acceptable to the client and incline her toward cooperative participation.

Motivation to Participate

Different paths to the interview suggest differences in levels of motivation to participate. Clients may even go beyond lack of motivation to positive resistance. They may see the agency as having no legitimate right to an interview with them and the scheduling of such an interview as an act of coercive authority.

Initial motivation or lack of motivation is, however, a transient factor. While it is admittedly easier to get a successful interview started with an interviewee who is motivated to engage in the encounter, this is no guarantee of success. The client might lose her initial motivation during the course of the interview because of the way it progresses. Conversely, clients who come with very tenuous, limited motivation may, and often do, develop the motivation to participate because of what goes on in the interview. There is empirical confirmation of these observations. Successful outcomes have been reported for interviews in which the interviewee was initially an involuntary participant; other studies have failed to show a clear relationship between high initial motivation and outcome of therapy (Volsky et al. 1965).

A group of young female probationers who were "directed" to accept treatment by a family service agency showed a favorable outcome as compared with a randomly selected, untreated group of probationers. The report notes that "these data would seem to cast considerable doubt on the assumption that voluntary initiation of casework treatment is required for successful involvement of the client" (Webb and Riley 1970:572).

The consequences of compulsory referral for treatment were studied by Gallant and coworkers (1968). Male alcoholics paroled from a state penitentiary were randomly assigned to either a voluntary or a compulsory treatment group. Those assigned to compulsory treatment were told that failure to attend even one weekly psychotherapy session at an alcoholism clinic over a six-month period would constitute a violation of parole. The voluntary group was required to attend only the first appointment, all subsequent appointments being voluntary. A follow-up study initiated a year after the first clinic visit indicated that the compulsory treatment group showed clearly superior performance in terms of abstinence from drink, subsequent arrest record, work record, and general social adjustment. While the results do not argue for the advantage of compulsory referral, they do clearly indicate that it may be followed by very good results in the treatment contact. Similar positive results were obtained by Margolis (1964) and his associates in a study of voluntary and compulsory referrals of probationers to psychotherapy.

These data suggest that initial motivation is neither a necessary requirement for a successful interview nor a guarantee of one. They emphasize the interviewer's responsibility to nurture whatever motivation the client brings and to develop motivation in those clients who come without it. Concern with motivation is a necessary and obligatory task of the interviewer. Motivation energizes behavior and gives an impetus to action in a particular direction. Motivation to participate cooperatively and collaboratively in the interview is the result of social and psychological forces that encourage the client toward cooperative-collaborative participation and social and psychological forces that make for opposition and resistance to such participation.

People will be motivated to participate in the interview when they anticipate that the inducements and incentives, the gains and the pleasures, will outweigh the penalties and the pains. The task of the agency and the individual interview is to initiate and conduct the interview so as to enhance and intensify the magnitude of the factors that motivate the client to participate and to reduce the factors that result in opposition and resistance.

In general, motivation will be higher if psychological penalties are reduced by agency procedure and the interviewer's behavior. For instance, some stigma is associated with becoming an agency client, although it varies with the presenting problem. Studies establish this feeling very clearly for the clients of the public assistance agency. As one public assistance client noted, "The hardest part of [being on welfare] is getting up the nerve to go up to somebody and say 'I'm poor and I need help.' That's very hard to say and it's real work to say it because no matter how you try to say it, it still seems to come out 'I'm no good' " (Zurcher 1970:213).

Marital problems and parent-child problems are still regarded by many as evidence of personal failure and inadequacy; somewhat less stigma is associated with services related to physical illness and disability. Consequently some of the prospective client's hesitancy to contact the agency is due to the stigma which he and others see associated with the role of social agency client. The sense of shame, guilt, and inadequacy which afflicts a prospective client may affect behavior in the interview once contact is made.

The psychological penalties that result when a prospective client defines herself as inadequate because she must seek help from a social service agency are reduced if the worker's attitude is one of respect for the individual. Fear of rejection by others because of inadequacy is reduced by an atmosphere of acceptance in the worker's approach. Fear of loss of autonomy and independence as the interviewee becomes dependent, in a measure, on the agency is reduced by the worker's respect of the client's right of self-determination to the degree that this is possible and permissible. Fear that the community will learn of her problem and that she might be shamed and rejected as a consequence is reduced by the promise and actuality of confidentiality. Fear of self-exposure, of learning about the more unpleasant aspects of oneself, is reduced in the context of an accepting relationship. Thus the interviewer's behavior designed to establish a positive relationship also has the effect of increasing the client's motivation to participate by reducing the negative aspects associated with participation.

More positively, however, the extrinsic rewards and the intrinsic gratification in the interview contact itself are prime considerations motivating the client to participate in the interview.

The prospective client is faced with a difficult problem causing pain. The hope is that the agency can help resolve the problem and reduce the pain. The more the interviewer can prove his utility to the client by helping her solve her problems and by providing a socially and emotionally satisfying experience, the greater the likelihood that the client's motivation will be enhanced.

The pull of hope and the push of discomfort are powerful complementary factors motivating the interviewee to cooperative participation. Cooperative participation is admittedly more difficult to achieve with some client groups than with others. Freud recognized that the treatment motivation of the poor may be less strong than that of the middle class since the life to which they return after giving up the comfort of their neuroses is less attractive than the life of fantasy. The drug addict needs to be convinced that the unexciting routine of daily existence is better than the euphoria of temporary blissful withdrawal, the hassle of getting the means to pay for the drugs, the cycle of arrest and release, and the probability of an early death.

Approaching the Interview

Having decided to come to an agency and having scheduled an interview, the prospective client prepares for the interview and rehearses it in her mind. Prospective clients talk to other clients, find out about agency procedures, what the social workers are like, what to say, what to avoid saying, how to present their story. A wealth of gossip about many of the social agencies is available to people living in neighborhoods where a high percentage of the people have had agency contacts.

Interviewing that takes place in a closed social system where prospective interviewees are in close contact with former and currently active interviewees faces a special hazard. There is an active informal communications network among the people in prisons, hospitals, schools, and institutions of every kind. A frequent item of information for sharing is the interview habits of the social work staff.

The interviewee may come prepared to manipulate the interviewer into a favorable response to her request. Clients who have some sophistication about the factors that determine the worker's decision about their request are likely to engage in managing the impressions received by the worker— as would anybody in a similar situation. For instance, many adoptive applicants have not only discussed with already adoptive parents how they should behave but may also have studied what the agency is looking for in books such as *Adopting a Child Today* by Jean R. Isaac. One section of the book is in effect a perceptive tip sheet on how to behave to ensure favorable assessment by the agency interviewer. The author advises a couple to use the pronoun "we" not "I," to confess to quarreling on occasion, to confess that infertility poses a problem for adjustment but "then go on to say that they adjusted to the situation through talking the matter out with each other." Both should indicate that they are "happy in their jobs but the wife should not be too happy," seeking fulfillment in motherhood; they should present a picture of a "reasonably active social life and be active in community affairs—but not too active" so that they will have time for children, etc. The suggestions are presented as a practical guide to a couple seeking to convince the agency that they have the capacity for adoptive parenthood (1965:6–24).

FINDING THE AGENCY

The interaction also begins before the two people meet, in terms of the events around scheduling and the immediate pre-interview situation. Prospective clients face frustration in trying to find the agency's listing in the telephone directory, in being shunted on the telephone from one person to another, and in having to repeat their request to a number of different people. This recurrent difficulty is confirmed in the following report:

A group of well-educated volunteers, competent in the use of the telephone and with easy access to it, tested the information system for us by calling agencies in a designated order, making standard, set inquiries. Many inquiries required a number of phone calls and much persistence before help was given. Many other inquiries led to a dead end. In fact, one-third of all attempts ended without conclusive answers or offers of help. The average request required 3.5 telephone calls and considerable time, thus reflecting agencies' specialized functions and rather narrow conceptions of their responsibilities. Agencies rendering one specific type of service often seem to know nothing about other fields of service, even related fields. In fact, even within a given field an agency may know little about services other than its own. (Kahn 1966:48)

An initial irritating experience in scheduling an interview might cause the prospective client to develop a negative attitude that contaminates the beginning of the actual interview.

The client may come to the interview after having experienced a number of false tries because she was not certain which agency offered the service she required. A process of sorting goes on between clients with particular needs and agencies with particular services. Some sorting is accomplished by the agency's name—Family and Children's Services, Society for Prevention of Cruelty to Children, Traveler's Aid. Some is accomplished as a consequence of agency auspices—Catholic Social Service Bureau, Jewish Child Care Association. Some is achieved because an agency is located as a social service department in a particular hospital or a particular school. People make mistakes, of course. Sometimes the agency title or auspices or location does not clearly communicate the kinds of people and problems to which it offers services. When this happens, the referral procedure is a second screening device to direct the applicant to the proper agency.

PHYSICAL IMPACT OF THE AGENCY

The physical accessibility of the agency is a determinant of the client's attitude at the beginning of the interview. Many clients have to come long distances dragging fretful children with them in subways or buses, to centrally located agency offices. It is, therefore, understandable that some prospective clients resist scheduling interviews or begin the interviews physically exhausted and emotionally enervated. Some agencies have responded by decentralizing their operations, opening district offices close to the client group, often in storefront locations in the immediate neighborhood.

The location of the agency, its physical appearance, and its state of repair (or more often disrepair) say something to the client about the community's attitude toward the service and the client group. Very often, particularly for public welfare agencies, the building suggests that the service has low priority among community concerns and that, inferentially, the client group which the agency serves need not be given any great consideration. This is disheartening and depressing to the interviewee and reinforces the supplicant attitude which many clients bring to the agency. Location of the agency in an older, run-down neighborhood may make some clients anxious and uneasy, particularly if they have late appointments which means that they leave the agency at night. The availability or the lack of parking facilities may lessen or increase feelings of frustration brought into the interview.

Maluccio (1979), in interviewing clients of a family service agency, found that many of them commented on the agency's physical environment—

mostly negatively. They remarked on the location and physical appearance of the agency, the size and condition of the waiting room and offices, and the lack of parking. Clients pointed out that the building looked run down and that the offices were old, too small, and looked cold. One client said:

> "I liked the location because of my job—but the building was something else. They should do something about it—fix it up a little bit—you know it made me feel worse about myself because I couldn't afford anything better." (Maluccio 1979:164)

Another client said:

> "The room was very small—just a desk and some chairs. The social worker put in some plants and tried to make it homey—but it was still an office. The room looked empty like I felt for quite a while. Sometimes, well, it made it hard to get going." (p. 165)

These may be transitory feelings of limited intensity but that they do have some effect on the interview needs to be recognized.

As Germain notes: "Space design and decoration in our agency settings communicate messages about their status and worth to users of services and affect self-esteem and psychic comfort" (1976:20)—and interview interaction. The interviewer may fail to note the effects of a dingy physical environment and thus may fail to give the interviewee an opportunity to discuss her dismay at the start of an interview. Anybody working in a place for some time becomes inured to the environment and so may overlook its effects on people encountering it for the first time.

Even color of office walls may affect interview interaction in a subtle way. Studies of reactions to color show that different colors evoke or intensify different moods. Black is somber and depressing, green is calming, and red has a stimulating, excitable effect.

The aesthetics of the interview room have significance for the interview. Mintz studied the effects of the aesthetics of work surroundings. Over a period of three weeks, two interviewers met with subjects in an interview-like situation. They alternately used two different rooms for these meetings. One room was "pleasantly decorated and furnished to give the appearance of an attractive comfortable study." The other room was "arranged to appear as an unsightly storeroom in a disheveled unkempt state" (1956:459). Observational notes showed that in the second, ugly room the interviewers reacted with "monotony, fatigue, headaches, sleep, discontent, hostility and avoidance of the room. By contrast in the first 'beautiful' room they had feelings of comfort, pleasure, enjoyment, importance, en-

ergy and a desire to continue their activity" (p. 466). Pictures in the interview room should be neutral and calming in their effect.

An interviewing room which displays some visual objective evidence of
the interviewer's expertise generally contributes to the client's feeling more
hopeful. The influence of diplomas, an NASW membership certificate,
and/or credential indicating membership in the Academy of Certified Social
Workers should not be discounted. These enhance the interviewee's perception of the interviewer as an expert.

For many social workers, the reality of the physical interview setting is,
however, often far from ideal.

> The new professional social worker's home base is usually a district office. His
> desk is one of many on an open floor. There is little or no privacy. He is
> surrounded by other workers, welfare assistants, clerks, and supervisors, all
> crowded together with one desk adjoining another. Telephones are constantly
> ringing and there is a steady hum of conversation, typewriting, and people
> moving from place to place. This office is not an environment in which a worker
> can think clearly and calmly about the complex and painful situations he faces
> and the fateful decisions he must sometimes make. There is no quiet place
> where one can go to think for a few moments or consult with colleagues. In-
> terviewing clients, which occasionally takes place at the agency, is carried out
> in small open cubicles. There is no privacy. In sum the setting is not one
> usually conceived of as professional; in fact the environmental image is more
> industrial than professional. (Wasserman 1970:95)

WAITING

Of more immediate impact and potential for carryover is the experience
encountered at the agency, while the client waits for the interview to begin. In public welfare agencies, clients wait for long periods in noisy, un-
attractive reception rooms, sitting uncomfortably on crowded, hard benches.
Even a half-hour delay may seem interminable to an anxious person, uncertain whether she will be granted the help she badly needs.

Waiting is felt as an indignity by everyone. In waiting you are controlled
by others, and there is nothing you can do but remain passive and available
until the other person is ready. It arouses feelings of competition and resentment against whoever or whatever is occupying the other person while
you wait. It evokes feelings of anxiety about being abandoned. Will "they"
remember that you are there waiting?

Because the reaction to waiting is primarily negative, lessening the waiting time ensures a better start for the interview. Administrative problems,

shortage of staff, and constant heavy intake may however make delays inevitable and, beyond a certain point, irreducible.

Letting the interviewee know just how long the wait might be is an elementary courtesy. If the wait is unavoidably prolonged beyond the given time, the receptionist should give the interviewee periodic reassurance that she will be seen.

When interviewer and interviewee finally meet, it takes some time and effort to dissipate the frustration and resentment generated by the period of waiting. The interviewer may be successful in communicating a genuine feeling of respect. Nevertheless, his job is made more difficult by the need to counteract the disrespect inherent in the agency procedure that results in people having to wait for an interview.

If the client has waited a long time, it might be helpful to recognize explicitly with her at the beginning of the interview that she is likely to be annoyed for having been kept waiting, to openly acknowledge that the client might have some strong feelings about this and invite discussion of these reactions. An interviewer says, "I began by noting that I knew she had been waiting a long time and that she might be feeling annoyed."

RECEPTION

Although the interviewer may not be explicitly aware of this because he does not live this experience, the fact is that the interviewee may have had some unnerving experience within the agency before she reaches the interviewer's desk.

While the first formal scheduled interview for a client coming to a social agency is with the staff social worker, receptionists or secretaries actually conduct an informal unscheduled initial interview. Some essential identifying data is usually obtained by the receptionists to find out what the client wants and whether the client is at the right place. This generally involves a series of questions.

Hall studied the reception procedures in several social agencies in great detail. The person at the reception desk acts as a gatekeeper and regulates border traffic flowing in the direction of the interviewer's room. The receptionist makes many discretionary decisions "at the point of initial contact between the agency and its clients" (1974:21). She decides whether or not the client is at the right agency, acts as a buffer between the interviewee and interviewer, keeping the interviewee from intruding until the interviewer is ready, and acts as an advocate of clients with workers, getting them to see a particular client.

Hall notes the lack of privacy and the violation of confidentiality, which is routine in many agencies during such pre-interview "interviews." He says:

Time and time again as I sat in a variety of waiting rooms I saw obvious distress on the part of visiting clients who were obliged to describe their problems in a room containing other people. The receptionists, accustomed to tales of misery and deprivation, were accustomed to most of the stories they were told and failed to see the lack of privacy as a problem. This was obvious from their attitude toward visitors and the way in which the clients were asked to "speak up" when they had obviously been trying to retain an element of intimacy between themselves and the receptionist. (p. 1974:120)

A social work student describing her experience applying for service at a social agency said:

We walked in the door and found ourselves standing in a hallway. The receptionist was located on the other side of the corridor wall in a secretarial pool of about eight women and spoke to us through a hole in the wall. Having to explain why you are there in the middle of a reception room and an opening in the wall was very embarrassing. Fortunately there was no one there when we showed up. (Walden, Singer, and Thomat 1974:283)

Such experiences cannot help but affect the beginning of the formal scheduled interview with the social worker. An attractive, comfortable waiting room with easy access to lavatories and with a friendly, understanding receptionist may help to get the interview off to a good beginning.

Scheduling and the Interview

Agency time schedules affect the beginning of the interview. The client who can be accommodated at a time when it is convenient for her is less apt to be resentful and hurried than the client who has to take time off from a job, with possible loss of pay. The availability of an evening or Saturday morning interview, although an imposition on the staff, may pay dividends in a more effective interview.

Promptness without undue rigidity in starting and ending not only is a necessary manifestation of courtesy and respect to interviewees but also permits participants in the interview to know clearly the time allotted for the work they have to do. It enables them to plan such work with some assurance of having a given block of time available.

Scheduling should allow for the fact that some interviews will run over the allotted time. It should also allow for some let-up so that the interviewer can catch his psychic breath. A break between interviews allows time for clearing the mind, changing the mental scenery, making the transition. It permits the reverberations of the last interview to die away and provides opportunity for emotional preparation for the next interview. A loose schedule of interview time is thus far preferable to a tightly scheduled program which squeezes production. Fewer interviews may be conducted, but those that are completed will be better.

Respect for time means respect for the interviewer's time as well as the interviewee's. It might be better for the interviewer to resist a temptation to yield readily to a client's sudden demand for an emergency appointment, or to the intrusion of an aggressive client who wants an appointment at will. Courtesy and firmness as well as an explanation may be required. Holding an interview at a time when the interviewer is preoccupied and distracted with demands of other scheduled obligations would not, however, be giving the interviewee a good hearing. Flexible scheduling may be needed in response to unavoidable emergencies, but this does not warrant a masochism which invariably puts a client's need ahead of every other consideration.

Preparation

The interview begins before it starts for the interviewer as well as the interviewee. It begins for the interviewer when he prepares, in advance, in a general way for all the interviewees he will encounter in his office.

SETTING

One aspect of preparation is the physical setting for the interview; it should optimize the possibility of undistorted communication and minimize the possibility of distraction. A comfortable but unobtrusive setting suggests that you are treating the interviewee as one might a respected acquaintance. Since an interview is not a social visit, however, the setting must also suggest a businesslike purposefulness. A quiet office with privacy is ideal. Chairs for all participants should be comfortable enough that people are not conscious of physical inconvenience (which would be distracting) and yet not so comfortable that clients are lulled into lassitude. The temperature should be comfortable.

There should be sufficient light so that the participants can clearly see any nonverbal communication but not so much as to hurt the eyes. While privacy is desirable, isolation may not be, particularly in those instances where one of the participants is male and the other a young female. The intrusion of telephone calls is an inevitable hazard unless explicit instructions are given to hold all calls.

Fortunately, the human capacity for adaptation to a less than ideal environmental situation permits one to conduct interviews effectively under all sorts of adverse conditions. But it would be best to reduce the distractions imposed by environmental irritants as much as possible.

If clients of an agency are likely to be accompanied by children, a playroom and toys should be available; otherwise the interview may be constantly interrupted by the child or disrupted by the mother's anxiety about what the child is getting into.

The physical distance separating the participants should not be so great as to preclude the interviewer's reaching over and touching the interviewee if this should prove desirable. Distance might also make for difficulty in seeing subtle changes of expression. Nor should there be physical barriers to nonverbal communication. A desk between the interviewer and the interviewee means that half of the interviewee's body is nonobservable. Any gestures of the lower part of the body—tapping feet, knees clamped together, tensely clasped hands in the lap—are masked from view. However, some people need the limited protection from interviewer observation which the table or desk permits. They are made anxious if too much of themselves is exposed and accessible to observation.

A desk or a table is helpful in other ways as well. You can lean on it and rest your hands on it. It is a convenience for ashtrays and pocketbooks which otherwise might have to be held in the hand or juggled on the lap.

A definite block of time needs to be cleared for the interview so that the interviewer can appear unhurried. A reasonably uncluttered desk helps confirm the impression that, in effect, the worker has cleared his desk so as to make his time and energy exclusively available to the client.

The setting of the interview should provide psychological privacy as well as physical privacy. A closed room may ensure physical privacy but thin walls which permit overhearing of the interview deny the interviewee assurance of psychological privacy.

BONING UP ON HOMEWORK

Preparation for the interview involves more than concern with scheduling and with the physical setting of the encounter. It involves the personal and professional preparation of the interviewer himself for the experience. It involves a review of whatever material is available on the interviewee. There may be a voluminous record of previous contacts or only the face sheet obtained by the receptionist. In any case, no one appreciates being asked questions she has already answered for the agency. Ignorance of essential data that have been previously acquired communicates a lack of interest. If the interviewer knows, as a result of such preparation, that the client is married and has three children of such and such ages, the interviewee's confidence in the concern and competence of the interviewer is increased.

A walk-in agency which accepts and schedules interviews without any prior arrangements makes for a different start of the interview. There is little opportunity for preparation and no prior information to guide the interviewer.

Preparation may involve doing some homework. The interviewer needs to know what information he needs, what purpose the information would serve if he obtained it, how it can be used to help the client. The interviewer needs to be aware of the premises which guide selection of information. This kind of preparation gives the interviewer a cognitive map of the area in which he will be traveling. It gives him a sense of the unity of the interview, a sense of its coherence. An interview without some such guidelines is apt to be disorganized.

The problem may be a mother's concern about a child's bed-wetting. If the interviewer has not recently conducted any interviews concerned with enuresis, he might do well to read some of the recent literature on the cause and management of the problem. If the medical social worker is scheduled to see a patient who has had a serious heart attack, it may be helpful to review the literature on the psychosocial consequences of this. If the assertion of the interviewer's need for knowledge has validity, preparation for an interview does involve a mental review of what the social worker knows about the problem of concern to the client and a search of the relevant literature.

Preparation involves getting specific information that might be needed, the addresses and telephone numbers of places to which the interviewee might be referred, the forms that might be used (with the social worker having some assurance that he knows how to fill them out). It involves a review of the requirements and technicalities regarding procedures that might be discussed during the interview—applying for vocational rehabilitation, making a job referral, dealing with housing regulations, getting into a retirement home, applying for assistance.

DIRECTION OR OUTLINE

The interviewer's preparation must involve a clear idea of what he hopes to accomplish in the interview. The worker needs to make the purpose of the interview explicit to himself before he can communicate his perception of it to the interviewee and before he can hope to establish a mutually acceptable purpose. Some thought must therefore be given to what the interviewee's purpose might be and how the worker's purpose and the interviewee's purpose, if they are likely to differ, can be made more congruent.

Preparation involves operationalizing and specifying the interview's purpose, translating objectives into the specific items that need to be covered. How, in general, can the purpose be achieved, what questions will need to be asked, what content will need to be covered, and what is the most desirable sequence with which such content might be introduced?

An interview outline prepared in advance is an organizing device, a memory jogger. It may be particularly helpful for beginners whose minds may "go blank" at some point in the interview. The following preparatory introspective comments illustrate the process:

Worker: female, 22, mental retardation unit.
The purpose of the interview was to get a clear picture of the reaction of the family to learning that Bobby was seriously retarded and not likely to change much. But that's a global sort of thing. I needed to know about reactions that related to specific aspects of their lives. I tried to list these in my mind as I drove out to the house—changes in Mrs. L.'s relationship to the other children, her changed perception of herself as a woman, the change in relationship between the siblings, changes in the marital relationship, changes in the family's goals now that finances had to be allocated differently, changes in family routines and allocation of roles and tasks in the family. I wondered what their reaction was to learning about the retardation. Did they feel mad, sad, guilty, frustrated, inadequate? Were they relieved to at least know definitely what the situation was? What was their feeling about Bobby—ready to abandon him, so sorry for him that they wanted to make restitution by breaking their backs for him, sore at him for spoiling things? These were some of the things I thought about, some of the things I might ask about in the interview.

The interview guide is, of course, to be lightly and flexibly applied in the actual interview, modified in response to what the interviewee says and does. Planning dictates the general outline for the interview. Tactical decisions involve the fine tuning changes of strategy during the course of the interview in response to what actually happens during the course of the interview. This does not, however, diminish the importance of advance preparation. There is an important difference between planning an interview and inflexible adherence to a routine.

Developing an interview guide requires some decision as to how much can be covered during a specific, allotted time period. Just as beginning teachers try to teach all they know in the first period, beginning interviewers are apt to plan to cover too much during any one interview. Whatever the ultimate goal of a series of contacts, each interview must have a proximate, immediate purpose which is clearly defined and limited enough to be achievable within the time set for the usual interview.

Interviewer preparation involves some effort at anticipatory empathy, an effort by the interviewer to imagine he is in the place of the interviewee coming to the agency for help. What does it feel like to be in such a position? What might one be thinking about? What kind of interviewer would one like to meet if one had her problem? What kind of help would one hope was available? We often say that the interviewer should start where the client is. Following this precept requires considerable thought as to where the client is, or might be.

Thus, preparation involves a recognition and resolution of some of the anxieties that every interviewer brings, in a measure, to every interview: Will I like the interviewee? Will she like me? Will I be able to help her? Will I be able to understand her? Will I be able to handle the demands she might make? Will I conduct a good interview? What areas are likely to present the greatest difficulty for interview management? What kinds of feelings is the interview likely to arouse in me which may make for difficulty?

ROLE IMAGE

Preparation involves something more subtle as well—an effort to delineate who one is in this interview. The interviewer acts in response to different images of what he thinks is his appropriate role, in response to his image of the client. A public assistance worker might see himself as the guardian of public funds, protecting the community from unwarranted raids on the public treasury. Or he might see himself as representing the community's conscience in aiding the needy. The correctional social worker may see the delinquent as tough, bad, ruthless, and lacking in control, or as a deprived, pathetic child, a victim of a stressful home life. He may see the delinquent as needing control and punishment or needing love, nurturing, and protection. The interviewer might see himself as an all-forgiving father confessor, as a crusader correcting social injustices, as a professional helper, neutrally and objectively assessing what is feasible in a situation, as a rescue worker snatching the child or dependent adult from disaster, as society's avenger, seeing that the deviant is brought into line, as an expert who subtly helps the client find the answers the worker "knows" are correct, or as an impartial judge.

Clients also perceive the social work interviewer in a variety of different images—as a bleeding heart to be "conned," as a lover to be seduced, as an ally against a hostile world and personal enemies, as a source of influence with access to establishment resources, as an antagonist to be outwitted or placated, as a source of help or absolution or punishment, as an authority figure representing society's sanctions, as a parent protector. The setting and auspices with which the interviewer is identified tend to define the client's selective image of him. The school social worker is apt to be regarded as a teacher; the social worker in the court setting tends to be perceived as authoritarian, the medical social worker in the hospital as a nurse and comforter, the child welfare worker as identified with children.

The fact is that we all have an image of ourselves. We have, indeed, a variety of images, each of which we regard as more or less appropriate for some specific situation. Preparation for an interview requires some self-explication of who we think we are and who we think we represent in this particular situation.

NATURE OF SERVICE

There may be different conceptions of the nature of the service to be provided. One adoptions intake worker may see his responsibility as selecting, out of the pool of applicants, those offering the most desirable qualifications. Another may see all applicants as acceptable and the interview as an opportunity of helping the applicant resolve any problems or ambivalence about adoption.

Preparation involves some thought about the nature of the service and the extent to which one may feel coerced into the scheduled interview. Just as there are degrees of voluntarism with which the client engages in the interview, there are interviews and interviewees that the worker more or less dislikes and others with which he is comfortable. If he had his choice, he would never engage in some interviews or interview certain groups of people. But he is obligated, coerced by his professional conscience, to conduct such interviews.

Preparation requires developing awareness of what we confidently, but unwarrantedly, presume to be true about the interviewee. One reason some questions are not asked in the interview and some essential areas not covered is that the interviewer presumes he knows the answers. Since we know many things about sick people, or delinquents, or older citizens, or unmarried mothers, we think we know them, as well, about this particular sick person or older citizen. As Mark Twain said, "It isn't what we don't know that gets us into trouble, it is what we know which is not so."

The ultimate significance of preparation for the conduct of the interview can be easily exaggerated, although it needs to be noted. Being prepared is not as good as not being prepared is bad, since not being prepared suggests to the interviewee that she is not of importance. Once the interview actually begins, the nature of the interaction takes precedence over any of these preparatory considerations.

Every interview is likely to be difficult. The interviewer is asked to be a member of the cast in a play being written while it is being performed. It is said that the interview is analogous to learning to play the violin in public while composing the music being played. Preparation involves tentatively writing some of the lines in advance, composing some of the music before you go on stage.

But adequate preparation increases the interviewer's confidence, diminishes anxiety, and ensures a more positive start to the interaction. Since many routine problems to be encountered in the interview are thought out and resolved in advance, the interviewer's mind is free to deal more adequately with unanticipated problems arising during the interview. Being at ease himself, he is less likely to stimulate anxiety in the interviewee.

Nonagency Settings

The social agency office is only one of a number of possible places where the social interview can take place. Each setting has a different effect on the beginning of the interview, and each presents its special hazards. Social work interviews may take place, for example, in the home of the client, in hospital wards, on street corners, or in institutions.

The location of the interview varies with the agency. Social workers associated with mental health centers and clinics are likely to do most of their interviewing in the agency office. Social workers in public welfare and child welfare agencies are likely to do much more of their interviewing in the client's home.

Office interviews have the advantage of permitting control of the physical setting to provide the features that are desirable for interviewing. There is continuity and familiarity with the same place from interview to interview. The technology which assists the work of the interview is available there—telephones, forms, record data, etc.

CLIENT'S HOME

The client's home as the interview setting furthers our diagnostic understanding of her and her situation. As a consequence, the interviewer is in
a better position to respond empathically to what the client says. Family
interaction *in vivo*, in the natural setting which shapes the client's daily
life, and the expression of her individuality in the way she arranges her
home, are open to educated observation. Verbal descriptions are often mis-
leading, and home visits have frequently resulted in changes in diagnostic
thinking as the worker sees the home situation as it actually is rather than
as it had been thought to be. Home visits give the worker the opportunity
"to supplement what people say, by seeing what they do" (Overton and
Tinker 1959:56).

The home visit offers the interviewer more opportunities for actually entering into the life of the interviewee as a participant and consequently
being perceived as less of a stranger. Holding a crying baby, opening a
stuck window, moving a heavy box, and having coffee together are the
kinds of events involving the worker's participation encountered in home
visits.

Clients may be gratified by a home visit, since it suggests that the interviewer is sufficiently interested to inconvenience himself to make the trip.
However, the additional investment of working time which travel requires
of the worker must be recognized as a disadvantage of home interviews.

In scheduling an appointment time for a home visit, it is necessary to
keep the client's home routines in mind. Visits early in the morning and
late in the afternoon are inconvenient, since they interfere with meal preparation. Many older people have favorite radio or TV programs and therefore resent having visitors at certain hours. Every home visit involves some
disruption of the family routine.

Respect for the interviewee requires that the worker be on time for a
scheduled home interview. This might necessitate checking how to get
there, knowing the route to take by auto, bus, or subway, and starting out
early enough to arrive on time. Social workers tend to schedule a series of
home interviews when out in the field. Delays and longer-than-anticipated
interviews frequently make adherence to the schedule difficult. It may be
necessary for a worker to call, in order to let a client know that he is likely
to be late. Sometimes the client may have forgotten about the interview or
may have needed to leave the house unexpectedly. In such instances it is
advisable for the worker to leave a note that he has made the visit.

In making a home visit interview, one may have to face the fact that in
some deteriorated urban areas, house numbers may be missing. Having

found the house, it may be difficult to find the proper apartment if there are no names on mailboxes and no numbers on apartment doors.

Older people are often anxious about opening doors to strangers. In making a home visit an interviewer should be prepared to show credentials which certify his affiliation with the agency he represents.

The home visit may be somewhat threatening to the social worker. A measure of control is transferred from the interviewer to the interviewee who hosts the interview. The interviewee is in familiar, friendly territory; the interviewer is now in an unfamiliar setting. The interviewee controls seating arrangements and interruptions; she can temporarily move out of the interview psychologically, and physically, by making some household excuse for moving.

The interviewee can exercise a measure of self-protection by "arranged distractions" such as a radio or TV going at full volume, a warm welcome to neighbors who drop in, or vigorous rattling of pots and dishes which are washed during the interview. Since it is the interviewee's home, she has to take the initiative in turning down the radio or TV, although the interviewer can request this for the sake of the interview. Of course the interviewer can, somewhat more subtly, gradually lower his voice until the interviewee is prompted to turn down the radio in order to hear. Visitors often persistently intrude in the interview. The interviewer, having listened to their comments, equally persistently must direct all of his responses to the client.

Pets can be a problem. Dogs that bark throughout the interview or who keep jumping at the interviewer either out of an excess of friendliness or in presumed protection of their owner make it difficult for the interviewer to concentrate. Trying to communicate the message that he likes dogs (even though he may not) while fending them off is a difficult juggling act to perform. It may require a polite request that the dog be given time out, sent to another room, because the interviewer wants to be as helpful as possible to the interviewee.

An interviewer making a home visit may have to accommodate to a degree of disorganization that might be routine for the interviewee but beyond anything in the interviewer's normal experience. One interviewer said:

From my standpoint, the interview took in total chaos. There was the radio, a record player—both on. The respondent's small son, her daughter's little girl, her husband and son (both embarking on what seemed like some rather dedicated drinking) were all there. A neighbor came in to use the phone, and there were two incoming phone calls. Chaos seemed an everyday occurrence and my respondent knew how to deal with it. (Converse and Schuman 1974:3)

During the home interview a woman may not be entirely free of competing role responsibilities as mother, wife, and homemaker. This multiple role assignment may lessen the woman's concentration on the concern with the interview while engaging in some household task that demands attention.

Invitations to a cup of coffee or a meal, which social workers handle without difficulty in their personal lives, pose a problem for them as professionals. In accepting these simple gestures of good will, is one in danger of converting an interview into a purely social occasion? What effect will it have on the interaction? Food might be used as a tactic for ingratiation, as a weapon in obligating the worker to the client, as a digression from the difficult concerns of the interview.

A correctional social worker visiting a female probationer.
BARBARA: Could I give you a cup of coffee? God, I gotta have one!
WORKER: Well, uh [pause] yes, maybe I will have a cup.

The worker commented afterward:

My first response to Barbara's question was the feeling that I had been caught off guard. For a brief second I was trying to recall the so-called professional "dos" and "don'ts." None came to mind! I then thought about the actual situation I was in and how the results of my response would add or detract from our already well established relationship. I felt that Barbara and I had established a strong relationship, and yet I knew she needed constant reassurance of acceptance. I sensed that my not accepting the coffee would seem as if I were not accepting her. I really did not want coffee because I had just had a cup at the office. However, *in this situation*, want it or not, professional or not, I felt it was best to accept.

The home visit, like the family-therapy session, poses the risk of having to respond to family conflict while it is being enacted. A public assistance social worker visits a 27-year-old white mother, receiving AFDC, about whom complaints of neglect and possible abuse have been made.

MRS. W.: (To her 3-year-old daughter who is saying "Want a cookie.") What? No, you don't need another cookie. (The child repeats her request.) I said no; you just had one. (In the background the child again says "Cookie.") No! (Again, "Cookie.") Don't open! (Child is saying "Open.") I said no. (Child still saying "Open.") No. (Again says "Open.") What did I say? (Child says "Mom." Mother takes object from child and the child cries.) There's your bedroom in there, young lady (angrily). (Pause, child is crying very hard, mother gets up and takes child's arm.) Now pick up this stuff. (There is a great deal of noise and crying and scolding in the background.) You stay in there and play, unless you can behave yourself. (The child is whining.) Do you want to go to bed? (Harshly.) All right, in there and go to bed, because I'm not gonna listen to it. (Mother takes the child by the hand and takes her into the bedroom; the child is crying.) Stay there too. (Mother closes the bedroom door and leaves the child in the room, crying at the top of her lungs. Long pause.)

The worker comments:

The problem for me at this point in the interview was deciding what to do about the whole incident to which I had been a witness and about which I was developing some strong feelings. It was clear that Mrs. W. was harsh and rejecting and at the same time unhappy about the situation. Choking a little bit on it, I swallowed my growing dislike for Mrs. W., made a conscious deliberate effort to separate the person and the behavior, and decided to respond to Mrs. W.'s unhappiness. When she came back into the room, after the long pause during which we both tried to pull ourselves together, I said something about it's being tough to be both a father and a mother to the children.

A home visit is sometimes regarded as regressive since it may feed into the client's inability to mobilize herself to come for an office interview. Accepting the opportunity of coming to the office is seen as a sign of responsibility and interested motivation.

Some interviewers feel uncomfortable about home visits because they suggest spying on the client. The sense of intrusion is intensified if the worker drops in without previously making arrangements by telephone or letter. Home visits, initiated without such advance preparation, may start with a greater measure of anxiety, suspicion, and resistance on the part of the interviewee. These initial responses are transitory in many instances, however.

INSTITUTIONS AND HOSPITALS

In addition to the agency office and the home, interviews also take place in a variety of other places. Each place may have connotations for the interviewee which reverberate to effect her feelings about the interview or the interviewer. "Borrowing" the warden's office or the school principal's office in interviewing a prisoner or a high school student may suffer from the images evoked in the interviewee's mind by the place of the interview.

Interviews also take place in hospitals, in institutions and, as in the case of the Life Space Interview, in a variety of other settings. The Life Space Interview permits the clinical exploitation of life events as these events take place. Such interviews take place wherever the significant event occurs—in a cottage, at the waterfront, on the street corner.

> When S., a thirteen-year-old youngster, was adamant in refusing to return to her group and marched up and down the institution's "campus," it was her [caseworker] who joined her in the march. The material handled during this time was not at all dissimilar to the content of their interviews; the child's feeling that she was too sick to be helped, that her rejection by the family was devastating and motivated these overwhelming feelings of hopelessness. When she marched past the gate, she said she could not control herself and not even the worker could control her. On the ensuing three-mile hike through neighboring towns and the final return to the grounds of the institution, the child received not only the demonstration of the worker's ability to control her, which diminished her feelings of anxiety, but also some insight into her current concern about her mother's illness and its relationship to the incident. (Shulman 1954:322)

In arranging for an interview in a hospital or in a prison the interviewer must need to know something about the routine of the place. It may be that an interview arranged for a certain time would make the interviewee miss a meal or some regularly scheduled activity in which the interviewee is interested.

In an institution or hospital ward it is difficult to keep confidential the fact that a person has seen the social worker. If the inmate's or patient's group derogates those who see a social worker, the prospective interviewee may hesitate to make an appointment or may be uncomfortable when the social worker comes to see her. Clients are explicitly aware that the interviewer has ties to other clients. If there is any feeling of possessive sibling rivalry about the interviewer, these observations outside the interview will reverberate in it.

In an institution, interviewer and interviewee are likely to meet and interact outside the context of the interview. They have a relationship in which they occupy other roles vis-à-vis each other. It is difficult to keep these out-of-interview experiences from intruding into the interview relationship. The interviewee may have seen and spoken to the interviewer on the grounds, on the ward, in the prison yard. As a consequence, even before the first interview contact, she may have developed some attitude toward the interviewer.

The social worker has probably been seen talking to and laughing with the executive director or the warden or the hospital administrator. His relationship with those who are responsible for running the institution or prison is thus firmly established. The interviewee brings these perceptions into the interview, and if she has any feeling about the establishment and its representatives, the feeling will affect her initial interview behavior. Particularly in correctional institutions and residential treatment centers there is apt to be strong identification with the inmate subculture in opposition to the administration.

Interview scheduling may be simpler in institutions, where the interviewee is an inmate or where patient time is at the disposal of the administration. In an institution an interview may be a welcome break in the boring, monotonous routine or a sanctioned short vacation from a job. These secondary gains help to make an interview a desirable event.

Some of the difficulties of interviewing in a prison setting are perceptively reviewed by Johnson:

> Many interviewers, though they have been in an institutional setting for a number of years, are very little aware of what the inmate goes through simply in coping with the mechanics of arriving for the interview and returning to his assignment. The searching by guards, the wisecracks of guards and inmates, the annoying red tape, a long wait in a stuffy anteroom, possibly changing clothes, being late for a meal or missing a recreation period because of the interview—these and other small things may make the prisoner less than anxious for the interview and may bring him to it in a bad frame of mind—antagonistic and irritable.
>
> The physical facilities for the interview itself are frequently poor, and undoubtedly affect the quality of the interview in many ways. For example, because of the internal routine of prisons, more often than not prisoners have a long wait in unpleasant surroundings prior to the interview. They may be sitting on benches in a stuffy hallway, subject to curious stares and deprecating remarks by passers-by. The talk among the men waiting for the psychiatrist or social worker frequently takes on a negativistic, cynical tone, probably a collective reaction against feelings of embarrassment and concern over contact with the "bug doctors," as all such professional workers are usually called. The writer has frequently overheard younger inmates affect an air of braggadocio upon leaving the interview, undoubtedly calculated to convince their cohorts that they are not a "bug" or a "rat" but, to the contrary, have put something over on the "doc." Such remarks can hardly be expected to put the waiting inmates in a receptive and constructive frame of mind for their interviews. . . .
>
> The stigma of staff contacts for the inmate likewise should not be underrated. Many prison officers and a great majority of prisoners look upon the frequent visitor to the "bug doctor," to the front offices, to the chaplain, or to the social workers with considerable suspicion. (1956:44–45)

Interviewing patients in a hospital ward requires a knowledge of hospital routines, a recognition that such people have less energy for a standard-length interview.

Interviewing a sick client presents some difficult status problems for the interviewer. The interviewee is lying down, the interviewer sitting or standing beside her. This accentuates status difference between worker and client as does the difference between the sick and the well. The interviewer is dressed in street clothes, the interviewee is dressed in night clothes, which makes her more childlike and dependent. The interviewee is immobilized while the interviewer is mobile, which once again puts the interviewee at a disadvantage.

The hospital-based interviewer may be asked by the patient for help in getting out of bed, turning over, etc. This may entail nursing know-how and care which might best be left to the nursing staff.

The Interview Begins

There comes a time at last when the interview actually starts; interviewer and interviewee meet face to face and the flow of communication between them is initiated. (In discussing beginnings I have the office interview in mind.)

The interviewer has to decide whether to go out to the reception room and accompany the interviewee back to the office, whether to shake hands, what to talk about when walking down the hall. A meeting in the reception room may not be necessary if the interviewee has been there before, but it may be a simple but necessary courtesy in an agency where there are many offices and complex corridors.

PRE-INTERVIEW AMENITIES

The interview may begin during this journey from the waiting room to the interview room. One interviewer makes use of this time noting useful nonverbal observations. He uses the time to see how clients greet him, and how they are dressed, but mostly to see how they walk and carry themselves.

Just watching Mr. W. walk to my office gives me an inkling to his mood. Sometimes, for instance, he walks in very determined and rapidly. I've learned that this means he is anxious or angry, and that most of our time together may well be spent in verbal sparring.

With Miss T., who's depressed, I watch to see how slow her gait is and how drooped her posture is; together with her apparel she relays to me how badly she may be feeling that day. (Hein 1973:159)

It is helpful if the interviewer can greet the interviewee by name. Forms of address suggest status and level of intimacy. The interviewer can more frequently call the client by his first name without violating the norms of interview etiquette. The interviewer generally needs to give explicit permission for the interviewee to call him by his first name. Initially the interviewer is addressed by title (Dr., Mr., Ms., Mrs.) and last name. This clearly suggests that in the interview the interviewer is first among equals. Each new step toward greater intimacy is either initiated by the interviewer or initiated by the interviewee only after receiving a clear signal from the interviewer that this is acceptable.

Inviting the interviewee into the office, the worker goes through the familiar, social amenities—taking her coat, offering her a chair, and demonstrating his concern that the interviewee is reasonably comfortable. The interviewer gives the interviewee a chance to get settled—to compose herself, to absorb first impressions, to get her bearings, to catch her breath. She needs a little time to get used to the room and the interviewer.

The interviewer acts in effect like a gracious host offering the elementary and expected courtesies to the interviewee, encouraging the establishment of a cordial relationship. The degree of hospitality needs to be tempered in recognition of the fact that this is not a social visit and needs to be appropriate to the client. An exuberantly cheerful greeting to the depressed client or a firm handshake with a 6-year-old are inappropriate. As Oldfield suggests, the interviewee may be made "uneasy by his perception that the interviewer is trying to set him at his ease" (1951:56). The admonition is to try not to try too hard. The ritualistic noises we make at each other at the beginning of a contact have been technically labeled "phatic" communications. "How are you," "Nice day," "Howdy," "What do you say," "How does it go," all mean "I see you, I greet you, I acknowledge you, I am friendly." Phatic communications serve primarily as a gesture of establishing contact.

It is helpful, particularly at the beginning and the end of the contact, to make general conversation rather than engage in an interview. At the beginning we are making the transition from the way people relate to each other in an everyday social relationship, to the formal interaction of the interview. It is, temporarily, a social occasion before it becomes an interview. At the end we are making the same transition in reverse—this time from formal interview interaction to the informality of an everyday social relationship.

During the initial conversation the roles of interviewer and interviewee have not yet been officially assumed and the rules which normally apply to conversational interaction are observed. Any event or situation which is widely shared may be the subject of this transitional period. The preliminary chit-chat may be about the weather, parking problems, cooking, baseball, or the high cost of living. Subject matter selected as an ice breaker should be of some interest to the interviewee and a topic with which she is likely to be acquainted. Saying something about the weekend All-Star game to a male interviewee who is not interested in sports may intensify his feelings of inadequacy and difference. That is why comment about the weather is so often selected. It is something everyone knows about and is interested in. The weather not only provides a topic which represents a shared experience, it also is a topic about which agreement is almost certain. It is the least controversial of topics that might be used to stimulate the feeling of togetherness in talking.

This socializing is not wasted time. It eases the client's transition from the familiar mode of conversational interaction into a new and unfamiliar role which demands responses for which she has little experience. The conversation has the additional and very important advantage of permitting the interviewee to become acquainted with and size up the interviewer as a person. This opportunity makes for a more comfortable start to the formal interview, which demands, by implication, that the client trust herself to the interviewer. Small talk establishes the interviewer's interest in the interviewee as a person and reinforces a sense of human mutuality as they discuss matters of common interest and concern. Like the small talk, cocktail party chatter sometimes called "circling," this is really talking about getting ready to talk.

Small talk serves an important and useful purpose in addition to permitting a graceful transition from a social encounter to the formal interview. It permits us the opportunity of exploring the possibilities of co-membership and shared social identities. Some shared membership in a significant social group is established on sight. We can see whether or not we share membership in the same sex, race, and age group. But small talk may further establish the fact that we share co-membership in a religious group, that we are both veterans, or that we are both fishing enthusiasts, etc. The more the participants find they have in common, the greater the reduction in social distances and the increase in the interviewee's expectations that he will be understood and accepted. "Co-membership involves attributes of shared status that are particularistic rather than universalistic" (Erickson and Shultz 1982:35) like age, sex, and race. And because they are more particularistic, they can come to light as a result of small talk.

If the transition to the interview is too abrupt, it may be disconcerting and throw the interviewee off balance, as the following hypothetical interview beginning suggests:

CLIENT: Where shall I hang my coat?
WORKER: Where do you want to hang it?

CLIENT: Where shall I sit?
WORKER: Does it make a difference to you?

However, too long a period of conversation robs time from the interview. It also tends to puzzle the interviewee and make her anxious. She
recognizes that although the interview is a social situation, it is not a social
visit. Prolonged conversation makes her wonder what the interviewer has
in mind. Undue prolongation might be regarded as indifference to the urgency of the problem the client brings.

Even in the initial informal social conversation, an effort should be made
to indicate the direction of attention of the interviewee. The emphasis is
on the interviewee's experience: "Did *you* have trouble getting the car
started in this freezing weather?" "Did *you* have any difficulty finding the
office?"

Smoking along with conversation may help to break the ice. It is for
many people a familiar, comforting activity; it keeps one's hands occupied
and permits pauses without awkwardness. Offering a cigarette, or granting
permission to smoke, bridges the gap between strangers and is a simple
gesture of hospitality. When both participants smoke, the shared activity
reinforces a feeling of mutuality.

THE OPENING QUESTION

The opening interview gambit, which signals the end of the conversation
and the beginning of the interview proper, should be a nonthreatening
general question to which the interviewee is capable of responding easily
and one that serves to develop the mutuality of interaction. "What do you
want to see us about?" "What do you have in mind?" "What do you think
we can do for you?" Words like "problem" and "service" in the opening
questions are less neutral, are somewhat more technical, and may have
negative connotations. "What's your problem?" may be resented. "How
can we be of service?" may sound too formal.

A general, unstructured question grants the interviewee the decision on
the content and manner in which she chooses to communicate. An opening
question that can be fielded successfully encourages the interviewee's confidence in her ability to perform creditably in her role.

Subtle differences in the opening question may determine differences in
the direction the interview takes. One might say "What brings you here?"
or "Why have you come here?" or "What would you like from us?" The
first puts the emphasis on a description of the trouble itself, the second on
the explanation of the trouble, the third on the treatment. The first question, in itself, can be delivered to focus on three different concerns. *"What*

brings you here?" focuses on the problem; "What brings *you* here?" focuses on the interviewee; "What brings you *here?*" focuses on the agency.

The opening question might be phrased so as to force greater specification in response: "Could you tell me what problems prompt you to see a social worker?" This question specifies that what brings the person are problems and that she is seeing a social worker.

CLARIFY THE PURPOSE

The initial phase of the interview should clarify the purpose that will engage the participants during the course of the interview. The purpose needs to be of manageable proportions and should be stated in such a way that its achievement is objective and identifiable. Frequently the stated purpose of an interview is either far too ambitious or too ambiguously stated. The following statements of interview purpose from social work interview protocols exemplify some of these difficulties:

My purpose in this interview was to become acquainted, to get to know Mrs. P.

During this interview I planned to help him with his anxieties.

The purpose of this contact was to get to understand the client's situation.

My visit with the client was to establish a relationship.

In contrast, the following statements of interview purpose are circumscribed and the objectives are definite. There is a greater probability that such purposes can be achieved and their achievement identified.

The purpose was to help the client more adequately budget both her time and her money.

To determine what service the client wanted from the agency.

The purpose was to help Art with his feelings about leaving the foster home.

My purpose was to establish Mr. Y.'s level of motivation for job placement and, if time permitted, to explore what type of work he felt he was suited for.

To determine the problems this family faced as a consequence of the mental retardation of their preschool-age son.

To obtain the information which would help the agency make a decision regarding future placement plans for Jenny.

To help Mrs. C. handle her discouragement about Joe's schoolwork.

The purpose was to obtain the needed information to make a decision on relicensing the foster home.

Not only is it helpful to make explicit the purpose of the interview, it is necessary to state the purpose clearly.

In the following beginning of an interview the statement of purpose is ambiguous and muddled. The social worker is interviewing an 11-year-old boy who was recently placed in a group home.

INTERVIEWER: What I wanted to talk to you about was to figure out how you are feeling about the home and where you see yourself going and if you want to stay here. If you don't want to stay here, what type of situation do you want so we can make a recommendation for placement. Have you been thinking about this?

Not only should the purpose be clear to both participants, but they should also make every effort to formulate the purpose in operational terms. What specifically are they attempting to achieve by the meeting, what will be accomplished, what will be changed—arrange for housing, find a job, select parents for adoptive children, prepare a mother to place her child in day care, resolve ambivalence about an operation, help a child to stop truanting, arrange a maternity-home placement for an unwed mother? If the participants know clearly and unambiguously the definite operational purpose of the encounter, they can know when the purpose has been more or less achieved.

If the interview is being conducted at the initiative of the interviewer, he needs to make clear as early as possible what his purpose is. "I asked you to meet with me today because the teachers are having a difficult time with Robert." "I scheduled this interview because I would like to discuss with you a possible job for one of my clients." "I wanted to talk with you because Dr. —— indicated you had some questions about your medicare entitlement."

In addition to stating his purpose, the interviewer must obtain some agreement on the part of the interviewee that she wants to engage in an interview directed toward this purpose. The interviewer actively searches for any basis for mutual engagement in the interview acceptable to both parties. In interviews with collaterals, and in advocacy interviews, the statement of purpose might also include the reason for choosing this particular interviewee for achieving the purpose. The statement should be simple and concise.

Interviewer: female, 23, white, school social worker.
I visited Tommy's second grade teacher. I said I had made this appointment because I should like to find out more about how Tommy behaved

in contact with other children. I said I thought that she had a good chance to observe this, since this was the second year she had had him in class, and I thought her observation could be helpful to us in getting to understand him better.

In beginning an interview it is helpful to make explicit how much time is available if needed. The last two words are important because while the time available sets some clear outer limit, less time may be adequate. It serves no useful purpose to stretch an interview only to fill the time available.

Characteristics of the Early Phases

Certain aspects of the interview are more prominent in the introductory phase than in other phases. During the introductory phase the authority of the worker's position is more important than the personal-relationship authority, since the latter takes time to develop. The interviewee's uncertainty, unfamiliarity, and confusion are likely to be greater, and the interviewer may have to offer greater direction and structure at this point.

More attention also needs to be paid to the expressive aspects of interview interaction. It is at this point that the interviewee is apt to be most anxious and most uncomfortable with the newness of the situation. Affect is likely to be high not only with regard to the client's problem but also with regard to bringing the problem for agency help. Consequently the demands for encouragement, support, and empathetic understanding are likely to be greater in the early part of the interview. During the body of the interview there is relatively more concern with instrumental problem-solving activities.

The opening phase of the interview is likely to include open-ended, general questions. The interviewer is trying to find out what the situation is as seen by the interviewee. He does not have enough information to warrant asking specific questions or responding to details.

The form for the entire interview is that of a funnel—nondirective, open-ended questions early in the interview, more detailed explication and discussion of specific areas of content later. The sequence with which material is introduced is an important aspect of planning interview strategy. In general, material at the beginning of the interview should be concerned with more impersonal, more recent, more familiar material having lower affective importance for the client. The movement over the course of the interview is from impersonal to more personal, from recent to developmental history, from the overtly conscious and familiar to content of less explicit awareness.

There is a good deal of truth in the folk saying that well begun is half done. A good beginning starts the interaction spiral in a positive direction. It is easier to establish a good first impression than to reverse a bad one. First impressions are strong and persistent; later perceptions tend to be assimilated to earlier ones and to be consistent with them.

All of this says something about what is characteristic of a first interview with a social worker and the differences between the early part and the latter part of such a first interview. But interviewees have multiple contacts with the interviewer. In a nationwide study of family service agency activity Beck and Jones found that the "average case received 7.2 interviews" (1972:60). It might be helpful to delineate some differences between first interviews and later interviews in the series of contacts.

The objective of many first interviews is to help an "applicant" become a "client" or, as Perlman puts it, help a "needer" of services become a "user" (1979:21). Components of this objective include: clear identification of the primary problem; establishment of a relationship with the interviewer and through the interviewer with the agency; motivation of the client to continue if it appears she wants to; and provision of information for the client about agency services and resources relevant to the problem. Some effort should be made to determine what the client attempted in order to deal with the problem up till now, with what effect, and what prompts her contact with the agency at this time. The interviewer should seek to determine the extent, the duration, the intensity of the problem.

Early interviews in the contact are more apt to have a greater component of exploration of the client's situation, more communication concerned with socializing the interviewee to her role in the interview, and greater use of techniques which maximize development of the worker-client relationship. The worker is likely to be more directive and active.

In later interviews there is likely to be less small talk, and participants move toward the start of formal interview interaction more quickly. Generally speaking, later interviews focus more on treatment rather than exploration, are less concerned with socialization since the interviewee by now knows how she is expected to act, and evidence more risk-taking interventions such as confrontation and interpretation. In the balance between being responsive and intrusive the interviewer is more responsive and less intrusive in early interviews, with a shift in balance toward greater intrusiveness in later interviews.

SUGGESTED READINGS

Anthony Hall. *The Port of Entry: A Study of Client's Reception in the Social Services.* London: Allen & Unwin, 1974 (147 pp.).

An empirical study of the experiences a prospective client encounters on way to an interview with the social worker.

Anthony N. Maluccio. *Learning from Clients: Interpersonal Helping As Viewed by Clients and Social Workers.* New York: Free Press, 1979 (322 pp.).

Stuart Rees. *Social Work Face to Face.* London: Edward Arnold, 1978 (154 pp.).

Both Rees and Maluccio are based on research interviews with workers and clients that illuminate the problems (and some solutions) in getting good communication going between the two groups. The emphasis is on what actually happens when workers and clients first get together.

CHAPTER 7

Developmental Phase: Range and Depth

The introductory phase of the interview involves getting acquainted, initiating the interview process, deciding on some mutually acceptable purpose for the interview. The next step, the main body of the interview, is concerned with accomplishing the agreed-upon purpose. Content is focused and the sequence of actions is guided toward that goal.

The interviewer has to employ her technical skill to move the interaction toward achievement of interview purpose while at the same time she intervenes in other ways to maintain the ad hoc social system resulting from the coming together of the participants. She has to keep the emotional interaction comfortable and satisfying and to establish and maintain a positive relationship.

In achieving these instrumental and expressive tasks the interviewer faces a number of challenges which we will discuss in turn. She must help the interviewee to talk about the broad *range* of concerns relevant to the achievement of interview purposes and make *transitions* when it is necessary to move the interview from one content area to another, she must help the interviewee discuss some of this content in greater emotional *depth*, and she must make those interventions which help the interviewee in the instrumental tasks of problem solving, interventions discussed in chapter 8.

Range

One of the principal difficulties encountered during the main body of the interview is to stimulate the interviewee to discuss freely all the relevant aspects of the problem for which he wants agency service. The interviewer needs to help the interviewee to cover adequately the range of material which might be pertinent to the problem-solving process. In appraising what needs to be covered, the interviewer again needs an expert knowledge of the particular social problem involved.

Range refers to the variety and amount of relevant data. It speaks to the adequacy of coverage of possibly explanatory detail of the data generally thought to be important and significant in providing understanding of a particular problem.

For any one interview, range and depth are antithetical. If the interview covers a lot of territory, it cannot deal with any one question in depth. If sharply focused on one area, it may sacrifice a discussion of other pertinent topics. The interviewer needs to plan the strategy of each interview to balance range and depth in achieving the purpose of the interview.

The interviewer employs a variety of techniques to encourage the client to talk and to maintain the flow of communication—1) attending behaviors and minimal encouragements; 2) paraphrasing; 3) summarizing or recapitulation; 4) making transitions; and 5) questioning. Because *questioning* is a general procedure not only used in broadening range, but in intensifying depth and implementing problem solving, I have reserved a separate chapter for the subject of questions and questioning (chapter 9).

Interview Techniques

ATTENDING BEHAVIORS AND MINIMAL ENCOURAGEMENTS (EXPRESSIONS OF ATTENTION AND INTEREST)

A first, prime requirement of a good interview is that attention is focused on the interviewee and what he is communicating. Attending behaviors are those observable actions of the interviewer which indicate that she is interested and paying attention. An important component of attending behaviors is nonverbal, manifested in eye contact and body posture.

The interviewer is comfortably relaxed but not casually slouched. The body faces the interviewee squarely and has a slight forward lean. Arms and legs are not crossed, suggesting an openness, a receptivity to what the interviewee is saying. The interviewer speaks in a clear, audible voice with variable inflection indicating animation and involvement and employs expressive hand gestures.

A distance between interviewer and interviewee is selected so that the interviewer is not too intrusively close and not too unapproachably distant.

Good attending behavior communicates the interviewer's involvement in and commitment to the task of the interview. It suggests an intensity of presence, attentive listening.

The interviewer initiates and maintains comfortable eye contact with the interviewee. A determined effort at constant eye contact, amounting to a studied stare, is not desirable. What is suggested is a willingness and readiness to maintain eye contact but that it is varied in response to the flow of communication which dictates an occasional break in eye contact at appropriate points. Constant eye contact is intrusive; frequent shifts in eye contact suggest the interviewer's discomfort with or rejection of the interviewee.

The verbal component of attending behavior is manifested in what has been termed "verbal following." Attentiveness to the client is demonstrated by the fact that the interviewer's comments and responses follow from and are related to what the client is saying. The interviewer in her responses acknowledges the content of the interviewee's preceding remarks and includes in her response content related to the client's preceding remarks. The client's preceding comment is accepted then as the stimulus cue for the worker's following response. Client stimulus and worker response share the same content.

Contrariwise poor verbal following is manifested by frequent interruptions of the interviewee and frequent changes of topic initiated by the interviewer which are unrelated or only peripherally related to what the client has been saying—the worker's responses do not have as their antecedents the client's immediately preceding statements. There is a lack of continuity in the interview because the worker has not been attending to what the client has been saying. The following demonstrates poor verbal following, giving the impression that the interviewer has not been paying attention. The interviewee on parole had recently lost his job as a hospital attendant and had been interviewed for a job in a laundry.

CLIENT: I told him about my experience in the prison laundry but they just didn't seem to be interested. I think they were turned off when they learned I did time and was on parole.
INTERVIEWER: How long have you been out now?

Good attending behavior also involves some slight pause—2 to 5 seconds—between interviewee's statements and interviewer response. It communicates the fact that the interviewer is not rushing the interviewee and has given some consideration to what has been said before replying.

Minimal encouragements are short utterances with little content which have the effect of encouraging the interviewee and reinforcing his desire to continue—"uh-huh," "hmm," "go on," "and then——," "so," "I see," "sure," "that's so," "and——." It includes nonverbal nodding.

These essentially meaningless sounds and phrases assure the interviewee that the interviewer is paying attention, is psychologically present, is involved and is, in effect, showing interest in what the client is saying.

Minimal encouragements are employed once the client has started talking and is actively involved in communicating. They are like the pats you give to a swing in motion to keep it in motion. They lubricate the interaction.

While the word "minimal" refers to the level of activity of the interviewer, the effect on the interviewee is more than "minimal." Such utterances have a potent effect in reinforcing the interviewee's behavior.

Because they are meaningless interventions without content they are nonintrusive. They do not impede the interviewee's flow nor do they induce any shift in the nature of the material being shared.

The "uh-huhs" and "hmms" are neutral but ambiguous encouragements. Unlike encouragements such as "good," or "that's interesting," or "fine," the "uh-huhs" and "hmms" do not as clearly indicate that this is the kind of content that the interviewer is looking for. They tell the interviewee little or nothing about the interviewer's reactions other than that she is interested, attentive, and acknowledging what the interviewee is saying. The responses of "yes," "go on," "I see," "I understand" also are ambiguously encouraging. "Good" and "that's interesting," on the other hand, suggest more explicitly that the interviewee should continue focusing on the kinds of content she has been discussing. The different minimal encouragements subtly convey different messages. Saying "uh-huh" assures the interviewee you are paying attention. "I see" claims that you understand the clients' meaning. "Yes," "ok," "of course" suggest approval of what the client is saying. "Go on" obligates the interviewee to continue. The interviewer may need to give more conscious attention to exactly what message he wants to communicate rather than, as so often is the case, responding automatically as though choice of the minimal encouragement employed made little difference.

These responses also are delaying tactics. They keep the interviewee talking and give the interviewer an opportunity to build up a picture of the situation. The responses permit the interviewer to refrain from committing herself before she knows enough to decide what is best to do, yet suggest that the interviewer is with the interviewee and is not ignoring him. Reaching an impasse in the interview, the interviewer says, "I didn't know what to say so I used a safe 'uh-huh.' "

Shepard and Lee recapitulate some additional functions served by "hmm-hmm," as follows:

[Hmm-hmming] allows the patient to hear the sound of the therapist's voice; allows the therapist to hear the sound of his own voice; provides the therapist with a feeling of usefulness; provides the therapist with an outlet for stored-up energy; makes the therapist sound non-committal and therefore extremely professional. . . . When the patient hears 'hhmmnn' he knows for certain that he is in therapy and getting something for his money. (1970:65)

These interventions are one step beyond an expectant and receptive silence. They are somewhat selective, whereas silence is indiscriminate. They emphasize a response to some content, highlighting and encouraging elaboration of the material to which there is an "uh-huh" response.

There is a danger that minimal encouragement can become ritualistic or automatic. A worker manifesting a "uh-uh" or "hmm" syndrome "uh-uh's" and "hmms" at every statement whether appropriate or not.

Minimal encouragements have a cognitive effect, a conditioning effect, and a motivational effect. The interviewer's encouraging response tells the interviewee that he is acting as a good interviewee should act, is talking about things that are relevant. The reward of an encouraging response acts to condition and reinforce the behavior. The interviewer's encouragement further motivates the interviewee to continue because the approval implied in the response is rewarding.

Sometimes merely repeating or echoing a word or phrase acts as a minimal encourager. Here however there is a greater element of direction since the word or phrase selected for repetition gives it greater visibility and focus for attention.

INTERVIEWEE: "My mother keeps after me about my drinking."
INTERVIEWER: "Drinking?"

The interviewer might have repeated "mother" or "keeps after you" rather than "drinking." The alternative choices propel the interview in different directions.

The repetitive comment indicates that one is ready and willing to hear more about a particular topic. However, injudicious use of such repeating might sound as though in parroting the client, one is mimicking or mocking the client.

PARAPHRASING

A step beyond repetition of a word as a minimal encourager is the technique of paraphrase. In paraphrasing, the essence of the interviewee's statement is restated, although not exactly as an echo. It is a selective restatement of the main ideas in phrasing which resembles, but is not the same as, that used by the client. "Para" means "alongside," and a paraphrase parallels what the client said.

INTERVIEWEE: "Ever since I've been taking the drugs they gave me to take when I left the hospital I just can't seem to keep awake. It's getting so I really neglect my kids."
INTERVIEWER: "Because of the effects of the drugs on you, the kids get less care."
INTERVIEWEE: "Ever since Bob lost his job he's around the house more and we get into arguments more frequently than before."
INTERVIEWER: "Bob's being unemployed and home increases the amount of conflict between you."

Paraphrase is a restatement of what the interviewee has said by the interviewer in her own words.

A paraphrase is different from imitative repetition. The following does very little, if anything, to help move the interview along. A 22-year-old woman says:

CLIENT: I should never have become a mother.
INTERVIEWER: You should not have become a parent.
CLIENT: That's right. I shouldn't have become a parent.

The following paraphrase is more helpful.

CLIENT: I should never have become a mother.
INTERVIEWER: You don't like being a mother.
CLIENT: Well, I like being a mother, I just don't think I have enough patience.
INTERVIEWER: You like it but you have some questions about your ability.
CLIENT: Yeah, I wish I could be less impatient with Sheri.

A well-chosen paraphrase highlights the significant aspects of the client's statement. It thus insures visibility, clarity, and pertinence of the important aspects of the client's communication. It is, if done well, an unambiguous distillation of the essential essence of the client's communication.

Since paraphrasing requires accurate restatement of the interviewee's communication in the interviewer's own words it requires that the interviewer listen carefully and digest and understand what is being said. Paraphrasing is thus not a mechanical process but a complex, cerebral one.

Paraphrasing indicates what the message means to the listener, how the paraphrasing interviewer has received the message.

A variety of different lead-ins avoids sounding mechanical in paraphrasing.

If I get you right . . .

It seems to me . . .

In other words . . .

As I understand it . . .

I hear you saying that . . .

I gather that . . .

In using the paraphrase the interviewer confirms that she is interested and attentive, that she is following the interviewee and is encouraging the interviewee to continue. It helps the interviewer check her understanding of what the client is saying. The paraphrase might be accepted and confirmed or corrected and modified by the client.

Paraphrasing also helps the interviewee to see more clearly what he has said since it holds a mirror up to his communication.

Even an incorrect paraphrase may be a productive response. It stimulates further elaboration by the interviewee who feels constrained to help the interviewer understand more adequately what he is trying to communicate.

Paraphrase responses are formulated as statements, not as questions. The reflecting statement is affectively neutral, indicating neither approval nor disapproval. The interviewee's thinking or feeling should be reflected as much as possible in his own words.

One danger in the use of paraphrase is that it may lead to finishing the interviewee's thoughts for him. Instead of reflecting accurately and without distortion, we add some gratuitous interpretive comment without intending to.

SUMMARIZING OR RECAPITULATION

Partial or detailed summaries and recapitulations help to extend the range of communication. The interviewer briefly reviews what has been discussed and gives the interview its direction. A summary tends to pull together a section of the interview, make explicit what has been covered and, by virtue of this, indicate what has not been covered. It clears the agenda of items which have been adequately discussed so that attention can be devoted to items which have not. It also indicates to the interviewee that the interviewer has been listening attentively and knows what has been going on.

Summarizing requires a sifting out of the less relevant, less significant material.

Throughout the interview brief periodic summarizations of sections of the interview are helpful in making transitions. Such brief summary recapitulations serve to give unity and coherence to a section of an interview and indicate the interviewer's intent to move on to something else. A more comprehensive summary recapitulation takes place toward the termination of the interview, giving an overview of what has happened.

Both the brief summaries during the interview and the general summary at the end have the advantage of highlighting and giving greater visibility and emphasis to important points covered in the interview. They provide an organizational structure for the variety of content that might have been covered and suggest patterns and themes. If there is a plan for continuing contact, a closing summary acts as a bridge to the next interview. "This is what we did this time; this is what we need to do next time."

An interviewer summarizes the first twenty minutes of an interview with a divorced mother of three children who is receiving AFDC.

Okay, this gives me a little of an idea of your situation. After your divorce, you were forced to go on AFDC because your former husband did not make the support payments he should have been making. All of this time you've been faced with the terrific and lonely responsibility of being a single parent.

A behavior modification oriented social worker summarizes her identification of problematic behavior of a 4-year-old girl which the mother wants to work toward changing.

Okay, well we've identified five or so areas of behavior that you see as problems. So far, we've got: Alice stools in her pants; Alice follows mom around and clings, cries, whines; Alice is frequently noncompliant with requests and commands made of her; Alice has shown dangerous behavior with the baby; Alice reverts back to babytalk, on occasion. Can you think of any other behaviors that you would like to see changed?

Since summarizing requires a sifting out of the less relevant, less significant material, summaries are, of necessity, selective. There may be a bias in the interviewer's selection of material to include in the summary. The interviewee however may regard other content as significant. Feedback from the interviewee is, therefore, important.

The interviewer, in moving into a summary or recapitulatory statement might say, "Let me make sure I understand you. As I hear you, your situation is like this," or "To sum up what we have been talking about . . ." or "During the past 10 minutes we have been discussing —— and it seems to me that you are saying . . . ." Having summarized the interviewer then asks "How does that sound to you?"

Mutual participation in summarizing is desirable. Not only does it actually engage the interviewee in thinking about the interview but ensures that both participants are together in identifying what has been discussed and covered. In confirming and/or connecting summaries the interviewer might ask the interviewee to modify the summary, or the interviewer can invite the interviewee to state his own summary.

You describe—I'll tell you how it sounds to me and you can correct me if I've misunderstood—you describe to me a little boy who was deserted by his mother and who was adopted. Things didn't go very well, especially between you and your adoptive mother. You felt pretty much rejected and alone. You felt thrown out to whoever would take you—that maybe you were the forgotten child. I get the picture of a really unhappy little boy.

Summarizing as a technique in termination is further discussed in chapter 10.

Transitions

At times during the interview the interviewer may decide that a change should be made in the material being discussed. The interviewer then faces a problem of engineering a transition without disturbing the relationship. Transitions help extend the range of the interview.

There are a number of reasons why the interviewer may decide that a change is advisable. The content under discussion may have been exhausted, and it would not be productive to devote further time and energy to it—there is a clear diminution in spontaneity and interest with which the interviewee discusses the material. The content area may have been introduced for exploratory overview by either of the participants but now proves to be a dead end. The interviewee may have introduced some clearly irrelevant material which cannot, in any conceivable way, further the purpose of the interview. Some material may have been introduced prematurely. The interviewee may appear to be distinctly uncomfortable, embarrassed, or threatened by the content and, rather than risk danger to the relationship, the interviewer employs transitional comments to move away from this sensitive material. Sometimes transitions are the result of a deliberate effort to avoid creating anxiety.

A social worker is interviewing a woman, Mrs. P., who is applying to become a foster parent.

MRS. P.: I would imagine it is a difficult thing if foster parents get too attached to their foster children, and no matter how hard you prepare for their leaving I would think it's still pretty hard.

INTERVIEWER: Yes it is. Could you tell me how you heard about our program of foster care?

Commenting on her question, the worker says,

This was an extremely poor question as I failed to acknowledge the interviewee's anxiety and in fact completely ignored it, making a transition to something entirely different. At the time I was thinking that I didn't want to make Mrs. P. more anxious about the need to give up the foster child. I didn't want to emphasize this by encouraging discussion. I think I went too far in my concern about her.

A transition may be initiated by the interviewer if she senses that the interviewee is sharing material of a more emotional nature than is desirable at this point in the interview contact. Recognizing that neither she nor the interviewee will be able to handle this much affect at this time, the interviewer might say, "You seem to be getting quite upset about this. Perhaps we can table it at this point and talk a little more about the job situation you were telling me about before."

Transitions frequently are initiated by the interviewer to serve her own purpose rather than the purpose of the interview. This is indicated in the following comments made by social workers in explaining transitions initiated by them during the course of interviews:

P. has been discussing the problems with her son and solutions that were suggested and/or tried. She is asserting herself as knowing what is best for her child. This is a common response given by natural parents. This is touchy ground with natural parents, and I was treading very lightly. I felt uncomfortable agreeing or disagreeing with her at this point, so I changed the subject.

I was physically and mentally worn out from trying to keep up with the client. I introduced a somewhat neutral topic in order to give myself a breather.

I was feeling frustrated since the client hadn't been giving me any answer I could work with or had expected. I introduced another subject in the hope that I would have somewhat greater success.

This last reply she made should really have been probed for further elaboration, but since I really did not know what further to ask, I hastily moved on to another topic.

We were getting close to an area we had discussed before and about which I knew the agency, because of lack of resources, could do very little. I therefore made a transitional statement, taking us further away from the area I wanted to avoid.

At this point we got about as far as I was prepared to go with this. I wasn't sure about the admissions situation and/or procedure for local residential treatment centers. I therefore introduced a transitional summary and moved the interview on to the new content.

The cardinal operative principle violated by such transitions is that whatever is done by the interviewer should be done because it serves the purposes of the interview and the needs of the client.

The problem of transition derives from the time-limited nature of the interview. Out of respect for both participants, time available has to be employed most productively. Consequently no topic area can be given truly exhaustive consideration. Limited time implies selective concentration. Interrupting the interviewee's flow of communication on inconsequential material and suggesting a transition to more meaningful material is not a derogation of the client or an exercise of arbitrary authority. It spares both the client and the worker a fruitless expense of time and energy and increases the confidence of the client in the worker's competence.

KINDS OF TRANSITIONS

Transitions refer not only to a change in topic but also to a change in affect level within a content area.

Woman, 26, black, upper middle class, family service, marital counseling.
WORKER: Well, let me kind of see where we are now. You have been telling me about your husband, the kind of man you think he is, his education, his work, the kinds of interests you have in common, the kinds of things you do together or the kinds of things you hope he would do along with you. But I am not sure what the feeling is between you, what about him makes you glad, what about him depresses you, what about him that makes you happy, what makes you sore as hell. Maybe now we can talk about the feelings between you and your husband.

One can also shift the time reference. One can discuss the same relationship in the past as well as the present, making a transition from one time period to another.

Psychiatric social worker talking to 20-year-old male about plans for release from mental hospital and return to his home community.
GEORGE: The thing I really hate is, when you're in a place like this, you get out and people call you stupid and nuts and everything. Tease you about being here and all that.

WORKER: I imagine that makes you pretty angry. (Client nods. Pause.) That hurts. (Pause.) That really does. (Pause.) But how about before you came here, George? They couldn't say that about you then. (Client shakes head, no.) What was the trouble then in your relationship with the guys back home?

Transitions are often preceded by steering messages, road signs which prepare the interviewee for a change in direction. "I would like to change the subject now," "there is something of importance that we haven't as yet had a chance to discuss."

Sullivan (1954) classifies interview transitions as smooth, accented, or abrupt; Merton (1956) labels them as cued, reversional, or mutational. The smooth or cued transition is one where the interviewer adapts a remark that has just been made in order to effect a transition. There is no, or little, apparent break in continuity but the concern of the interview has been shifted as a consequence.

One form of cued transition is a short question or comment that leads the interview back from irrelevant to relevant material by linking the two. In effect such a question or comment makes the irrelevant become pertinent. The smoothest transitions are, technically, related associations rather than real transitions. The interview is really concerned with the same content, but in another context.

Transitions may result from the association between psychologically related topics. The classical transition from talking about one's father to talking about one's employer or supervisor is based on the emotional association of one's father with other authority figures on whom one is dependent.

Reversional transitions employ content touched on but not discussed at some earlier point in the interview. The interviewer exploits the comment previously made by using it to introduce the new topic.

WORKER: You remember, a little while ago, near the beginning of the interview, we were talking about the foster home you were in before you came here. And you said it wasn't an easy place. Remember that? What difficulties did you have there?

It is best wherever possible to use the comments and even the exact wording of the interviewee. This suggests that she has shared some responsibility for the decision and that it is being made to some extent with her consent.

A mutational or abrupt transition is a clear break with what is currently under discussion. It has no obvious associational ties with the material which preceded it, as in a cued transition, nor with anything previously raised in the interview, however briefly.

INTERRUPTION

Having made the decision to effect a transition the interviewer has to watch for a logical choice point in the interview flow when the topic under discussion can be smoothly terminated and a new topic introduced. This raises the question of perhaps the most abrupt "transition" of all—interruption of the interviewee by the interviewer.

In the face of a determined, nonstop interviewee, interruption to effect a transition may be difficult. The interviewer may need to be unequivocal in regaining the initiative. This may require a sentence like "Permit me, I know I am interrupting, but I wonder if I can say something about this," or "May I interrupt for a moment, please?"

There are occasions when the interviewer needs actually to interrupt the interviewee. If the interviewee has embarked on a prolonged digression which the interviewer is convinced is not likely to contribute to achieving the purposes of the interview, an interruption is called for. The interviewer needs to do this gently, but firmly and insistently. At the same time she owes the interviewee an explicit explanation for the interruption.

Permitting the very talkative interviewee to ramble on when it is clear that what is being said is repetitious or inconsequential is a disservice to the interviewee. It is an intrusion on the time that might be available to other clients and is a threat to the relationship. If the interviewer is like the rest of us she is likely to get increasingly impatience and annoyed at the interviewee who talks and talks.

But, caution is advised. Interrupting the interview when the interruption cannot be justified in terms of the needs of the interview is a derogation of the interviewee's autonomy and becomes a struggle for status and control of the direction of the interview. The interviewee feels he has been squelched, and that what he has had to say is of secondary importance. It is desirable then for the interviewer to keep interruptions of the interviewee to a minimum and make certain that the interruptions are necessary and justifiable.

Frequently, however, inexperienced interviewers tend to interrupt when such an intervention is not clearly warranted. The interviewer intervenes and takes control of the interview before it is clear that the interviewee has finished what he wanted to say. The tendency to make unwarranted interruption is once again a carryover from some of the habits of our conversational interaction where we interrupt each other frequently with impunity and without apology. There is some ironic justice in the oft-made comment that nothing is quite as annoying as to have somebody go right on talking when you are interrupting.

TRANSITION CAVEATS

A transition is like a scene change in a play. One topic is ended, another is introduced. Sullivan (1954), a psychiatrist, in a book on the psychiatric interview comments as follows:

> When I talk about how to make transitions I simply mean how to move about in the interview. It is imperative if you want to know where you are with another person that you proceed along a path that he can at least dimly follow so that he doesn't get lost completely as to what you are driving at. . . . It is ideal, if you can, to go step by step with sufficient waving of signal flags and so on so that there is always something approaching a consensus as to what is being discussed. (p. 46)

Transitions which are abrupt, transitions for which there is no preparation, transitions which might appear to the interviewee to be illogical, are apt to be upsetting and confusing. The interviewee knows what he was doing and why; suddenly he is moved to something else, and he isn't clear how he got there or why.

If the relationship of the new content to the purposes of the interview seems clear, it may be talking down to the interviewee to note it. Frequently, however, the significance of the topic being introduced is not clear to the interviewee, no matter how obvious the relationship is to the social worker. Preparation for transition then should include some explicit statement of the relationship between new content and the purpose of the interview.

Couple, white, upper middle class, man aged 33, woman aged 28, adoption application interview.
WORKER: We have been talking about the different kinds of children for whom you both seem to have a preference. Perhaps we might discuss now your feelings about unmarried mothers and illegitimate children. You might wonder what relevance this has to your wanting to adopt a baby. You may know, however, that most of the infants we have available for adoption are illegitimate, so that your feelings and attitudes about illegitimacy are relevant to our meetings together. What comes to mind when you hear the words "unmarried mothers"?

When a transition leads to a new frame of reference the act of making the transition has to be more explicitly raised to consciousness. This is because frames of reference of previous content tend to persist. For instance the interviewer might say "we have been talking about how you feel about having the abortion. Try now to shift in your mind to thinking about the putative father. How do you think he feels about it?"

The interviewer should be aware that the need for focus that is served by use of transitions may be antithetical to the need for rapport. Transitions employed by the interviewer tend to restrict the spontaneity of the interviewee and emphasize that the contact is interviewer-controlled. In some instances it may be necessary to sacrifice focus for rapport and permit the interviewee a greater freedom despite the fact that this is clearly unproductive in achieving the specific interview purposes.

It is best not to make a transition to other content unless some time can be spent on the new material. Every time the context of the interview shifts, both participants have to readjust their perception of the situation. It takes a little time, and some psychic energy, to get accustomed to the change. Unless there is time available to work on the new content, there is no return on the investment.

Too rapid and too frequent transitions may indicate that the interviewer has no clear idea of how to conduct the interview, does not know what is most relevant to discuss, and is seeking some direction. It suggests a buckshot approach, trying many things in the hope that one topic or another will prove productive.

Before actually initiating a transition, the interviewer should mentally review the area under discussion to check for failure to cover any significant aspects. The interviewer than checks with the interviewee to see if there is anything else of relevance to the content area that he would be interested in discussing.

A mother with a 14-month-old daughter, Sue, and a 4-year-old retarded son, Andrew, is discussing with the worker the problems she is having rearing her children as a single parent. The discussion has first focused on Sue and after some talk about feeding and toilet training, the mother says:

INTERVIEWEE: I really don't have many problems with Sue, not like I have with Andrew.
INTERVIEWER: Right. I'd like to talk about that in a minute. Anything else about Sue?

Commenting on transitions the worker says:

I wanted to get some closure on the subject of Sue before we moved on to Andrew, yet, still assure the client that she would be provided the opportunity to discuss him.

Effective transitions result from mutual agreement among participants in the interview. Hackeny and associates (1970) perceptively divide the interview into "islands" and "hiatuses." An island is a section of the interview where both participants are mutually engaged in attending to some content. Having momentarily said all they need or want to say about this, they reach a hiatus, a respite. The hiatus is "a period of negotiation between the counselor and the client, a negotiation in which new response classes or topics are sought" (p. 343). In short, it is a period of transition. The client may tentatively offer something as new content; the worker may tentatively suggest new content by a question or a comment. Each waits to see if the other responds with interest, acceptance, and approval, or disinterest and rejection.

Male, 20, white, parole interview.
WORKER: That's about it on the job situation then.
ANDY: Yep, that's about it. (Pause.) It's sure been hot lately.
WORKER: Yeah (pause).
ANDY: Good weather for swimming. Carol [girlfriend] and I were at the lake last night, and there sure was a big crowd out.
WORKER: I would imagine so.
ANDY: Saw a couple of guys from [the correctional school] there.
WORKER: What did they have to say?

In the above extract there is closure on the topic of the client's job. The client offers the weather, his relationship with his girlfriend, and leisure time activities as possible topics of interview continuation. The worker is indifferent to these possibilities. She picks up, however, on the client's contact with boys he knew previously in the institution. This became the topic on which the interview was focused during the next fifteen minutes.

In making a transition, even with the apparent agreement of the interviewee, the interviewer must be sensitive to any changes in interview interaction immediately following the transition. If the interviewee subtly reverts to the previous content area, if the flow from the interviewee seems to indicate a resistance that was not encountered earlier in the interview, if the interviewee seems to display some resentment, it may be necessary for the interviewer to reconsider the transition. It is more efficient for the interviewer to be flexible and follow the interviewee's lead back to the previous content area than to stubbornly dragoon him into discussing something else.

INTERVIEWEE-INITIATED TRANSITIONS

Transitions are not the exclusive prerogative of the interviewer. The interviewee often takes the initiative in making a transition. He may be bored by the topic under discussion; he may have something else to discuss that worries him more; he may want to flee the topic under discussion; he may feel a need to exercise some control over the interview situation.

With interviewee-initiated transitions, the interviewer has to decide whether to go along with the change and, accordingly, to modify her ideas about the content and sequence of the interview. She also has the problem of understanding what prompted the transition. Sometimes, of course, this may be obvious. At other times the emotional logic of the interviewee's thinking may not be apparent. Often an interviewee-initiated transition seems warranted. When the interviewer goes along with it, however, she needs to make a point of mentally filing for future reference the material she wanted to discuss but was now withholding in preference for the interviewee's choice of content.

When the interviewee introduces apparently irrelevant material, it is advisable to stay with it long enough to explore whether a transition is necessary. Sometimes apparently irrelevant material has a pertinence that only gradually becomes clear. The interviewee's interest in the material, manifested by his introducing it, acts as a constraint on rapid transition away from it. Rejection of the new content area is sometimes perceived as rejection of the interviewee. It may be necessary to accept the topic and by implication, the interviewee, in making the transition.

If it is unclear what prompted the interviewee-initiated transition and if the interviewer is uncertain about what to do, it might be helpful to raise an explicit question about the transition.

Male, 19, white, lower middle class, parole preparation interview.
WORKER: Help me out here. I think I lost you somewhere a little further back. We were talking about the guys you used to know at [the reformatory] who got out and made it. Now we're talking about the changes your father plans to make around the farm. I don't get it.
GEORGE: Yeah, how did we get to this?
WORKER: As I say, I don't know, but maybe you could think back on this.
GEORGE: Well, I don't know either. (Pause.) What was I saying about this? (Long pause.) Yeah, oh hell, I don't know.
WORKER: Okay, maybe you don't.
GEORGE: It may be that those guys who made it, some of them got a lot of help from their family, money for things they wanted to do or needed, so if my old man puts all that dough in the farm, maybe he can't help me out so much, or maybe I feel I can't ask him because he won't have it, see.

The interviewer's comments on the exchange follow:

George had me puzzled on this. I really didn't know how we got from his reformatory peer group to his father's farm. I turned over a couple of things in my head as he talked, but nothing seemed to click. I didn't want to cut him off because he seemed to want to talk about it, but I couldn't see that this stuff about the farm was going to get us anywhere. That's when I decided to risk having it out with him. For a while I thought he didn't know either. The pauses seemed long, and he seemed to get more annoyed. He fidgeted a lot in his seat. That's why I decided to let up the pressure by saying "Well, maybe you don't [know why you shifted the focus]." But maybe my letting up on him by saying that helped ease his tension so that he was able to tell me.

If the digression is apparently unproductive, the interviewer may want to acknowledge it but not accept it as a focus for discussion. She might say, "That is very interesting and may be helpful. Perhaps if you like, we can come back to it later. However, it may be more helpful to you if we could talk about the way you get along on your job."

Sometimes the interviewee-initiated transition is designed to frustrate achieving the purposes of the interview. It is an attempt to evade painful work of the interview that must be done. In instances where an interviewee-initiated transition seems clearly designed to be an escape, it may be advisable to go along with a temporary digression to neutral material. This provides the interviewee with a breather, a rest break, during which he can pull himself together for another try at difficult content. But if the difficult content is relevant and important, the interviewer should try again. If she fails to make this return transition, the client may be pleased, but disappointed, at the interviewer's collusion in his evasion of painful material. He may be annoyed, but gratified, at the unyielding but compassionate interviewer who holds him to the purpose of the interview.

The client may initiate a transition to meet his own needs and the interviewer may decide, for good reason, to accept the transition even though it might unfocus the interview. An interviewer notes the value of apparently unproductive digressions initiated by interviewee transitions.

I learned that I had to be flexible in response to a person's concentration ability. At first, when a person started in on a story about life in the Navy during the war, or an account of the dog's prowess as a watchman, I panicked a little: I felt that the interview was going to splinter off into small talk and long stories. Then I began to realize that this was an integral part of the process. The interview was a strain for some of the people and they needed a chance to retreat from it for a short time. They seemed to need a shift in focus and I usually drifted with them until they seemed ready to return to the questions. (Converse and Schuman 1974:46)

Sometimes a rambling digression is merely the equivalent of a mental coffee break. Good interviewing is hard work for both participants. The

interviewee may just need time to talk about something pleasant, less painful, even if it is not relevant. The interviewer who recognizing this sighs
and settles back to listen is ultimately likely to get where she wants to go
faster than if she tried to stop the process.

ROLE-REVERSAL TRANSITIONS

The role-reversal transition presents a recurrent problem for interviewers. The interviewee initiates a question, or series of questions, and becomes the "interviewer" temporarily. Although the interviewer might well
ask herself what explains the interviewee's shift in role, she should respond
by a willingness to share, simply and briefly, the information the interviewee wants. The interviewer should answer the questions asked, without
apology, and should keep as much as possible to factual data.

As soon as it is feasible, however, the usual interviewing roles should be
reestablished. The interviewer, if she is true to her responsibilities, has to
reclaim her position, not to exercise authority or to emphasize the subordinate status of the interviewee, but because the interview exists to serve
the purposes of the interviewee. They can only be accomplished if the
worker interviews the client, and not the other way around.

Interviewers frequently feel uncomfortable with role reversal because it
may mean sharing information that puts them at a disadvantage with the
interviewee. Finding out that the interviewer is unmarried, or childless,
or a student may erode, it is felt, some of the worker's potential for influence.

For the interviewee, such a reversal turns the spotlight away from himself and onto the interviewer. It gives him a break from having to talk,
having to consider his situation; it acts as a diversion and digression. It may
be symptomatic of interviewee hostility and a desire to make the interviewer uncomfortable by asking personal questions. It may be a test of the
worker's willingness to share. It may be a challenge to the interviewer's
control of the interview or resentment at the inequality of the relationship.
More frequently, perhaps, the role reversal is a response to the interviewee's need to know better the person with whom he is sharing so much of
importance. Knowing more about the interviewer helps him "place" the
interviewer. The interviewee may also want assurance that the interviewer
is as human, as fallible, as himself.

The interviewee can engage in role reversal not only by asking the interviewer for personal information but also by frequently asking for greater
clarification and specification about the interviewer's questions or comments. He may ask what the interviewer has in mind, or what use the

interviewer will make of the information, or for a justification of the interviewer's questions. Interview reversal is sometimes effected by frequent and specific requests for advice or by soliciting the interviewer's opinion.

So when she said that, I just walked out of the house. What do you think I should have done?

We were all together in this and everybody was kinda feeling good, and when the marijuana came around again to me, I took a puff. What could I do? What would you have done if you were me in this situation?

The discussion presented above, of attending behavior, minimal encouragements, paraphrases, summarization, and transitions is concerned with extending the range of the interview. Each of these interventions helps the interviewer obtain greater and more varied detail about the client and his situation.

Depth

A second major problem encountered during the developmental phase of the interview is depth. Having covered the range or general content areas of relevance to achieving the purposes of the interview, the participants have identified some particular areas that need to be discussed at a more intense emotional level. The problem posed for the interviewer is to focus on a particular subject and move vertically from a surface statement of the situation to the more personal, emotional, meaning of the content.

Depth refers not only to the intensity of feelings associated with events and people but also to the level of intimacy of such feelings. It encompasses those feelings the interviewee regards as private, those that are shared with some reluctance and resistance. In sharing this material, the interviewee feels a greater risk of self-revelation. Depth implies an affective response and a personal involvement with the content, as against impersonal detachment. Range is concerned with what happened; depth is concerned with how the interviewee feels about what happened.

Attending behavior, minimal encouragements, paraphrasing, summarizing, and effective use of transitions help to extend the range of the interview. Identifying and calling attention to feelings and reflections of feelings are interventions that intensify the depth of the interview.

IDENTIFYING AND CALLING ATTENTION TO FEELINGS

Various techniques have been developed to help the interviewee move from a superficial affective level to a more intense, more intimate level in discussing interview content. Encouraging the discussion of feelings by ask-ing about or commenting on feelings is the simplest and most frequently employed technique for achieving depth. The "How do you feel about it?" response, which has almost become an identifying slogan of social workers, is a good example. Such questions or comments tend to focus the inter-viewee's attention on feelings and feeling contexts. They offer stimulus and invitation to discuss content at greater depth. They "reach" for feelings.

Female, 32, black, upper lower class, juvenile court.
The mother had been describing at some length the experiences her son, 16, had with drugs. He had been recently arrested for possession and sale of heroin, and at this point the mother was detailing the arrest and the efforts she had made to obtain legal assistance.
WORKER: A lawyer is very important, and I am glad you were able to get such help. But what were your feelings when they told you that William was arrested?

Social work interviewers are sensitive to and quick to call attention to feel-ings.

Woman, 29, black, lower lower class, foster care agency.
MRS. Y.: So when the doctor said I needed the operation and I knew I had to go to the hospital, I thought what am I going to do with the kids? Who will take them, take care of them I mean, there's nobody. Half the people, like relatives, I know, far away, they can't come.
WORKER: You feel all alone.

In response, the interviewee shifted from the problem of child care to discussing her own feelings of fright at being alone and facing an operation without the support of anybody close to her. The worker here responds not to the external details of the mother's problem but rather to the unex-pressed feelings associated with it. The interviewer's comments on the emotional aspects of the situation encourage the interviewee to discuss them. The worker identifies the feelings, gives them recognition, and attempts to keep the interviewee's attention centered on her emotional responses.

A 30-year-old Mexican-American mother on public assistance, discussing her relationships with her children.
MRS. D.: And John more or less is inclined to favor Mary, and my mother-in-law favors the twins. Everybody favors the twins, and Mary. But then these two are left out. I guess I'm more or less inclined to favor Mary, too.
WORKER: What makes you feel this way?

MRS. D.: Well, we all love them the same. We buy them things, we buy
them all nice things, but yet when that one's hurt or something, I just
sort of ache more. I don't know why, is that selfish, or something? I
don't know. I even feel guilty about that and maybe I'm doing wrong.

WORKER: You feel guilty?

MRS. D.: Yes, but as long as I try there's nothing wrong. Okay?

WORKER: I think so, but how do you mean wrong?

MRS. D.: Am I doing wrong because I favor Mary above the others? I don't
try to favor her. Well, I think I have my own answer, really. But I hate
to look at it sometimes.

WORKER: What's your own answer to what makes you feel this way about
Mary?

Once the interviewee begins to discuss material with some intensity of
affect, rewarding encouragement may help him to continue. "I know it is
hard for you to talk about this, and it's a sign of your strength that you can
discuss it"; "It must be painful for you to discuss this, and I admire your
courage in making the effort." Part of what may be involved here is a process of modeling. The interviewer demonstrates that she is not afraid of
feelings, is ready and willing to discuss feelings; she acts as a model for the
interviewee to emulate by being open about her own feelings.

SANCTIONING FEELINGS

One of the barriers to self-revelation is that such sharing makes a person
vulnerable to rejection by others. Content about which the client is sensitive, about which he has considerable feeling, is often content which is
likely to seem, at least to the interviewee, to be self-incriminating, embarrassing, associated with shame, guilt, or blame.

One approach to such content is to sanction, in advance, feelings which
might provoke shame or guilt. It makes acceptable the seemingly unacceptable and frees the interviewee to share that which she would have
withheld. A legitimate explanation or excuse may preface the comment or
phrase which is offered as stimulus to the exploration of feelings. Thus the
interviewer might say to a mother of a large family, who is considering
institutionalizing her mentally defective child, "It must be hard caring for
the other children, given the extra burden of care that John requires. How
do you feel about the care you have been able to give the other children?"
Or to a daughter struggling with the problem of helping her elderly parents
find a place to live, "I can understand that there might be a conflict between what you feel you owe your children and what you feel you owe
your parents. How do you feel in looking for a nursing home for your

parents?" Such prefacing has a face-saving effect; it softens the potential threat involved in self-disclosure of feelings.

Another sanctioning procedure is universalization of emotional responses which are known to be very common. Thus one might say to an unmarried mother, "Most girls are anxious about many things related to pregnancy. How do you feel about it?" Or to a woman recently divorced, "Many women feel lost and lonely right after the divorce. What are your own feelings about this?" Or to an unhappy wife, "All married people hate each other on occasion. How do you feel about your husband?"

Kinsey used such a procedure to encourage discussion of material about which the interviewee might otherwise have been reticent. Instead of asking whether or not the interviewee masturbated, followed by a question on frequency, his interviewers asked only, "How frequently do you masturbate?" The question incorporated the presumption that the practice was universal.

One can sanction socially unacceptable responses by prefacing which indicates the interviewer's awareness that people feel this way and that such feelings are understandable. What is involved here is projection of such feelings onto others and a depersonalizing of what are regarded as socially unacceptable feelings. "Some people feel that parents cannot always love their children. How do you feel about your child?" "Even happily married men think of extramarital adventures. Have you ever felt this way?" "Some people feel that going for an operation is scary even to adults, and they feel frightened. What is your reaction to this?"

The interviewer may explicitly sanction feelings and at the same time present herself as a model for emulation by indicating her own response to the situation. "If anybody treated me like that, I know I would really get sore." "I don't think I could face a situation like the one you mention without feeling depressed and upset."

Explicit expressions of empathy help the interviewee to verbalize feelings. "I can understand how anxious it might make you feel to know that Jim is getting into drugs and not knowing what to do to stop it." "I can imagine how frustrating it must feel to be ready, willing, and able to find employment, only to find no jobs are available."

By explicitly articulating the different kinds of feelings that might possibly be associated with some problem, the interviewer indicates that all are equally acceptable. "Some families do institutionalize their mongoloid children. Some maintain them at home. What is your own feeling about this at this time?" "Some unmarried mothers keep their child. Some unmarried mothers give up their child for adoption. How do you feel about it?"

The interviewee has no difficulty in sharing positive, socially sanctioned feelings. Encouraging the articulation of such feelings about some content under discussion might then make it easier for the interviewee to verbalize feelings that he perceives as negative and unacceptable. Having discussed what he likes about his marriage, the interviewee might be ready to discuss what he dislikes about it. The child might be ready to express his dislike for his parents after having described some of his affectionate feelings for them. The interviewer then moves gradually from focusing on the acceptable feelings to asking about less acceptable feelings.

EUPHEMISM

The use of euphemism is helpful in moving into more sensitive areas. Euphemisms are a way of communicating tabooed or offensive words or ideas in a socially acceptable form. "Euphemism" is derived from the Greek word which means "good-speak." Social workers who previously talked of the "retarded child" now speak of the "exceptional child." Workers in adoption replaced the "hard-to-place child" with "children with special needs," which was then replaced by "the waiting child." A mother who is reluctant to discuss her feelings about "hitting" a child may be ready to discuss her feelings about "disciplining" a child. An adolescent who retreats from talking about his feelings associated with "stealing" may talk more readily about his response to "taking things." Euphemism and metaphors soften the threatening impact of the question, trigger less anxiety and resistance, and reduce the probability that the interviewee will avoid discussion of certain feelings. For example, in talking with an older client about a possible move to a group home, the worker refers to it as a "nursing home." The client reacts negatively to the connotations of such a term and shifts the interview to more neutral material. A little later in the interview the worker reintroduces this content but now refers to a "home for senior citizens." The client picks up on this and readily engages in a discussion of planning for the move.

One may approach personal emotional reactions gradually and indirectly. One way of doing this is by initially depersonalizing the discussion. Instead of asking a mother how she reacted to the experience of accepting a homemaker after her return from the hospital, the worker asks about her husband's feelings in response to the homemaker and about her children's feelings. Only after such discussion, desensitizing the mother to any reluctance to discuss the emotional aspects of homemaker service, does the worker ask the mother about her own feelings.

Sensitivity to and labeling of latent content is one approach to depth content in the interview. The latent content behind the manifest comment suggests the accompanying deeper, more intimate feelings associated with the content. The very sick patient who says to the medical social worker, "This has been a very hard winter. I wonder what next winter will be like," may be asking for assurance that she will live to see another winter. The 6-year-old child who asks the foster-care worker, "Did my brother cry when you took him to the [foster] home?" may be asking for acceptance of his own need to cry.

Although the interviewer may stimulate the interviewee to introduce more intense emotional content, she may also block further exploration of feeling. As is true to some extent for all of us, the beginning interviewer is more comfortable with concretely factual material than with affective content. The initial tendency, then, is to retreat from emotional material into the reportorial, factual "who," "what," "when," "where" kinds of response. The interviewer fails to respond to the feeling the client is attempting to communicate, thus discouraging further discussion of feelings.

A 13-year-old boy describing a family fight involving his parents and older brother to worker of family service agency.
PHIL: Jim wanted to go out; some one of his friends called him up and he wanted to go out. But Mom didn't want him to go out, and he pushed her away and he slapped her, and then they just started fighting and hollering, and it was all sort of scary.
WORKER: What day did this happen?
PHIL: I think it was Wednesday, no Thursday. I can't picture it in my mind.
WORKER: What time was it?

The following example illustrates the worker's feelings effecting an interview. The mother of an emotionally disturbed 3-year-old boy is discussing the child with an intake worker at a day care center for disturbed children. She has just suggested, with considerable affect, that the child was unplanned, unwanted, and is rejected. She feels guilty about her attitude as a possible explanation of the boy's behavior. She is leaning forward tensely in the chair, twisting her hands together, looking at the floor. The worker, in response, introduces a series of questions about the onset of walking, talking, and toilet training by saying, "Let me ask you some questions we need for our records." The worker says in retrospect:

I felt that the mother and myself needed the emotional relief of a fairly objective line of questioning. But what made me feel that? As I think about it, she seemed ready to explore it further. Maybe I wanted out.

Asking about the emotional reactions of everyone but the interviewee is another evasive procedure. It permits discussing the issue but not risking any strong display of feelings by the interviewee himself, to which the interviewer will have to respond.

Correctional social worker talking to a 19-year-old white male charged with drug abuse.
WORKER: So when you dropped out of school, how did your parents feel about this?
GREG: Well, they didn't like it, of course. They were upset and hollered a lot and we argued.
WORKER: What was your girlfriend's reaction?

The worker fails to ask about Greg's feelings about his decision.

The interviewer can also avoid discussion of emotionally laden material by shifting the focus to a person outside the interview.

MARY: I was over at my boyfriend's house, watching TV, and my father came busting in and said I had to go home with him. He was shouting and everything and made a big scene. I was so embarrassed.
WORKER: Why did he do it?

REFLECTION OF FEELING

Reflection of feeling is an interventive procedure designed to intensify depth in the interview. Reflection of feeling is similar to paraphrase since both procedures feed back to the client the interviewer's perception of the communication. They differ in that they are focused on different aspects of the communication.

Paraphrase relates to the content component of the communication, information about the client and his situation, a description of an incident or event; reflection of feeling elicits from the interviewee feelings about the incident, the event, the information being shared. Paraphrasing is a restatement of the content component of the interviewee's statement; reflection of feeling is a restatement of the affective component of the communication. Consequently reflection-of-feeling interventions are more appropriately related to depth in interviewing.

Attending behavior says "I am with you." Minimal encouragers says "I am with you, please go on." Paraphrasing says "I am with you, please go on, I understand what you're saying." Reflection of feeling says, "I am with you, please go on. I understand what you are saying and recognize how you are feeling."

The distinction between paraphrase and reflection of feeling is illustrated in the following:

An aged client applying for Supplemental Security income.
CLIENT: The inflation is killing us. We had to come here because we just can't get along on the lousy small company pension.
WORKER (paraphrase): You need to apply for supplementary income because it's difficult to make ends meet.
WORKER (reflection of feeling): You seem to feel uncomfortable and unhappy about having to apply for the help.
A young adolescent talking to a social worker at a shelter for runaways.
CLIENT: I had it at home—up to here. I wanted out but it's hard to know where to go, what to do and be sure you're going to eat.
WORKER (paraphrase): You wanted to get away from your family but it's not so easy once you do.
WORKER (reflection of feeling): Sounds like you feel confused and scared.

Accurate reflection of feeling is more difficult than paraphrase. In paraphrasing you are acting on words the interviewee has actually said. There is an objective communication which provides the base for the response. In reflection of feeling the communication to which the interviewer responds is more ambiguous. The client does not, for the most part, identify or label his feelings. The translation of the emotion being displayed by the client requires some inference on the part of the interviewer. Acting in a certain way, speaking in a certain tone of voice, gesturing in a certain manner, are signs the interviewer "reads" to learn what the interviewee is feeling—sad or glad, friendly or hostile, hurt or delighted. Having made some decision as to how the interviewee is feeling the interviewer reflects it back to the interviewee.

In reflecting feelings the intensity of affect communicated by the interviewer should be in line with the intensity of affect communicated by the interviewee. If the client is only mildly annoyed or irritated, it would be inappropriate to reflect hate or disgust.

There is admittedly a possible overlap between paraphrase and reflection of feelings despite differences in intended focus. It is hard for a paraphrase not to include some reflection of feeling and equally difficult for reflections of feeling not to include some of the objective, contextual elements of the client's communication.

Both paraphrasing and reflection of feeling tend to increase the bond between interviewer and interviewee. Both intensify the feeling of sharing, of mutual understanding. The fact that the interviewer is in tune with the interviewee in reflecting accurately is a confirmation of her empathy. Accurate reflection is the optimum way of communicating that the interviewer is, in fact, empathetic. The reflective comment affirms that the interviewer does understand the interviewee's thinking and feeling.

Hearing the interviewer's accurate and sensitive reflection of the thinking and feeling gives the interviewee an opportunity of listening to themselves through the echoes of the interviewer's reflective comments. A social worker in a planned parenthood clinic is interviewing a 16-year-old high school senior who, having missed her period, suspects she might be pregnant.

INTERVIEWER: What do you think you might do if the tests confirm the fact that you are pregnant?
INTERVIEWEE: Oh, I don't know—I guess I am not sure.
INTERVIEWER: You're not sure?
INTERVIEWEE: No, I've thought—um about an abortion—but it's just—I don't know.
INTERVIEWER: Uh-huh, so although you have thought about an abortion, it seems like you are not totally comfortable with that option.
INTERVIEWEE: Right (silence). I guess that in a lot of ways an abortion would probably be the best, but it's just that—even though I think women should be able to get them—abortions—I just wish that I didn't have to even think about it.

A senior citizen in a nursing home is discussing her reaction to group activities.

INTERVIEWEE: Well, it gives us something to do, I guess. Like the awareness group, I don't know if I like that group or not. I don't like hearing other people's problems. I feel uncomfortable in the group sometimes.
INTERVIEWER: You feel uncomfortable when other people are talking about their problems?
INTERVIEWEE: I don't like hearing all that stuff.

Good reflection of feelings is associated with some concern for concreteness and immediacy. The interviewer's reflection has greater credibility if it is clearly tied to some definite stimulus situation evoking the feeling which the client has discussed, as in the above illustrations.

Reflection of feeling, like the previously discussed responses, has the effect of assuring the client the worker is attentively listening and striving to understand, but it has the additional effect of reinforcing discussion of feelings. The interviewer's response gives additional emphasis to the feeling content communicated by the interviewer and suggests the interviewee should continue with it.

Reflection of feeling has the additional effect of clarification. In reflecting feeling the interviewer attempts to give a name to unclear emotional sensations.

The interviewee may become more aware of what he feels as the interviewer explicitly labels feelings in reflecting them.

Accurate reflection of feeling also has the advantageous effect of sanctioning negative feelings. The interviewee may express the feelings indirectly. The interviewer, in reflecting, identifies and shows acceptance of the feelings more directly.

A woman discussing her problems in getting a sibling to share responsibility for the care of aged parents.
INTERVIEWER (with some exasperation): He doesn't want to know about it, he doesn't want to help me with them, he leaves it all up to me, he is completely and totally uncooperative.
INTERVIEWER: It sounds to me like you are mad at him and resent him now for what he is doing.

Two additional aspects of depth in interviewing might be noted.

We need to be aware that we tend to use the word *feel* loosely. It often is used to ask what the person *thinks* about something. "How do you feel about protective tariffs," or "How do you feel an advanced degree will be helpful" is really asking what people think about this.

Second, it might be noted that the interviewer is often the deliberate target of the interviewee's expressed feelings. Feelings are not only "expressed," giving us some relief, they are also communicative displays designed to influence others. They are intended to evoke pity or guilt or assistance in the person toward whom they are directed. We use displays of feeling to influence others, to manipulate, even to coerce others. The interviewee may use the expression of feelings to control the interviewer.

We have given in detail the interventions the interviewer employs in helping the interviewee extend the range and the depth of the interview. Research analysis of interviews indicates that such interventions are employed in achieving these objectives.

Detailed studies of thirty-six videotapes of interviews with clients in a psychiatric clinic indicated that different interventions were employed when the interviewer was focused on eliciting information (range) and that other interventions were employed in eliciting feelings (depth). The interviewer was more successful in eliciting information when she talked more, took the initiative in raising topics, used a high rate of probes, and asked for detailed descriptions. The interviewer was more successful in eliciting feelings when she used more open than closed questions, when she made direct requests for feelings, when she used expressions of sympathy and made interpretations. Direct requests for expressions of feelings were helpful in initiating expressions of feeling and interviewer response to emotional cues were helpful in sustaining expression of feelings once they were initiated (Cox, Hopkinson, and Rutter 1981; Hopkinson, Cox, and Rutter 1981).

A matter-of-fact request for expression of feelings coupled with the interviewer giving the interviewee an uninterrupted opportunity to express feelings was more effective when the interviewer expressed warmth and nonverbal displays of acceptance and encouragement (Hopkinson, Cox, and Rutter 1981:412). Successful gathering of information in extending the range of the interview required a more active stance by the interviewer. Soliciting feelings and self-disclosure in extending the depth of the interview required more passivity on the part of the interviewer. However, the research indicated that the same interviewer could successfully use different approaches at different points in the interview. The different approaches when skillfully used are not necessarily in conflict. The research also showed that optimal rather than maximal use of warmth and sympathy was more effective. Some clients responded with greater reticence to excesses of warmth and sympathy (Cox, Holbrook, and Rutter 1981:150–151).

SUGGESTED READINGS

Steven J. Danish and Allen L. Hauer. *Helping Skills: A Basic Training Program.* New York: Behavioral Publications, 1973 (122 pp.).

A manual of programs designed to teach basic interviewing skills that reflects the micro-counseling orientation.

Gerard Egan. *The Skilled Helper: A Model for Systematic Helping and Interpersonal Relating.* 2d ed. Monterey, Calif.: Brooks/Cole, 1982 (324 pp.).

Written by a professor of counseling and counselor oriented. An introductory section on theories of helping is followed by the major part of the book devoted to specific helping skills, e.g., empathy, confrontation, self-disclosure, etc. Readers will find themselves on familiar ground. The book is accompanied by a separately published handbook of *Exercises in Helping Skills: A Training Manual.*

Dean H. Hepworth and Jo Ann Larson. *Direct Social Work Practice: Theory and Skills.* Homewood Illinois: Dorsey Press, 1982 (559 pp.).

Although not directly focused on the interview, many of the direct practice skills discussed and aptly illustrated are, in effect, interview-related skills. The illustrations are primarily from social work, the authors being faculty members of a graduate school of social work.

Allen E. Ivey and Jerry Authier. *Microcounseling: Innovations in Interviewing, Counseling Psychotherapy, and Psychoeducation.* 2d ed. Springfield, Ill.: C. C. Thomas, 1978 (584 pp.).

The granddaddy of the microcounseling texts. It presents an overview of microcounseling and an exposition of specific skills such as attending, reflecting, confrontation, as well as associated attitudes such as empathy, warmth, and genuineness. The book then goes on to describe microcounseling training. The microtraining group also publishes microtraining manuals devoted to *Basic Attending Skills* and *Basic Influencing Skills* by Allen E. Ivey and Norma Gluckstion, available through the Microtraining Associates, Inc., Box 641, North Amherst, Mass. 01059.

Lawrence Shulman. *Identifying, Measuring, and Teaching Helping Skills.* New York: Council on Social Work Education and Canadian Association of Schools of Social Work, 1981 (146 pp.).

Written by a professor of social work who has done extensive research on the nature of the worker-client interpersonal interaction.

CHAPTER 8

Developmental Phase: Problem-Solving Interventions

The manifestation and effective communication of facilitative attitudes toward the client help the interviewer develop the necessary positive relationship with the client. Attending behavior, minimal encouragements, paraphrase summarization, and effective use of transitions extend the range of the interview. Identification of and calling attention to feelings and reflection of feelings help the client deepen the emotional level of the presentation of her problem. But no matter how skillfully the social worker has demonstrated his acceptance, empathic understanding and warmth, no matter how competently he has helped the interviewee to broaden and deepen her sharing of the problem(s) that brings her to the agency, the purpose of the contact is yet to be achieved. Skills relating to helping the client communicate the nature of the problem are necessary but only halfway steps in discharging the responsibilities of the agency to help the interviewee move toward resolving her problem. The interviewer, in addition, needs to demonstrate problem-solving skills. Clarification and interpretation, confrontation, information sharing, advice, and support are among the skills that interviewers need to achieve the problem-solving objectives of the interview. This chapter focuses on a discussion of such interview interventions.

Clarification and Interpretation

Clarification and interpretation go a step beyond mechanical reflection and selective restatement. Clarification mirrors what the interviewee has said but translates it into more familiar language so that it can be more clearly understood; it amplifies without falsifying. Clarification involves helping the client restructure her perceptual field. Unlike interpretation, in clarification all the elements of such restructuring are already within the interviewee's level of awareness. Clarification distinguishes subjective reality from objective reality and presents various alternatives for consideration, with a delineation of the consequences of different choices. The dominant note is cognitive understanding.

Interventions directed at clarification have the objective of bringing into sharp focus and giving clear visibility to otherwise vague communication. Many of the interviewer's interventions discussed earlier, such as reflecting and paraphrasing, as a side benefit also clarify what the client is thinking, feeling, and saying to herself and to the interviewer. When the interviewer says "do you mean that . . . ," "in other words . . . ," "let me see if I have this right . . . ," "if I understand you correctly . . . ," the response is a further clarification of what has been said.

Clarifying efforts have the effect of increasing specificity. When the client says, "I think my husband really dislikes me," and the interviewer asks, "What does he do or say that suggests this to you?" the interviewer is asking for clarification through specificity. When the client says, "I feel depressed," and the interviewer asks, "What depresses you most—your job, your marriage, your children, your social life?" the interviewer is attempting clarification through specification.

The interviewer requests clarification when he wants to check out his understanding of what the client is saying and/or when he feels the client is not clear in her thinking and feeling. The request for clarification is then designed to help both participants in the interview.

The interviewer's requests for clarification appeal to the interviewee's help in dispelling the interviewer's confusion and/or ignorance and have the positive effect of increasing mutuality in the interaction. The interviewee is "helping" the interviewer at this point, and the interview becomes more of a joint endeavor. It also motivates the interviewee to participate more actively in the interaction. It is difficult not to respond to another person seeking to do a good job.

A word of caution. Here, as always, the art of interviewing calls for a *judicious* use of such intervention as "I don't understand," "I am not sure I know what you mean," "I am not clear about. . . ." Too frequent use of these phrases may suggest to the interviewee that the interviewer is not particularly bright or that he is not listening carefully.

Interpretation goes a step beyond paraphrasing or reflecting or clarifying. In paraphrasing, reflecting, and clarifying, the frame of reference of the interviewee is maintained; in interpreting a new frame of reference is offered for consideration. The interviewer renames or relabels the client's comment so that it has a different meaning. A clarifiction or paraphrase or reflection stays very close to the message as presented. Interpretation takes off from the message and includes an inference derived from the message, one added by the interviewer. It is what was heard plus what was inferred.

This inference is based on other information offered by the interviewee at some other point in the contact. Using theoretical constructs about human behavior, the interviewer puts different pieces of information together so that they make psychological sense. The result is an interpretation.

In arriving at an interpretation, the interviewer is more directive than in either clarifying or reflecting. In effect, he is attempting to lead the client to an explanation (developed by the interviewer) that he thinks has some validity.

Clarification and paraphrase are more descriptive. Interpretation adds explanation of causality. In reflection, the worker does not seek to suggest an explanation for the behavior being highlighted and does not go beyond what has been presented by an interviewee. To "go beyond," however, is the essential feature of interpretation. In interpretation, the worker deliberately seeks to suggest an explanation, a rationale for the interviewee to consider, by using information provided by her.

In the following excerpt from an interview with a 12-year-old boy the social worker in a residential institution for emotionally disturbed children is faced with a resistive interviewee. He reflects the client's statements a number of times and then makes an interpretation in the form of a question.

CLIENT: I don't like talking to grown-ups, I like talking to kids.
WORKER (reflection): You don't like talking to grown-ups. How come?
CLIENT: I don't like to talk seriously . . . I just like to talk "goofing around."
WORKER (reflection): Um-hum . . . you don't like to talk seriously.
CLIENT: Nope.
WORKER (interpretation): Kids don't ask you a lot of personal questions?
CLIENT: Yeah, that's part of it.

In making an interpretation the worker offers a connection the client may not be aware of.

A high-school student is having difficulty in a chemistry lab class supervised by a male teacher. She resists following the teacher's instructions in doing the required lab work. She discusses her anxious feelings about her relationship with her rigid authoritarian father:

CLIENT: My father makes me feel uneasy. Even when he's not criticizing me, I feel he's criticizing me.

WORKER: As you talk about this I keep wondering if there is any connection between your feelings about your father and your antagonistic behavior toward Mr. P [the lab teacher].

If the above example showed the interviewer reflecting or paraphrasing, the interviewer would merely have described in somewhat different words the way the client was relating to her father and her feeling response in this relationship. Instead it shows the interviewer interpreting previously unlinked but psychologically related items of information, suggesting an explanation for the problem in the lab.

Interpretation can be hazardous because the "explanation" only partly depends on what the client has actually said at different points in the contact—it also depends on the theoretical constructs basic to the inferences.

Applying different theoretical constructs to the same client's statements could result in varying interpretations. For instance, the interviewer in the example just given had preconceived ideas about parents and teachers as authoritative figures and about displacements and transference. The client's behavior toward the teacher was seen as a result of transferring feelings in the parent-child context to the teacher-pupil context because teachers are identified with parental figures. A behavioral-oriented interviewer using the same information may "explain" the problem as a result of learning certain patterns of behavior in the family that are being repeated in the school setting. An interviewer with a feminist orientation might interpret the conflict as another illustration of problems in socialization of women to a subservient role in relation to men. A transactional-oriented interviewer might have made an interpretation of the child-self in conflict with the adult-self.

Since different explanations have somewhat equal plausibility depending on the explanatory cosmology applied, the ultimate determinant of its utility in helping the client is the client's reaction to and use of the interpretation. The process is once again illustrated in the following.

The worker has been discussing with a foster mother the possibility of converting the status of the foster child, Norman, age 11, to that of a subsidized adoption. The foster mother has had an ambivalent relationship with the child during the five years he's been in her home. She is resistant to the idea of adopting Norman despite the guarantee of a maintenance subsidy. She says: "I don't want to do it, but then I wonder if maybe Norman will reject us if we don't."

The worker, putting his knowledge of some of the mother's feeling of rejection toward Norman together with concepts of projection, interprets by piecing this together and saying: "Could it be that some of your reluctance about this is related to the fact that you sometimes can't really accept Norman as a child of yours?"

Interpretation requires not only a conceptual framework for ordering behavior, which the interviewer brings with him to the interview, it also requires a sufficiency of information from the interviewee about his specific situation. Unless an interpretation is firmer grounded in information provided by the client, it is likely to be more of a guess than a valid inference.

Every interpretive statement has an element of inference. The interviewer is establishing some connection between thoughts, feelings, and attitudes that previously had not been perceived as being related. It is often, in effect, a translation of "manifest behavior into its psychodynamic significance."

Every inference is more or less conjectural. The best interpretation is the one that has fewest components of conjecture, that is most clearly substantiated by evidence from the client's communications. It is what the client has almost said but has not yet said. The interviewer anticipates her by just a little.

Interpretation makes explicit that which the interviewee had communicated at such a low level of awareness that she was not aware she said it. It is often a latent affective message translated into words. Fromm-Reichmann defines interpretation as the translation of the "manifestations of that which is barred from awareness into the language of consciousness." The dominant note is emotional understanding.

In interpreting, the interviewer may make explicit something the client knows and does not explicitly know she knows. The interviewer acts as a mental obstetrician, helping the client give birth to an understanding that is on the edge of her recognition. It makes explicitly conscious, preconscious understandings. If accepted the interpretation has the effect of providing the client with a different perspective or a broadened perception of her behavior and perhaps a different angle on how to deal with it.

The goal of interpretation is that the interviewee herself accepts the interviewer's definition of the situation as valid and accurate. The worker cannot force or even "give" an interpretation. It needs to be achieved by the client. When achieved it may lead to insight, a different understanding of the situation.

Because interpretation comes partly from what the client has said and partly from the sense the interviewer gives to the message, it is best presented tentatively. It is often offered as a suggestive question: "Would it be fair to say that . . . ," "Might you consider the possibility that . . . ," or introduced by qualifiers such as "I wonder if . . . ," "maybe," "perhaps." It is presented as a hypothesis for consideration rather than as a conclusion for acceptance.

An interpretation is introduced with greatest probability of acceptance when it is within the grasp of the interviewee—"sensed but yet not clearly understood"; if it results from a shared understanding developed cooperatively to which client and worker each makes a contribution.

The introduction of an interpretation may be preceded by the interviewer's efforts to help the interviewee work toward it by asking questions that stimulate the interviewee's ideas of possible connections between seemingly separate events and seemingly unrelated behaviors and feelings: "How do you figure it . . . ," "How do you understand this . . ."; "What are your own ideas about this . . . ," "How do you size that up . . . ?"

If the client disconfirms the suggested interpretation—"no that's not the way it is," "I don't buy that,"—the interpretation was either off the mark or presented before the client was psychologically ready to consider it. The client may not reject it overtly, but may ignore it or respond defensively or with resistance, or become confused. In these instances it would seem desirable for the interviewer to back off from the interpretation and not press it. Negative reactions suggest that the client is not as yet ready or that the interpretation is invalid.

In the following interchange an interpretation is tentatively offered, explained, and finally accepted. A social worker is talking with a young mother who is anxious about continuing conflict with her 6-year-old daughter.

INTERVIEWER: Okay. Just to help me understand, when she complains like that and she's feeling miserable, and you get angry at her, is there a feeling that somehow for you that you have to, want to, make things ideal for her so that she's happy?

INTERVIEWEE: Yeah.

INTERVIEWER: And that when she then complains like that, it makes you face the fact that things are less than ideal.

INTERVIEWEE: Yeah.

INTERVIEWER: And you get angry because they're not ideal, that there are difficulties and limitations in your situation.

INTERVIEWEE: That's really accurate. Cause I—you know, I fantisize that— in my fantasies everything is, you know, peaceful, loving, happy, and— and—it is. It's like a slap in the face when these disappointments come up. And then I think—I brush 'em off, like, you know, it's not going to be this way all the time. And I keep struggling to make things better. Even though it's just a minor thing like, you know, getting upset over not, you know, having broken a promise or something. It just seems too much to look at.

In the following, the interviewer recognizes the danger of making interpretations for the interviewee. The client is a teen-age, single, pregnant white girl.

RUTH: Like, at a party I can talk to people, but inside I am afraid.
WORKER: Of what? (Pause.) Maybe you're afraid that people won't like you?
RUTH (blowing her nose): Yes, I guess so.

The worker comments:

I think I could have waited out a longer pause before giving an interpretation. Perhaps she might have stated this reason herself—or maybe another reason—if I had let her.

The construction of interpretive statements or interpretive questions is usually that of a statement linked by the word "because" or a similar conjunction. The statement following the bridging conjunction embodies the inference that the interviewer recognizes but which is supposedly unrecognized or only partially recognized by the interviewee.

You spank Roger the way you do because this is the way your parents disciplined you.

You feel guilty and anxious about your brother's accident because sometime you hoped he would be out of your way.

As I get it, while you knew about contraceptives you failed to take precautions because maybe you wanted to get pregnant.

One can tie one piece of data in the present to another piece of data in the present. One can tie something happening in the present to something which happened in the past, perhaps during childhood. In either case, two apparently separate and unconnected events are hypothesized as having some connection, some relationship.

Interpretations can be offered at various levels of psychological depth and distance from the content presented by the client. Since the interpretation has to be acceptable to and accepted by, the interviewee if it is to have any effect, the initial interpretations of data should, advisedly, be close to the data presented.

INTERVIEWEE (15-year-old girl): My parents fight all the time and they talk of divorce. If they do, which they might, what's going to happen with me? I just feel terrible.
INTERPRETATION (level 1): You're worried about who will provide the love and care that you still need?
INTERPRETATION (level 2): You're worried about being abandoned like the time we talked about when you were in foster care.
INTERPRETATION (level 3): You're feeling upset about the things you did that might have increased the fighting between your parents like your dropping out of school.

Confrontation

Confrontation deals with incongruities between what the client says at one point and a contradictory statement made later on, between what is said and how it is said, between the fantasy of how the client sees herself and the reality of the impact of her behavior on others, between what the client says she wants and behavior which suggests otherwise. It sets, face to face, contradictory elements in the client's presentation. A confrontation presents discrepancies for acknowledgment and explicit examination. The definition of the word *confront* implies "bringing together to the front" so that what is communicated is clear and visible.

Confrontation has the effect of pulling the interviewee up short. The confrontation itself does not change behavior. It does, however, initiate reconsideration of behavior and suggests a possible need for change. By acting contrary to the usual social expectation that discrepancies and inconsistencies will be ignored, the interviewer sets up a new situation which requires resolution.

The interviewer calls attention to observed discrepancies, to inconsistencies, contradictions, distortions, evasions, and "stinking-thinking" rationalizations. It makes denial more difficult.

Confrontation stimulates self-examination. It presents the interviewee with a contradiction that she is invited to attempt to resolve. It is a challenge to the interviewee to face herself more honestly and realistically—an unpleasant, difficult exercise. The invitation to deal with it is often made explicit by concluding the confrontation statement with, "What do you think about what I just said?" or "What do you feel about this?"

The use of confrontation has gained acceptance and sanction as a result of the use of the "hot seat without an escape hatch" in encounter groups, sensitivity groups, EST, etc. It has gained incremental visibility through the use of confrontation in sociopolitical contexts as a technique in forcing social change.

Confrontation as contrasted with interpretation is more focused on description rather than explanation. Confrontation invites the client to provide his own explanation for contradictions, discrepancies, conflicts between the reality and fantasy. Interpretation provides for the interviewee's consideration of the interviewer's explanation of the meaning of the interviewee's behavior. Confrontation goes a step beyond interpretation. It is a more forceful, more active presentation of a hypothesis for the interviewee's validation or rejection presented not so much as an understanding that might possibly be true but as a conclusion that the interviewer believes is true.

Confrontation may be a necessary intervention with nonvoluntary interviewees who deny any problems and are very resistive to any attempts at helping. It is employed *deliberately* to develop some anxiety and uneasiness in the client.

Confrontation calls unmistakable attention to what is being avoided or not being said. It lets the client know what the interviewer thinks he knows about the situation and what needs to be openly talked about. To the client who was referred for counseling because of neglect of her children and who spends the first twenty minutes of the interview consistently talking about the rise in the cost of living, the interviewer might say directly: "I think we both are aware that we are together to discuss your care of the children. We would need to begin to discuss that now."

The interviewer may confront a client by pointing out clear differences between what the client says and what she does. "Talking the talk, and not walking the walk." To the client who details the great satisfaction and pleasure she gets from having her aged mother-in-law living with her after inquiring about nursing homes, the worker says: "The way you tell it it sounds wonderful. But then why a nursing home? I would imagine that it's not all that wonderful."

A 17-year-old girl, going to college in a small city and living with her parents, is complaining to the worker that her parents do not understand her, restrict her freedom, and are always "down on her." It's getting so she "can't stand it." The worker says, in confrontation:

But, it seems to me, you must be able to stand it, because you are talking about living here next year rather than finding an apartment or a dorm maybe.

A client who has been unable to hold a job for more than a few months because of his heavy drinking persists in describing himself as a "social drinker." In confronting the client, the worker says:

I notice that you keep calling yourself a "social drinker," as you did just now. You have been drinking about a quart a day for some time now. How much do you think you would need to drink in order to consider yourself an alcoholic rather than a social drinker?

The worker uses confrontation by pointing out differences between verbal and nonverbal behavior.

A lesbian is talking about her relationship with other women in the bank where she works.
CLIENT: Since I accept my sexual preference and feel comfortable about it, I am pretty relaxed when I have to work with other people.
WORKER: I wonder if you noticed that when you said what you just said

you lowered your eyes, turned your head away from me, and clenched your right hand into a fist. What you said doesn't seem to go with all of that.

One can confront by suggesting disbelief. "Did I understand you to say that you *never* felt any anger toward your children?"

There is a very natural, very human, tendency to say the socially acceptable things in our discussion of personally significant and/or socially controversial matters. We talk in platitudes about love for children, satisfaction on the job, happiness in our marriage, etc., so that we "look good." If rapport is sufficiently well established and there is some intimation that the interviewee might feel differently about such matters, it is helpful for the interviewer to say, "I know most people say that. But what do *you really think* (or feel) about that?"

A good confrontation involves not only explicitly pointing out that there appears to be some discrepancy or contradiction in the client's presentation. It also includes some details which provide the basis for the worker's statement that there is some inconsistency or discrepancy.

A mother of a 6-year-old boy, Carlo, who is so fearful of other children that he has been unable to remain in school, sees herself as an accepting, loving, permissive mother. The boy recently received a bike from his grandmother for Christmas. The mother has just finished detailing the fact that, fearful that Carlo may have an accident, she locked up the bike until he is older. This is one of a number of overprotective actions on the part of the mother. In response to the details of the story about the bike the social worker says:

You know, I don't get it. On the one hand you say that you would like Carlo to grow up and help him to be less dependent, and on the other hand you do things like this thing with the bike and your not letting him sleep overnight at a friend's house that we discussed last week, that tend to keep him dependent. The two things seem contradictory to me. How do you explain to yourself the inconsistency between what you say you want and what you tell me you do?

The social work interviewer is obligated to raise the questions for discussion that the interviewee would rather not think about. There is an element of confrontation in forcing the interviewee to consider these questions.

A college senior, Gail, with a long-standing relationship with a boy friend by whom she is pregnant, is discussing the possibility of abortion with a social worker in a family service agency. The worker raises the question as to whether or not the putative father has been involved in the decision. Gail indicates that she has not told him she is pregnant and does not plan to tell him. The worker asks:

Have you thought at all about how you would feel later on? That is, like . . . do you think that by not telling him, it would affect your relationship later in the future? I guess what I am asking you is if, say, you stayed together and got married, would it bother you in later years to have a secret from him and how would it affect your relationship, say, if you told him or he found out about it after it was done?

In commenting on this intervention, the worker notes that:

The way I came at the question was hesitant and somewhat garbled, but the idea behind the question was good. I felt it important to confront Gail with this type of question since I didn't think she would confront herself with it.

The decision to confront a client is based on something the interviewee actually said or did as observed by the interviewer. There should be less inference in a confrontation as contrasted with an interpretation.

The principle of contiguity suggests that confrontation use the client's most immediately antecedent statements and behavior: "Thinking about what you just said . . .," "Seeing what you are doing now with your hands and feet and your facial expression, and comparing that with what you are saying, it seems to me that . . ."

A male adolescent in a training school for boys has had a preliminary discussion with the residential social worker about his suppression of feelings about his parents. The worker is attempting to follow this up in the next interview, but the client is resistive, saying he really doesn't feel strongly about his parent. The worker, attempting confrontation, says:

WORKER: What about your angry feelings?
CLIENT: Aaagh . . . I stopped that . . . Oh God, let's talk about something else.
WORKER: Like the weather, bowling, snowmobiling . . . fun stuff, huh? It sounds to me like you don't feel safe talking about your angry feelings, so you want to change the subject.
CLIENT: I don't get angry anymore. (Joe's face is turning red; he is very angry right now. His voice is raised almost to a shout.)
WORKER: Oh yeh? Aren't you angry at me right now?

Like interpretation, intervention by confrontation is best made after a relationship is firmly established and when the interviewer has enough information to feel confident that there is some validity to the confrontation statement, when the client has herself indicated some beginning perception of the discrepancies, inconsistencies, mixed messages, etc., at which the confrontation is directed.

A young battered wife is very ambivalent about leaving her husband and has discussed her feelings a number of times with the worker without having taken any action. The worker in confrontation says:

You've got to make up your mind, Dolores. Every time we talk about it you say the same thing, but you never do anything about it. I realize that you might not be able to make that decision for good right now, but you have to do something to keep yourself from getting so upset all the time.

In commenting on her action, the worker says:

I'm pushing her pretty hard. I can only do this because my love and approval are very important to her. When her psychiatrist starts pushing her, she walks out on him. I was pretty sure of my position, or I wouldn't have been quite so strong.

A presumption in making a confrontation is that the interviewee is able but unwilling to deal with the contents to which attention is called. If the client is unable to deal with it, confrontation would be futile and injurious.

Confrontation must openly violate the etiquette code of social conversation whereby we make a deliberate effort not to face people with such observed discrepancies and inconsistencies. Because we have been trained to regard such probing as impolite and because it is contrary to our patterns of learned social behavior, confrontation may be difficult for the interviewer. The fact that it tends to evoke a hostile reaction in the interviewee reinforces reluctance to use such an intervention.

Since confrontation does involve a measure of unmasking self-deception necessary to the maintenance of a client's self-esteem, we need to recognize that it is a painful process for the interviewee. We need to recognize the pain being imposed and feel some concern. The interviewer should be candid and open but not coercive or punitive. The principle is to "confront without affronting."

Confrontation is not forced. It is not designed to "break down defenses," to shove unpalatable content down the interviewee's throat, to "make" her face facts squarely. It is designed to stimulate the interviewee to take a careful look at what needs to be considered and to help her feel free and safe enough to take that look.

There is a difference between assertiveness which makes for a helpful confrontation and aggressiveness which arouses anxiety, defensiveness, and hostility. The most important consideration is the spirit, the feeling tone, in which the intervention is made. The spirit of the good confrontation is not assault or intimidation but rather a desire to do whatever can be done to help the client. It is a neutral description of a significant aspect of the client's behavior presented forcefully and unambiguously, making it difficult for the client to avoid dealing with it.

Confrontation risks alienation. An approach sympathetically attuned to the effect the confrontation is likely to have on the interviewee reduces the possibility of alienation. If confrontation is an attack merely to provide ego satisfaction for the interviewer, or to force the interviewee to make a change to meet the needs of the interviewer, it is likely to evoke defensiveness and hostility. If engaged in out of empathic understanding of the needs of the client, out of understanding of what may induce client change to meet client needs, it may still be resisted but less actively and with less animosity.

Confrontation is a "loaded word" and rightfully so because it can be, and often is, used as a sanctioned opportunity for acting punitively and hostilely toward the interviewee. The interviewer can justify saying some punishing, nasty things, telling people off and putting people down, by rationalizing that it is in the service of a helpful confrontation.

Once again the basic attitude associated with the confrontation is as important or even more important than the content of the confrontation itself. If the challenging statement is said out of narcissistic desire to display how smart the interviewer is ("see how I can psyche you out, how I can read you"), it is likely to be resented. If it is said with an intent to satisfy the worker's aggressive feelings toward the client ("Now I gottcha—how are you going to weasel out of this"), it is likely to be communicated as a desire to hurt. If, however, it is said out of desire to understand the client better, out of a sense of puzzlement, a hope that it will enable the client to more effectively deal with his problem out of a concern to be helpful, it comes across differently and is likely to be reacted to differently. As Hammer says, "It is important not to get used to tearing away people's masks so that you no longer hear the rip" (1950:150). The best confrontation mirrors the Bible's admonition to "speak the truth in love."

Confrontation creates less of a threat to the worker–client relationship if the confronting statement can be selected so as to focus on strengths rather than limitations. Mr. P, a supervisor in a machine tool plant, is very assertive on the job when supervising his men or when facing plant administrators about worker grievances, but he expressed considerable resentment over the fact that he generally feels he has to go where his wife wants to go and do what his wife wants to do, on his time off the job. The interviewer says:

Look. How is this. You act one way on the job—assertive, talking-up, kind-of-courageous, and another way off the job—unassertive, meekly going along. It's like you're two different people.

Because confrontation nakedly exposes what the interviewee is often most anxious to hide from herself and others, a successful confrontation depends not only on the interviewer's skill in confrontation or from a relationship which provides an effective context for confrontation, but it also depends on the interviewee's readiness to explore whatever the confrontation invites.

Little of value is gained for the client if a confrontation results in a change of client behavior out of a desire to please, placate, or appease the worker. This is a fake acceptance of the confrontation message.

Sharing Information

While almost every interview involves some flow of information from the interviewee to the interviewer, some interviews involve a reverse flow of information. Social work interviewers provide necessary information to the client, information about the eligibility requirements of some social service programs, procedures to be followed in applying for benefits, the nature of foster care service, the legalities of adoption, family planning alternatives, etc. Some interviews may involve sharing information about the diagnostic findings of a team assessment, as in the case of a mentally retarded child. Such interviews have been termed "informing interviews" (Svarstad and Lipton 1977). Providing information is an intervention which contributes toward problem solving.

The significance of sharing information relevant to the problem may be too easily dismissed. Sometimes people have difficulty in effectively dealing with their problems simply as a result of a lack of knowledge. Providing information may show the client the problem in a new perspective or may provide unrecognized alternate possibilities to consider. Correcting misinformation by providing accurate information may prevent mistakes. Sharing specialized information is an important and relevant intervention procedure in social work interviewing.

Wherever possible the worker should provide information, if available, to ameliorate fear and anxiety based on misinformation. Providing the factual assurance that masturbation does not lead to insanity or that most children born to teen-agers are not deformed, or that the disabled child of a retiring worker will continue to draw social security benefits after the worker's death is itself reassuring and supportive.

In communicating information the interviewer has to clearly and accurately know the factual details—the specific eligibility requirement of a program that might be helpful to the client, the actual procedures in making application, etc. The nature and amount of detail to be communicated should be judiciously selected so that only the most pertinent and relevant information is shared. There is a danger of information overload and too much, too quickly, may leave the interviewee more confused than ever. Timing is important since receptivity to information depends on interviewee readiness to hear it. Communication of information should come at the point of the interview when it is most meaningful and when the interviewee is highly motivated to listen. Information should be provided incrementally in digestible dosages as the client needs additional information. There may be some necessity for patient repetition. What is crystal clear to the interviewer because of familiarity may be very confusing to the interviewee. Solicitation of feedback while providing the information may help the interviewer determine what is getting across and what is being missed.

If available, printed notices, brochures, pamphlets, etc., are helpful supplements to the interviewer's communication of information.

Special care needs to be given in sharing information felt to be hurtful or derogatory. In protecting the interviewee and in self-protection the interviewer may be purposely vague and indirect. Having to tell parents that their child has been found to be mentally retarded, or a couple that their application for adoption has been rejected, can create anxiety for the informing interviewer and hostility in the interviewee. But just because clients are more likely, in such instances, to deny and distort the information communicated, the interviewer has to be more than ordinarily clear in what he says.

Advice

Advice is an intervention which contributes to meeting the problem-solving responsibilities of the interviewer.

Reviewing tapes of interviews and categorizing interviewer response indicates that some 5 to 8 percent of social work interview interventions can be classed as advice (Mullen 1968; Reid and Shyne 1969; Ewalt and Kutz 1976).

Giving information is neutral. It provides resources for decision making. Advice is biased and directs a decision. However interviewers advise and suggest by selectively presenting information that favors a particular course of action. In doing this the interviewer is often not explicit that he is advising.

The word *advice* covers a number of different, albeit somewhat similar, activities. It covers explicit directions as to what the client "should" or "ought" to do. It includes "suggestions" of alternatives for the client's consideration, and it includes questions worded in such a manner as to point in the direction the interviewer hopes the client will go.

Thus, one can say "It seems to me that, having heard how senile your parents are, you should find a nursing home for them," or "It seems to me the physical condition of your parents as you described it is like many other families I have known who found a nursing home to be a desirable solution to their parents' problem," or "Given the physical condition of your parents, have you ever thought of a nursing home as a possibility?"

The recommendation is essentially the same in each instance. The gradation is, however, from an imperative directive statement which dictates to the client, through a tentative suggestion which raises the recommendation for consideration, to an even more tentative question which manipulates the client's mind-set to focus on the recommendation. The interventions are progressively less directive.

Advice can vary in the degree of directiveness and also in the degree of explicitness, some being more subtle than others. The technique of "modeling" is, in effect, a subtle nonverbal form of suggesting the client's adoption of certain behavior.

There are a variety of attenuated, soft, forms of advice giving. As a question: "How do you think it might work out if you tried . . . ?" As self-disclosure: "I once faced a similar kind of problem and what worked for me was that . . ."

Interviewers often make suggestions and give advice without being explicitly aware that they are doing it.

INTERVIEWEE: So I had to work late and Doris had to stay with the baby-sitter till 7 o'clock, and she was very upset, and I felt very sorry and guilty.
INTERVIEWER: You really shouldn't feel guilty because coming late wasn't your fault.

The interviewer is advising the mother to change her feeling about the incident.

Simple statements like "Perhaps you need to get out more by yourself," or "You should try picking up on your knitting again because it seemed to give you so much satisfaction," or "It might be helpful to continue taking the medicine regularly" all embody advice.

In each instance the intervention seeks to influence the interviewee to take a particular course of action. This is the essence of advice. It is designed to encourage or discourage some behavior attitude or feeling on the part of the interviewee through the open expression of the interviewer's opinion. It is, in its varied forms, a procedure of direct influence.

The advisability of offering advice has been a controversial matter in social work for some time. It was felt that offering advice to the interviewee on how she might solve her problems and how she should deal with her life was a manifestation of arrogance on the part of the interviewer. How could he possibly know enough about the interviewee's total situation to be able to advise her? Objections to giving advice were also based on the fact that the tactic shifted responsibility for solving the problem from the interviewee to the interviewer and that it encouraged greater dependency on the part of the interviewee. Furthermore, giving advice has been viewed as futile and ineffectual—the interviewee is not likely to take it. It is a violation of social work ethics since it denies the client the right to her own decisions.

Even when advice is offered by professionals who have very considerable specific expertise for the problems they deal with it is often ignored. Studies of medical patients' adherence to the doctor's advice show that "an estimated one-third to one-half of all patients fail to follow fully the treatment prescribed for them" (Stone 1979:36).

However, it has been recognized that giving advice might be justified in some situations and with some groups of clients despite its dangers and shortcomings. In stressful crisis situations where the client is immobilized and very depressed, with mentally incompetent and with younger clients, the need for giving advice is reluctantly acknowledged.

Empirical studies of clients' expectations regarding advice and their response to it indicate that such interventions are useful problem-solving procedures. Although some interviewees do not expect advice, do not welcome it, and resent it, the majority of interviewees come to the social agency with some expectation that advice will be offered. They are receptive to the offer of advice and generally make effective use of advice in working on their problems (Reid and Shapiro 1969; Mayer and Timms 1970; Ewalt and Kutz 1976; Davis 1978; Maluccio 1979).

Feedback from clients indicates that they were more frequently dissatisfied when too little advice was offered but almost never complained of having had too much advice given to them. Maluccio, in summarizing client feedback, notes:

Clients from diverse socio-economic groups indicated that they expected the worker to play a more active role by expressing opinions, giving advice and offering suggestions. While they accept the ultimate responsibility in resolving their problems, they clearly looked to the social worker as the expert to suggest options and guidelines. Over half of the clients expressed dissatisfaction with what they perceived as the worker's failure to offer advice and guidance. (1979:74)

A study by Davis (1978) demonstrates that while the initial reaction of many clients to advice-offering interventions was negative, critical, or resistive in the interview, the same client, in a follow-up research interview, indicated that the advice had been helpful. Even if the advice itself was not followed, the explicit suggestion stimulated alternative efforts to solve the problem. The advice had the effect of actively engaging the client in problem solving if only by giving her something specific to react against.

Withholding advice the client expects has its disadvantages. The client may feel that there is a lack of interest, a lack of concern, a lack of willingness to help and may evaluate the worker as someone without understanding who is incompetent to help. Consequently if there has been a request for advice which the interviewer plans to ignore, some explicit and convincing explanation for the decision needs to be given to the client.

We are expected to have some knowledge, some expertise, about social problems and the variety of alternatives to their amelioration. We are supposed to have had some repetitive experience with the probable consequences of the various solutions available. All of this gives the social worker the legitimate grounds for offering advice and making suggestions.

Failure to offer advice where appropriate may follow from an excessively rigid interpretation of self-determination. The worker might hold the attitude that unless the client herself initiates a plan it is in every case doomed to failure. Withholding advice when appropriate may also be punitive—a denial to the client of what might be helpful.

Interviews in child guidance clinics around parent–child problems showed more frequent use of advice-giving interventions than was true for interviews in a family agency around marital problems. Workers are apparently more certain of their ground discussing child discipline and child rearing than they are discussing marriage and divorce decisions.

It would seem, then, that rather than be rejected out of hand as an intervention procedure that has no legitimate place in the social work interview, advice and its variations need to be given more positive consideration. Here are some guidelines to observe in offering advice.

1. It should be clear that the request for advice comes from the client and is not a manifestation of the needs of the worker. Giving advice, whether

or not it is accepted and acted on, is intrinsically pleasurable: it parades the worker's smartness and wisdom; it is a gift to the client with the expectation that the worker will be liked more for having offered it; it enables the worker to "do" something for the client if the client isn't sure how the worker can be of help. All of these speak to workers' needs for offering advice without reference to whether or not clients expect it, ask for it, or want it.

2. The advice offered in response to client need should be grounded as much as possible in the knowledge base of the profession. The advice should derive from some knowledge that what is being suggested has a high probability of having the desired effect, the nature of the effect being shared with the client. If we advise the parent to take some particular course of action in dealing with a hyperactive child, we should know something of the research and/or practice wisdom which shows that certain ameliorative effects are quite likely to result.

3. However objectively sensible a recommendation might be, the particular context in which the client has to implement the suggestion may make it difficult if not impossible. Consequently, consideration must be given to the client's situation, frame of reference, the social norms of her group, the degree of support or opposition the suggestion is likely to elicit from the client's significant others.

4. Advice in most instances should be offered tentatively, giving the client freedom to reject it and encouraging honest feedback about the client's reaction. It should be offered in such a way that the client does not feel obligated or coerced to accept it. This implies that the interviewer has to feel comfortable about having his advice rejected. The most desirable approach is to use the least coercive, least restrictive degree of influence necessary to achieve the objective.

5. Wherever feasible advice should be given in conjunction with other interventions such as support: "If you do decide to attempt to learn an occupational skill through the WIN program, as I am suggesting, I think you are capable of succeeding in the program."

6. Advice should be offered only after the client has been helped to explore her own suggestions for dealing with her situation. Doing this answers the objection that giving advice preempts the client's opportunity to solve her own problems by herself, which is clearly desirable.

7. Receptivity to and acceptance of advice is maximized in the context of a good relationship (Stone 1979:39; Evalt and Kutz 1976:16). Consequently advice should not be given early in the interview or early in the series of interviews. Some opportunity for the participants to get to know each other is not only important in giving the relationship an opportunity to develop and solidify, it also gives the interviewer the op-

portunity to learn enough about the situation so as to offer sensible advice.

Support

Another kind of interviewer intervention has sustainment or support of the interviewee as a primary objective. Support is evidenced by overt expressions, both verbal and nonverbal, of understanding, reassurance, concern, sympathy, encouragement. It includes expressions of praise and appreciation of the client's abilities, qualities, coping efforts. Such intervention gives active recognition and approval of the client's qualities and achievements.

The atmosphere of psychological safety and acceptance of a good relationship is in itself supportive. The facilitative attitudinal approach toward the interviewee discussed earlier is, in and of itself, supportive. The interpersonal atmosphere created by behaving in accordance with this approach makes the client feel comfortable, safe, relieved. The very fact that the worker is available, involved in helping with the problem, is in itself supportive. The interviewee is no longer struggling alone with her problem.

However at this point the discussion focuses on more explicit acts of support in facilitating problem solving. Specific supportive interventions go beyond a general supportive context. They are designed to affirm, validate the fact that the worker sees the client as capable, on the right track, having some of the strengths necessary to deal effectively with the problems (Nelsen 1980). This is what the interviewer is saying, in effect, when he praises the client, indicates approval of certain things the client has done or said, expresses confidence in the client's plans.

Sustainment or support intervention communicates confidence in the client's ability to cope with her problems. The hoped-for outcome is that the client then is in a better position to mobilize resources for problem solving.

The intent of support is to relieve psychological pain, to affirm and reinforce the client's ego strengths, and to replenish depleted self-esteem.

Support is demonstrated in communicating an appreciation of the interviewee's efforts to solve her problem in a recognition of the real difficulties she is encountering in dealing with her problem. They include short interactions, such as: "I think I can understand that," or "That must have been very difficult," or "I think anybody would get upset as you did about a situation like this," or "You seemed to have handled that very well."

Following a client's statement that she thinks her son's daydreaming in school is related to the fact that she and her husband have been fighting, the worker says: "I see you have given this a great deal of thought. You might be right."

An older client who has joined a senior citizens club after considerable hesitancy is supported by praise by the worker: "I know that it takes a lot of courage to do this, and I am glad that you were able to join."

An inhibited pre-teen who had previously expressed very little of his feelings became very agitated when he learned that he might be removed from a foster home that he liked very much and returned to his own home. He expressed considerable feeling about the move and very openly talked about his negative feelings toward his own parents. The interviewer, throughout, nonverbally showed encouragement to his continuing by nodding and facial gestures. At the end the interviewer complimented the client on his awareness of his feelings and his ability and willingness to articulate them.

A young adult in remission from a psychotic break for which she had been hospitalized began to dress more neatly and carefully as she moved to full recovery. The worker recognized this and complimented her on the gradual improvement in the way she dressed. She said, "You look very nice in that dress. I have been noticing recently you seem to be giving more care to the way you look. It really looks good."

Because such interventions come easily and naturally and have been frequently previously employed by the interviewer in nonprofessional interactions, they present a danger of indiscriminate overuse in the interview. If misused they might lead the client to feel that her problem was disrespectfully minimized or that the interviewer failed to understand the real difficulties in her situation.

Rather than helping a client feel less anxious they might increase client anxiety because they suggest that the worker perceives the client as more capable than she actually is. This might be felt as an increased burden of having to live up to the worker's unwarranted expectations.

The principal caution to observe in the use of support intervention is that it must be based in reality. Praise, approval, expressions of confidence that the client is capable or that the situation will get better should only be offered if the assessment squares with the facts.

Expressions designed to comfort and "cheer up" based on little but hope and faith are viewed by the client as a dishonest, disrespectful con. "Don't worry. I am sure things will get better and that you're going to be all right" has a hollow ring and leads the client to worry about the worker's understanding of the seriousness of the situation. To be effective, support requires some conviction on the part of the client in the worker's sincerity and accurate judgment.

Congruence between verbal and nonverbal communication, although important in all situations, is of critical importance in offering support.

Most studies of the relative frequency of sustainment or supportive intervention show it to be from 5 to 10 percent of the worker's efforts. It is supposed that this is supplemented by much nonverbal and hence unrecorded supportive intervention. However, in a study of casework service to families of children at risk for foster care placement, support was clearly the most predominant casework technique used. Of the variety of interview interventions only "support" showed a statistically significant relationship with "outcome," and the client's perception of the helpfulness of the agency (Sherman et al. 1973:126–27).

Supportive interventions have an element of evaluation associated with them. The worker has made an assessment of what the client has done or is planning to do and has found it desirable and worthy of approval. This makes some interviewers hesitant since it seems to be inconsistent with a neutral nonjudgmental stance. However, the empirical evidence available tends to show that supportive interventions do have a generally desirable effect in helping.

Empirical Studies of Interventions Employed

Having reviewed the variety of interventions that social workers might make in the interview, what does the research show about the kinds of interventions social workers actually do make?

Hollis (1967) developed a systematic categorization of the activities of the social work interviewer. The system was applied in her own research on what social workers did in the interview and modifications of the system were applied by other social work researchers in their examination of social work interviews (Mullen 1968; Reid and Shyne 1969; Cohen and Krause 1971; Sherman et al. 1973; Reid 1978; Fortune 1979; Rosen and Mutschler 1982). Other social work researchers have employed alternative systems of categorization in studying what workers do when interviewing (Shulman 1973).

Human service professionals associated with disciplines other than social work have developed other categorization schemes of interview activity. The microcounseling group (Ivey and Authier 1978) talk of attending skills, designed to stimulate and sustain the interviewee in sharing. These include "minimal encouragements," paraphrase, reflection of feeling, closed and open questions, and summarizations. A second group of skills is designed to influence the behavior, attitudes, and feelings of the interviewee. These include giving directions, advice, suggestion, information, interview self-disclosure, confrontation, and interpretation. Despite differences there is some considerable overlap in the activities engaged in by the interviewer as seen by different groups studying the interview in human service context.

While the definitions of interventions are not standardized and differ somewhat from study to study, there is some general overall agreement regarding the frequency with which various interventions are employed.

The findings of such research tend to be very diverse depending on whether the interview selected for analysis is an interview early or late in the contact with the client and the nature of the client's problem. In general, however, the workers were found to be involved, with varying degrees of frequency, in four different kinds of activity. They say and do things to *explore* the client's situation, to learn about the nature of the problem. They say or do things to *structure* the interview situation in clarifying the role of interviewer and interviewee. They say and do things in providing emotional *support* to the client, reassuring, encouraging, sympathizing, showing concern, understanding, acceptance, and they say and do things designed to *effect some change* in the client's perception of his situation, some change in the client's attitudes, feeling and behavior. In doing this they offer directive advice and suggestions, provide information, raise questions and make comments that encourage selective reflection, engage in clarification, interpretation, and confrontation. Thus, interventions are classified as exploratory, supportive, structuring, directive, or reflective.

Exploration of the client's situation (receiving information from the client "about relevant or past situation attitudes and behavior" and giving information to the client about resources and services) and supportive interventions during which the "worker expresses reassurance, understanding, encouragement or sympathy with the client's feelings, situations and efforts to cope with the situation" were among the interventions very frequently employed (Sherman et al. 1973:259; Grinnell and Kyte 1975:315; Jones, Neuman, and Shyne 1976:68). While receiving information may have therapeutic, cathartic, and reassuring implications, the primary purpose of the worker's intervention was to gain knowledge rather than effect change in the client's behavior or attitude.

Directive interventions during which the worker attempts through "advice, recommendations or suggestions to promote or discourage particular client behaviors and courses of action" (Sherman et al. 1973:59, 138; Jones, Neuman, and Shyne 1976:68) is frequently employed in social work interviews.

Reflective interventions during which the "worker raises questions or gives explanation to increase the client's understanding of his own behavior attitudes, of his situation, the consequences of his behavior and the reactions of others to him," are less frequently employed. These include interventions such as confrontation and interpretation.

Fortune (1981) recapitulated and organized the findings of a total of nine different research projects which had, by 1981, attempted to explicitly identify through the use of the Hollis or Reid typologies what social work interviewers do when they interact with the client in the interview. The summarization of findings suggests a somewhat different picture of the worker activity than that outlined above.

Combining the research results of the various projects, Fortune found that the worker's principal communications, by far, were concerned with exploration with the client of her current reality situation and her behavior and attitudes regarding it (40 percent overall) and with communication designed to help the client understand cognitively the causes and consequences of her behavior (38 percent overall). Little emphasis was given to exploration of early life developmental data. Somewhat more emphasis (6.4 percent overall) was given to direct influence—suggestions, advice, and recommendations designed to influence client's decisions and behaviors in a specific direction.

The fact that the more recently completed studies in the group indicate a greater use of direct influence (advice–suggestion) interventions may indicate a changing attitude toward the use of such techniques.

Sustainment and reassurance "expected to be a fairly large component of practitioner activity was surprisingly infrequent" (p. 99) (4.6 percent overall). That such communication was so infrequently noted is explained by the fact that the typologies depend on verbal communication and that sustainment and reassurance may be more frequently communicated nonverbally.

The difference in frequency with which particular interviewer interventions are found in different studies may depend on the time in the point of contact when the interview took place. The balance of intervention in the first or second interview is likely to be considerably different from the balance of intervention in the fifteenth or sixteenth interview.

One might envision a sliding scale which reflects a change in the nature of interventions employed over the course of a number of sequential interviews. At the beginning of the contact there is more emphasis on interventions which are supportive and accepting, which express concern and a willingness to help. Intervention at this point follows rather than leads the client and employs the client's frame of reference. These include interventions such as reflection, paraphrasing, minimal encouragements. As a relationship is developed the emphasis on the sliding scale gradually shifts to more leading rather than following activity by the interviewer. These include more active interventions designed to effect change, more frequent challenges to the client's frame of reference. The emphasis shifts from activity concerned with establishing a relationship and learning about the client situation to activity concerned with actively using the relationship to effect change, to a problem solving orientation, while still being supportive, accepting, respectful, and empathic. There is increasingly greater emphasis on interventions designed to move the interviewee from where she is in reference to her problem to where she wants to be. Advice, suggestion, interpretation, and confrontation are more actively employed in this stage of the process.

Within the frame of a single interview the same shift might take place in an attenuated form. The early part of the interview is located at the acceptance end of the sliding scale emphasizing communication of the core facilitative conditions and those interventions designed to assist the interviewee to share her problems as openly as possible. As the interviewer confirms for the client that this is a psychologically safe, understanding, respectful context, and as the interviewer develops a clearer picture of the problem that needs to be resolved, there is a shift toward the directive end of the sliding scale. The shift is toward more active involvement of the interviewer in problem solving, active involvement in helping, actual employment of interventions directed toward influencing changes in feelings and behaviors. At this point the interviewer may sound less accepting and more judgmental. If early in the contact the client was free to be herself, however she was, if changes are to take place, being as she is needs to be challenged. If early in the interview the interviewer needs to communicate a caring willingness to help, in the later part of the interview, he has to demonstrate an ability and competence in actually being helpful.

CHAPTER 9

Developmental Phase: Questions and Techniques of Questioning

Asking questions is a multipurpose intervention. As a consequence of the variety of purposes it serves in the interview, asking questions is probably the most frequently employed intervention in the social work interview. Questions are used to extend the range and depth of the interview, to help in problem solving, to make transitions. Questions stimulate and energize the interviewee to share both factual and affective information which the interviewer needs in order to be helpful. Questions instigate exploration of different content areas and particular content areas at different levels of emotionality.

Questions are used to encourage the interviewee to tell his story. Once the interviewee starts his presentation they are used in obtaining elaboration, clarification, explanation of what is being said. Good questioning helps the interviewee to organize his presentation and ensures that he will include all the relevant material.

Questions are also used to stimulate problem-solving thinking and feeling. They help stimulate the interviewee to think about his problem situation in an explicit, systematic way. Questions directed to clarifying the situation for the interviewer also have the effect of clarifying the situation for the interviewee to himself.

Questions have a latent training function. They model, for the interviewee, the interviewer's approach to problems. For instance, a series of questions which directs a client's attention to how he reacted to a particular situation, what he thought about dealing with it, how he finally decided on the action taken, implies that his behavior was not haphazard or accidental, that people's behavior is purposive. The sequence of the questions is based on the interviewer's presumption, implicitly communicated by her questions, that there are reasons that might explain people's behavior.

Questions have the function of socializing an interviewee to the requirements of his role. A question asked about some content communicates the differential significance of this content. If the interviewer elects to ask about it, it must have some importance. Questions which focus on feelings indicate to the interviewee that this is a matter of relevance to social work interviews. A question which follows up on what the interviewee is saying, requesting further information, indicates that the client is on the right track and what he is talking about has relevance.

General Classifications: Open and Closed Questions

Questions may be classified in terms of a number of dimensions. One is the amount of freedom or restriction the question offers the interviewee. By focusing on specific aspects of the situation, the closed question restricts the scope of the answer the interviewee can offer. The open question, on the other hand, gives the interviewee the responsibility, and opportunity, of selecting his answer from a larger number of possible responses. The interviewee has the opportunity of revealing his own subjective frame of reference and of selecting those elements in the situation which he regards as of greatest concern. Open-ended, nondirective questions also communicate clearly that the interviewee has considerable responsibility for, and freedom in, participating in the interview and determining interview content and direction.

"What brings you to the agency?" "What would you like to talk about?" "Where would you like to begin?" and "What seems to be bothering you?" are all relatively open-ended questions. "What seems to be bothering you about the children?" "What seems to be bothering you about what the doctor told you?" and "What seems to be bothering you about school?" are all more restricting questions that define the frame of reference for the content of the response.

It might be well to note that questions are not dichotomously either open or close ended. There is a whole continuum of different degrees of freedom between wide open questions such as "Tell me what brings you here" to very restricted questions such as, "Do you have any children?" Questions then might be open-ended, moderately closed or tightly closed.

"What would you like to talk about?" "Where would you like to begin?" are the most neutral nondirective openings. "Could you tell me something about your problem?" directs attention and focuses on "problem." "Could you tell me how you think we can be of help?" directs attention to what the client wants from the agency. As contrasted with the first two openings, the second two are more restrictive.

The following series of questions moves from an open to a progressively more closed format. The setting is a child guidance or family service interview.

Before this happened, what was your life like?

What was your life like as a child?

When you were growing up, how did you get along with your family?

When you were a child, how did you get along with your parents?

When you were a child, how did you get along with your mother?

When you were a child and you did something wrong, what did your mother do in disciplining you?

When you were a child and you got into fights with your brothers and sisters, how did your mother handle it?

When you were a child and you got into fights with your brothers and sisters, how did you feel about the way your mother handled the situation?

Each question successively narrows the area of the interviewee's experience to which attention is directed. The first question is open to any period prior to the event which brought the client to the agency. The second question restricts the scope temporarily to childhood but permits the interviewee to select for discussion any sector of childhood experience—relationship with parents, with siblings, with peers, school experience, leisure time activities, attitude toward the community, economic situation at home, etc. The final questions direct attention to one particular relationship, during one time period, i.e., the mother-child relationship during childhood, in a very specific context, disciplining in response to sibling conflict. The scope of answers solicited by the final questions is more narrow than that permitted by the first questions. The next to the last question calls for an objective description of the mother's handling of the situation. The last question calls for a subjective emotional response to the same situation.

Open-ended questions have their advantages and disadvantages. While appropriate in some situations, they are clearly inappropriate in others.

ADVANTAGES OF OPEN-ENDED QUESTIONS

Open questions have the advantage of giving the interviewee a measure of control over the interview. The interviewer invites the client to talk about some very broad area of concern, but suggests to the interviewee that she is interested in anything the interviewee might select to say about this. Such questions permit the interviewee greater discretion, maneuverability, choice, and thus permit the interviewee to introduce significant material that the interviewer may not have thought to ask about. The interviewer may, as a consequence, learn more of pertinence about the interviewee's situation than if she had asked a series of more closed questions.

Open questions have the advantage of not limiting the interviewee's response through the restrictiveness of their formulation. Much of interest and concern to the client may be missed because pertinent questions were not raised and the client had no autonomous opportunity to introduce these considerations.

Open-ended questions permit the interviewee to select for early discussion the matters which are of greatest concern to him. If these matters are not raised early in the interview, the interviewee's strong, unexpressed concerns interfere with his ability to focus on the questions raised by the interviewer.

Open-ended questions are more likely than closed questions to provide information about the interviewee's feelings and intensity of feelings about his situation and are more likely to provide information about the interviewee's explanation of his attitudes and behavior.

Open-ended questions have a positive effect on the expressive-relationship aspects of the interviewee. An interviewee is gratified when given a greater measure of freedom in permitting to tell his story in his own way. He responds warmly to the implication communicated by the interviewer that he is capable of adequately exploring his situation and that the interviewer has confidence in his ability to tell his story in his own way. Such questions further communicate a respect for the individuality and uniqueness of the interviewee. A standardized series of questions tends to suggest uniformity in the problem configurations people face. Open-ended questions imply that this interviewee and his problem is somewhat different.

Open-ended questions permit a greater degree of catharsis than close-ended questions, providing a greater element of support and relief.

Open-ended questions generate an atmosphere of greater mutuality in the interview interaction. By contrast a series of closed questions evokes a feeling that the interviewee's role is that of passive supplier of answers to the questions that are of interest to the interviewer.

Because closed questions can be and often are answered with a limited response on the part of the interviewee, such questions impose a heavy burden of activity on the interviewer. She has to be constantly formulating the next question. Open-ended questions shift the burden of activity to the interviewee.

DISADVANTAGES OF OPEN-ENDED QUESTIONS

Open-ended questions have a high component of ambiguity. The interviewer is deliberately unspecific about the answer she is trying to elicit. Ambiguity encourages interviewee verbal productivity. At the same time, it may be puzzling to the interviewee who has a limited tolerance for ambiguity.

Open-ended questions are threatening to the interviewee who has little experience and/or competence in the role of interviewee. For such an interviewee, open-ended questions give him little structure, little direction, little guidance about what he is supposed to talk about and how he is supposed to talk about it. He may be embarrassed because he does not know how to organize his presentation and finds that he has little to say.

If the interviewee responds to an open-ended, nondirective question with a detailed account of some relevant significant aspect of his situation, the interviewer has no problem. However, the answer to a beginning question such as "Could you tell me about the situation which brings you to the agency?" may be "Well, I really don't know where to begin." The interviewer then faces the problem of helping the interviewee to tell his story. A more specific general question is required, such as "What has been troubling you recently?" or "What made you decide to come here?"

In one case the open-ended question, "Would you like to tell me something about your situation," was answered by the following request for clarification, "What would you like to know?" Moderately broad close-ended questions might help such a client to focus, to recall relevant material, and to structure the presentation.

CLOSE-ENDED QUESTIONS

Closed questions have their utility and appropriateness when the interviewee is uncertain as to how to proceed, where the situation appears confusing, and where definite information is needed by the interviewer.

Closed questions are appropriately employed to provide greater clarity and greater focus to the interview. The interviewer uses the closed question at some point to exercise greater control of content and give direction to the interview.

The closed question helps narrow the scope of the interview and limits introduction of extraneous and irrelevant content by the garrulous interviewee.

Close-ended questions can help the reticent interviewee to get started and develop some momentum in participating in the interview.

A series of closed questions can be used to slow down the interaction and reduce the degree of emotionality of an interviewee who is displaying an intensity of feeling which might create problems for achieving the purposes of the interview. Closed questions help "cool" the interviewee who is too open too early, sharing content he may later resentfully regret having shared.

On the other hand close-ended questions may sometimes be used in introducing a sensitive topic which the interviewee may be hesitant to bring up in response to open-ended questions. A more direct question may appropriately be employed to introduce content that the interviewee needs encouragement to discuss. Such content would then not likely be spontaneously introduced by the interviewer in response to an open-ended question.

Closed questions provide cues which stimulate the memory for retrieval of information. Open questions require information retrieval without much stimulating or guiding cues.

An interviewer with limited time available may deliberately opt for closed questions. Open questions may be time consuming in that much of the client's talk in response to open questions may have limited relevance to the purpose of the interview.

As is true for most interview techniques, the different kinds of question formulations are not, in themselves, good or bad. They are merely appropriate or inappropriate at different stages of the interview and at different stages with different kinds of interviewees.

Nondirective, open questions are generally more appropriate in the early part of an interview. At this point, when the interviewee knows everything about his situation and the interviewer knows nothing, maximum freedom should be extended to give the interviewee the opportunity to talk about whatever is of concern to him.

Having helped the interviewee say what he wants and needs to communicate, through a few broad open questions, the interviewer then can use more restricted, closed questions to fill in details. Even later in the interview, as a new subject area is introduced for discussion, it is best to start with an open-ended question to give the interviewee the choice of approach to the new content.

The interview as a totality may resemble a funnel beginning with more frequent open-ended questions, ending with more detailed, closed questions. But within the interview itself there may be a series of smaller funnels, as each new area is introduced by an open-ended question. Within the exploration of this particular segment, this is followed by increasingly ss open-ended questions.

he appropriateness of open or closed questions varies with the interviewee. Nondirective, open questions may be very appropriate with so-phisticated interviewees who have a clear grasp of their role and the capac-ity to implement it. They need very little direction and structure from the interviewer to fulfill the purposes of the interview. Open questions impose heavy demands on the interviewee to select and organize his responses, demands that experienced interviewees can meet.

OTHER DIMENSIONS

Questions may further be classified in terms of *responsibility*. Direct and indirect questions are differentiated in this way. Direct questions ask about the interviewee's own response to a situation, a response for which he takes responsibility. Indirect questions solicit a response for which responsibility is diffuse. The following questions are presented first in the direct and then in the indirect format:

How do you feel about your job?
What's the feeling in your unit about the job?

What's your feeling about applying for assistance?
How do you think most people feel about applying for assistance?

Questions are also differentiated by the *level of abstraction* to which they direct attention. A question such as "What hobbies do you have?" is some-what more abstract than "What do you do in your leisure time?" "How do you discipline the children?" is more abstract than "Think back to the last time one of your children did something which made you mad. What did you do then?"

Questions may be classified in terms of *antecedents*. Those questions that derive from interviewee communications are said to have interviewee an-tecedents. Questions that derive from what the interviewer has said might be labeled questions with interviewer antecedents. Whenever possible and appropriate, once interaction has been initiated, the interviewer's ques-tions or comments should derive from and respond to what the interviewee has said, his interests and preoccupations. Furthermore, questions and comments are most understandable when they use the interviewee's own words or phrases.

Questions can be classified in terms of *differentiated focus*. For example, they can focus on different time periods. The interviewer can ask about past events, current events, or future events. Questions can have the thinking, feeling, and behavior of the interviewee as their point of refer-ence, or they can focus on the thinking and behavior of significant other persons related to the interviewee. "How does your husband feel about having a homemaker in the home?" (time: now; person focus: other; activity: feeling). "Once the children are placed in foster care, in what ways do you think your husband's feeling toward you might change?" (time: future; person focus: other; activity: thinking). "What was your feeling when you learned your wife had been hurt in the accident?" (time: past; person focus: interviewee; activity: feeling). "What do you think is the cause for your reluctance to go to school?" (time: present; person focus: interviewee; activity: thinking).

Probe Questions

Probing by the interviewer ensures that significant but general statements are not accepted as such. It is not a cross-examination technique. It is rather a judicious process of explication which permits the interviewee and interviewer to see the situation in greater, more clarifying detail. If an adoptive applicant says that she loves children and gets pleasure from her contacts with them, the interviewer tries to fill out this statement through probing. What kind of contact has she had with children? Under what circumstances? What exactly did she do with them? What was pleasurable in the contact for her? What was difficult? What kinds of children did she like best? Which children did she find hardest to like? How did the children react to her? What were her feelings at the termination of contact? What initiative did she take to bring her in contact with children? What kinds of volunteer work does she do that involves children?

A school asks the protective agency to visit a mother whose children come to school hungry and inadequately dressed, and the mother says, "That's a damn dirty lie; my kids are as well taken care of as anybody's." The worker replies, "Perhaps you're right," but then goes on to probe the behavioral aspects of the mother's statement. "What did the kids eat yesterday?" "How regular is mealtime?" "Who takes responsibility for preparing the food and seeing that the children are fed?" "What do you consider a decent meal?" "What problems do you have in giving the children the kinds of meals you think are desirable?" "What kinds of cold-weather clothes do the children have; what kind of rainy-weather clothes?" "What difficulties do you have in getting proper clothes for the kids?"

Probe questions seeking additional, more specific information may be necessary because the initial answer is insufficient, irrelevant, unclear, or inconsistent with some previously offered information. The general picture of the client's situation has emerged but specific consequential details may be missing. Unless clear, complete relevant information is obtained regard-

ing content of significance for achieving the interview objectives, the interviewer may incorrectly presume she accurately knows what the interviewee had in mind.

Keeping the content on a general level does not permit an understanding
of the individual client in his individual situation. General statements like
"It's a hard job" or "marriage is very complicated" or "being a parent has
its drawbacks" need more specific follow-up questions: "What specifically
is hard for you about the job?" "What complications have you encountered
in your marriage this past week?" "What kinds of drawbacks are you thinking of?" These are probe questions.

Probe questions are successive approximations to the detail the interviewer needs to know if she is to be helpful. They direct the interviewee
in shaping a response. Open-ended questions followed by probes permit
the interviewee to tell his story in his own way, and then helps him supplement it with amplifying details.

While questions are the most frequent kind of probe intervention, silence, minimal encouragements, paraphrasing and reflecting can also have
probe effects. These varied interventions also result in communication of
greater detail and more specific information.

The words "probe" and "probing" tend to evoke a negative reaction among
social workers. The words suggest to them the very antithesis of the kind
of emotional response to the client which they regard as proper and desirable. Probing implies an active interviewer and a passive interviewee who
is involuntarily required to answer questions. The probed interviewee implies an object, valued as a source of answers to questions. In reality, it is,
most often, a gentle follow-up on what has been said in order to obtain
more information needed by the interviewer. Most frequently it is a legitimate request for further concreteness and specificity. It is distinguished
from a prying question which would be characterized as more unwarranted, more coercive, more intrusive. While probe questions may often
be circumscribed and direct, they do not have to be asked in a demanding
manner or in a way which denies the interviewee the right to refuse a
response.

Probe questions are employed when the 1) relevance of content is not
clear, 2) there is a need for clarification of ambiguous content, 3) there is
need for more detail, and 4) there is need for greater specificity.

Different kinds of probe questions are asked in response to different
problems in the interview.

Completion probes are directed toward neglected or inadequately covered content and call on the interviewee to elaborate and amplify details
and to fill in omissions. They include such questions as "And then?" "What
else can you think of about this?" "Does anything else come to mind?"

"What happened then?" and "Could you spell that out a little more?". "I know you said you left the job because you didn't like it. Could you tell me what you didn't like about it?" "You said you left the hospital after the operation without the doctor's approval. What prompted you to do this?"

While completion probes are designed to obtain further elaboration of what is being said, clarity probes are designed to elicit a clearer explanation of what is being said.

Probes for clarification are designed to reduce ambiguities and conflicts in details; they help to further explain the situation. They include questions such as "Can you help me? I don't understand that." "Could you explain that a little more?" "Could you give me an example of that?" "What do you mean by that?" "Could you tell me what you think leads you to feel this way?"

A psychiatric social worker discusses a mentally retarded 4-year-old girl with the mother.
WORKER: What problems did you have with her during this past year?
MRS. M.: No problems, but only that I feel she was too good a child, that there had to be something wrong.
WORKER: Well, when you say too good a child, could you give me some examples?

Some clarity probes permit further specification of response so that the interviewee, with the help of the interviewer, more clearly defines his situation. "When you think about the shoplifting incident, what feeling seems dominant, shame or guilt?" "Do you feel anxious about Roger [a mentally defective child] only when he is out in the street or when he is in the house as well?"

Vague or inconsistent responses to an open-ended question lead to probes asking for greater clarification: "What did you have in mind when you said your relationship with your mother left a lot to be desired?" "What do you mean when you say the doctors in the hospital are close-minded?" "When you said we didn't have sex 'very often,' how often was it?"

The use of completion probes suggests that the interviewer senses that the interviewee might say more if given additional encouragement. The use of clarity probes suggests that the interviewer is sensitive to the ambiguities, contradictions, and qualifications of the interviewee's response.

Woman, 44, white, lower middle class, AFDC because of husband's disability, vocational counseling service.
WORKER: How does your family feel about your going back to work?
MRS. H.: Well, the kids are all for it.
WORKER: All for it? [Clarity probe through reflecting.]

MRS. H.: Well, they think it would be good for me. I would get out and be less concerned about the house and have some interests. They know it will mean more cooperation on their part in the housekeeping. They say they are ready to do this.

WORKER: And your husband? [Completion probe—question was around family reactions, and interviewee had answered in terms of children only.]

Reaction probes focus on the interviewee's own thinking and feeling and serve to increase the emotional depth of interview content. "How did you react to it?" "What do you think about it?" "What are your own feelings when this happens?" "How did you feel while this was going on?"

Answers to open-ended questions may *suggest* an attitude or feeling which is not clearly explicit. Probe questions are designed to make these attitudes and/or feelings more explicit. "I got the idea from what you said that you had a strong reaction to the doctor's suggestion that you consider placing Ruth in an institution. What did you feel when the doctor said that?" "You said you thought you had good reasons for objecting to your mother's coming to live with you. What were the reasons?"

The following interview excerpt with the worker's introspective comments indicates the value of follow-up exploratory probes.

INTERVIEWEE: I get upset about the decision to break away from the church and to miss mass and confession.

INTERVIEWER: What's upsetting about it?

INTERVIEWEE: I don't know.

(INTERVIEWER: Maybe she really doesn't know but maybe it's something she's afraid I'll laugh at or be shocked at—so I probed further.)

INTERVIEWER: What comes to mind when you think about it?

INTERVIEWEE: Well, ah I guess I really know. It's well, I guess I'm, well I'm afraid of going to hell.

INTERVIEWER: That can be upsetting.

(INTERVIEWER: I had to be careful to treat this very seriously, because it is a real fear of hers.)

The timing of probe questions is important. It would not be advisable to stop the interviewee who has developed some momentum in telling his story and ask questions for clarification or elaboration. Allowed to continue, the interviewee may go on to answer some of the questions the interviewer intended to ask. Waiting until the interviewee runs down poses a problem, however. A worker may need clarification or elaboration of some details that appeared early in the client's presentation. By the time he ended he might have moved the focus to other areas. Attempting to probe the material introduced earlier requires a contextual lead-in. "When you first started to tell me about this, you said that you felt . . . Could you tell me what led to your feeling that . . . ?"

Formulation and Phrasing: Some Common Errors

Questioning is a much abused art. It appears to be very difficult for interviewers to ask a clear, unequivocal, understandable question and then be quiet long enough to give the interviewee an unhampered, uninterrupted opportunity to answer.

Questions need to be understandable, unambiguous, and short enough that the interviewee can remember what is being asked. Any question of more than two sentences is apt to be too long. One sentence may permissibly set the context for the question, or explain the reasons for it, or prepare the interviewee for the question, or motivate him to answer it. The second sentence should be the question itself. After which the interviewer should stop and wait, expectantly listening for the response and comfortable in the period of silence between the question and the response.

Among recurrent errors in question formulation are the following: the leading or suggestive question, the yes or no question, the double question, the garbled question, and the "why" question.

THE LEADING OR SUGGESTIVE QUESTION

A frequent error is to phrase a question so as to lead the interviewee to make a specific or particular answer desired by the interviewer. The formulation of a leading question is based on a preconception by the interviewer of what the answer should be or on a strong expectation of what the answer might be. Leading questions make it difficult for the interviewee to respond freely. He has to oppose the interviewer's question-answer if he is offering a response that contradicts the anticipated answer implied in the question. Leading questions are not really questions at all, but answers disguised as questions. The interviewer is not asking for an answer but soliciting a confirmation.

A social worker talks to a 12-year-old boy who has run away from and been returned to an institution for emotionally disturbed children.
WORKER: You might as well face it, John, you're going to have to learn to deal with your anger in other ways. I can understand that you're very upset, but you saw how running away didn't accomplish anything. Don't you agree?

A school social worker talks to a 7-year-old girl about her relationship to classmates.
WORKER: You play just with these two girls in the class. But you want more friends, don't you?

The worker's introspective comment follows:

As soon as I said, "But you want more friends, don't you?" I wished I hadn't. I felt I was putting words in Helen's mouth. It is true that she wants more friends, but I shouldn't be telling her; she should be telling me.

The interviewer can suggest a response through negative phrasing of the lead-in to the question itself.

A worker in the social service unit of a public assistance agency asks a young mother receiving AFDC:
WORKER: I don't suppose you have thought about working while the children are so young, have you?

The context in which the question is framed, rather than the question formulation itself, may suggest the interviewee's answer.

WORKER: Do you think Roger and Ruth [client's preschool children] receive enough attention and care from your neighbor while you are working when she has three children of her own to take care of?

A parole officer asks a parolee:
OFFICER: How about some old friends with a prison record that you aren't supposed to associate with. Do you see any of them?

A question can be biased by the interviewer through omitting an alternative in the question formulation.

A worker in a service for single pregnant adolescents interviews the prospective mother.
WORKER: As you think about abortion or placing the child for adoption, which way seems the best to you?

The question is biased because it omits the alternative of the mother keeping and caring for the child herself.

Omissions are subtle but nevertheless significant. An interviewer can ask questions about a mother's reaction to her getting custody of the children following a divorce and follow this up by questions about her reactions to the husband's obtaining custody. No questions about the possibility of joint custody bias the interview by virtue of neglect of this consideration.

A leading question may influence the response on the basis of the associations it seeks to evoke. "As a mother concerned about the welfare of her child, do you think it would be good for him if you go to work so soon after his birth?" "As a considerate son, do you think your mother would be happy in an old-age home?" "Do you, as a good husband and father, help your wife with the care of the children?"

Sometimes selective emphasis suggests the answer. "Do you *really* feel that your plans to keep the baby and find a job and housing are realistic?"

Questions may prejudice a response by communicating the interviewer's annoyance. "What made you think that spanking Billy was going to do any good?"

However the bias is incorporated in the question, biased questions imply that certain answers are more acceptable than others, gently pressuring the interviewee to respond with the preferred answer.

The following are some question-answers taken from social work interviews, with the more desirable neutral formulation of the question offered:

Biased Formulation	Neutral Formulation
If you leave Mark at the daycare center now, won't he act up again?	How do you think Mark will react to the day-care center now?
Won't Sue be the most difficult one to care for?	What difficulties do you think you might have with Sue?
Well I see you're making good progress. Don't you think so?	What progress do you think you are making?
I suppose Mrs. A. [the foster mother] treats all the kids the same?	How does Mrs. A. treat the different kids?
You feel pretty comfortable with younger children?	What's your reaction to younger children?

The dangers of such kinds of question formulation can be exaggerated. Leading questions can be and are employed by highly competent interviewers, and when used properly they do not result in a distortion of the interviewee's true response. Clients with well-crystallized points of view and with some self-assurance are not likely to be intimidated by the statement of interviewer preference embodied in a leading question (Dohrenwend 1963, 1965, 1970). However, the research just cited was conducted with a general group of respondents. Social work interviewees are a particular group of respondents—particular in a sense that most of them want something from the agency. The power differential in the relationship is clearly in the interviewer's favor, and the interviewee is vulnerable. Consequently his readiness to disagree, to oppose, to contradict is likely to be somewhat more attenuated in this situation than it might be in other interview situations.

Leading questions are least appropriate with those interviewees who are anxious to please or "con" the interviewer, who are afraid to disagree with the interviewer, or who have little motivation to participate actively and responsibly in the interview. In these instances the interviewee will be ready and willing to parrot back whatever the interviewer suggests she expects to hear. For such interviewees, this is the least painful way of fulfilling what is required of them.

Some questions which suggest an answer are not only objectionable on this ground but may be formulated in a way which makes them even less desirable: "Don't you think that — —?" "Shouldn't you have — —?" "Wouldn't it have been better to — —?" are phrasings which not only suggest an answer but also critically evaluate the interviewee's behavior. Such question formulations impose the "tyranny of the should" and are likely to be resented by the interviewee.

Leading questions can be useful in communicating the social worker's position. They consequently tend to ally the worker with that aspect of the client's ambivalence which favors the alternative supported by the directive question. The worker may deliberately select the leading question "Don't you think it might be better to consider other methods of discipline than refusing to talk to Sally?" rather than the more neutral "What methods of discipline would you consider, other than refusing to talk to Sally?" because she wants to emphasize that she favors an alternative procedure.

Sometimes, a question which suggests a response is a result of the interviewer's desire to be helpful. Rather than impose on the interviewee the burden of formulating his own answer, the interviewer makes it less difficult by offering both the question and the answer simultaneously.

THE YES OR NO QUESTION

Beginning interviewers often make the mistake of phrasing questions in a way that calls for a simple yes or no answer and thus cuts off any further, useful elaboration.

Yes–No formulation	*Formulation requiring elaboration*
Do you feel that when you go home your visits with your family are successful?	Tell me about your visits with your family.
Did you have to miss work a great deal?	What about absenteeism on the job?

| Do you think there are some advantages in having this operation? | What do you see as the advantages in having this operation? |
| Do you ever do anything together with your children? | What kinds of things do you and your children do together? |

In general, closed questions can more frequently be answered in a few words than can open questions. Questions which start with "is," "did," "have," or "does" are more likely to get a simple yes or no answer and a limited response yield. "Have arrangements been made for maternity-home care?" "Is he generally this way when his mother visits the foster home?" "Did you ever make application for adoption previously?" "Does the fact that you have been in prison make for difficulty in applying for a job?" Similar questions starting with "what" or "how" are likely to require more detailed communication of the interviewee's experience. "What arrangements have you made for maternity-home care?" "How does he generally behave when his mother visits?" "What contacts have you had with adoption agencies previously?" "What difficulties have you encountered in applying for a job as a result of your having been in prison?" Similarly, the formulation is not "Does he like his sister?" but "How does he get along with his sister?"; not "Did retirement from the job lessen your contact with people?" but "What contacts with people have you had since retiring from the job?"; not "Is it difficult for you to manage on this budget?" but "How have you managed on this budget?"

THE DOUBLE QUESTION

The beginning interviewer frequently asks more than one question at the same time. Hearing her first question as she speaks, the interviewer decides that it is not really what she wanted to ask. Before the client can begin to answer it, the interviewer asks a second question. The situation is confusing because the interviewer asks her question, then qualifies it, then explains it, then qualifies the explanation. By the time the interviewer is through nagging at the question, there is not much of it left. Frequently, the second question changes the frame of reference, or shifts the content, or asks something quite different from the first question. The interviewee then has the problem of deciding which of several questions he should answer. Given a choice, he often answers the easiest question, ignoring the others. The least difficult question to answer is often the least productive since it encounters the least emotional resistance. For the interviewer, multiple questions pose another hazard as well. Having asked a series of questions, she may forget that the original question was not answered. She may remember only that the question was asked and write it off his interview agenda. Often it is not clear which question has been answered.

WORKER: Are you managing better with your crutches, and how about your glasses, do they fit?
MR. W.: Oh my, yes.

The following are some examples of double questions asked during social work interviews.

Have you found the changes in customs from your country hard to deal with? How have you gone about adjusting to them?

What happened when you had a nervous breakdown? By the way, what do you mean by a nervous breakdown?

When do you think you and your Dad started fighting? How long has it been? Has it been since your Mom died or before that? Have you always not got along with your Dad?

The worker, commenting on his question says, "The client chose to answer the last question with a one-word answer 'yes'—about what I deserved."

Sometimes a single sentence can involve a double question because it offers more than one frame of reference for response.

Since coming home from the hospital what difficulties have you had in finding a job, or finding housing, or even getting back in with your friends?

Were you angry at what you were doing then or at the way you were treated then?

How do you and the children feel about moving out of the state? ("You" and "the children" are distinctly different reference points for an answer.)

A good interviewee can save a poor interviewer from her imperfections. In the following a double question asked by the interviewer is answered sequentially by the interviewee.

INTERVIEWER: Okay, and then do you and your boyfriend live here, and do you work, or do you have any job that takes you out of the house much of the time?
INTERVIEWEE: Yeah.
INTERVIEWER: You do? Okay—
INTERVIEWEE: And he's living here, too.

THE GARBLED QUESTION

Sometimes it is impossible for the interviewee to know what the interviewer is asking.

When the interviewer is unclear about what she wants to ask, the message is more or less garbled. The interviewee would be justified in asking "What did you say?" or perhaps, less kindly, "Would you please get the marbles out of your mouth." The following are verbatim examples from tape-recorded social work interviews:

INTERVIEWER: Yeah. So (pause) okay (pause) you said in the beginning of the interview that the frustrations that you are having (pause) are you finding that, well, is it cyclical? Have you noticed that? (lights up a cigarette). Is there any, you know what I mean?

A social worker in a divorce-court setting, interviewing a 40-year-old male with regard to a possible reconciliation.
What do you think, what do you suppose she wants to do, like why do you suppose she's acting the way she does?

The worker comments about this question as follows:

My question was uncertain to the point of being incoherent. I felt something should be brought out and clarified, but I wasn't sure what and so I stumbled around. I am not sure what point I wanted to make—possibly something about his wife's deeper motive for [sharing his infidelities with the children], to justify herself or punish him, or erode the children's loyalty to him. What? I guess I had several ideas in mind but wasn't clear about how I wanted to develop this.

It takes an assertive interviewee to request clarification as in the following interchange. The client has said that he has learned to control his feeling of embarrassment at hearing himself praised. Earlier the client had discussed problems in controlling anger. The worker attempts to establish a connection between the handling of the two kinds of feelings:

WORKER: How do you see to maybe perhaps learning from that experience of expression, transferring that to anger or anything that you can think of that would work in a similar way?
INTERVIEWEE: Would you repeat that? I didn't follow.

THE "WHY" QUESTION

One kind of question that is used more frequently than it should be is the "why" question. This is a very difficult kind of question for the interviewee. It asks for a degree of insight and understanding which, if possessed by the interviewee in the first place, might have obviated the necessity of coming to the agency. In asking "why," we are requesting the *interviewee* to provide the insights into his own behavior. A why question demands of the interviewee that he explain or account for his behavior in rational terms, but very often people really do not know why they felt or behaved in a certain way. This discovery of explanation is often one of the objectives of the therapeutic contact. The truth is, we often do not know "why."

Most people find it difficult to explain "why" they behave in the way they behave, particularly when the behavior is self-destructive and self-defeating. The "why" question increases their feelings of frustration, inadequacy, and defensiveness, and a sense of having disappointed the interviewer.

If sophisticated enough, the interviewee may attempt to provide reasons in retrospect to satisfy the questioner. The "why" question thus encourages a tendency toward a rationalization of behavior that may falsify the actual reality, the disordered impulses which, in fact, prompted his behavior. That behavior may have been in response to unconscious or preconscious needs, to socially unacceptable impulses which the interviewee is trying to repress or suppress, and so is unable to share the more accurate answer to "why" with the interviewer.

As rational people most interviewees feel a need to defend their rationality by devising a rational answer in response to the question—and one "why" question leads to another.

A school social worker, talking to an 8-year-old girl.
WORKER: What happens when you try to play with the other girls?
LIL: They say, "go away."
WORKER: They tell you to go away. Why do you think they say that?
LIL: 'Cause they don't want more people to play with.
WORKER: Why do you think they don't want *you* to play with them?
LIL: 'Cause they have too many friends, and I was just learning how to jump rope, and I can't jump good. I always hafta take an end. I never get to jump.
WORKER: Why do the other girls always make you take an end?

Psychiatric social worker in an institution for emotionally disturbed children, discussing attitudes toward institutional personnel with a 16-year-old boy.
WORKER: You just said you're not going to, uh, like anybody around here again.
WILLARD: I'm not (hostile tone of voice).
WORKER: Why do you feel that way?
WILLARD: I just feel that way.

WORKER: Have people disappointed you?
WILLARD: Nobody's disappointed me.
WORKER: Then why do you think you feel that way?
WILLARD: I just do (matter of factly).

The worker comments:

I continue to try to get Willard to verbalize his reasons for not liking any-one. I make a serious assumption here, and probably an erroneous one. I assume that Willard understands, or at least is aware of, the dynamics of his behavior. I push him to reason on a cognitive level as to the origins of his feelings.

Workers find that asking "why" is often counterproductive.

A social worker in a drug abuse center is discussing peer relationships with a young adult male. She asks why the client always has to follow what the group wants him to do since it often gets him into trouble.

I got the usual response: "I don't know." Then it dawned on me in the middle of the interview that Jack became defensive whenever I asked the question "why?" The word "why" seemed to imply that Jack had to justify his behavior, to hold himself accountable for his feelings. I realized then that asking "why" all the time was like pointing a finger at Jack and only resulted in his becoming more defensive and upset in the interview.

It is difficult to formulate a question in "why" terms without suggesting overtones of accusation, condemnation, and blame. Reasons and explanations formulated in response to such a question may appear to the interviewee as answers submitted to the interviewer for evaluation. Do the reasons appear solid and acceptable to the listener? "Why" has a critical component as well as an information-seeking component. As a consequence, the interviewer may be prompted to respond defensively and focus counterproductively on justifying rather than explaining the behavior.

There are effective alternatives to a "why" question which might elicit the same kind of information being sought. Instead of "why," it might be better to ask "what." "What" is easier for most people to answer than "why," which calls for self-analysis. "What" calls for explanatory description. Not "Why do you have difficulty in telling your husband about the things he does that annoy you?" but "What do you think would happen if you told your husband about things he does that annoy you?" Not "Why are you afraid of the medical examination?" but "What scares you about the medical examination?" Not "Why didn't you use contraceptives since you knew you might become pregnant?" but "What prevented you from taking precautions so that you would not become pregnant?" Such interventions direct attention to some explanation of behavior without the direct challenge incorporated in "why."

Additional Guidelines in Question Formulation

At this point, some additional caveats and suggestions in question formulation might be noted.

The best questions are those which arise organically and almost spontaneously out of what the interviewee is saying. The interaction is responsive. Facts and feelings are not so much actively sought as much as they are permitted to emerge. Such a developmental pattern shows the worker is following the client and listening attentively. The relevance of the question is clear, there is greater likelihood for continuity in thought and mood. Such an approach reflects the worker's concentration on getting a client to talk rather than getting him to answer questions, on having a greater interest in listening to answers rather than in asking questions.

A well-formulated question requires some precise thinking on the part of the interviewer. She needs to know exactly what she wants to ask, exactly what she wants to find out.

Questions should be crisp, lean, clearly phrased, and focused. They should be phrased with regard to the interviewee's frame of reference and vocabulary level and the social psychological accessibility of content. Thus asking a female interviewee with a third-grade education to discuss the "attitudinal orientation of her husband which creates difficulties in the role allocation of responsibilities in their marital relationship" is likely to be met with a blank stare—and should be.

Questions should be formulated with concern as to whether or not the interviewee is likely to know the answer. A question should not be asked if it is likely that the interviewee does not have the information at hand to answer it. Asking a man in a marital counseling interview whether his wife's parents were generally emotionally accepting of her during her childhood is asking for information that the interviewee may not know.

Rather than being hesitant, timid, or apologetic about the questions to be asked to find out what she needs to know if she is to be truely helpful, the interviewer should be convinced of her entitlement to the information and communicate a sense of confident expectation that the interviewee will respond to the question. "Would you mind if I asked whether or not you are married?" "May I ask if you have any children?" suggest apologetic hesitancy on the part of the interviewer.

Asking a question potentially activates a variety of risks. The interviewer has to weigh the need for the information the answer will provide against the nature and degree of discomfort, anxiety, resistance, defensiveness, etc., the question may evoke. The instrumental value of the question has to be balanced against its expressive costs, its impact on the relationships. Such risks can be mitigated by the use of appropriate introductory *lead-ins.*

Prefaces, or lead-ins, to questions can make the question more palatable, or less likely to arouse hostility or resentment. "Face-saving" prefaces and prefaces which universalize problems are employed. A protective service worker asks: "It must be difficult for you without a husband to share the care of the children and to have to be always patient with them. What was happening just before you struck the child?" A worker in a mental health clinic serving adolescents asks: "Many young people have a problem in the differences in attitudes between their parents and themselves about pre-marital sex. What differences did you have with your parents about this?"

Lead-ins are employed to motivate client participation. A school social worker asks a mother: "As Ed's mother, you have had the most continuing contact with him and know him better than anyone else. Could you tell me what he is like to live with?"

Lead-ins are used to raise a client's self-esteem in preparation for dealing with a question that is apt to be self-deflating. A social worker in a corrections facility says in a first interview with an adult paroled offender: "From what you've told me there are many problems you encountered which you've dealt with successfully on your own. Which situations were hardest for you?"

The *attitude* with which a question is asked is perhaps as important as the question itself. The context and spirit of the question should reflect the emotional tone of the interviewee at that moment. If the interviewee is depressed, the question should indicate a supportive understanding; if he is anxious, reassurance; if he is hostile, recognition and acceptance of his hostility. In each instance the interviewer demonstrates by the lead-in that she is paying attention not only to the content of what the interviewee is saying by asking a relevant, appropriate question but also to the feelings which accompany the interviewee's statements.

Male, 78, white, lower middle class, Old Age Assistance.
MR. Q.: At our age we have to depend on each other. As long as I'm around, she has somebody to depend on. But I don't know. . . .
WORKER: It worries you. [Pause.] How do you think your wife would manage if she survived you?

Male, 19, white, upper lower class, probation interview.
MR. D.: And my mother is another one. She gives me a stiff pain in the ass.

WORKER: She really makes you sore. What does she do that gets you so mad?

Where the subject matter is unfamiliar to the interviewee, it might be best to introduce the question by offering essential information.

The mother's group has about six to eight people, all in their early thirties, meeting for two hours every Wednesday evening to discuss the problem of how to live on a public welfare budget. What is your reaction to the idea of joining such a group?

Phrasing should avoid common words with vague meanings—"most," "much," "many," "frequently." The answers are easy to misinterpret because the interviewer's standards with regard to such words are generally unknown. "Do you frequently use corporal punishment in disciplining your children?" "Frequently" may mean once a day to the respondent who only punishes once a week who then answers, "No, not frequently." To obtain information sought by such questions, the use of precision is required. "In the last month, how often have you used corporal punishment in disciplining your children?"

Questions need to be formulated with some sensitivity to "buzz" words— words that have high affective connotations and carry a lot of emotional freight. Acceptable formulation can get the same information without the accompanying flak induced by such words. "As you grow older, what kinds of things do you do more poorly?" is likely to evoke more defensiveness than "As you grow older what kinds of things do you do less well?" "How do you feel about your wife's asserting her desire to work" is not as neutral as "How do you feel about your wife's desire to work?"

Questions and variations on questions can be transformed with only subtle change in wording from neutral, inoffensive requests for information to offensive, antagonizing formulations. To a client with a long-standing problem who comes for help at a point of crisis, the question "Why did you wait so long to get some help about this?" is antagonizing; "What made you hesitant about coming to the agency previously?" is more neutral. "Were you a school drop-out?" is offensive; "What was your last grade in school?" is less so.

A skilled interviewer will vary the format of the way questions are phrased so that no one pattern characterizes the interaction. If possible and appropriate some direct questions should be interspersed with indirect questions, and varied with comments as questions. Even a series of open questions should have a few closed questions tucked in. Some effort should be made at novel question formulation such as projective hypothetical questions or alternate choice questions.

Projective questions present a hypothetical situation that requires a decision. Such a question directed to a child might be, "If you were going on a vacation and could take either your mother or your father with you, whom would you take?" Hypothetical probes pose hypothetical, but realistic, situations for reaction. "Suppose she did. . . ." "Suppose you had. . . ." "What do you think would happen if you said. . . ."

Worker in a correctional agency is talking to a 17-year-old white male.
BILL: They urged me to try it [shooting heroin] and so I thought, what the hell.
WORKER: Suppose you had refused. What do you think would have happened?

Questions can sometimes be formulated in hypothetical terms in engaging the interviewee vicariously in experiences she is likely to encounter but has not as yet done so. The worker asks a male adolescent about to be discharged from a mental hospital, "Suppose you were to go back and live with your parents again, how would you imagine it would be now?"

Indirect, projective questions have the advantage of permitting the interviewee to answer without personalizing the responses. It then permits the introduction of sensitive material without increasing anxiety unduly. It has the disadvantage of assuming that the answers represent the way the interviewee actually thinks or feels. This may not be the case.

WORKER: Think about a girl your age watching a favorite TV program. Her mother says, "turn the set off, it's time for supper." What do you think the girl does—turns the set off and comes to supper, or sits there and continues to watch the program?

Alternative-form questions provide choices from which the interviewee is invited to select a response.

INTERVIEWER: How do you feel about your job?
INTERVIEWEE: It's ok!
INTERVIEWER: It's ok?
INTERVIEWEE: Yeah, that's about it.
INTERVIEWER: Well, as you know for some people the thing they like best about their jobs is the work that they have to do; for another, the best thing may be the people they work with; for others it's the pay; for others it's the location; or the hours; or the status and prestige of the job title. What aspects of your job do you like most?

The use of the plural rather than singular noun in the question asked above gives the interviewee more freedom and nets a bigger answer since it permits the interviewee to talk about a number of different related aspects of the job situation.

Alternate choice questions need to offer approximately equally desirable alternatives. To ask "Would you rather make application for general assistance or continue without any money?" poses alternatives that lead to one answer in most instances.

The alternate question form is sometimes used in conjunction with hypothetically posed situations. In trying to clarify the preferences of a foster parent applicant, the social worker says:

We have many different kinds of children who need a home. For instance, Bill is a shy, quiet, withdrawn 7-year-old who tends to play by himself and doesn't talk much. Timmy is very active, outgoing, talkative, 7 years old, always on the go. Which kind of child is more in line with the kind of child you feel more comfortable with, Bill or Timmy?

Questions can be imaginatively formulated in terms of comparisons and contrasts: not "How do you feel about Bob?" (a mentally retarded child) but "In what way is your feeling for Bob different from your feeling about the other children in the family?" "What do you like better about being married than about being single?"

One can ask questions by making statements rather than using the interrogative mode. Rather than asking, "What are some of the difficulties in caring for a handicapped child?" one can ask by indirection saying, "I imagine it can be really tough in a number of ways to care for a handicapped child." Rather than asking, "What prompted you to separate from your husband?" the interviewer might say, "I would be interested in the reasons which prompted you to leave your husband."

Questions can often be reformulated by a remark that might appear less challenging. The question, "What do you think would be the difficulties you would face if you did go through with the divorce?" might translate to "You probably have given some thought to the difficulties you would face if you went through with the divorce. We could discuss your thoughts about this." "What difficulties have you encountered in being both a mother and a fully employed teacher?" might translate to "Being both a mother and a fully employed teacher probably presents some problems. Tell me about those you have encountered."

The remark is an indirect question without the question mark inflection characteristic of the direct question. The reformulation of the question as a general remark reduces the danger of having the interview give the impression of a question-and-answer session. It increases the feeling of the interaction as a comfortable informal conversation.

The art of asking questions like the art in the use of any group of inter-ventions depends on the interviewer's sensitivity to what is appropriate for the situation at the moment of the intervention. It involves the judicious variation in the formulation of questions to fit the occasion.

Relentless consistency in the use of any one particular style of question is likely to be counterproductive, however comfortable the interviewer feels with it. Because the demands at different points in the interview are so varied, the consistent use of one type of questioning is likely to be more appropriate at one time, but much less appropriate at another.

A final word of caution. Despite the general multi-purpose applicability of questions, it might be wise for social workers to use this kind of inter-vention sparingly. Interaction based on a persistent question-answer format tends to confirm a kind of relationship between interviewer and inter-viewee which contradicts the cooperative-collaborative mutually participa-tive atmosphere that is most often helpful.

A series of questions develops an undesirable perception of the respec-tive responsibilities of interviewer and interviewee. It suggests an unreal-istic situation in which, if the interviewee answers the questions, the inter-viewer will provide a clear, solution to the problem.

CHAPTER 10

Termination and Recording

The final phase of the interview is termination. Preparation for termination begins at the very beginning of the interview. The interviewee should be informed explicitly at the beginning that a definite period of time has been allotted for the interview, that she is free to use some, or all, of this time but that going beyond the time limit is clearly discouraged. Unless an unusual situation develops, it is understood that the interview will terminate at the end of the allotted time.

Another aspect of preparation for termination is linked to the mutually agreed-upon purpose of the interview. The interview is an ad hoc social system created to achieve a purpose. When the purpose is accomplished, the system should dissolve. The purpose should bear some general relation to the time available, so that it probably can be accomplished within the time scheduled. If this is not possible, the general purpose should be broken down so that some subunits are achieved in one interview, and an additional interview, or interviews, scheduled. In a sense, the interview has not been terminated at the end of the first meeting; it has merely been interrupted.

Research findings regarding long-term and short-term worker-client contacts may be applicable to the interview situation. Such research suggests that if the agency establishes a limited time period for contact with the client, both worker and client tend to mobilize their efforts more effectively to accomplish the tasks of the contact within the time designated. If there is a clearly limited time period for the single interview, similar mobilization of effort may take place.

Termination Techniques

Throughout the interview the social worker has to be aware of time spent and time yet available. Since he is responsible for seeing that interview purposes are accomplished, he needs to pace the interview so that there is some reasonable expectation of success. He may decide to make more rapid transitions; he may decide to focus less time on some areas; he may make less effort to evoke affect if time is growing short. If the pace toward accomplishment of purpose is quicker than anticipated, he may decide to conserve the interviewee's time as well as his own by ending early. It might be well, in moving toward termination, if the interviewer occasionally checks with the interviewee.

It seems to me that we have done what we set out to do and that we are coming to a close. How do you see it?

It might be noted that the interviewee is as free as the interviewer to terminate the exchange. If she feels her purposes are accomplished or if she feels that there is little real likelihood that her purpose will be achieved, the interviewee may not want to spend further time.

There is preparation for termination in the pacing of affect as well as content. In moving toward the end there should be an easing of feeling, a reduction in intensity of affect. Content that is apt to carry with it a great deal of feeling should not be introduced toward the end of the interview. The interviewee should be emotionally at ease when the interview is terminated, in contrast with the following.

A worker is discussing marital planning with a young adult. The woman is a carrier of a genetically transmitted anomaly and has discussed how this might be handled if she became pregnant. Toward the end of the interview the worker says: "Another option is just not having children, being married and having a husband but not having kids, remaining childless."

Commenting on this intervention at the end of the interview the worker says:

I wanted to be complete, and by stating this final option I was completing the spectrum of options for Ruth. Yet, it was very unfair of me to so casually drop this bomb on Ruth when I knew we wouldn't have time to deal with her reactions to the idea of never having children. Her facial reaction showed that this thought made her very sad. I wonder if I might have subconsciously waited with this option until the end of the interview so that I wouldn't have to deal with Ruth's hurt.

The interview should terminate before the participants become physically or emotionally fatigued and the interview suffers. An hour to an hour and a half is a long time for most participants. It is said that "the mind can absorb only as much as the seat can endure." Highly charged emotional interviews may fatigue participants even earlier. If fatigue sets in, the risk of interviewer error is greater.

It would be best, of course, if the decision to terminate was mutually acceptable to both participants, that both recognized that the purpose of the interview had been achieved and there was little reason for continuing.

If it becomes clear that the interviewee is unaware of the limited time available, some gentle reminders may be necessary. The interviewer might signal movement toward closure by explicitly noting that he perceives the interview as coming to a termination. "Well, I guess that's about as much as I think we can cover today." This legitimizes and sanctions termination. The tentative "I guess" and "I think" permits the interviewee the possibility of shaping her own, perhaps different, perception as to whether or not she sees the interview as coming to an end. The interviewer might say "Now that we are coming to the end of the interview, perhaps you. . . ." Or "I wish we could get into this more fully now, but given the time we have left it seems that. . . ."

One can signal movement to closure by explicitly noting external circumstances for terminating. "I am sorry, but there is another interview scheduled to begin in five minutes." Or "I think we have to finish up now. I am due at a committee meeting shortly" (Knapp 1973).

Verbal reminders are reinforced by nonverbal gestures which suggest that the interview is drawing to a close. The interviewer collects the papers or forms used during the interview; he looks at his watch rather than glances at it. Grasping the arms of the chair, placing palms on knees, moving to the edge of the chair, assuming a readiness-to-rise stance are all nonverbal messages indicating an intention to end the interview shortly. It is a courteous preparatory signal to the interviewee that things are coming to an end without having to verbally articulate this.

These verbal and nonverbal movements toward closure release people from contact with each other in a courteous manner, permitting each to go his or her own way without feeling dismissed. Such termination rituals preserve a sense of cordiality between participants and emphasize the element of solidarity in the relationship. We are leaving each other now, but we will make contact again.

If the interview is terminated abruptly and without considerate warning, the interviewer may be perceived as discourteous and rejecting. Separation is easily confused with rejection; the interviewer should make clear that termination of the interview is not the equivalent of wanting to get rid of the interviewee—although sometimes the worker may want to do so.

Sometimes despite the interviewer's best efforts, the interviewee fails to respond to the verbal and nonverbal signals communicated. The interviewee runs the risk of continuing beyond the point where the interview should have been terminated.

There needs to be concern for, and understanding of, the interviewee's reluctance to leave. Sometimes this reluctance is a hostile gesture toward the interviewer. Sometimes it reflects the long time needed before the interviewee feels comfortable enough to bring up the most important problem. This may be delayed until the end of the interview to avoid having time to explore it fully. Sometimes the reluctance to end the interview expresses a desire to prolong a satisfying experience; sometimes it is an expression of sibling rivalry and reluctance to share the interviewer with the next sibling-interviewee. The problem may result from different perceptions of how the interview has progressed—the interviewer seeing the purpose accomplished, the interviewee, from her point of view, seeing much that still needs to be done.

The interviewee's reluctance to terminate and the worker's difficulty in handling it is illustrated in the following account.

She began to talk about the boys, and as I began to break in at a pause or start a concluding sentence which would indicate a termination of the interview, she became extremely tense, talking faster and in a dissociated manner. I asked what she thought of my getting hold of her again, and she replied that she would be able to hear the phone ring. I then stood up to indicate termination and she began to list relatives and their careers. I perhaps should have stated that I must return to other work, but I was rather cowed by her sudden extreme talkativeness, and so I just walked her to the stairs and she continued to talk all the way downstairs and as she walked out onto the street. I had avoided interrupting her or being firm—those are not my usual ways of dealing with people—and I also was afraid to, but I did no favor to her to allow her to become so anxious at that point.

Whatever the interviewee's reasons for failing to perceive the warning preparations for termination and for acting to prolong the interview, the interviewer needs to follow some specific procedures in terminating. Here, as always, the worker would do well to recognize explicitly the manifested behavior.

I can see that you would like to continue longer.

It seems like you are reluctant to end the interview.

It appears to me that you wished we had more time.

While holding, without equivocation, to the need to terminate, the interviewer should indicate a desire to maintain communication. It is not that he does not want to hear more, it is that he does not want to hear it at this particular time. Consequently an offer is made to continue during another specified time period. The offer confirms the interviewer's continuing interest. If there is already an understanding that this is one of a series of interviews, there is an implicit promise of continued discussion. The interviewer might say, "I am very sorry but we have to wind this up. I would like to continue now but it's not possible. I would be glad to schedule another appointment so that we could continue talking together about this." If there is some intent to continue with another interview, recognition and support of the continuing relationship is made explicit by saying "till next time," "see you next week," "see you soon," rather than "good-bye."

When a subsequent interview is scheduled, specific arrangements should be made for the next steps, such as time, date, and place of the next interview or the time, date, place, the person to see, and how to get there, if the interview terminates in referral to another agency. If there is no plan to continue, termination of the interview and signaling a break in contact might seem like an impersonal dismissal unless softened by supportive comments: "Well, I hope things work out for you." Or "Good luck in your efforts to deal with this."

If the interview is with a collateral, or is an advocacy interview, it is advisable to thank the interviewee, recapitulate the significance of the contact, and reassure her about how the interview content might be used.

All these suggestions need to be applied flexibly, with sensitivity to the individual situation and with a generous helping of common sense. The interviewer should consider the interviewee's needs in moving toward termination. He must also give some consideration to his own needs, since they may indirectly affect the interviewee adversely. The interviewer's balanced concern for his own schedule is the highest courtesy to the interviewee. If the interviewer is too compliant, too yielding, too compassionate, and the interview runs beyond the scheduled time, he begins to worry about the next waiting interviewee, he begins to worry about the things that need to get done and will not get done if the interviewee continues to talk, he begins to listen to his own mounting anxieties and forgets to listen to the client. The extra time is then spent inefficiently and unproductively.

The least desirable alternative is one where the interview is, in effect, terminated for the interviewer but he does not have either the courage or the skill to say so to the interviewee. Withdrawing attention, preoccupied and disengaged from the interview, the interviewer leaves the interviewee "forgotten but not gone."

Sometimes it is the interviewee who takes the initiative in signaling what is, for her, the end of the interview. An interviewee might say, "Well, that kind of wraps it up for me. I think I know how to take it from here." Or "Well, that's about what I wanted to discuss—that's what was on my mind." Nonverbally the client might take off her glasses, or stand, gathering up her belongings, or open her purse, searching for her car keys. The client may prepare the interviewer for termination by expressions of appreciation. "Well, this has really been helpful." Or "Thanks very much for giving me your time."

SUMMARY AND POST-INTERVIEW CONVERSATION

As part of the termination phase, the interviewer briefly recapitulates what has been covered in the interview, what decisions have been reached, what questions remain to be resolved, what steps for action, if any, are to be taken. A summary tends to consolidate the work of the interview and give participants a feeling of satisfaction as they look back over what they have achieved. If nothing much has been accomplished, however, it may lead to a sense of despair.

Summarization is always a selective process as noted above. Consequently a summary tends to highlight and emphasize those aspects of the interview which the summarizer, generally the interviewer, regards as most significant. For this reason the interviewee's response should be actively and explicitly solicited. She should be invited to revise the summary if it does not accord with her perception of what was significant during the interview. Or the interviewer may ask the interviewee to recapitulate what *she* thought was accomplished. Such recapitulations might include a statement of what still needs to be done in subsequent interviews. The summary should enable both participants to get a perspective on the interview, highlighting the relationship of the many different, perhaps seemingly unrelated, aspects that have been discussed. It is an opportunity to give a sense of coherence to what has taken place.

Just as the interview itself may be preceded by a short social conversation as a transition, the termination of the interview may be followed by a similar short conversation. It acts as a transition out of the interview. It helps, further, to restore emotional equilibrium if the interview has been emotionally charged. Such post-interview conversation permits the interviewee time to regain composure and restore her ego, which may have been somewhat battered during the interview.

A correctional social-worker has been discussing the best fishing spots with a male client toward the end of an interview. He notes later, listening to the interview on tape:

The content is pretty much small talk. However, Bob seemed to need this neutral conversation after expressing the previously emotional material. It also gave me an opportunity to learn something about his interests and show him I was interested in him as a person with hobbies, etc., and not merely interested in him as a probationer.

As at the beginning of the interview, if such a conversation goes on too long however it tends to confuse a formal interview with a social encounter. Since there are different rules for communication in the two situations, the interviewee may be puzzled about which rules are appropriate. Even though the conversation may be pleasant, pleasure and gratification are not the factors that bring people together for the interview and should not be the determinants of when it ends.

The best termination is accomplished in a friendly, collaborative, and definite manner, indicating that the interviewer knows what he is doing. Adherence to the suggested procedures will ensure a greater likelihood that the interview will terminate rather than just stop or peter out.

The following is an example of how one social worker in a university counseling center employing a summary moved toward termination of an interview.

INTERVIEWER: Okay, that's fine, okay. Anything else you can think of that might be helpful?

INTERVIEWEE: Nothing more right now.

(Period of silence.)

INTERVIEWER: Okay. I think I'm starting to get a general picture from this early information, which is where we have to start. And, right now I'm seeing two or three areas that, that I see as potential areas of importance as far as, uh, exploring with you. Definitely your relationship with your boyfriend—I think it's something we have to talk about more in depth. Uh, I think perhaps, too, another area I would like to explore a little bit, uh, your perceived expectations which you might feel are based in reality, or how much aren't based in reality. Uh, I think that's just going to take us a little bit of time to look at. Um, that's what I see as the important areas. How do you feel about that?

INTERVIEWEE: Um, I agree.

INTERVIEWER: Another thing that I see is that you seem to have an excellent support system—friends, family, etc. That should be most helpful to you.

(Pause.)

INTERVIEWER: So I'm getting a few ideas. What I'd like to do now is assimilate what you've told me and ask you to think about these things also, and also set up a time for next week. Then we can start to look into some of these situations in more depth. How does that sound to you?

INTERVIEWEE: Yeah, that really sounds great.
INTERVIEWER: Okay, then let's set up that appointment for next week.

Just as an interview starts before it begins, it terminates before it ends. Both participants carry something of the interview away from them, mulling over what was said, continuing the interview in their minds after they have separated. The interviewer may deliberately stimulate postinterview rumination by assigning some "homework." He might suggest that the interviewee think over something they discussed, in preparation for continuing the exploration of the problem, as in the above excerpt.

TERMINATION CONTRACTS

More frequently now than in the past beginning interviews with clients may end in written contracts. The contracts detail what the agency expects the client to do, what the worker promises to do in behalf of the client, the time frame in which these obligations are to be achieved, and the consequences of failure to fulfill the contract. The following is an example of such a contract from a child welfare agency.

I [client] have agreed that I am interested in working on becoming less neglectful in the case of my children, Harry, 6, and Marie, 4.
I agree to meet each week with Ms. ———— at [child welfare agency] to discuss progress.
I agree to spend at least 1 hour each day with the children reading with them, playing games with them, taking them to a movie or a museum during the next 3 weeks.
I agree to spend at least 2 hours each day with the children during the following three weeks.
Each morning for the next 3 weeks I will see that a breakfast is prepared for the children before they go to school.
I agree to be home each day during the next three weeks when the children come home from school.
I understand that failure to meet the terms of the agreement may result in Petition of Termination of Parental Rights to my children.
I [social worker] agree to meet with [client] at a regularly scheduled time at [child welfare agency].
I agree to provide teaching homemaker service to [client] to help her develop homemaking child caring skills.
I will make an effort to locate an acceptable day care placement for Marie, 4.

Note-Taking

The more notes taken during the interview, the less note-taking is required after termination. The immediate caveat is that note-taking presents a possible distraction to interview interaction. While the interviewer is taking notes, he risks diminishing his contact with the interviewee and the attention he can devote to what the interviewee is saying. If he looks down to write, he breaks eye contact, indicative of a shift in his field of awareness. His focus in note-taking is generally on what *has* been said rather than on what *is* being said.

With eyes of the interviewer on the writing pad, some possibly significant nonverbal information is lost.

Note-taking also risks an increase in the interviewee's selective attention to certain content. If, after talking for some time, the interviewee says something which mobilizes the interviewer to make a note, the interviewee will naturally wonder about the significance of this item and begin to focus on it. This focusing may be good if the interviewer's deliberate intention is to reinforce concern with this particular item and to single it out for emphasis. However, focusing may be an inadvertent, unintentional by-product initiated by note-taking.

As the interviewee sees the interviewer taking notes, she is unsure whether she should continue to speak. She hesitates not only because the interviewer is apparently not listening but also because she does not want to interfere with what the interviewer is doing. It may be necessary to assure the interviewee that taking notes does not affect the conduct of the interview and that she should continue to talk.

Note-taking is, in some measure, self-defeating. When the most important things are happening, when involvement in the interview is greatest, the amount of attention that can be devoted to note-taking is minimal. When what is happening is less significant there is more time for notes. Hence the most complete notes may highlight the less important interchanges.

There are exceptions. Some interviewers can take notes unobtrusively without looking away from the client and without seeming to shift their attention. They have learned to set down key phrases or words that serve as adequate reminders of blocks of interview content. And they have learned to write without looking at the note pad. They take notes easily and without much show. On the other hand some interviewers may use note-taking as defense against contact with the client, hiding, in effect, behind the notebook.

Pencil poised over a notebook is a nonverbal artifact communicating the message "tell me more." As such it emphasizes the difference in status between interviewer and interviewee. The interviewee usually has no pencil, no pad, and takes no notes.

These considerations need to be applied differently with regard to different content. If the interviewee is offering specific, necessary information such as dates, names, addresses, and telephone numbers, it is essential that the interviewer note them. If he does not, the interviewee, recognizing that they will probably not be remembered, concludes that the interviewer is disinterested and indifferent. She might well wonder why the interviewer asked about these matters in the first place. Taking notes at this point validates the importance of what the client has said and indicates that it has been taken seriously. Notes about the actions the interviewer has promised to take are essential. If he has promised to obtain an interpretation of some regulation, make a hospital appointment, or check the availability of a homemaker, a note should be made.

If the interviewer is planning to take notes during the interview, this should be shared with the interviewee and her permission requested. Generally this is done in a manner which suggests that the interviewee will have no objections and includes some explanation of the purpose for note-taking. "You don't mind if I take some notes while we're talking? I'll need to do this if I am going to be most helpful to you." Especially with a suspicious interviewee, the request for permission may, further, include a statement of a willingness to share the notes if the interviewee wants to look at them. The interviewer may even encourage the interviewee to take her own notes on the interview. Notes should be taken in full view of the client rather than surreptitiously.

The effect of note-taking needs to be assessed periodically during the interview. If at any point the interviewee appears to be upset or made hesitant by note-taking, this reaction should be raised for explicit discussion. If, despite the interviewee's stated assent, notetaking appears to be a disruptive tactic, one might best forget it.

The principle is that the purpose of the interview has clear priority over note-taking and in any conflict between the two activities the interview interaction is given decided preference. Taking notes then should be done selectively, inconspicuously, flexibly, and openly. If it is difficult to take notes during the interview, it may be necessary to make some notes immediately after the interview. To wait until the end of the working day risks a considerable loss of essential detail. It is easy, after a series of interviews, to confuse interaction that occurred in one interview with interaction in another.

Taking notes during home interviews presents greater problems. The interviewer may have to make notes in his car after the interview or during a coffee break at a near-by restaurant.

Review and Evaluation

The interviewer needs to schedule some client-free time between interviews to enable the interviewer to clear his mind in preparation for the next interview. We noted the importance of this in discussing the beginning of the interview. Time-out also is necessary, however, to serve the needs of the interview just concluded. The worker may need time for review and evaluation of this interview, time to absorb some of the less obvious aspects before closure. Evaluation is a responsibility of the interviewer. The interview is not ended until the interviewer recapitulates the encounter in his mind and attempts to assess his performance critically. There are a number of questions that the interviewer may want to ask of himself in making such an evaluation.

1. In retrospect, what were the purposes of this interview—for the interviewee and for the agency?

2. To what extent were the purposes achieved?

3. What interventions helped to achieve the purposes? What intervention hindered the achievement?

4. What was my feeling about the interviewee?

5. At what point was my feeling most positive? Most negative?

6. How might these feelings have been manifested in what I said or did?

7. If I now empathize with the interviewee, how did she seem to see me? What seemed to be the reaction of the interviewee to the interview?

8. When did the interview seem to falter? When was it going smoothly?

9. At what point did the interviewee show signs of resistance, irritation? What had I said or done just prior to that?

10. At what point did it cease to be an interview and become a conversation, a discussion, an argument?

11. If I had the opportunity of doing the interview over again, what changes would I make? What justifies such changes?

12. What, in general, did this interview teach me about myself as an interviewer?

Recording

Having conducted and completed the interview, the interviewer is faced with the responsibility of recording it in some manner. Considerable amounts of staff time and agency finances are absorbed in recording and keeping records. In addition to the time spent by the worker, such expense involves clerical transcribing time, filing time, and time spent in record reading.

Keeping accurate records ensures a continuity of client-agency contact that transcends the client's contact with any individual social worker.

Recording of the interview spares the interviewee and collaterals from having to repeat the details of their situation to another worker who might subsequently be involved. The case record also implements the agency's accountability to the community. It provides a permanent, documented account of services to clients.

The interviewer about to record the interview faces the essential question, What should be recorded and how should the recording be organized? Just as purpose guides interview interaction, so it guides selection for recording. Traditionally, social work recording has been designed to meet a number of different purposes. We record to achieve more effective practice; we record to meet the needs of supervision and administration; we record to provide material for in-service training and teaching; we record for research. There is no consensus on the principal purpose of social work recording; consequently, recording has served these various purposes with limited effectiveness and has served no one purpose well.

Use of case records suggests that they are an integral aspect of practice and interviewing. The caseworker responsible for a case is the person most likely to use the records. Studies of record use indicate that their principal use has been in preparation and planning for direct or indirect service to the client. Records are used less frequently for supervision and administration, rarely for teaching training, and even less frequently for research.

Miles' empirical study of usage of correctional case records further confirms that the use of records for teaching and research is minimal and that their use in supervision has been overemphasized.

According to Miles, the worker uses the record "to organize his thinking about the case and to plan future courses of action. Through reading the record and recording his contacts with the case in the record, the [worker] organizes his thinking and prepares his plans for the case" (1965:290).

Recording helps the interviewer toward more effective interviewing. Recording the interview imposes the need to order and structure the information obtained in the interview. Recording not only requires a more precise, systematic formulation of the experience, it also helps to more clearly individualize the interviewee and her situation for subsequent recall. It helps the interviewer recognize what he did well, what was covered adequately, and what was missed. Recording the interview in whatever form permits opportunity for and contributes to, analytical reflection about the interview experience in retrospect. It encourages cognitive and affection integration of the experience.

Computerization of agency operations and documentation of activity for third party payments, as in Medicare and Medicaid, peer review of worker performance as exemplified in the Professional Standards Review Organizations (PSROs), and the courts' definition of evidence in actions in which social workers are frequently involved (e.g., termination of parental rights, divorce proceedings, adoption, etc.) have affected the way information obtained in the interview is recorded.

The interview may be recorded so as to justify a decision the worker has made, such as petitioning for movement of a child to foster care and to "cover" the worker in case an action is challenged.

The recording purpose dictates form and content. If recording is primarily designed to serve the needs of the practitioner, it might include content which focuses on the extent to which the purposes of the interview were achieved, worker interventions which helped or hindered achievement of purpose, client strengths and weaknesses in relation to interview purpose, work completed, and plans for the next contact. The practitioner's record would include all the essential identifying data which would enable him to review the client's situation at a glance.

Record content and organization will naturally differ from agency to agency. However, at least one definite prescription may be justifiable. The agency needs to be clear and explicit as to the purpose, or purposes, for which it requires the records. The agency should be able to communicate to the workers its unambiguous expectations as to what is wanted, how much is wanted, why it is wanted, how it should be organized.

The time lag between the interview and the recording should be as brief as possible. The longer the passage of time between the interview and the recording, the greater the danger that interview content will be forgotten or distorted. No matter what the purpose, selectivity is inevitable; even in the most detailed process records, a large part of what happens goes unrecorded. An hour's interview, when transcribed in full, generally covers thirty-five to forty typewritten pages. A great deal of selectivity is clearly involved in reducing it to a process recording of six or eight pages, which is a long record by any standards. Selectivity and consequent distortion are empirically confirmed by comparing process recordings with tapes of the same interviews (Wilkie 1963).

Most often the interview is briefly summarized or included in a brief statement as part of a recapitulation of a series of interviews. Criteria often cited for efficient recording of the interview include brevity, clarity, accuracy, selectivity, utility, and easy retrievability of information—a tall order.

Various attempts have been made to summarize the interview through a preformulated code. More recently there has been extensive adoption in social work of the Problems Oriented Record developed originally in medical practice but standardized for other professions (Burill 1976; Hartman and Wickey 1978). This involves a procedure for: 1) systematic recording

of the relevant data; 2) identification of the principal problems derived from
the data; 3) assessment and development of a plan for each identified problem; and 4) implementation of the plan. It provides an operational framework, with some flexibility, for making explicit in the record what has gone
on in the interview.

Care needs to be exercised in what is chosen to be recorded about the
interview. When recorded, what transpired in the interview acquires per-
manence and an element of authority, freezing a picture of the interviewee
at one point in time. Furthermore, records may be opened by court order,
as noted above (see discussion of confidentiality in chapter 3). Once the
interview is recorded, the interviewer loses control over how the information obtained might be used and possibly abused.

The rights of clients to have access to their records gained considerable
support during the 1970s through two federal acts—the Federal Privacy
Act of 1974 and the Federal Educational Amendment of 1974 (more popu-
larly known as the Buckley Amendment)—both mandating opening agency
records to clients who request access. As a consequence, many social agencies receiving federal government support were required to make their
records available to the client on request. The demands by organizations
of adopted persons who fought for open records so they could learn about
their background further contributed to changes in agency attitude and
policy regarding client access to records.

Abel and Johnson (1978) did a survey of attitudes of social workers regarding clients' access to records. They found the majority of practitioners
favored an open access policy. Workers felt that clients were entitled to
access, that access would increase client involvement in the relationship,
and would improve the quality of recording. The minority opposed to access felt that it might have a negative impact on the client and on the
relationship, and that workers would be prompted to "sanitize" the record
and include only innocuous material. There was concern that confidentiality would be violated since material in the records from other professionals
would be available as well. While most of the agencies had a policy making
access available, it was mitigated by the fact that clients were often not
explicitly informed of their prerogatives.

Reports of actual experience by social agencies indicated that permitting
client access to records generally worked out well, the open records foster-
ing mutual confidence and understanding (Houghkirk 1977; Freed 1978).
However, as Freed notes, implementing access is accompanied by great
care in recording the interview and greater selectivity in what is included
in the recording.

Because of the vulnerability of agency records two kinds of record keeping are sometimes suggested. One group of official records consists of more

objective data—demographic, face sheet data, health and test records, summaries of interview contacts and actions taken. A second group of unofficial records, belonging more to the interviewer for interviewer use than to the agency, consists of workers' progress notes, subjective impressions, and diagnostic inferences relative to interview interaction.

SUGGESTED READINGS

Suanna J. Wilson. *Recording: Guideline for Social Workers*. New York: Free Press, 1980 (238 pp.).

A detailed account of social work recording with an interesting variety of examples of recording.

Part III

Special Aspects of Interviewing

Feedback, Self-Disclosure, Immediacy, Humor

Throughout the interview, the competent interviewer recurrently uses some procedures which have been identified in the literature as expediting the interview, as helping to achieve the objectives of the interview.

Feedback, self-disclosure, immediacy, and humor have been cited as among the more significant of such helpful procedures. This chapter is concerned with a discussion of these procedures.

Feedback

Throughout the course of the interview, the interviewer provides feedback to the interviewee and solicits feedback from the interviewee. Feedback is a special form of communication. It is designed to let the participants in the interview know the extent to which they are accurately reading each other's communication. The necessity for feedback is exemplified in the admonition, "I know that you believe you understood what you think I said, but I am not at all sure you realize that what you heard is not what I meant."

Feedback is a distinctive form of communication. It is a communication that enables the participants in the interview to interact and check how close they are to achieving the objectives of their communication.

Positive feedback is a confirmation that, yes, they are communicating what they have intended to communicate. Negative feedback tells them that they have missed the mark and need to adjust their communication technique and make corrections for the deviation. Feedback enables the interviewer to more effectively monitor her communications.

Feedback is both internal and external. Internal feedback involves critically listening to yourself to check if what you are saying is what you meant to say. Internal feedback is, of necessity, a subjective assessment. External feedback, the response of others, is an objective determination of one's success. In a sense every response of the interviewee has an element of feedback associated with it since it shows how the interviewer's comment or question was received. The term *feedback*, however, is generally reserved for those explicit communications concerned with how the message was received. The client might say, "I don't understand your question," or "It isn't clear to me what it is you want to know" or "You keep putting words in my mouth." Feedback is communication about the communication.

The need for an occasional solicitation of feedback is based on the supposition of ignorance. The interviewer cannot know how she is coming across to the interviewee unless she checks. And while she wants to make certain that she understands and is understood, it is almost equally, if not more, important to make certain that she does not misunderstand and is not misunderstood. "Did I understand you correctly when I said that you didn't want to consider a homemaker?" Or, "Is the question clear to you?" Or, "I think I might be missing you. Can you tell me what you think about what I have just said?"

To be effective, solicitation of feedback has to be more than perfunctory. Frequent interjection of "Do you understand?" "Do you get me?" without pausing for a response raises questions in the client's mind of how much feedback is really wanted. In the usual one-downmanship position of the interviewee, it takes more than average courage and self-security for him to confess to the interviewer that she seems garbled and vague.

In soliciting feedback, the worker should be as specific and descriptive as possible, while sticking with the immediate interaction. "I noticed that, just now, when I raised the question of contacting your stepfather you clenched your fist and turned away from me. How do you feel about my asking about this?" Or, "You seemed to frown and you waved your hand impatiently when 'welfare' was mentioned; am I right in thinking you got sore at my mentioning it?"

The interviewer not only solicits feedback to check on the accuracy of her communication and her perceptions, but she also offers positive and negative feedback to the client. "Good," "that's right," are positive feedback comments indicating the client is on target. On the other hand the interviewer may share with the interviewee her feeling that the interviewee seems to be digressing or rambling and avoiding the difficult specific problems that need to be dealt with in the interview. "It seems to me that most of what you have said during the last 10 or 15 minutes doesn't say much about the problem you say you want help with."

When offering negative feedback to the interviewee, the interviewer should realize that, however innocuous the nature of the feedback, some criticism of the interviewee is implied. The interviewee is not doing what is expected of him, or he is communicating less effectively than hoped. Consequently, it would be well if negative feedback is primarily descriptive and depersonalized. Not, "You seem to jump around a lot in telling your story," but rather, "A moment ago you were talking about your mother and then you switched to your job, and now you're talking about school. I have some trouble following you. Could you help me on this?" Not, "You come across to me as argumentative and aggressive," but "When you keep shouting at me as you are doing now, I find myself getting sore at you."

Self-Disclosure

Feedback and self-disclosure are related. In self-disclosure, the interviewer feeds back to the interviewee how the interviewee is affecting her in the here and now, what feelings the interviewee is evoking. But self-disclosure goes beyond this. It also involves sharing with the interviewee some personal details regarding the interviewer's own life and experience.

Self-disclosure by the client is the expected norm in the interview. It is recognized as a necessary cost for obtaining the help the client seeks. Self-disclosure by the interviewer to the interviewee is not generally expected.

Interviewer self-disclosure is related to an interviewer's authenticity and genuineness, as described in chapter 3. The feelings of openness, spontaneity, and congruence predispose toward a willingness to self-disclose. However, although related to interviewer authenticity and genuineness, self-disclosure is a separate intervention.

Authenticity and genuineness are *intra*personally focused. They suggest that the interviewer is aware of her negative as well as positive feelings toward the interviewee, that she accepts responsibility for these feelings, and undefensively accepts ownership of them. These feelings may or may not be communicated or disclosed to the interviewee. If, however, it is necessary to disclose such feelings to the interviewee in response to a direct question or in response to what is needed to accomplish the purpose of the interview, the interviewer shares her feelings openly and honestly without defensiveness or apology. Self-disclosure is thus *inter*personally focused. It is an interactional, social act in which the interviewer, intentionally and voluntarily, shares personal information about herself, her experiences, feelings, beliefs, attitudes.

Of course the interviewer may unintentionally and not always entirely voluntarily disclose a good deal about herself. Sex, age, race, class are disclosed on observation. A marriage ring discloses marital status. Diplomas and membership certificates from professional organizations hanging on the wall disclose information about education and experience. But parenthood status, life failures, frustrations, disappointments, and satisfactions can only be voluntarily and intentionally disclosed. Thus "self-disclosure" generally refers to these aspects of communication.

The interviewee may seek information about the interviewer that is not available through casual observation. In orienting himself to the interviewer as a real person outside of her professional life, the client may ask direct questions about the interviewer's personal life.

Clients raise questions indirectly which solicit interviewer self-disclosure. Remarks such as "I sometimes wonder how people feel about me," "I am uneasy about whether or not most people really like me," "I wonder if men can really understand what women have to go through" might validly be interpreted as requests for some idea as to how the interviewer feels about the interviewee.

There are ideological commitments to self-disclosure. Some humanist oriented interviewers are uncomfortable with the inequality of a relationship in which sharing of personal information goes only one way. To redress the inequity of such a situation, to restore a greater sense of mutuality, and to reduce social and psychological distance between interviewer and interviewee, they feel impelled to share with the interviewee personal information about themselves.

OBJECTIVES

Interviewer's engage in self-disclosure to achieve a variety of objectives.

1. Authenticity coupled with a readiness toward self-disclosure facilitates the client's willingness to communicate and reduces barriers to intimate communication. The interviewer cannot fully expect openness and readiness-to-share from the interviewee unless she herself sets an example of such openness, spontaneity, and responsiveness.

There is considerable research support for the contention that disclosure by the interviewer of some information about herself, her difficulties and deficiencies, encourages a greater flow of such disclosures from the interviewee (Chelune et al. 1979). Shulman found that clients felt that the workers' sharing personal thoughts and feelings enabling the client to get to know her better as a person was highly associated with perception of the social worker's helpfulness as well as being important in developing the worker-client relationship (1977:78). Research from psychology tends to suggest that moderate, judicious, appropriate self-disclosure by the interviewer facilitates the development of an effective working relationship and encourages increasing self-disclosure by the interviewee (Murphy and Strong 1972; Bandza and Simonson 1973).

This interaction is generally known as the *reciprocity effect*—the interviewee reciprocates self-disclosures offered by the interviewer. A variety of explanations have been offered.

There is a socially felt norm of reciprocity which operates. Self-disclosure by the interviewer obligates the interviewee to share as well. Personal information is the price of the exchange and to keep the situation equitable the sharing of one needs to be matched by the sharing of the other. Another explanation derives from the effect of modeling. Since the social work interview situation is an ambiguous situation the interviewee is not always clear as to what is expected of him. The worker's self-disclosure presents a model as to the kind of behavior that is appropriate in the social work interview.

It should be noted that the reciprocity formula—"disclosure begets disclosure"—does not invariably work. Interviewers who seem cold and distant do not always get interviewee disclosure in response to their own. Once again, the nature of the interactional relationship is a powerful mediating variable.

2. The interviewee, in being selected as a receiver of self-disclosure by the interviewer, gets the sense that he is liked, respected, and trusted. This reaction is therapeutically supportive. Interviewer self-disclosure can be designed to be additionally therapeutic by helping the client know how his behavior affects other people, the impression he makes on other people.

3. Self-disclosure by the interviewer can relieve the interviewee's anxiety. Sharing similar negative experiences gives the client the feeling that he is not alone in the problems he faces.

4. Interviewer self-disclosure can encourage client self-disclosure when other, less intrusive, measures have failed.

In response to a client's telling her she had to have an operation for an ovarian cyst a medical social worker began by saying: "From what you said I get the feeling that the operation scares you." When the client was silent the worker universalized by saying: "I would imagine that most women would be frightened in thinking about having the operation." After a pause and continued silence the worker said: "I think I know a little bit about how you might feel because I remember when I had a hysterectomy last year I was really nervous and upset for a week before the operation." As the worker reported later: "After a short pause Ms. P. asked some questions about my operation and after I briefly answered what she wanted to know she began slowly and in a depressed voice to talk about her own feelings."

5. Interviewer self-disclosure can be used to support the client and reassure him that the worker is capable of understanding the situation because she too has "been there."

An adolescent girl has just shared with the social worker the fact that she "told her mother off in no uncertain terms" when her mother objected to her going out with a certain boy.

CLIENT: I don't think she was mad, but she was upset. I don't think she's going to leave me alone. Sometimes I hate her.

The worker, self-disclosing, says:

WORKER: I've felt the same way about my mother sometimes. The worst times were when I was trying to break away from her and form some opinions of my own.

The worker, commenting on her decision to share this with the client, says:

I think Ann feels very guilty, and hates her mother for making her feel guilty, but probably also might feel guilty, because she shouldn't hate her mother.
I think she needed to be reassured that she isn't the only one who has ever had feelings of hatred for a parent. I also want to let her know that I know what it is like and can understand her feelings.

6. Self-disclosure can be employed to relieve, through sharing, feelings that are getting in the way of interviewing effectively.

A female social worker in a mental health center was engaged in an initial interview with a middle-aged engineer who was considering divorce and who was anxious about its implications. Throughout the interview the interviewee had made a number of classic male chauvinist remarks. The social worker noted that she was becoming increasingly upset. She felt that she was expending energy in controlling herself to the detriment of the interview.

I felt that I was not acting as effectively as I might have in the interview because of the feelings the client generated by his remarks. When he said that he thought a woman's place was in the home taking care of the kids I took advantage of this to raise the question with him of how he thought I might be responding to his remarks. I said I wondered what he thought about my working since I was obviously "not home caring for the kids." In response to his ambiguous answer I pursued it further by wondering if given his feelings about this he thought I could be helpful to him. While I did not disclose directly how I felt about his male chauvinist remarks, raising it indirectly for discussion permitted me to resolve some of my feelings so as to be able to conduct the interview more effectively.

7. Self-disclosure can be used deliberately to provoke catharsis on the part of the client.

A worker in a protective agency had helped an abusive mother obtain a job as a typist along with day care for her child as a relief from child care. A short time later Mrs. F. was laid off because her typing speed was too slow. The worker said:

As we discussed what happened, she seemed unable to express any feelings about being let go. She discussed it in an indifferent matter-of-fact way although I had the feeling she was hurt and upset. So I said, "Gee if I were in your place I think I would feel lousy, upset, angry, sad. I know I would feel that way because I once had your experience and I know how it affected me." I then told her about the time I had been fired from a job in a dress factory because I couldn't sew a straight seam and how lousy this made me feel. Sharing this seemed to help Mrs. F. open up. Even before I finished telling about my experience, she started to slump, hunched over the desk and started to cry.

In summary, genuineness, congruence, and related discreet, appropriate self-disclosure manifested by the interviewer do facilitate the development of a productive relationship contributing to achieving the purpose of the interview. Like acceptance, warmth, and empathic understanding, the attributes of genuineness, authenticity, and self-disclosure encourage the client to share more fully and help develop a greater sense of liking for and trust in the interviewer. They help support, reassure, and confirm the worker's ability to empathize with the interviewee.

DANGERS AND DISADVANTAGES

There can be dangers and disadvantages in the use of self-disclosure. Attention needs to be paid to timing, appropriateness, and relevance. The worker should be aware that self-disclosure may impede rather than facilitate relationship development with some clients. The question is in what situation, with what interviewees, might the interviewer appropriately disclose what kinds of information about herself, with what precautions. The interviewer who indiscriminantly engages in self-disclosure to encourage self-disclosure by the interviewee may not always be doing the client a service. As Parloff says: "Not everybody is benefitted by the opportunity to let it all hang out. Some indeed may need help in tucking it all in" (1970:203).

1. There is a danger that, unless controlled, worker self-disclosure may shift the primary focus away from the interviewee and his problems on to the interviewer and her problem.

A female social worker in a child welfare agency was discussing day care with a divorced mother of two young children:

WORKER: I lost control of the interview for an extended period because I talked too much about myself and had to struggle hard to get back on course (which I am not sure I really did).
Mrs. B. asked me where I lived and if I had a family. I said on the west side and have one child but, I went on to say I was divorced too. Mrs. B. then wanted to know if I was divorced for some time. I told her three years. And before I knew how it came about I was discussing the problems which led to my divorce and the problem I had in being a single parent now.

A client deserves honest answers to his questions but the interviewer's responsibility then is to return the focus of the interview back to the interviewee. For example, a middle-aged white client in a family service agency says that he is having trouble in his marriage and supposes that "everyone has difficulty."

WORKER: Yes, I think you're right. I know that in my own marriage despite the fact that we generally get along, there are many moments of conflict. How does that compare with *your* experience?

Too much interviewer self-disclosure blurs the boundaries of who is interviewer and who is interviewee.

2. The interviewer may need to make a diagnostic assessment of the client's questions to determine what exactly is being asked of the worker.

The client, a young female adult whose mother was mentally ill for years, asks the worker: " 'What is your opinion of me?' She looked up at me. I said I was beginning to like her a lot. I said we've just known each other a short while but she's really done some good work" (Urdang 1979).

The interview then moves away from the question. Note that in asking, "What's your opinion of me?" the client may be asking, "Do you think I am crazy like my mother?" Returning the interview to the client in exploration of this question may have been the more productive option. In this instance the latent significant implication of the client's question got lost in the eagerness of the interviewer toward self-disclosure.

3. If an interviewer shares personal information in self-disclosure, she increases her vulnerability. Offering a picture of herself as humanly fallible leaves her open to derogation and criticism. However, it has been noted that the interviewee can more easily excuse weakness than he can deal with a worker who, by her failure to share, projects an image of perfection and invincibility.

4. The worker needs to be judicious about disclosing honestly felt feelings of shock and disapproval in response to what the client is saying.

A young female worker in a protective service agency interviewed a middle-aged man reported for committing incest with his seven-year-old stepdaughter. The worker reports:

This really was a hard one for me. As he talked about what had happened I kept saying to myself "how could you? how could you?" In my own mind his behavior was unacceptable and despicable. I had to exercise conscious, deliberate control over what I said and how I thought I sounded. I knew that if he could "read" how I felt he would clam up and withdraw from the interview.

Weiner, in a careful evaluation of his prolonged clinical experience with self-disclosure, concludes that "one cannot naively be one's self with patients in spite of the Rogerian notion that genuineness is the sine qua non of successful psychotherapy" (1978:2). Self-disclosure is not a license for a full expression of feelings by the interviewer. The interviewer is obligated to be in control of feelings which, if expressed, may be contrary to the therapeutic needs of the interviewee.

There are a wide range of alternatives between absolute honesty and downright dishonesty, between rigid self-effacement and lavish openness. There is selective self-disclosure, partial self-disclosure, and refusal to disclose with an explanation by the interviewer as to why she thinks refusal is best for the purposes which bring interviewer-interviewee together.

In avoiding destructive openness and insensitive sensitivity, the dictum is not to "tell it like it is," but rather "don't tell it like it isn't" (Pfeiffer and Jones, 1972:197).

5. Self-disclosure may compound the interviewee's problems.

The personalization of the interaction resulting from the interviewer's self-disclosure may be felt as a burden. The interviewee may feel he has to be supportive or reassuring to the interviewer who has just told him that she, too, has similar problems. Specific communication by the interviewer of her thoughts, feelings, and problems may be regarded by the person interviewed as an intrusion into his life-space. The interviewee may be primarily, if not exclusively, interested in a professional rather than a personal relationship with the interviewer.

6. Self-disclosure by the interviewer may be perceived by the interviewee as a demanding pressure for reciprocal self-disclosure from him. He may feel coerced to comply with the implicit demand and resent the felt pressure.

7. There is a danger of unintentional manipulation.

When the interviewer, in telling about a situation she experienced that is analogous to the one faced by the client, indicates how she resolved it, her account could be interpreted as a strong hint to the client to go and do likewise.

8. Self-disclosure can be misused by the interviewer as a tactic in ingratiating herself with the interviewee, in seducing the interviewee into liking her, by offering her personal secrets as a present.

Indiscriminate self-disclosure not obviously related to the requirements of the interview situation may then be perceived negatively by the interviewee as manipulative.

There is, further, the conceit that willingness to self-disclose is an indication of maturity and superior mental health. An interviewer's self-disclosure may be in a subtle way of the interviewer's reassuring herself that she is indeed mature, mentally healthy, openly human. Thus undisciplined self-disclosure may be disguised narcissistic gratification in exhibitionistic self-display.

GUIDELINES

Given the fact that interviewee self-disclosure involves danger as well as advantages, some guidelines might be useful.

Research on self-disclosure suggests that too much self-disclosure too soon by the interviewer is as bad as too little, too late. While the interviewee may be uncomfortable and anxious with the interviewer who remains sphinxlike herself, carefully, protectively, and defensively safeguarding her anonymity, he is equally discomforted by an interviewer who is a Niagara of self-disclosure, who seems ready and eager to let it all hang out. Interviewees see the latter as indiscreet, self-preoccupied, indiscriminate, and unstable and are concerned about her competence to be of help.

Timing is important. Intimacy in the relationship needs to be developed gradually and the client's need for some psychological distance early in the relationship needs to be respected.

The context, the dosage, and the timing of self-disclosure are the principle factors that determine if and when self-disclosure might be helpful. The most important question is Whose needs are being serviced by self-disclosure? Only if it answers the client's needs is interviewer self-disclosure justifiable. This implies, too, that failure of the interviewer to disclose when the needs of the interview already require it is as much a failure as over-disclosure that impedes the interview.

Self-disclosure needs to be used sparingly so that it does not overwhelm the interviewee. It needs to be offered discriminately and selectively, delicately and cautiously with some sensitivity to the client's readiness for such information, with a conscious idea as to what is likely to be helpfully achieved by such self-disclosure. It needs to be made in such a way that the interviewer does not, in the digression, become the focus of the interaction rather than the interviewee.

Since each interview is a highly individualized encounter and since no interviewee is like any other interviewee, the effects of any interviewer's self-disclosure should be monitored. Feedback from the interviewee helps the interviewer to adapt, adjust, tailor self-disclosures so that they are timely, appropriate, and helpful.

While self-disclosure by the interviewer facilitates self-disclosure by the interviewee, this is only one of the ways the interviewer achieves interviewee revelation. And given the dangers inherent in self-disclosure it may not be the best or most effective way of facilitating self-disclosure by the interviewee. The atmosphere of psychological safety, the acceptance, respect, and manifestation of empathic understanding, all have the effect of facilitating interviewee self-disclosure. Well-timed, well-formulated questions, open invitations to talk also have this effect. It may be better to depend on these kinds of intervention rather than the trickier tactic of interviewer self-disclosure. Most social work clients are aware that in order to use the service they need to share with the interviewer many intimate aspects of their lives. The interviewee generally needs less prompting toward self-disclosure since he recognizes this as an obligation of his role as a client and that his sharing of personal information is not contingent on the interviewer's reciprocal sharing of such information. Affective neutrality may then be the safest initial orientation of the interviewer discarded briefly and temporarily for self-disclosure when it is clear that the needs of the interview would be best served by the change.

The fact that self-disclosure implies an increasing intimacy in the relationship has consequences for the frequency with which some social workers self-disclose. Bradmiller, in a study of self-disclosure by social workers, found that unmarried female social workers were least likely to share information about themselves with clients. While married female social workers might feel that the fact that they were married "offered a form of protection against misrepresentation of their personal or intimate disclosures" (1978:33), unmarried female social workers might have some anxiety that self-disclosure might be perceived as an invitation to greater familiarity outside the interview situation.

A recent study of the use of self-disclosure by social workers (Borenzweig 1981) echoes Bradmiller's finding (1978) that social workers are guarded in their use of such intervention. Borenzweig found this particularly true of social workers who regard themselves as psychoanalytically oriented. Social workers showed reluctance to share with their clients information about their political, sexual, or religious orientation. Information was more freely shared about marital status, parenting, and significant experiences of loss such as divorce and death. There was a feeling expressed by respondents that they resented being manipulated and/or coerced by the clients into self-disclosure. There was further the feeling that emphasizing the elements of a common humanity in disclosing secrets about themselves diminished some of the clinician's charismatic power to help the client.

Immediacy and Concreteness

In interviewing to extend the range and depth and stimulate the client's problem-solving efforts, the interviewer makes choices to stimulate immediacy and concreteness in the interviewee's response (Weiner and Mehrabian 1968). The interviewer's subtle differences in choice of wording in formulating questions or responses tends to make communication more or less concrete, more or less immediate.

Immediacy is the degree to which the focus of attention is on the "here and now" rather than on time past or time future. Thus one can ask the client how he felt about his children at the time they were born, or during the time they were growing up. Asking about how he feels about Johnny now, at this point in time, focuses the discussion on the immediate parent-child interaction.

Concreteness in expression is the extent to which the interviewer or the interviewee is involved in what is being discussed, and the explicitness with which the content of the discussion is defined. Some emotional distance between the client and the situation persists if the worker says: "People generally have some difficulty with their marriage," or "It is probable that people sometimes have conflicts with their marital partner."

It is much more concrete to say: "From what you have been telling me, it seems that you have problems in your marriage." Concreteness implies that the content discussed is specific and relevant to the individual interviewee's concerns.

When the client expresses his problem in terms which suggests greater concreteness and immediacy, it indicates a greater willingness to accept ownership of the problem and greater responsibility for his situation.

In expressing a commitment to some action discussed in the interview, the interviewee may choose to say any one of the following: "I should take care of my family," "I must take care of my family," "I need to take care of my family," or "They want me to take care of my family." He may preface any one of these variants by "I think," "I feel," or "I believe." Every variation in use of "think," "feel," or "believe" in combination with "should," "must," "need," or "they want" makes a sentence with distinctively different meaning.

An interviewee discussing a previous interview might choose to say "in the interview," "in your interview," "in our interview," or "in my interview." The last phrasing indicates the most intimate acceptance of involvement and immediacy.

Sequence has significance. "My wife, our children, and I went . . ." rather than "I, our children, and my wife went . . ." may suggest something of who is accorded seniority in the interviewee's perception of the family.

The interviewer, in seeking concreteness, follows up vague or abstract or evasive questions or comments and translates these into content that is specifically relevant to the interviewee's individual, particular situation. Universal statements applicable to everybody are personalized. Not "most people do" or "most families do," but "what do you do," "what does your family do."

There is a difference in immediacy and concreteness between a client's saying: "He was really being hurtful when he said that," and saying: "I felt very hurt by his comments."

Modeling communication which emphasizes an active orientation in which the person does the acting as against a passive orientation in which the person is acted upon, increases the level of concreteness.

INTERVIEWEE: I was overcome with shame.
INTERVIEWER: You feel ashamed.

INTERVIEWEE: A feeling of remorse came over me at that point.
INTERVIEWER: You felt guilty.

INTERVIEWEE: My boy friend kept after me till I had to give in.
INTERVIEWER: You did have intercourse with him then.

The use of vague modifiers: "perhaps," "kind of," "sometimes," "it seems that," "I wonder if," tend to reduce the level of concreteness of communication. "Usually," "at most," "probably," are other examples of qualifying language that limit concreteness and increase ambiguity.

There is an element of avoidance involved in talking in general terms. The worker, attempting to achieve concreteness, needs to ask a series of probing questions or make ambiguity visible.

BOB: I seem to have difficulty in getting along with everybody now about everything. And it just makes me feel lousy.
WORKER: Everybody?

Reflecting "everybody," the worker seeks to identify some one specific person for discussion. Having difficulty in getting along with "about everything" presents an obstacle for the interview unless it can be further identified. Specifically, what is *one* situation in which Bob has had difficulty in "getting along"? Further, since "feeling lousy"is very vague, what are some of the specific feelings Bob has about his situation?

It may be softer but also more ambiguous to say, "I didn't pass" as compared with "I failed," and to say "I felt happier before" as against saying "I feel sad now." The phrasing amounts to the same thing in both instances but they amount to the same things in different ways. The difference in expressions reflects different approaches to dealing with the problem.

The use of lower levels of immediacy and concreteness may be the desirable option in some instances. If there is a desire to soften the impact of the communication, to approach a sensitive area indirectly and obliquely, than saying "one does" rather than "you do" would be the most helpful choice.

Concreteness and immediacy are not unmitigatedly desirable. Sometimes it is helpful to be deliberately vague and indirect. Qualifying words soften the impact of a message. This may be just what is needed by an anxious defensive interviewee.

Humor

The judicious use of humor can facilitate the achievement of the purposes of the interview. The use of humor has received very little attention in social work, there being only a few scattered references available in the literature (Orfanidis 1972; Dewane 1978; Rhodes 1978:128; Nelson 1975).

Humor and accompanying laughter is likely to be more frequent and more appropriate at the beginning and end of the interview. It tends to be less frequent during the body of the interview when the participants are actively involved in the serious business bringing them together.

Humor serves a variety of significant purposes in human interaction. It permits indirect expression of ideas which are generally irreverent and impertinent. The meta-communication which accompanies saying what is normally prohibited is "it's all a joke; don't take it seriously." This function of humor was institutionalized in the role of court jester and is currently institutionalized in April Fools' Day. Humor here serves the purpose of a safety valve permitting the release of feelings which need to be suppressed but are difficult to suppress. It is a momentary sanctioned liberation from everyday inhibitions. It helps explain why so many jokes are based on sex and aggression.

The use of humor permits worker or client to act as though the ordinary norms of the interview interaction are temporarily suspended and either or both can act with impunity outside the ordinary constraints of logic, language, and conduct. The fact that humor gives an element of indirection to communication, the fact that each can disallow something by implying, while saying it, that one does not really mean what one is saying, makes humor a useful tactic for transitions in the interview. Sensitive or potentially embarrassing material can be tentatively introduced through humor. If it proves too threatening, the fact that it was humorously stated permits the speaker to back off from it, to withdraw without penalty. Thus humor might be used by the interviewee to challenge the authority and status of the interviewer. Because such an approach is anxiety-provoking the use of humor permits doing so while denying that one is doing it. Humor permits us to circumvent inhibitions through ambiguity, metaphors, and symbols.

Humor enables us to objectify and cope with some of the absurdities of the human condition, the injustice and capriciousness of life. Humor enables us to deal with and express feelings that we find too painful to confront directly. Humor relieves anxiety and makes us better able to handle situations which are frightening by making them appear less frightening. This function is exemplified in gallows humor. We joke at death when we talk about the man who, about to be executed, refused a last cigarette, and explained his refusal by saying he was trying to give up smoking. In laughing at the paradoxes, the absurdities, the intractable difficulties of everyday life which are typical of the human condition, we transcend them. Humor thus has a cathartic effect.

Humor, artfully used, provides a gentle way of dissolving tension that is making participants in the interview uncomfortable.

A young worker with Red Cross assigned to a rural area hit by a tornado felt uncomfortable about asking clients a series of detailed factual questions about background when "The whole world around them lay in ruins." The client said he was a Creole. I questioned, "Creole?" "What," he said, "you never heard of it?" I said, "No, I have led a sheltered life." This broke both of us up and the laughing made us feel easier with each other.

Humor can be used as a compassionate kind of confrontation. Satirical humor is used to "unmask" inflated pretensions, to indicate that you're not buying what the client's saying. The use of humor softens disagreement with the client. If successfully employed in such instances, honesty in the relationship is increased as sham and affectation are reduced.

A male social worker describes such use of humor in a contact with a very intelligent high school student underachiever in conflict with his parents.

Robert went on at great length all about how good he had been the past weeks and how unappreciative his parents were and how they still kept criticizing him. I got the feeling that much of what he was telling me was B.S. and a con. Wanting him to face what he might have contributed to how it went between him and his parents these past weeks, I said jocularly (and maybe somewhat sarcastically), "No good deed goes unpunished, eh?" Rejecting the implication, he said, "No, he had really been an exemplary son"—so I dropped it at this point.

Because humor makes a point in a comical, sharply focused manner, it can help the client make sense of his situation from a novel perspective. Humor is potentially insightful. It is not a trivial distraction but can be a potent procedure for facilitating interview objectives. Levine cites such an instance:

A forty-year-old female patient constantly complained about her unfaithful and inconsiderate husband. The marriage was a failure since she disliked her husband, found sex with him disgusting, and generally considered his behaviour contemptible. The therapist felt moved to comment that she still chose to live with him and did not consider divorce. The patient responded that she was afraid that she would not be able to replace him and as bad as he was she felt that loneliness would be worse. The therapist remarked that he could under-

stand her fears of loneliness but felt that there was another aspect of her preference for remaining married which was suggested by the story of the man
who worked in the circus cleaning up after the animals and giving enemas to
constipated elephants. An old friend of his observing the menial type of work
that he was doing offered to help him get another job. To which he replied,
"What, and give up show biz?" The patient at first was indignant about this
analogy but then began to laugh about it. She was able to come to grips with
some of her covert motives in her complaints about her husband. She came to
recognize that despite these constant complaints her marriage had some re-
deeming features and did satisfy some of her needs, not the least of which was
the opportunity to complain and to blame others for her unsatisfied needs.
(1977:133)

The joke is in the nature of an astute interpretation offered to the client
for thoughtful consideration. Use of humor in an interpretative or confronting intervention by the interviewer gives the message a more benign, less
threatening quality.

Incongruity often provokes laughter. Playfully violating habitual patterns
of thought about things, a joke has an element of insightfulness associated
with it since it puts two ideas together that generally do not go together.
Consequently this kind of humor might be used by the interviewer to stimulate clarification or insight.

In addition to qualifying and/or disguising the latent meaning of the communication, joint laughter tends to increase the sense of solidarity between
interviewer and interviewee in their participation in a joint activity. It
heightens the sense of being involved in a special unique small social system, the sense of "we" as contrasted with "them." Humor here has the
effect of being supportive.

The use of humor tends to reduce social-psychological distance and formality between interviewee-interviewer. Laughing together increases a
sense of mutuality and the joint appreciation of the joke solidifies a sense
of common membership in the human race. The psychiatrist who tells a
patient about a postcard he had received from a fellow psychiatrist on vacation, "Having a wonderful time. I wonder why?" seems more humanly
accessible as a consequence. Humor, like self-disclosure, increases the sense
of intimacy between interviewer and interviewee.

Humor tends to intensify group identification, making people feel closer
to each other. Much humor is concerned with disparagement of out-group
members by in-group members, making in-groupers feel better about
themselves. Ethnic humor has an element of this. Disparagement of self
and particularly of others is a frequent cause for laughter. In both cases it
is an expression of hostility and aggression made socially acceptable by virtue of the fact that it is expressed in humor. On the other hand humor

directed against oneself may be used as a weapon of appeasement or ingratiation.

Because humor comes in all shapes, sizes, and colors, having different effects on different people, it needs to be employed and used with considerable caution and care (Kubie 1971). What seems funny to one person can be felt as sarcasm, mockery, derision, or ridicule to another. Humor is clearly a double-edged weapon.

The potential dangers in the use of humor increase with the developing self-consciousness of additional groups in society. Jokes about women and minorities that were previously acceptable, or at least not regarded as unduly offensive, are now seen as unacceptable manifestations of racism and sexism (Meitz 1980).

The need for caution is particularly acute in the social work interview. Since the interviewee is there because he has a consequential problem, the situation is inherently not funny. No matter how bad a problem is generally it is worse for the person who has it, so that the client is least inclined to see any humor in his situation. The joking interviewer may appear insensitive and unfeeling to the interviewee.

Humor should never be used at the expense of the client and laughing with a client is very much different from laughing at the client.

The interviewer who maintains her "superior" position through the use of supposedly humorous sarcasm or ridicule is using humor inappropriately. But every intervention lends itself to abuse in the hands of a punitive interviewer, and humor is no exception.

Because the effects of the use of humor are difficult to predict, the interviewer is on safer ground if she responds to humor introduced by the client rather than if she herself initiates an intervention she regards as humorous. A female social worker helping a mother on AFDC with difficulties in budgeting says,

One of the things Mrs. W. said early in the interview helped increase our sense of support with each other. She said she keeps struggling with the budget and it seems to her that it's like trying to help elephants have intercourse. She just can't seem to get on top of things. The picture this spontaneously seemed to invoke in both our minds had us laughing together uproariously.

Dosage timing, sensitivity, and good taste with regards to this as well as other aspects of the interview, are important considerations. Humor is most effectively used when it is spontaneous and relevant to the specific content offered by the client. Dosage of humor has been likened to yeast in bread—an appropriate amount leavens the bread making it more digestible; too much yeast spoils it.

Some might object to the use of humor if the encounter is perceived as a very serious matter which is not likely to be effective unless it is painful. Interviewers who use humor may be regarded as frivolous or insensitive. Worse it might be regarded as unprofessional—the deadliest of sins. Yet laughter contributes to the objectives of the interview by highlighting contradictions, challenging sacred ideas and feelings so that they become approachable and discussable. Humor enables us to see our situation from new perspectives and makes the unbearable bearable.

The very nature of humor makes it difficult to discuss abstractly. Context and timing are most important. It is by nature spontaneous and unplanned. All we can do here is to raise the reader's consciousness about the possible contributions humor might make to a good interviewer and to encourage its use as an acceptable and appropriate interview procedure.

SUGGESTED READINGS

SELF-DISCLOSURE

Gordon J. Chelune and Associates. *Self-Disclosure: Origins, Patterns, and Implications of Openness in Interpersonal Relationships*. San Francisco: Jossey-Bass, 1979 (394 pp.).
An edited text which presents a sophisticated analysis of what is involved in self-disclosure, the implementation of self-disclosure interventions, and the effects of self-disclosure. The book includes a comprehensive bibliography of resources on self-disclosure.

Myron F. Weiner. *Therapist Disclosure: The Use of Self in Psychotherapy*. Boston: Butterworth, 1978 (175 pp.).
An engaging presentation of the implications of self-disclosure for the interviewer. The author, a psychiatrist, shares his doubts and problems.

HUMOR

A. Chapman and H. Foot, editors. *Humor and Laughter: Theory, Research, and Application*. New York: Wiley, 1976 (348 pp.).
Sometimes humorous in the seriousness with which it discusses humor. The readings attempt to define and explain humor and shows its applicability to the therapeutic situation.

CHAPTER 12

The Technique of Listening, the Sounds of Silence, and the Telephone Interview

Listening

It is estimated that if the interviewer spends less than two-thirds of an interview listening and more than one-third talking, he is more active than he should be. A common error of inexperienced interviewers is to talk too much and to listen too little. Overactive talking makes for underactive listening. Listening is deceptively simple; effective listening is difficult, an active rather than a passive technique. Good listening requires following carefully what is overtly said as well as the latent undertones. It requires being expectantly attentive and receptive. It requires a relaxed alertness during which the interviewer reaches out mentally to bring in what the interviewee is saying.

Because the listener is externally quiet we tend to think of listening as a passive function. The apparent passivity of the listener is accentuated by the overt activity of the talker. Actually, despite the fact that the listener appears passive, good listening requires a considerable amount of internal activity.

HEARING VS. LISTENING

Hearing and listening, while related, are in fact two different processes. Hearing is a physiological act—the apprehension of sound. Listening is a cerebral act—that of understanding the sound which has been heard. It is the act of deriving meaning from sounds. Unlike hearing, listening requires deliberate attention to sound. Just as you can look without seeing you can hear without listening.

Listening is the dynamic process of attaching meaning to what we hear, making sense of and understanding aurally received raw verbal-vocal symbols. It is a purposive, selective process in which sounds communicated by a speaker are received, discriminately screened, given attention, recognized, comprehended, and interpreted by the hearer. Listening is not the passive reception of sound but the active processing of sounds we hear. It involves not only listening *to* sounds but listening *for* sounds that would further our understanding.

From all the words uttered by someone speaking to us, all of which we hear, we select a limited number for attention, focus, and awareness. Until we actually receive and attend to the communication, we have only heard but have not as yet listened. We then actually engage in a process of ascribing meaning to the limited number of sentences we listen to and then go on to interpret meaning from that to which we have listened. Listening involves the cognitive structuring of the message to which selective attention was given.

Giving meaning to the sounds we hear requires not only attention but the intelligence to comprehend, a reasonably large vocabulary, a knowledge of the subject matter being presented. One can hear a foreign language, but there is no listening involved, no meaning derived, unless one knows the language.

Since listening, unlike hearing, is not an automatic process we have to make a conscious, deliberate and continuing commitment to listen. It almost requires that we occasionally deliberately command ourselves to listen to make ourselves receptive to listening, to stop to listen.

Listening involves attention not only to the words per se but the vocalizations accompanying the words. This permits us to distinguish a command from a request or from a question. I will discuss the vocal nonverbal aspects of interview communication more fully in chapter 14.

Although listening is distinct from hearing, it depends on good hearing. If you cannot hear the sounds you cannot process them for listening. Any distractions or impediments to good hearing affects listening adversely. A quiet room with a minimum of competing sounds is a necessary prerequisite to good listening. Poor speech habits make hearing difficult and may require some adjustment to the interviewee.

The interviewee who speaks through clenched jaws holding a pipe or around a cigarette dangling from the corner of the mouth, the interviewee who slurs her words because she is under the influence of drink or drugs or who speaks in a very low voice, present problems for hearing and listening. Gently and courteously telling the interviewee she cannot be heard is a helpful communication and one that might be accepted without resentment because it indicates the worker's sincere interest in trying to listen. The interviewer has the responsibility of helping the interviewee present her situation in a way that helps him listen effectively.

Listening is basic to a good interview. Unless the interviewer listens carefully to what the client is saying he cannot "follow" her, he cannot reflect or paraphrase accurately, summarize correctly, or offer feedback in line with what she said. Listening is not only basic to implementing the instrumental aspects of interviewing, it is also related to the interview's expressive aspects. Listening requires effective attending and indicates respect and concern for the interviewee. Careful listening demonstrates that the interviewee is worthy of the full attention of the interviewer.

Not only is it important to listen, but the interviewer needs to present an attitude of listening, to visually communicate the fact that he is listening. The interviewee needs such confirmation that the interviewer is listening to her. An attending stance, eye contact, a forward lean, a physically related and attentive orientation show that the worker is listening. More to the point in confirmation is the interviewer's accurate reflecting, correct paraphrasing, and summarizing on target. These indicate that the interviewer has not only heard but has listened because he manifests understanding of what was said.

While careful to communicate positive nonverbal manifestation of attentive listening, the good listener is equally careful to refrain from any indications of inattention. Furtive glances at the clock, idle doodling on the note pad, sorting material on his desk top, a glance directed at the window to check the weather, all suggest wandering attention.

Admittedly, some interviewees make listening more difficult. They talk in a flat monotone. There is little drama in their presentation. They are repetitive, redundant, and present their problem in the least imaginative, most uninteresting manner. There are long pauses and frequent interjections of "you knows" or "eh, eh." Some interviewees are easier to listen to and consequently require less concentrated effort in listening from the interviewer. But the obligation to listen to the presentation of the least interesting interviewee is as great as in the case of most interesting. Greater self-monitoring by the interviewer is required, however.

PROBLEMS AND GUIDELINES

Typical day-to-day social interaction encourages the development of poor listening habits. Social interaction involves a considerable amount of hearing but only a limited amount of listening. Most often we courteously feign listening but pay only peripheral attention to what we hear, as we do to background music in department stores and restaurants. We know from experience that to listen to everything we hear is a regrettable waste of time involving a considerable expenditure of effort for the return provided. We have learned that it is functional not to listen because much that is irrelevant is said by many people to whom we have only limited obligation to listen. Much of what we hear is in the nature of ritualistic noises we make to one another.

The tendency toward redundancy by people engaged in social conversation further encourages the development of dysfunctional listening habits. The fact that people repeat themselves means that we do not pay a high price for failure to listen the first time around. We have learned that we will catch anything important the second or third time around. For good reasons and in self-protection we have, as a consequence of long experience in commonplace social interaction, developed listening habits that are bad for good interviewing. In learning to listen most effectively in the interview it is helpful to consciously identify our habituated patterns of listening and to determine what needs changing.

In everyday social situations, listening usually involves communication interaction with somebody we know—spouse, children, friends, co-workers. Our knowledge of patterns of past interaction help us to listen, to make sense of what is being said. We can anticipate, with some validity, some of the things they are likely to say. We can correctly fill in gaps in listening. This makes for listening with diminished concentration since heightened concentration is not required. We therefore, once again, tend to develop lazy listening habits. Interviews with strangers, as is often the case in social work, require a greater effort of concentrated listening. There is no history of previous patterns of interaction on which to draw in understanding the communication.

In social situations we often listen defensively. We busy ourselves with preparing our rebuttle to ideas, attitudes, and values being expressed which are in opposition to our own and which, consequently, threaten us. Preparing our own counter-presentation interferes with full effective listening. A considerable amount of energy is devoted to formulating an answer rather than to listening. Consequently we often listen inattentively waiting impatiently for the opportunity to have our turn to talk.

Sometimes we do not listen because we cannot afford to listen. To listen with a willingness to understand what is being said may risk for us the development of internal conflict and dissonance as our cherished beliefs are challenged and perhaps contradicted. Or we may learn things that make us feel inadequate or inferior or call attention to a problem we are trying to suppress.

A social worker in corrections was checking an interview with the wife of a prisoner in a state penitentiary which she had taped:

As I listened to the tape I was chagrined to find that a whole section of the interview had drifted out of my mind. Mrs. N. talked about the sadness she felt on separating from her husband after a recent visit. She went on to talk about the emptiness of the house and the effect of his absence on the family. I recalled none of this. Apparently the word separation triggered for me my own feelings about my impending divorce and I kind of turned myself off at this point or tuned her out.

The example illustrates the fact that reactions related to listening (or in this case not listening) may be triggered by stimuli about which we are not consciously aware, but which have significant ego involvement for us. Perceptual discrimination, screening what gets listened to, occurs both in terms of feelings as well as information. True listening implies a readiness to accept hearing what challenges our preconceptions. It involves a willingness to lower the psychic barriers that might impede undistorted perception of what the interviewee is saying.

In the interview, listening requires a different approach in contrast to social listening habits we have developed. The interviewer needs to feel comfortable and unthreatened by anything the interviewee says so that he can devote all his energy to listening freely to what is being said. While recognizing that what is being said may be contrary to his own values and attitudes he is not called on to defend them in the interview.

The nature of spoken communication presents a special hazard, seducing the interviewer into an easy nonlistening mode. The hazard is the great discrepancy between the number of words that are normally spoken in one minute and the number of words that can be absorbed in that time. Think-speed is much greater than talk-speed.

The average rate of spoken speech is about 125 words per minute. We can read and understand an average of about 300–500 words per minute. There is, then, a considerable amount of dead time in spoken communication, during which the listener's mind can easily become distracted. The listener starts silently talking to herself to take up the slack in time. Listening to the internal monologue may go on side by side with listening to the external dialogue. More often, however, it goes on at the expense of listening to the external dialogue. The interviewer becomes lost in some private reverie—planning, musing, dreaming.

Client, female, 68, white, upper middle class, medical social work interview.
MRS. M.: So maybe because of the experience on the trip, Arnie has a

better appreciation of how inconveniently crowded it might be with another person living in their relatively small house.

WORKER: Arnie?

MRS. M.: Yes Arnie, Arnold, my daughter's husband. I told you this before.

The worker's introspective comment on this follows:

I felt ashamed about this. I was caught woolgathering. Mrs. M. has been telling me about a trip her daughter's family had taken recently out West. It didn't seem particularly consequential to the problem for which she was referred [helping her accept a post-hospital living situation with her daughter], and so I began to think about my coming vacation and a trip we were planning. I just monitored the cadence of what Mrs. M. was saying but really was not listening. I was thinking about what needed checking on the car and some of the reservations that needed to be made yet. Somewhere along the line, Mrs. M. must have switched from the trip to the reactions of the family, living crowded together in motel rooms. Somehow I must have become aware that the content was becoming more relevant, but I surfaced slowly from my own trip plans, and when she said Arnie, for the moment I couldn't place the name. She generally refers to him as "my daughter's husband." When she had to explain who he was, she must have sensed I had not been listening, because she was irritated and annoyed. Not so good.

The supposition is that if you are not talking, you must be listening. Actually, one may not be talking and not be listening either—at least not to the interviewee.

The following analysis by a male psychiatric social worker of his pattern of listening is instructive:

I have become aware that I carry over to the interview some defensive listening patterns I have developed in general social interaction. It is a way of faking listening while permitting yourself the opportunity of enjoying your own private thinking. You look expectantly directly at the person, nod occasionally, or say "Yes, yes," smile when he smiles, and laugh along with him—at what, you don't know, because you haven't been listening. To protect my relationship with the speaker, I half-listen or listen sporadically. Every once in a while I'll really listen to check if I know what, in general, he is talking about. This is in case he should ask me a question. I listen for questions by the inflection. If the tone changes and I catch a rising inflection, I know I am being asked something. In social encounters, this gives me a lot of time for myself, and saves me from having to listen to an awful lot of BS. But I tend to slip into this pattern in the interview when the client bores me with repetition or with inconsequential detail. It bothers me because, unless I keep listening, how do I really know it's repetitive stuff or inconsequential?

The great possibilities for distraction from listening require considerable self-discipline from the would-be listener. Rather than becoming preoccupied as a consequence of the availability of the spare time between the slow spoken words, the good interviewer exploits this time in the service of more effective listening. The listener keeps focused on the interviewee but uses the time made available to the mind by slowness of speech to move rapidly back and forth along the path of the interview, testing, connecting, questioning: "How does what I am hearing now relate to what I heard before? How does it modify what I heard before? How does it conflict with it, support it, make it more understandable? What can I anticipate hearing next? What do I miss hearing that needs asking about? What is she trying to tell me? What other meanings can the message have? What are her motives in telling me this? How can I use what she is saying in order to be helpful to her? What does she want of me?"

We hear much more than we listen to. We could not conceivably really listen to all that we hear—to all of the sounds that impact on our ears and make for the physiological changes we define as hearing. Nor would it be functionally efficient to listen to all that we hear. We are inevitably selective. From the variety of sounds that we hear, we pay attention to and process relatively few for recognition, cognition, and understanding. Someone once described the average listener as a narrow necked bottle over which the speaker tosses water. Some goes in but much more goes by. If the interviewer felt compelled to listen to everything that was said, he would be overwhelmed with stimuli. The ear, like the eye, receives more than the mind can efficiently process.

Since listening involves the cerebral process of devising meanings from the sounds heard, the more a worker knows about the social problems the client is concerned with the more likely he can listen effectively. Being knowledgeable about the problems of old age, or single parenthood, or adolescence, or physical handicaps, or adoptions permits the worker to make mental connections that enable him to make sense of what he hears. It makes listening less difficult. The interviewer finds that he understands the client's situation better through listening because of the background knowledge he brings to the situation. This is rewarding and sustains motivation to continue to pay the close attention required for effective listening.

General knowledge of the content area also guides selectivity in listening. Having some expertise regarding some particular social situation for which the agency offers service permits us to assess what is of importance and significance in what the client is saying and what we can let go by because it's not particularly relevant.

A clear idea of purpose of the interview acts as an important filter for selectivity in listening. Knowing the objective of the encounter, a worker is in a better position to center his attention on certain things the client is saying that most need listening to because these are the ones that might conceivably contribute to achieving the purpose of the interview. A clear conception of purpose acts as a magnifying lens which selectively amplifies for attention and perception these points. Purpose structures attention.

A worker should listen for recurrent dominant themes rather than focus on detail. T. Reik's admonition to "listen with the third ear" repeats Freud's advice to listen with "free floating attention." Listening to the essence of the interviewee's communication with an "ever hovering attention" suggests this kind of approach; it is an approach which focuses on listening to what the interviewee means rather than what she says.

While it makes for more efficient productive listening to pay attention to dominant themes rather than unassorted details in the client's presentation, formulation of such themes should be allowed to develop slowly over the course of the interview rather than be set down too early. Although the interviewer actively organizes the material listened to, he holds the developing configuration lightly, provisionally.

An effective interviewer suspends closure in his mind, holding everything he listens to tentatively and subject to revision by what the client might say next. This is not only true for immediate interactions, but over the longer course in the interview. Making up one's mind about the interviewee and her problem early in the interview is a decision which, in itself, acts like a screen filtering subsequent listening. A worker can fall into the trap of tending to listen to those things which confirm the assessments made early in the interview and failing to listen to those communications which contradict the conclusion he has come to and which require a revision of those conclusions. It takes a deliberate effort to listen to the unexpected.

A middle-aged blue-collar worker was referred by a high-school teacher to a local family planning service when his 14-year-old daughter, Ruth, was found to be pregnant. The female social worker said:

The way he talked early in the interview . . . I guess my stereotype of blue-collar workers' attitudes leads me to think of him as conservative in his thinking. Everything he said and his whole approach to problems seem to confirm it for me. He was a living twin of Archie Bunker of "All in the Family." Consequently I strongly anticipated that he would be against abortion. So when it came to discussing it, I actually heard him say in response to my question, that he was against it. I was beginning to present, for consideration, some of the reasons which might make it an option in this instance when he interrupted. He said emphatically: "You didn't listen. I didn't say I was against an abortion for Ruth. I said I was in favor of it."

Here adherence to the stereotype raised expectations which distorted what was heard.

The stronger, more persistent, more inflexible, the stereotype a worker brings to the interview, the more certain he is that he knows what the interviewee will say, the less inclined he will be to actively and flexibly listen. To know the stereotypes one holds is a step in making for more effective listening. To be ready to modify and revise the stereotypes is another giant step. It is said that the human mind is like a parachute—it functions better when it is open.

Undistorted listening requires some recognition of the stereotypes, preconceptions, mind-sets, one brings to the interview. The client cannot be expected to discard her stereotypes, preconceptions, or mind-sets. All that can be expected is that the interviewer is aware of his own and treats them with sufficient freedom and flexibility so that they are subject to modification in contact with the individual interviewee. Stereotypes not subject to change, sometimes called "hardening of the categories," make for high risk of distorted listening.

Good listening requires an assumption and acceptance of ignorance. If a worker knew what the interviewee was going to say, he would not have to listen and would feel little motivation to listen.

If a worker makes assumptions about what the interviewee will say, rather than listening to what she is actually saying, he will find himself interrupting to finish her thoughts for her, in anticipation of what she is likely to say assuming he can "see" what she is driving at.

A 47-year-old man has been sharing his paranoid thoughts with a psychiatric social worker.
MR. A.: These things I've told you are—
WORKER: [Interrupting] strictly between you and me, confidential.
MR. A.: [Continuing] are the way I think most of the time, and I hope you don't misinterpret me.

In order to listen a worker must control his desire to speak, assume ignorance of what the speaker is likely to say, and intensify a desire to learn what it is that she wants to say. As Schulman says, the good listener "develops large eyes, big ears, and a small mouth" (1974:121).

Specific obstacles to good listening are: anxiety about one's competence in interviewing; listening to oneself formulating the next question rather than listening to the client's answer to the last question; resisting listening when one feels that the interviewee is being deliberately manipulative.

Interviewers sometimes communicate an unreadiness to listen out of their consideration for the interviewee's feelings. For example, parents of mentally retarded children indicated that one of the most difficult aspects for them in social work student interviews was that the workers did not permit them an adequate opportunity to express their sadness. The interviewers did not appear willing to listen to this. While parents felt the workers were afraid of these painful feelings and wished to avoid them, the interviewers explained their reluctance to listen as a response to a concern about the emotional fragility of the parents (Wikler 1979).

Focused and attentive listening is made more difficult by virtue of the redundancy that all speech includes. To ensure being understood, people will say the same thing in several different ways. The listener, thinking he has received the message the first time, finds that his mind wanders as the message is repeated.

The client who tends to repeat herself is a special hazard; as soon as the worker recognizes that this is the second time around on some detail, he is apt to turn off his listening. The following introspective responses to taped interviews indicate this problem:

The tape shows that I am temporarily not aware of what is going on. The client is repeating a story he told me in the last interview, so the absent-mindedness is understandable but still indefensible. Concentrate or else you risk many things—missing subtle changes in the repeated version, conveying an impression to the client of not caring much, losing an opportunity to respond to the client when he is making some effort to both talk to and interest you.

As the client had already gone into this earlier [the effect of her illness on her relationship with her husband] and is repeating the details, I only half listen and plan ahead to find out about other problems in the marriage. As a result I miss the cue she gives me that, while she doesn't want her daughter in a foster home, it is really nice when she's not around.

External noise which masks speech is as distracting to listening as is the inner noise of absorption in a private reverie. Just as an interviewer tries to control distraction from inappropriate internal digressions, he tries to focus on the sounds coming from the interviewee. Looking at the interviewee while she is talking focuses attention and concentrates one's mind on these sounds. Lip reading, which supplements hearing, is possible only if one looks at the interviewee.

Frequently, the interviewer has to accept a poor hearing-listening situation as given—poor acoustics, interviewees who have speech defects, or a difficult accent, or who talk at an inaudible level, or in rapid jerky tempo. These difficulties mean, however, the expenditure of more energy in merely hearing what is said, and therefore result in fatigue and a wish for relief from the work of listening.

Because listening is an active process requiring considerable expenditure of mental and emotional effort, fatigue reduces one's ability to listen. Attention span is decreased, concentration is more difficult, and motivation is attenuated. Listening is apt to be less efficient toward the end of a long interview. This argues for interviews of reasonable length—not much more than one hour without a break.

Silence

The principal therapeutic activity of most kinds of social work interventions involves talking. Even providing a social utility such as day care or homemaker service, a foster home, or housing involves a considerable amount of talk between client and worker around acceptance of the concrete service, preparation for use of the service, and adjustment to the service. All of social work, but particularly casework, may be listed as one of the "talking cures." Talk is the medium of exchange, the raw material for the work of the interview. Consequently silence, the absence of talk, gives the appearance of frustrating the achievement of the purpose of the interview.

The social work interviewer frequently perceives silence as a hindrance and a hazard to the progress of the interview, which needs to be removed or resolved. The professional presumption is that talking is better. Sometimes, however, silence may be more effective for achieving the purposes of the interview.

The American cultural emphasis on self-expression, on speaking one's mind, having one's say, makes silence seem an unacceptable form of behavior. In general social interaction, we feel compelled to talk even if we have nothing to say. The silent one is suspect and regarded as unfair for his failure to contribute to the conversation. The usual social meaning of silence is rejection. We use the "silent treatment" to punish by denying ourselves to others. Silence also is used to communicate the fact that we think so little of the other person that we will not exert ourselves even to talk with him.

The norms of interpersonal etiquette define silence as impolite. We are unnerved by silence that suggests we are boring others. We regard it as a manifestation of social failure—as a measure of social acceptability. To suggest that you should never break a silence unless what you have to say would improve on it would be regarded as un-American.

Silence generates social anxiety, felt as embarrassment, in people who have come together with the intent of talking to each other. But the social worker, in addition, feels a professional anxiety at the thought that continued silence signals a failing interview. It is no surprise, then, that inexperienced interviewers tend to feel uncomfortable with silences and tend to terminate them prematurely. It takes some measure of confidence and security for the interviewer to let a productive silence continue. It also requires that the interviewer accept the fact that a silence is not necessarily an attack against him.

Because, as has been noted, think-time is faster than talk-time, silence seems to expand time. Five seconds of silence seems considerably longer than five seconds of talk. Even silence of actual limited duration builds up anxiety in interview participants.

Sometimes a distinction is made between pauses and silences. Pauses are regarded as a "natural rest in the melody of speech," a kind of verbal punctuation analogous to a change of paragraphs or a new topic heading in printed communication. Silence, unlike a pause, is a temporary deliberate withholding of speech. Silence is a paradox, in that ostensibily nothing seems to be happening. But something is happening all the time, even when the participants appear totally passive in their silent interaction. It is a period filled with nonspeech, in which both interviewer and interviewee participate.

One of the most significant sounds which needs listening to is the sound of silence and the associated messages of omission. What the interviewee does not say, avoids saying, is as important as what she does say. Silence is not an absence of communication. It's a rather special form of communication. Not talking is a special way of talking.

It goes without saying that pauses and silences are important aspects of communication. Just as speech can conceal as well as reveal, silence can reveal as well as conceal.

The words used to describe silences graphically illustrate the fact that there are many different kinds. We speak of "tranquil" silence, a "pregnant" silence, an "ominous" silence, a "cold, stony" silence, an "empty" silence, a "tense" silence, a "contemplative" silence, a "reverent" silence, a "taciturn" silence, a "peaceful" silence, an "embarrassing" silence, a "solemn" silence, a "disapproving" silence, an "assertive" silence, a "reserved" silence, an "attentive" silence. One can be silent out of reticence or indifference. The catalog of silences includes, in addition, the silence of rebuke and the silence of defiance. While the act is in each case the same—refraining from talking—the meaning that each of these different silences communicates is far from the same. A silence is dynamic, subject to change. What was a "pregnant" silence can gradually become an "embarrassing" silence; what was a "tranquil" silence can become a "tense" silence.

Silence as resistance is in the service of self-protection; silence as denial is in the service of provocation. The problem for the interviewer is to decide which kind of silence is being manifested because the response required in dealing with each of the varieties of silence is quite different.

The interviewer's response needs to be predicated on some understanding of the meaning of the interviewee's behavior in maintaining her silence. Silence is itself a communicative gesture. Its meaning varies from interviewee to interviewee and may be different for the same interviewee at different points in the interview.

Differences in social status between interviewer and interviewee in some social work interviews may result in silences which are culturally determined. Silence in the presence of a higher status person of some authority may be a consequence of learned patterns of respect. The admonition "don't speak until you're spoken to" and the silence in the courtroom and the church are similar expressions of silences of respect. This might suggest that lower-class clients need more active encouragement to break their silence and talk.

Silence can result from uncertainty as to who has the responsibility for continuing the interview. It is a nonverbal way of jockeying for status in the interview. The interviewee controls the situation by her silence. Silence, more effectively than words, can often hurt, discomfort, create anxiety. It can be a very effective form of passive aggression.

The interviewee might be silent because nothing further readily occurs to her to say about the topic. She stops to think things over, to review this content in her mind, to see if there is anything else that needs to be said.

Silence may be the result of normal difficulties encountered in enacting the complicated and demanding role of interviewee. The interviewee may have reached a point when it is not clear to her which of a number of different directions she might want to take. Her silence is an expression of her indecision, and it gives her time to resolve her uncertainty.

Silence may have an organizational aim. The story is a complicated one; the response to the question raised is difficult; and the interviewee is silent while trying to organize her answer in a coherent fashion.

Sometimes silence permits the work of synthesis. Having talked about material that has considerable emotional meaning, the interviewee wants a chance to pull herself together, to reduce tension and to gain a measure of composure. She sits in silence to give herself an opportunity to sort out her feelings, to absorb them and assert control over them. The following illustrates the need expressed by the client for a period of silence following discussion of highly charged material. The interviewee is discussing possible divorce and breakup of the family.

Client: male, 9 years old, white, middle class, child guidance clinic.
RICKY: If that happens, I don't know what I'm going to do, I'm just gonna keep. . . . If that hard to face, I'm just going to jump in the Susquehanna River, or, or. . . .
WORKER: Or just not face. . . .

RICKY: Or just go, or just climb in a hole, or. . . .
WORKER: Or cover yourself up.
RICKY: Yeah, just climb in a hole and maybe put a blanket there.
WORKER: Hide.
RICKY: Or just starve to death. Because I don't want to live in a world if the world is going to be like that when I grow up.
WORKER: Like what?
RICKY: Well, say, the way it is now, you know, it's not going to be too nice to face.
WORKER: What is not going to be nice to face?
RICKY: Well, say, if that . . . ah . . . if that ever happens.
WORKER: If what ever happens?
RICKY: If my mother and my father departed, well. . . .
WORKER: Yeah. . . .
RICKY: You know, I'm just a. . . .
WORKER: You're just a. . . .
RICKY: Where am I? I'm just a. . . . I'm just a. . . . I'm just nowhere. I would have been better. . . .
WORKER: You would have been better. . . .
RICKY: I would have been better. . . .
WORKER: You would have been better off dead?
RICKY: Yeah.
WORKER: Is that what you think?
RICKY: Yeah. I would be better off. . . . [R. is really agitated, and the therapist offers him candy.] No, thank you, I don't like candy.
WORKER: Why?
RICKY: Oh, I, well, I'm thirsty. May I?
WORKER: No. [Long pause.] How do you feel about my not letting you go for a drink?
RICKY: Well, I, I don't feel like you're punishing me. I could probably go and get a drink. I would just like to stop and review my thoughts. You have me kind of mixed up or under a barrel.

Silence follows sharing of highly emotional material, intense grief, sorrow, disappointment, not only because time is needed to control the feelings evoked, but also because words are difficult to find to do justice to what has been said. "Silence is the language of all strong passions: love, anger, surprise, fear" (Bruneau 1973:34). The fact that we talk of strong feelings as "inexpressible" suggests that silence is an appropriate response.

Silence can be the pensive consideration of some interpretation, some explanation of the dynamics of her behavior, which the interviewee has encountered in the interview discussion. The interviewee needs a period of silence in order to think over the validity of interpretation.

Silence may be a deliberate effort on the part of the interviewee to solicit, or provoke, some response from the interviewer. The interviewee may have asked for advice, or a suggestion, may have requested information, or may have subtly solicited support or approval. Her silence at this point is a pressure on the interviewer to give her what she asked for.

Silence may indicate an effort to frustrate the interviewer and hence has the nature of a hostile attack. The interviewee spitefully withholds what the interviewer needs to conduct the interview. The interviewee who is requested to come to an interview against her wishes may demonstrate her opposition by frequent and prolonged silences. Here motivation rather than silence is the problem.

Silence may reflect an effort by the interviewee to exert control over the interview and the interviewer or an attempt to defend himself against control by the interviewer. In silence the interviewee is beyond any outside control. Silence, in these instances, is an act of protective antagonism and has a quality of anger not associated with other, more comfortable, silences.

Silence may be a defense against anxiety, a resistance to saying what should not be said. One series of studies empirically establishes an association between anxiety-provoking content and subsequent silences (Goldenberg and Auld 1964). Speech affirms, to ourselves and others, the existence of thoughts and feelings and makes perception of them more difficult to evade. To convert thoughts and feelings into speech, so that one hears oneself articulate them, is to intensify the conscious knowledge that one harbors them. Conversely, refraining from putting such thoughts and feelings into words makes them easier to deny. Silence is an act of refusal to give speech to some thoughts and/or feelings so that they cannot be heard either by ourselves or others.

The tendency is to interpose resistance to those thoughts and feelings which we are reluctant to recognize. Speech is interrupted and a silence maintained when the interview approaches such content. The interviewee needs time to think things over to consider whether or not she should divulge the things she came perilously close to saying. Thus a clue to understanding the silence may lie with the material being discussed immediately preceding the silence and with the associations and recollections such content might evoke.

It is the function of silence as a defensive withholding which suggested the frequent theoretical equation of silence with oral eroticism, words with feces, the mouth as a sphincter maintaining selective control over what is shared.

The following excerpt illustrates the use of silence to give the interviewee a chance to catch her psychic breath, after which the interviewer permits a transition. He then holds the interviewee to the anxiety-provoking material that she was reluctant to disclose and that prompted the initial silence. The interview excerpt not only illustrates the correct use of silence but also the correct use of transition. The interviewer permits the interviewee to make a transition away from painful material but then, recognizing the need for dealing with the evaded material, he moves the interview back to this material. The client has been discussing the causes for her conflict-filled marriage. Each pause is a substantial period of silence.

Patient: female, 30, white, middle class, psychiatric outpatient clinic.
Interviewer: a psychiatrist.
PATIENT: (Sighs.) I don't think he's the sole factor. No.
WORKER: And what are the factors within. . . .
PATIENT: I mean. . . .
WORKER: Yourself?
PATIENT: Oh, it's probably remorse for the past, things I did.
WORKER: Like what? (Pause.) It's something hard to tell, huh? (Short pause.)
PATIENT: (Sighs, moves around. Pause, sigh, pause.) I've had one psychiatric interview before, but it wasn't anything like this.
WORKER: Where did you have that one?
PATIENT: Oh down——. (Sniffs.) I was depressed, and this doctor took a history on me. (Interviewee, who is a nurse, gives some detail about the examination.)
WORKER: So, how is this interview different?
PATIENT: Oh, he asked me routine questions.
WORKER: Mmmmhnnn.
PATIENT: How. . . . Then he asked me how I liked the Army and so forth. But you know (sniffs). . . . I dunno. I think I had a tendency to cover things up.
WORKER: Yeah. What is this thing you had so much remorse about? (Pause.)
PATIENT: (Sighs.) It seems to me I'm going around in circles. (Sniffs.) In 1946 I met a man. He was married but I loved him anyway. (Sighs.) I became pregnant. (Gill, Newman, and Redlich 1954:194–98)

While resistance is frequently offered as an explanation for silence, studies show that silence is more frequently used by interviewees for nondefensive purposes. The interviewee falls silent because there is nothing more to be said about the matter under discussion, or because she is organizing her thoughts, or because she is not sure which direction to take.

Interviewers use silence in response to their uncertainty and frustration in the interview. In retrospective review of their own periods of silence interviewers said:

I would like to say that this long period of silence was maintained because of its therapeutic, thought-provoking potential, but actually I felt frustrated because my questions weren't getting the material I thought we needed to discuss and I couldn't think of how I could get the client to discuss this.

This silence meant that we had reached the end of a thought and both did not know what to say next. I had lost my way temporarily and did not know how to proceed. This made me feel nervous and out of control.

Silence is uncomfortable for many interviewers because it heightens a sense of their own inadequacies. For a moment, they are not sure of what they want to do, or should be doing.

Some interviewers feel compelled to talk even when it might be best for achieving the objectives of the interview to remain silent because they regard silence as a dereliction of duty. They feel they are paid to respond to the interviewee and unless they are talking, they are not earning their salaries. They then model rejection of silence which makes it more difficult for the client to be silent when it would be desirable for him. The interviewee needs to learn that silence is an acceptable form of communication and that she can be silent and still be accepted.

More often, however, interviewer silence is deliberately employed. Silence on the part of the interviewer acts as a stimulus encouraging the interviewee to continue talking. The interviewee, who knows and accepts her role, is conscious of the fact that she has the major responsibility for talking. The major channel for interaction in an interview is verbal communication. If the interviewer refrains from talking, the interviewee feels a pressure to fill the silence in response to her recognition of her role responsibilities. The interviewer's silence communicates his clear expectation that the interviewee will interrupt the silence and accept her obligation to talk. The normal role relationship between interviewee-talker and interviewer-listener can then be resumed.

Judicious use of silence slows the pace of the interview and gives it a more relaxed mood, a more informal atmosphere. The fact that it does slow the pace may make use of silences counterproductive in an agency where time for interviews is very limited. A relaxed pace eats up limited time.

Interviewer silence is an ambiguous interventive technique. It gives the interviewee no direction, no specification of what is wanted or expected other than the general expectation that she will continue talking. If the interviewee needs some direction, a silence enhances anxious uncertainty. For the interviewee who is capable and desirous of taking the initiative, however, interviewer silence offers the freest choice of selecting the content she wants to discuss.

Silence is like a blank screen. It can be filled in in any way. It is a neutral nonverbal probe which neither designates an area for discussion nor structures what might come next in any way.

Since one can get lost in silence, and since too much is as bad as too little, impeding the work of the interview, the interviewer sometimes has to accept responsibility for ending the silence. Tension as a consequence of too prolonged a silence might make it difficult for the interviewee to continue. If the silence results from some uncertainty about what to say next or from the fact that the interviewee has said all she can say about a particular matter, there is little point in letting it continue. If silence is the result of hostility, prolonging it might engender guilt; if silence is due to resistance, prolonging it might solidify the resistance. In these instances, instead of a "pregnant pause" that leads to productive communication, one has an unproductive, embarrassed silence.

The problem for the interviewer is not only to help the interviewee resume the flow of communication but also to help her understand, if this is appropriate to the goals, what prompted the act of silence.

Rather than "nagging," the interviewee out of her silence the interviewer can engage her in a joint search for an understanding of her silence.

Wolberg has offered a series of graded responses to silence in psychotherapy that is equally applicable to the social work interview. When an appreciable pause is encountered (more than five seconds) so that it might be regarded as a silence, Wolberg suggests the following:

a. Say "mmhmm" or "I see" and then wait for a moment.

b. Repeat and emphasize the last word or the last few words of the patient.

c. Repeat and emphasize the entire last sentence or recast it as a question.

d. If this is unsuccessful, summarize or rephrase the last thoughts of the patient.

e. Say "and" or "but" with a questioning emphasis, as if something else is to follow.

f. If the patient still remains silent, the therapist may say, "You find it difficult to talk," or "It's hard to talk." This focuses the patient's attention on his block.

g. In the event of no reply, the following remark may be made: "I wonder why you are silent?"

h. This may be succeeded by. "There are reasons why you are silent."

i. Thereafter the therapist may remark, "Perhaps you do not know what to say?"

j. Then: "Maybe you're trying to figure out what to say?"

k. This may be followed by: "Perhaps you are upset?"

l. If still no response is forthcoming, a direct attack on the resistance may be made with "Perhaps you are afraid to say what is on your mind?"

m. The next comment might be: "Perhaps you are afraid of my reaction, if you say what is on your mind?"

n. Finally, if silence continues, the therapist may remark, "I wonder if you are thinking about me?"

o. In the extremely rare instances where the patient continues to remain mute, the therapist should respect the patient's silence and sit it out with him. Under no circumstances should he evidence anger with the patient by scolding or rejecting him. (1954:164)

The interviewer has the responsibility for the effective management of silence, to use silences so that they contribute to achieving the purposes of the interview. Instead of a threat, silence should be seen and utilized as an opportunity.

Interviewing by Telephone

There is increasing interest in the use of the telephone in offering social work services. Telephone interviewing requires some adaptation of general interviewing principles and approaches.

For some time now social workers have conducted a considerable amount of worker-client transactions over the phone. In 1954 Shyne reported on a study of the use of telephone interviews in casework. It was estimated that telephone interviews "constituted about half of all casework interviews in family service agencies" conducted "by a member of the casework staff with a client or collateral for the purpose of discussing the client's problem in the client's interest" (p. 342). About half of the telephone interviews were with collaterals, (relatives, employers, school personnel, other agency personnel, doctors, lawyers, etc.) involved with the client's problem.

A study of family service agency activity in 1970 confirmed the fact that a very considerable amount of casework was being done over the phone. In one census week 140 family service agencies throughout the country reported a total of some 3,000 initial intake contacts handled by telephone (Beck and Jones 1973:48). In most social agencies telephone interviews are frequently employed to supplement personal interviews.

Crisis and hotline agencies have proliferated dramatically during the 1970s increasing the use of telephone interviews. From an organization established in 1953 in London, "The Telephone Samaritans" (concerned with preventing suicide), there developed by 1973 a network of more than 1,000 telephone crisis intervention centers in the United States. Different crisis hotline agencies were concerned with a wide variety of problems—teenage pregnancy, drug addiction, child abuse, alcoholism, battered wives, etc. In the crisis intervention agencies telephone interviews are frequently the principal contact with the clients (Lester and Brockopp 1973). Because it offers the possibility of immediate contact, it is most likely to be used at time of crisis. Obliterating space, the telephone maximizes the use of limited time available.

CHARACTERISTICS, ADVANTAGES, AND DISADVANTAGES

The telephone makes the interviewer accessible to the client at any time. The telephone quickly circumvents all of the obstacles between the interviewee's mouth and the interviewer's ear while preserving the anonymity of the interviewee. Access to an interview without delay is as close as the nearest phone. Phone contacts are characterized by maximum immediacy and accessibility.

Unless barriers are carefully interposed, the client can initiate an interview with the worker at home or at the office at a time when the worker is unprepared for such an interview. Access at the office can be controlled through switchboard operators or receptionists who ask who is calling and then get signals from the worker as to whether or not he is available. Preparation for the contact can be safeguarded by the worker's indicating that he will return the client's call later. Interviewers can give appropriate instructions to the receptionist and have calls selectively screened, accepting calls from other agencies or other professionals, but rejecting calls from clients.

Calls by clients to workers at home at any hour cannot be so easily controlled and indicates the heightened accessibility to the worker which the telephone makes possible. An unlisted home phone number can control client accessibility to the worker but also presents problems for the worker's personal social life.

Another unique aspect of phone contacts that applies to office and home is the insistence and anonymity of the signal initiating interaction. The ring demands to be answered, it cannot be ignored. Incoming rings sound alike so that the caller is not identified until the interaction begins, too late to courteously refuse the contact.

Easy accessibility of contact through the telephone encourages client dependency and the dependent caller may become a chronic caller. Clients may cling to phone interviews in rejection of the more difficult, but more productive, face-to-face interview.

The telephone permits people to come to a social agency while not coming to a social agency. It combines psychological mobility with physical fixity. If there is a resistance to identifying oneself as a client of a social agency a telephone contact permits a happy initial compromise.

Some clients prefer the safety of the phone interview to the feeling of greater exposure and vulnerability in the personal interview. This "allows the ambivalent client to achieve closeness at a safe distance" (Grumet 1979:577). It may be easier for some interviewees to discuss intimate details of their lives without the personal face-to-face encounter—as in the church confessional. A caller ready only to explore the possibilities of obtaining help can be more positively assured of anonymity through a phone contact. This anonymity permits disclosure without threat of embarrassment or humiliation. The telephone interview is characterized by anonymity as well as accessibility and immediacy.

Engaging in an interview while physically at home in familiar territory is easier for some than is the visit to the worker's office, an unfamiliar and less friendly location.

The phone restricts the information the client has to share. A personal appearance provides obvious information about age, sex, race, looks, handicaps, etc. In addition it provides information through body and facial gestures over which the client has limited awareness and control. Access to all of this information is controlled by the interviewee when she selects the telephone as the channel for the interview.

It is much easier for an ambivalent interviewee to terminate a phone contact than it is to terminate a personal interview. If she wants to withdraw she needs only to hang up the phone. The interviewee is consequently much more in control of a phone interview than she is of a face-to-face interview. If the interview proves to be too threatening, or the interviewer disappointing, the interviewee can terminate at will. There is no struggle as in a face-to-face interview with the need to make an explanation and extricate oneself from an embarrassing situation in abortive termination of an interview.

Since one of the advantages of a telephone contact for the client is the anonymity it provides, asking for identifying information from the client might well be delayed until identification is necessary to helping or until the client is willing and ready to provide it.

Despite the distance separating phone interview participants and despite the fact that contact is made through a cold mechanical contrivance, voice-to-ear phone contact lends an unusual degree of auditory intimacy and visual privacy to the interaction. The speaker's lips are, in effect, inches away from the listener's ear and a client can take part in the interview in the nude.

Since the interviewer is not visible the interviewee can fashion an image of him in line with her needs. If the interviewee feels most comfortable in talking to an avuncular older man who looks like Walter Cronkite she can imagine that that is the interviewer with whom she is talking.

Telephone interviews preclude visual nonverbal sources of information. Words and vocal accompaniments are the only channel available. One is even denied the assistance to hearing given by lip-reading. This increases the demand on concentrated listening.

The loss of visual cues may tend to make the interviewer uneasy. He is faced with the responsibility of understanding the interviewee without having available much of the information he normally depends on. It creates a "telephone blindness" for the interviewer (Miller 1973).

The loss of nonverbal channel information from the interviewer to the client also presents a problem for the interviewer. It means that whatever impression the interviewer wants to communicate depends on careful word choice and vocalization. The words cannot be modified by facial expressions, smiles, positioning. The interviewer has to sound warm, interested, sincere, and concerned as communicated only by voice tone and inflection.

Because the telephone carries a limited range of frequencies, high-pitched voices come across as screechy, so pitching the tone of the voice as low as possible makes for more pleasant communication.

The fact that our nonverbal gestures cannot be seen by the interviewee presents a danger as well. A worker often needs to take calls while engaged in an office interview with another client. Because he cannot be seen he might gesture impatiently, raise his eyebrows in disgust, or fidget irritably. While these gestures are unseen by the caller on the phone, they are seen by the client in the office. As a consequence an interviewee may revise her impression of the interviewer.

Telephone *interruptions* while interviewing are difficult to handle because they require attention to conflicting obligations to both the person calling and the person being interviewed (MacKinnon and Michaels 1970). An interview interrupted by a telephone call risks a breach in confidentiality. Talking on the phone within earshot of a client in the office inevitably means that the client overhears information to which she has no entitlement. Client trust in the assurances of confidentiality is eroded as a consequence.

If the call is a welcome interruption to an interview which is boring or difficult, the tone in answering the incoming call may betray to the interviewee the interviewer's delight in having been "saved by the bell."

In receiving a call while interviewing, a rapid assessment needs to be made of priorities. Generally priority is and should be given to the needs of the interviewee in the office and the phone interruption recognized very briefly. However, a call often suggests some urgency on the part of the client and this should be explicitly recognized if a call needs to be returned later. "I know you are upset about this but you caught me at a very inconvenient time. I will call you back shortly."

Silences over the phone seem longer and more ominous than equal length silences in face-to-face communication. Face-to-face verbal silences are "filled" with nonverbal gestures, facial expressions, body movement, none of which are available over the phone. Since phone communication tends to make every pause or interruption seem longer, any break in contact requires some periodic reassurance that worker and client are still connected. Sometimes the worker has to go look for a file or a form or some information in answering a question, which is likely to take some time. Then, it might be best for the worker to tell the client he will call back. If the interviewee is on "hold" and it is taking longer than anticipated, an occasional reminder that the worker is still looking reassures the interviewee that she is not forgotten and that she is not holding on to a dead line.

PROCESS IN TELEPHONE INTERVIEWING

Interviewers often use the telephone to initiate contact with collaterals and with personnel at other agencies. Here it is of key importance that the social worker identify himself, his agency affiliation, and state clearly the purpose of his call, particularly if it is long distance. Any call from a stranger to a relative or friend of the client is apt to be upsetting until the recipient of the call knows what it is all about.

In initiating telephone interviews with collaterals, the worker should make sure he is talking to the person the client has authorized him to contact. Otherwise he might reveal knowledge about the client to someone she does not want to know about her problem.

Making a call is like making a visit to the recipient's office or home. There are times when calls may be more convenient, less intrusive, or when the person called is more likely to be available.

Preparing for calls initiated by the interviewer is as important as preparing for any interview. Listing the questions and content areas he plans to cover during the call may eliminate the necessity for calling back.

Telephone interviews are generally shorter than face-to-face interviews. This is in deference to the courtesy norms of telephone interaction as against face-to-face interaction and is partly a result of the tendency of telephone interviews to be more sharply focused. It seems discourteous to terminate face-to-face interaction within five or ten minutes after meeting, but not discourteous to terminate a phone call within that time. Shyne (1954) notes that while face-to-face family service interviews were slightly less than an hour, phone interviews averaged somewhat more than ten minutes. Telephone contacts are not only shorter, they tend to be more focused, less diversified, and more formal than face-to-face contacts.

Because of the nature of telephone interviews, particularly in crises or hot-line agencies, interviewers are apt to be problem-centered rather than person-centered, tending to stress problem solving rather than relationship building. Because they are time limited and because help may have to be given quickly the interviews generally tend to be sharply focused on identifying and dealing with the presenting problem and its specifics. The interviewer in crisis intervention telephone interviews tends to be more active than is usually the case, more directive rather than reflective.

There is a conviction among social workers that telephone interviewing is most appropriate under specific conditions. Such interviewing is appropriate with collaterals who generally are busy professionals with no personal stake in the interview and with clients whose request for service does not depend significantly on the development and maintenance of a worker-client relationship. "The more practical depersonalized and objectified the problem, the more appropriate" (Shyne 1954:345) is the use of the telephone interview. The appropriateness of the use of the phone presumably decreases with the need for the client's emotional involvement with the service. Diagnostic assessment of the client requires face-to-face contact.

The telephone has been effectively used for interview contacts where the primary purpose is support and/or reassurance. For instance, older clients who are homebound can easily be contacted by the worker providing such a service (Greene 1976). For the very dependent client who needs the assurance of frequent contact with the worker, telephone interviews can be an efficient substitute for time-consuming face-to-face scheduled interviews. The phone provides an immediately accessible safety valve for anxious clients.

Telephone interviewing can be surprisingly effective. Research comparing information obtained by telephone interviews with information obtained via face-to-face contacts shows very little difference in the nature of intimate details obtained (Simon et al. 1974; Rogers 1976; Bradburn and Sudman 1979). Simon concludes that "the information elicited by one method was not significantly different from the information elicited by the other method in either quantity or quality. Our results indicate that the amount or quality of historical psychiatric data collected was not related to the technique used" (1974:141). And Dilley et al. (1971) show that counselor empathy can be effectively communicated in telephone interviews.

Summarizing the results of 30 different empirical studies of the differences between face-to-face and telephone interactions Reid concluded that "in information transmission and problem solving conversations the withdrawal of vision has no measurable effects of any kind on the outcome of conversation" (1981:411).

RECAPITULATION

In recapitulation the telephone has characteristics which provide particular advantages to some clients or potential clients—accessibility, immediacy, anonymity, and a greater measure of control than in the face-to-face context. For housebound dependents, anxious clients, telephone interviews provide supplementary contacts. They provide advantages for the interviewer in contact with collaterals but deny him the understanding available from nonverbal communication and present some hazards of which he needs be aware.

Effective telephone interviewing requires adherence to some simple precautions since the client cannot see who she is talking to.

Clearly identifying who you are at the start of the call is important.

Since communication depends solely on speech, clear unimpeded articulation is important. Talking around a cigarette or pipe or while eating makes it difficult to understand what you are saying.

Extended silence on the phone is more unnerving than in face-to-face interviewing where bodily gestures, head nodding, etc., can fill in the silence.

While talking to you, the interviewee cannot know for certain that you are still at the other end of the line unless you frequently make some sound indicating you are there.

If a call is made at a time when you are heavily involved with someone or some thing, there is no way for the caller to know this unless you politely but firmly share the information that the call is inconveniently timed and you will call back. Take the necessary information that will enable you to return the call and indicate when this is likely to be. The problem of priority and preference is handled differently than in face-to-face contacts where an interviewee is not likely to intrude into your office if you are occupied.

When you as interviewer initiate a call, be sure to ask if the timing of the call is convenient for the interviewee.

An incoming call should be answered promptly but if the caller is put on "hold," an explanation should be offered and frequent assurances at intervals during the delay should be made.

Manuals put out by phone companies emphasize developing a pleasing telephone personality communicated by a pleasant sounding voice with vitality, expressiveness and naturalness—qualities hard to define but recognizable when you hear them.

SUGGESTED READING

LISTENING

Larry L. Barker. *Listening Behavior*. Englewood Cliffs, N.J.: Prentice-Hall, 1971 (154 pp.).

Carl Weaver. *Human Listening: Processes and Behavior*. New York: Bobbs-Merrill, 1972 (170 pp.).

Both books present a good overview of the process of listening, the problems encountered in listening, and the things that might be done to improve our listening.

CHAPTER 13

Cross-Cultural Interviewing

This chapter is concerned with the problems that frequently result from the separation between the world of the social work interviewer and the world of the interviewee. Class, color, age, and sex are some of the significant subcultural differences that separate interviewer and interviewee, increase social distance, and limit empathy and understanding. There are those who doubt that people can, in fact, bridge these gaps which separate them.

Beyond compatible matching of such variables as race, class, age, and gender the question has also been raised regarding compatible interviewer-interviewee matching of sexual preference. Gay and lesbian social workers have suggested that they are more likely to be able to offer gay and lesbian clients the necessary understanding and acceptance required for good interviewing (Hart 1979).

The statistically typical social worker is different from the statistically typical client in significant social characteristics. The statistically typical social worker is middle class, college trained, white, young, and female. The statistically typical client is an older, lower-class female member of a minority group with less than high-school education. The only significant social characteristic they hold in common is that the typical social work interviewer and the typical social work interviewee are both females.

In discussing the effects of group membership differences between the social worker interviewer and the client interviewee who is significantly different in some consequential social characteristic—age or sex or race or class—some general considerations need to be noted. These considerations are applicable across the board to all of the significant variables of difference.

The research on these differences and the literature deriving from it always lag behind the current reality. The chance for misstatement is greater in such a transitional period. A rising consciousness and greater pride and self-acceptance on the part of members of minority groups, females, and the aged in their blackness or femaleness or age may require continuing modification of the content presented here.

There is, inevitably, an element of stereotyping in characterizing the interviewee by age, gender, race, class, or ethnicity. In doing so we give primary emphasis and visibility to group designations which are, in truth, a limited number of broad categories making up the complex personal, highly individualized, multifaceted configuration of any one interviewee. Content presented in terms of these group designations violate the interviewee's unique individuality. Just remember that although any interviewee can be described in terms which are characteristic and typical of the group he is affiliated with, he is, at the same time, uniquely dissimilar from every other member of that group. There is as much difference between individuals who are aged as there is between the aged and the young.

There is a growing recognition and appreciation of the effects of differences in race, age, class, gender, and ethnicity on interview interaction. These factors do tend to intrude into the interviewer-interviewee relationship despite the worker's awareness and vigilance.

There is, however, a need for balance in assessing the importance for the interview of these key identifying characteristics. An approach which ignores age or gender or race or class and suggests that none of these makes a difference is as erroneous as the approach which holds that these attributes are the total difference. One extreme denies the significance of vital shared group experiences; the other extreme denies the unique psychodynamics of individual response.

A knowledge of the client's cultural milieu is necessary in understanding the client as well as in helping in problem solving. A client who may appear to be withdrawn and excessively passive may be only reflecting the norms of his group. Advice and suggestions which may seem eminently serviceable in the interviewer's group context may be inappropriate and inapplicable in the interviewee's cultural situation.

More subtly, there may be differences in attitudes toward some key values between members of different groups. Attitudes toward sex and sex roles, toward child-rearing and child discipline, toward competition and achievement, toward autonomy and dependence in personal problem solving, toward the definition of success and failure and desirable life-styles may be different for people of different ethnic backgrounds.

It would be difficult if not impossible for the interviewer to study the wealth of material that is currently available on the variety of the different ethnic subcultures that she is likely to encounter. Even if the interviewer were to have a clear cognitive understanding of the different groups as a result of such study, affective understanding would still be lacking. This kind of understanding comes only after living the life of group members. Consequently what may ultimately be more important than knowledge is an attitude. The interviewer needs to feel with conviction that her culture, way of life, values, etc., are only one way of doing things; that there are other equally valid ways, not better or worse, but different. Cultural differences are easily transmuted into cultural deficiencies. There needs to be an openness and receptivity toward such differences and a willingness to be taught by the client about such differences. There are differences in the way the different ethnic groups define their problems, explain their problems, prefer to solve their problems. The "ethnically sensitive" interviewer needs to actively accept the help of the ethnically different client in understanding how he sees his situation and what he wants to do about it.

Because the interviewer is less likely to have had the experience which permits empathic understanding of the racially different interviewee, she needs to be more ready to listen, less ready to come to conclusions, more open to guidance and correction of her presuppositions by the interviewee. The presumption of ignorance, needed in all interviews, is even more necessary here.

Good interviewing in contact with a client who differs from the interviewer in some significant characteristics requires more than a knowledge of the culture and life-style of the interviewee. It also requires an adaptation of interview techniques—pace of interview, activity level, choice of appropriate vocabulary, modification of nonverbal approaches—to be in tune with the needs of the interviewee.

The question of objectives as well as technique is often raised in interviewing minority groups, lower class, female, and/or aged clients. Radical social workers contend that these are all members of socially and economically oppressed groups. The interviewer should then have consciousness raising as an explicit objective, i.e., developing greater awareness on the part of the clients regarding their oppressed situation and advocating effective change.

The nature of the problem that is the focus of the interview is a determinant of the significance these attributes may have for the conduct of the interview. The problem may be clearly related to the race or sex or age or class of the interviewee, in which case the effect of these attributes would have greater significance.

Race

Racial differences between interviewer and interviewee are a potential source of problems in interviewing. Most often the interviewer is white, the interviewee non-white. Although this difference most frequently involves a white interviewer and a black client, non-white also includes Asian-American and Native American interviewees. In some instances, the interviewer is non-white and the interviewee is white, posing special problems for interview interaction.

Interview participants of different races are keenly aware of racial differences between them, nevertheless, the racial factor is rarely discussed openly. It is not clear whether race is not discussed because it is regarded as truly irrelevant to the work that needs to be done or because both participants conspire to ignore a potentially touchy issue. One study of racially mixed interviews found that "tape recorded interviews revealed almost no overt or veiled references to racial matters" (Miller 1970:19). However, race, like any other significant factor which intrudes to contaminate interview interaction, needs to be at least tentatively raised for explicit discussion. Being "color-blind" is denying the real differences which need to be accepted.

If interview content is not concerned with matters that may call attention to race relations, there is likely to be less distortion in the interaction. While conscious of the racial difference between them, interviewer and interviewee can relate themselves to the neutral interview content. If, however, interview content does have racial significance, participants may become uneasy. The difficulty is that so much in the non-white interviewee's life today may be regarded as implicitly related to the racial problem.

WHITE INTERVIEWER—BLACK INTERVIEWEE

Because blacks are by far the largest single non-white group and because most of the descriptive, clinical, and experimental literature concerning race as a factor in interview interaction focuses on the black interviewee, much of the following discussion is concerned with black-white interviewee-interviewer participants. Many statements are, however, relevant and applicable to other non-white racial groups.

The black interviewee often presents the interviewer with differences in socioeconomic background as well as differences in racial experience. Although the largest group of poor people in the United States are white, a disproportionate percentage of the black population is poor. The median income of the black family is substantially below the median income of the white family, and a large percentage of blacks lives on incomes below the poverty level. The material on interviews with the poor is thus applicable to most black interviewees. But over and beyond the difference in socio-economic background between the middle-class interviewer and the lower-class black is the racial factor—the differences that stem from the experiences of living white and living black. This is a factor affecting the interview with middle-class as well as lower-class black clients. Color is an additional problem.

If trust and confidence and openness between participants are necessary ingredients for a successful interview, how can they be achieved in the face of the long history between the races in this country in which trust was exploited, confidence betrayed, and openness violated? If blacks feel paranoid in their mistrust of whites, this is not pathology but a healthy reaction to the reality they have long experienced, it is asserted. Concealment and "putting the white man on" have been elaborated and institutionalized as a way of life, a necessary weapon contributing to survival, but one which is antithetical to the requirements of an effective interview. Conditioned defensiveness in response to anticipated prejudicial attitudes based on expectations which have been repeatedly confirmed in the past may impede development of rapport between the white interviewer and black interviewee. "Playing it cool," maintaining a cover, a distance, and a reserve is a stance adopted by some ghetto militants in contact with whites which needs to be accepted and respected.

If understanding and empathy are crucial, how can the white interviewer imagine what it is like to live day after day in a society that only grudgingly, half-heartedly, and belatedly (if at all) accords the interviewee the self-respect, dignity, and acceptance that is his right as a person? How can the white interviewer know what it is to live on intimate terms with rejection, discrimination, harassment, and exploitation?

If a feeling of comfortable, untroubled interaction is required for a good interview, how, it is asked, can this be achieved in an atmosphere in which the black interviewee feels accusatory and hostile as the oppressed and the white interviewer feels uneasily anxious and guilty at her complicity with the oppressor? It is anticipated that the black interviewee in such a situation would tend to resort to concealment and disguise and respond with discretion or "accommodation" behavior. Often there is open refusal to share, as expressed in "Impasse" by the black poet Langston Hughes.*

I could tell you,
If I wanted to,

*From Langston Hughes, *The Tiger and the Lash* (New York: Knopf, 1967), reprinted with permission of the publisher.

> What makes me
> What I am.
>
> But I don't
> Really want to—
> And you don't
> Give a damn.

The attitude toward permeability of the racial barrier for the social work interview has shifted over the last thirty years. In 1950 Brown, in a questionnaire to social agencies, attempted to assess the importance of race in the casework relationship. The response of 80 percent of the practitioners, assessing their experience, was that race intruded into the relationship but that it did not present much of a problem to the experienced worker with some sense of self-awareness.

By 1970, disillusionment with the integrationist stance and a greater accentuation by blacks of their special identity separate from the white culture, of the unique effects of their historical experience, had resulted in frequently repeated assertions that no white can understand what it means to be black. Consequently, it is said, an effective interview with a black interviewee requires a black interviewer. Many who have studied this problem, while not ready to go this far, concede that the racial barrier in the interview presents a much more difficult problem for rapport and understanding than had previously been imagined (Miller 1970; Vontross 1970; Banks 1971; Burns 1971).

There has been a movement over time affecting interracial interviews from disregard of race as inconsequential to an orientation of cultural pluralism and beyond that to a greater respect for ethnic identity. A black mental health worker, retrospectively analyzing her personal experience, concludes that rapport is possible although not easy to achieve:

In answering the question of whether a white middle-class psychiatrist can treat a black family, I cannot help but think back over my own experiences. When I first came to New York and decided to go into psychotherapy I had two main thoughts: 1) that my problems were culturally determined; and 2) that they were related to my Catholic upbringing. I had grown up in an environment in which the Catholic Church had tremendous influence. With these factors in mind, I began to think in terms of the kind of therapist I could best relate to. In addition to being warm and sensitive, he had to be black and Catholic. Needless to say, that was like looking for a needle in a haystack. But after inquiring around, I was finally referred to a black Catholic psychiatrist.

Without going into too much detail, let me say that he turned out to be not so sensitive and not so warm. I terminated my treatment with him and began to see another therapist who was warm, friendly, sensitive, understanding, and very much involved with me. Interestingly enough, he was neither black nor Catholic. As a result of that personal experience, I have come to believe that it is not so much a question of whether the therapist is black or white but whether he is competent, warm, and understanding. Feelings, after all, are neither black nor white. (Sager et al. 1970:210–11)

The fact that a cross-racial contact is inherently more difficult, however, may help to account for the higher attrition rate of black clients applying for many kinds of social services. This is true for black clients in family service and black applicants for adoption.

The question "Can cross-racial contact be established?" is more correctly redefined as "How can such contact be established?"

What can be done to ease the real difficulties inherent in the white interviewer–black interviewee interaction? On the most practical level, because the white worker may be initially regarded with suspicion, as a potential enemy until proven otherwise, it is necessary to observe with singular care all the formalities which are the overt indications of respect.

Discussion of racism has left every white with the uneasy suspicion that, as a child of her culture, she has imbibed prejudices in a thousand subtle ways in repeated small doses and that the symptoms of her racism, if masked to herself, are readily apparent to the black interviewee. It may be necessary to accept such uneasy suspicions as true. The worker needs to acknowledge frankly to herself the possibility of racist attitudes and the obligation to make the effort to change. This suggests a paraphrase of a Chinese maxim. The prospective white interviewer who says "Other white interviewers are fools for being prejudiced and when I am an interviewer I will not be such a fool" is already a fool.

A good interview requires some sense of security on the part of the interviewer that she knows her subject area. The white interviewer who is sensitive to her unfamiliarity with the black experience and blackness certainly can make efforts to dispel her ignorance by reading about, and becoming familiar with, black history, black culture, black thinking and feeling. This is a professional responsibility. Here again, lack of knowledge about the interviewee's situation makes the interviewer appear "innocent." There is less respect for such an interviewer, she is more likely to be conned, and she is less likely to be a source of influence.

It may help for the white worker to be explicitly aware of her own reaction to racial difference in the interview. In making restitutions for felt or suspected racism, a white worker may be overindulgent. She may tend to simplify the problems and attribute to race some behavior which she hesitates to ascribe to personal malfunctioning, although the difficulty objectively belongs there. Where color is exploited as a defensive rationalization, race is a weapon in the interview. The worker may be "too sympathetic to be of assistance; too guilty to be of help" (Heine 1950:375). Burns points out that black children "have learned how to manipulate the guilt feelings of their white workers for their own ends. They have also learned to exploit the conceptions most white workers have about the anger of black people" (1971:93).

Some white liberal activists may be anxious to validate their credentials as being nonracist or antiracist and might seek to achieve validation by an overconcerned, oversolicitous approach. There is the counterproductive danger of being paternalistic, excessively benevolent, and overly compliant to interviewees' demands and wishes.

Some workers feel a need to be visibly nonracist and shift upward in their expression of liberal attitudes when the interviewee is of another race. Thus in one study white social workers evaluating a black and a white client from the same class background presenting the same problem in the same way tended to perceive the black client in more positive terms. In an attempt to explain this finding the researchers note that "perhaps this can be seen as a kind of 'leaning over backwards' by predominantly white social workers in an effort to assume that their judgments were, at the least, fair" (Fischer and Miller 1973:108).

The interviewer who is likely to be least uncomfortable and most flexible is one who has resolved her own sense of racial identity, who does not need to deny racial differences but is accepting of them, and who does not see them as threatening. She has no need to romanticize the racially, ethnically, or socially different, making others better than they are.

The white interviewer has to have some familiarity with black English and the black vernacular in interviewing the black client. Studies of speech behavior in the black ghetto of "rapping," "sounding," "jiving," suggest great imagination and skill in the use of English with patterned variations.

Although it is somewhat of a digression from the central focus on racial aspects of the interview, this may be the most appropriate place to discuss the problem of speaking the client's language.

There is a good deal of speculation, but little empirical material, about the consequences of the worker's efforts to "speak" the language of the client. The general conclusion seems to be that unless the worker can speak the language, the jargon, the argot, of the client naturally and easily, unless it is genuinely her own language, any attempt will come across as an insincere put-on. Assuming the language of the client in contrast to one's own is to risk "coming on too strong." Not only the phrasing used but also the style of delivery has to be natural to be accepted without ridicule by the interviewee. The "tone" is very difficult for an outsider to come by. The effort of a white, or even an educated, middle-class black, to talk like a lower-class black will sound forced and unnatural. It may appear patronizing and devious to the interviewee and generate contempt and suspiciousness at the interviewer's apparent attempts to con him.

Whyte, studying the social structure of an urban community as a participant observer, encountered this difficulty.

> I bumped into that problem one evening as I was walking down the street with the Nortons. Trying to enter into the spirit of the small talk, I cut loose with a string of obscenities and profanity. The walk came to a momentary halt as they all stopped to look at me in surprise. Doc shook his head and said: "Bill, you're not supposed to talk like that. That doesn't sound like you."
>
> I tried to explain that I was only using terms that were common on the street corner. Doc insisted, however, that I was different and that they wanted me to be that way.
>
> This lesson went far beyond the use of obscenity and profanity. I learned that people did not expect me to be just like them; in fact, they were interested and pleased to find me different, just so long as I took a friendly interest in them. Therefore, I abandoned my efforts at complete immersion. (1955:304)

Although the interviewer should refrain from speaking the language of the client when it is not native to her, she needs to be familiar with the language and indicate her understanding of it. If she is going to be working with black interviewees or lower-class interviewees, she should make an effort to learn something of the idioms and vocabulary of that group.

BLACK INTERVIEWER–BLACK INTERVIEWEE

In dealing with the needs in the interview of the ethnically different client the agency can help by hiring black clerical and professional staff. Seeing people who are members of his group at the agency gives the black client a sense of greater assurance that he will be accepted and understood.

Yet black interviewers working with black interviewees present problems as well. The fact that black social workers have achieved middle-class professional status suggests that they have accepted some of the principal mores of the dominant culture—achievement motivation, denial of immediate gratification, the work ethic, punctuality, self-denial, etc. To get to where they are, more likely they have been educated in white schools, have read white literature, and associated with white classmates, as they are now associating with white colleagues. Some black middle-class social workers may feel estranged not only from whites but also from their own blackness.

The black social worker returning to the ghetto after an absence for professional training may be viewed with suspicion. An "alien" returning from the outside world where she has been "worked over" by the educational enterprise to accept white assumptions, values, and language, she has, in the interim, supposedly lost contact with the fast-changing ghetto subculture. Whereas the black interviewee may see the white worker as representing the enemy, he may see the black social worker as a traitor to his race, a collaborator with the Establishment. Barriers toward self-disclosure and openness may therefore be as great in the black interviewee–black interviewer combination as in the interracial combination.

The pervasiveness of the negative cultural definition of blackness also affects the black client. He may feel that being assigned to a black interviewer is less desirable, that a white interviewer may have more influence and be in a better position to help him. The black worker may be the target of displacement. The hostility felt by the black interviewee toward whites may be expressed toward the black worker simply because she presents a less dangerous target.

Recently some black social workers may have felt pressured into a greater militancy, a more vehement espousal of blackness, as against being Negro, than they genuinely feel. Such a stance is a defense against the implied accusation of having deserted their race and is an effort to retain their identification with their black brothers. In such a situation, the black interviewer may find it difficult to be relaxed and at ease in the interview. On the other hand, a militant black interviewer may be annoyed by the passivity of some black interviewees and feel an obligation to stimulate a sense of racial consciousness.

The black interviewee is a source of anxiety to the black interviewer in other ways as well. As one black psychiatrist says, "For the therapist who has fought his way out of the ghetto, the [black interviewee] may awaken memories and fears he would prefer to leave undisturbed" (Sager 1970:228). It is, therefore, not surprising that Brown (1950) found black social workers to be less sympathetic toward black interviewees than toward white clients. They were made anxious by failures on the part of black clients to live up to the standards of the dominant culture. They felt that such deviations reflected on the race as a whole, decreasing the acceptability of all blacks, including themselves. A black AFDC client talking about black social workers said: "Sometimes the ones that have had hard times don't make you feel good. They're always telling you how hard *they* had to work—making you feel low and bad because you haven't done what they done" (Mayer and Timms 1969:153).

The danger of overidentification is greater in the black interviewer–black interviewee situation. In this context, overidentification is aptly defined by Calnek as "a felt bond with another black person who is seen as an extension of oneself because of a common racial experience" (1970:42).

One clear advantage, however, in the black interviewee–black interviewer situation is that the black professional makes possible the identification with a positive image. "A black counselor who has not rejected his own personal history may be most able to inspire a feeling of confidence and a sense of hope in his black client" (Kincaid 1969:888). Some black interviewees might respond positively to the black interviewer as a source of racial pride and as an ally and a model for emulation.

BLACK INTERVIEWER–WHITE INTERVIEWEE

A situation where the interviewer is black and the interviewee white poses its own kinds of problems. The black interviewer in contact with a white interviewee has to control any hostility she feels toward whites generally so that it does not distort the interview. She is likely to be tense, fearing expressions of antipathy from the interviewee.

The black worker may derogate the white client because she is sensitive to the special advantages the white client enjoys. She might then be impatient with the white client's complaints and inadequacies. The black interviewer has an advantage however in that she has been forced to learn about and attempt to understand the dominant white culture. The white interviewer has never been subjected to the same necessity of learning about and understanding the black subculture.

A white client who sees himself as lacking in prejudice may welcome assignment to a black worker. It gives him a chance to parade his atypically unprejudiced feelings. He may feel that he has been assigned to an unusually competent worker, since only an unusually accomplished black would have, in his view, achieved professional standing. Also, because whites who come to social agencies often feel inadequate and inferior, they may in some cases more easily establish a positive identification with the "exploited" and "oppressed" black worker.

The white interviewee having some problems in social functioning may feel more comfortable with a minority member interviewer whom he perceives as also marginally acceptable to the normative culture.

Many white interviewees, however, may be reluctant to concede to the black interviewer a presumption of competence. They may wonder if the interviewer is as good as the agency's white workers and feel as though they had been assigned second best. The white interviewee, especially from the South, may be sensitive to the reversal in usual status positions. Where the interviewee brings a prejudicial attitude against blacks into the interview, he is less likely to regard the interviewer as a source of influence and, hence, less likely to respond to the interviewer's efforts to socialize him to the interview situation or guide him in the interview. A prejudiced interviewee in such a situation is less responsive to overt and covert conditioning cues communicated by the interviewer. This is only one aspect of a general resistance to submit to any kind of influence from a negatively perceived interviewer. Prejudice produces a functional deafness, reducing receptivity to communication from the interviewer.

Just as the variables of class and race overlap to determine interview interaction, the variables of race and sex present a complex interrelationship. The black male interviewee may feel resentment toward the black female interviewer. The relationship in the interview may reflect problems deriving from the frequency of female-headed households in the black community. Perhaps the most problematic combination for a good interview is a white female worker and a black male client. This combination intensifies all of the threats to masculine pride involved in the subordinate position of interviewee and evokes all of the menacing mythology of interracial sex.

It needs to be recognized that race, however significant, is only one component in a person's social identity. And different people give different priorities to this aspect of their social identity as compared with other aspects. A middle-class black college graduate interviewee interacting with a white middle-class college educated interviewer may give higher priority to class and educational comembership with the interviewer than to the racial non-co-membership. The interviewee might feel a sense of solidarity with the interviewer in response to these shared aspects of identity.

There is considerable heterogeneity among blacks and much of the above needs modification as applied to subgroups among the black population. Studies have indicated that minority group members who identify themselves as blacks respond differently than those who identify themselves as Negro or colored or Afro-Americans. The different terms indicate differences in levels of racial consciousness and differences in approaches to interracial interaction. Differences in age may reflect differences in race consciousness and degree of militancy. Young blacks who grew up following the civil rights movement react differently to interracial encounters than do blacks who grew up under overt segregation.

HISPANIC, NATIVE AMERICAN, AND ASIAN AMERICAN CLIENTS

There is considerable heterogeneity in groups which are lumped together by a single label. The phrase American Indian or Native American, which evokes a single image, comprises some 478 different tribes, as recognized by the federal government. Asian Americans comprise such diverse groups as Chinese, Japanese, Filipinos, Koreans, Vietnamese, and Indonesians.

Hispanic Interviewees   Hispanic American includes Cubans (who are concentrated in Florida), Puerto Ricans (more often situated in the Northeast-
ern states), Mexican Americans (primarily in Southwestern United States),
and South Americans. While all of these groups have Spanish as their primary language, they are significantly different from each other. And second
generation Hispanics are different from newly arrived immigrant groups in
values and attitudes.

For many Hispanic clients English is a second language. Communication
has to be clear, simple, and slow, with frequent solicitation of feedback by
the interviewer to determine if she is understood. The interviewer may
need to be more active and directive.

Even clients who seem fluent in English may do quite a bit of mental
translating as they talk. This is demonstrated in studies which show that
bilingual clients when communicating in Spanish show greater spontaneity,
more active gesturing and increased voice animation as compared with
communicating similar material in English. Nuances of feeling and communication of emotions require a richer vocabulary more likely to be available to the client in his primary language.

The interviewer who speaks and understands Spanish has a definite advantage in conducting interviews with Spanish-speaking clients. The interviewer who is not fluent may need to use an interpreter. The danger in
use of interpreters, in addition to distortions of meaning involved in translating and retranslating the original communication, is that a dominant assertive interpreter may take over direction of the interview. Or, an interpreter may identify with and be protective of the client and distort
translation in response to these currents of feelings.

The interpreter needs to be acceptable to and respected by the client as
well as the worker and agency. If the client is suspicious of or mistrustful
of the interpreter, he is likely to restrict what he says. Guarantees of maintaining confidentiality need specifically to include the interpreter, particularly if he is a member of the client's community.

The interpreter who focuses on exact literal translation may fail to communicate to the interviewer some subtle significant aspects of the interviewee's communication. This leads to correct translation but inadequate
communication.

The best interpreter is one who collaboratively participates in the interview under the direction of the interviewer and who communicates not
only the client's words but also the client's meanings.

The interpreter should sit at the side of the interviewee and the interviewer should face both of them. While realizing that the client may not
be able to understand her, the interviewer should speak directly to the
client. This is more desirable than speaking at the client through the inter-

viewer in the third person. Asking the interpreter to ask the client about the problem depersonalizes the relationship between interviewer and interviewee. The interpreter should be cast in the role of assistant rather than principal informant on whom the interviewer is dependent.

The correct pronunciation of Hispanic and Asian names might present a problem for the interviewer. It is important that an effort be made to pronounce names correctly. This pronunciation not only communicates disrespect, it also communicates disinterest. Checking with minority group staff before the interview and with the client at the start of the interview may help in learning correct name pronunciation.

For better or for worse, there is a need to recognize the persistence of adherence to the machismo configuration by many Hispanic males. Anglo interviewers tend to define machismo solely as supermaleness and hypermasculine sexual assertiveness. To Hispanics, the concept includes much that is positive, protective, and expressive. It includes a tender and benevolent concern for those who are in need of care and support by someone confident of his sense of masculinity. It involves providing leadership in the family. It includes elements of manhood, honor, and dignity. The macho image also suggests independence, strength, and self-sufficiency so that asking for help is difficult for the man in the family. But by the same token, the man cannot be ignored and offering help to the family must involve his participation and acceptance. Adhering to the idea of machismo, the male interviewee may be turned off and find it difficult to relate to an assertive female interviewer.

It seems to be true that sex roles are more distinct, more defined, and perhaps less flexible than among Anglo families. Any change suggested by the interviewer regarding sex roles is thus apt to encounter considerable resistance.

The worker needs to be aware of the importance of religion and the significance of the extended family to the Hispanic interviewee.

An orientation toward personalism in a relationship suggests that the Hispanic and Native American interviewee discounts bureaucratic rules and regulations. The expectation is that the interviewer will go beyond rules and regulations in respecting the interpersonal relationship. Personalism suggests an expressed willingness on the part of the interviewer to do something, however inconsequential, for the interviewee as a guarantee of sincerity in helping.

Native American and Asian American Interviewees   The Native American client requires patience and a slower pace in interviewing. There may be longer periods of silence, a reluctance to verbalize feelings and a considerable reserve about sharing personal information. Interventions which are intended to be helpful might be regarded as unwarranted interference and

meddling by Native American clients who value autonomy and self-determination very highly. Much eye contact and reduced physical distance are
perceived as communicating disrespect.

The etiquette of deference and respect operates against assertiveness in
taking the initiative. Native American and Asian American interviewees
may wait for the interviewer to provide leadership and direction and continue to look to the interviewer to keep the interview going.

Unawareness of the slower pace of presentation and the more frequent
use of silence by Native Americans and Asian Americans may result in
premature "turn-taking" by the interviewer. The silence is less frequently
a "floor-yielding" signal on the part of such clients.

Without realizing it, the interviewer may apply inappropriate culture-
bound values in assessing the normality of the client's behavior. Among
Native Americans siblings are often given the responsibility for the care of
their younger brothers and sisters. A Caucasian social worker unaware of
this might regard such a procedure as indicative of parental neglect.

Tied more closely to the family, Asian Americans as well as Hispanics
may not value autonomy, independence, separation from the family as highly
as the American interviewer. Even as an adult, the client may still be dependent on and living with his family. Viewing this as pathology reflects
the interviewer's ethnocentrism rather than a problem of adjustment for
the interviewee.

Since the Asian family is highly structured, the supposition is that the
Asian American interviewee is less comfortable in an unstructured ambiguous, open interview situation. The value placed on compliance with fam-
ilial authority may clash with the interviewer's objectives of helping the
Asian American interviewee move toward greater self-fulfillment, a more
individualized sense of self-identity.

Asian American clients are more apt to be sensitive and deferentially
responsive to hierarchical differences in status. They are also more likely
to be characterized by self-effacement, modesty and, reticence in sharing
opinions, shame in sharing feelings. They are very hesitant in disagreeing
with the interviewer, whatever their own opinion. This is part of a pattern
of respect and deference to ward authority figures, but also an aspect of
the code of etiquette and interpersonal courtesy.

Asian Americans and Hispanics tend to define relationships in hierarchical patterns and may be disconcerted by interviewers who attempt to structure the interview relationship in equalitarian terms. Expecting and accepting the interviewer as having higher status, the interviewee expects
"answers," "advice," suggestions. He also expects the interviewer to be
formal in behavior, dress, and form of address.

Different ethnic groups may have a preference for different approaches to problem solving deriving from differing value orientations of the group. Asian Americans seem to "prefer a logical rational structured approach over an affected reflective ambiguous one" (Atkinson, Maruyama Matsui, 1978:80).

Because of the high value placed on self-control, the inhibition of display of strong feelings and a traditional respect for personal information that belongs only within the family, Asian American interviewees may have strong feelings against self-disclosure and sharing emotions. The concern with self-mastery results in a presentation of a seemingly calm, deceptively bland facade, even when under strong emotional stress.

Hesitancy about revealing personal information is reinforced by the fact that in sharing such material, secrets about other members of the family are likely to be revealed as well. Cultural reluctance to share family secrets with strangers may be regarded as resistance, inhibited defensiveness or emotional constriction by an interviewer not aware of this aspect of the client's culture.

Subtlety in expression and indirectness in presenting a problem are more typical of Asian American approaches to social relationships. Hence, interviewer frankness, bluntness, and openness may make such an interviewee feel uncomfortable. Asian Americans, and to a somewhat lesser extent Native Americans, regard directness in speech as disrespectful. The use of less immediate phrasing is not necessarily, then, a personal evasion of directness but is rather a culturally oriented approach to interview content.

Confrontation is perceived as rude and disrespectful. Questions about sex, finances, intimate family matters may be regarded as an unwarranted infringement on privacy and personal modesty. The Asian American interviewee may be reluctant to tell the interviewer "what he thinks" because open expression of one's different opinions violates the value of humility.

Class

The social work interviewer is generally middle class in identification and orientation. The interviewee is frequently lower class. "Lower class" and any of the other identifying labels that have been employed—"low income," "working class," "the poor," "the disadvantaged"—are vague and ambiguous. They tend to include diverse subgroups which are distinguishable. There are differences between the well-organized poor and the disorganized, demoralized poor; between multiproblem families that are overwhelmed by their situation and more adequately functioning families with money problems.

As used here, the term "lower class" refers to that sector of the population that has lived under low-income conditions over a long period of time. Low income is not a temporary, atypical situation for them but a prime fact in their lives. Consequently, in defense and adaptation, they have developed a life style, a set of values, a configuration of attitudes, and a repertoire of behavior that is identifiable and characteristic.

The poverty environment acts as a particular socializing matrix which influences and determines the ways people believe, think, and behave. Low-income life style, "the culture of poverty," is, of course, a convenient fiction, much as the middle-class life style is. It would be difficult to find any middle-class or low-income family that exactly mirrored the life-style configurations detailed in a sociology textbook. Still, there is sufficient empirical material to suggest that low-income people do have beliefs, attitudes, and patterns of behavior that are distinguishable from their middle-class counterparts.

SCHEDULING AND ACCESS

For instance, scheduling, a relatively routine problem for the middle-class interviewee, is likely to be a special problem for the lower-class interviewee. There are persistently noted differences in time sense among the social classes. For a variety of reasons there is less concern with scheduling, with punctuality, with time-related regularity among lower-class interviewees. Consequently, while making the effort to schedule interviews, agencies offering service to lower-class clients might also consider an open-door arrangement. Such an arrangement permits the interviewee to come for an interview at unscheduled times with some assurance that an interviewer will be available. It might involve availability at the times most convenient for the lower-class male—evenings and weekends. Walk-in arrangements are, furthermore, in line with another facet of lower-class use of agencies. The motivation to use the agency is highest when the individual or family faces a crisis. Anticipating problems is a middle-class exercise; lower-class people are likely to respond to the problem when it is causing maximum discomfort. It is at this point that the client wants to see an interviewer and that one should be available if the opportunity for helping is not to be lost.

The open-door policy needs to be supplemented by a "revolving door" policy, making possible an easy return for later contacts. Lower-income interviewees are likely to have definite immediate goals for any contact. They are apt to want immediate alleviation of discomfort rather than to work toward any elaborate, long-range objectives. Consequently, once their limited goals are achieved, they may have little motivation for continuing the contact. At the time of the next crisis, however, they may want to return; agency policy should make them easily welcomed. Such a policy implies a willingness to be concerned with symptoms rather than with causes and a readiness to attempt to alleviate symptoms rather than eliminate causes. Each problem situation would be viewed as a distinct entity, and there would be acceptance of the probability that problems would recur.

Whenever the low-income interviewee is ready to come to an agency, physical inaccessibility is more of a deterrent than it is for the middle-class interviewee with a car. A woman has to count on long, inconvenient rides, the expenditure of badly needed money on carfare, arrangements for babysitters, etc. A man has to get his boss's permission to take time off and may lose pay. The physical accessibility of an agency which has offices in a low-income neighborhood is, therefore, an important prerequisite for effective service.

Coming to the agency at all, wherever it is, however flexible the schedule, may pose a problem. However brave the attempt at informality, an agency is still a place of middle-class strangers. The lower-class interviewee may be uneasy about his clothes, language, and conduct, uncertain about acceptability, and anxious about doing the wrong thing. He may have doubts about whether he has the social skill required to initiate and maintain such a contact. With lower-class interviewees, therefore, the social worker should be more ready to consider a home interview. The interviewee is then on his own ground, in a milieu in which his clothes, language, and conduct are appropriate.

Attitudes toward the agency prevalent in low-income neighborhoods also may reduce motivation to arrange for or accept an appointment. The agency may be viewed as an institution of social control, representing the Establishment, the oppressive, depriving society.

CONCEPTIONS AND GOALS

The interviewer and the interviewee bring different preconceptions into the interview. Lower-class clients are apt to come with a general cynicism which suggests that everyone is out for himself, everyone has an angle. Their whole life experience generally confirms such an assessment of human interaction. The exploitation, indifference, and rejection experienced by low-income people at the hands of members of the dominant culture exacerbate the difficulties in developing a relationship of trust and confidence between a middle-class interviewer and a lower-class interviewee.

A lower-class person is apt to be much more concerned with consequences of behavior than with explanations of causation. Where causation is considered, it is in terms of a single simplistic explanation rather than a complex, multiple one. "Why?" or "What explains . . ." is less likely to hold attention for discussion than "What has happened?" or "What will happen if. . . ." The client's orientation is more likely to be external and fatalistic. "Acts of fate" and "environmental pressures" are apt to be seen as causes for difficulty, in contrast to the psychological orientation to problem origin likely to characterize the worker's thinking. For the lower class, threats to sheer physical survival in the midst of pervasive physical deprivations take clear priority over concern with difficulties in personal relations.

Limited income interviewees are more likely to be concerned, as they have to be, with day-to-day survival. Consequently they are more likely to be sharply focused on dealing with the presenting problems, the immediate situation. Such clients are likely to discount intra- and inter-personal difficulties as explaining their situation because the pressures of deficiencies in their physical environment are so overwhelmingly obvious. At the very minimum, the interviewer has to be receptive to the idea that the interviewee's definition of the situation may be right. She must initially try to orient the interview to consider the solutions that the lower-class interviewee thinks are necessary.

These brave statements simplify a complex problem. Agency workers often redefine the client's problems in their own terms not because they want to arbitrarily deny the lower-class client's definition of the situation but because, unless they redefine it, there isn't much they can offer the client. The agency may not be able to help the client in the way he wants to be helped. There is not much it can do about solving the problems of poverty, lack of housing, lack of satisfying, self-actualizing, well-paying jobs, drugs in the streets, rats, falling ceilings, and plumbing that does not work. So the social workers try to help in the ways they think they can—mainly by exploration of feelings, attitudes, understanding. They often redefine the situation so that they can help in the only way they are equipped to help.

LANGUAGE

The lower-class client's communication patterns pose problems for productive interviewing. Language generally is used within a limited group of people who share assumptions and interests that make elaboration unnecessary. Most people employ a restricted code for primary-group communication; they use shorthand speech which depends on considerable shared experience to fill in what is left unsaid but is mutually understood. People outside the group may find the speech difficult to understand because meanings are condensed and dislocated. A more elaborate, less particularistic communications code is generally used with outsiders in deference to their lack of understanding of the private language. The lower-class interviewee, however, is likely to use the restricted code even with outsiders, such as the interviewer, which hampers the interviewer's efforts to follow what she says and to understand her experiences.

One problem is simply a difference in word usage, as we have noted earlier in chapter 2. But often the problems are complex and structural. A study of the contrast between middle-class and lower-class interviewees, all of whom had faced the same crisis experience (a tornado), revealed a number of significant differences (Schatzman and Strauss 1955). Middle-class interviewees seemed to grasp what the interviewers wanted and presented reasonably well-organized, coherent accounts of what had happened to them. They built structure into their stories and were responsive to relevant probes. There was a tendency to generalize from their experience. The lower-class interviewees had less tendency to take themselves as objects of introspective reflection. There was less inclination to empathize with the interviewer. Lower-class interviewees responded more to their own internal imagery than to the questions posed by the interviewer. The interviewees tended to personalize and concretize their experience. Their accounts of their experiences were apt to be rambling and unorganized, lacking a coherent focus. The interviewer had to be much more active and controlling if focus was to be maintained and the interview purpose accomplished.

The researchers concluded that these were differences in communicative styles that directly affect behavior in the interview. Other studies of lower-class speech support their conclusions. Such speech tends to "reflect a sender-centered, particularistic style of speech as against a more topic-centered style in the speech of the higher status speakers" (Williams and Naremore 1969:97). Bernstein (1964) notes significant discrepancies between the lower-class speech system and the communication code characteristic of the social work interview. The lower-class speech system puts less emphasis on a vocabulary of feelings. There is a preference for concrete rather than abstract propositions. Parenthetically, it might be noted that the lower class interviewee has less concern with confidentiality although he is not altogether insensitive to the invasion of privacy.

SERVICES OFFERED

These differences in orientation help explain the unanimous conclusion of numerous earlier studies which detail the reaction of lower-class clients to "talking cures" (casework included). The studies available show clearly

that, when compared with middle-class clients, lower-class clients are offered psychotherapy less frequently, accept psychotherapy less frequently,
drop out earlier and at a higher rate when they do accept it, and tend to
benefit less from it (Meyers and Roberts 1959).

Stereotyped characteristic patterns of thought and behavior previously
attributed with some confidence to the low-income client has been found
to be only partially true. These were characteristics that supposedly made
for difficulties in effective deployment of traditional social work interview
approaches. Lower-income clients were characterized as limited in verbal
skills, impulsively focused on immediate gratification rather than long-range
goals, unoriented to introspective psychologizing as an approach to personal problem solving, more preoccupied with somatic complaints, tending
to act out and externalize blame, and distrustful, suspicious, and resentful
of authority. Manifesting these characteristics, the lower-income interviewee was a more difficult client to work with. There were, consequently,
problems in service delivery.

The national development of community health centers grew partly out
of concern for earlier failures to effectively reach low-income populations
in providing mental health services. Insurance coverage for out-patient
therapy included in many union contracts and the support of such services
by the Medicaid program for the medically indigent has likewise resulted
in increases during the 1970s and 1980s of contacts between lower-income
clients and social workers offering mental health services.

Although some of the differences between low-income and middle-income interviewees have more recently been reaffirmed "directionally, their
extent appears to have been markedly reduced"—"undoubtedly television,
the movies and the popular press have provided much information to the
public about the psychotherapy process" (Lorian 1978:913, 915).

Lerner's research report on the services of a mental health center in a
low-income community, *Therapy in the Ghetto* (1972), indicates that such
services could be offered effectively to such a population of clients. The
crucial factor in this case, making for success, was the democratic, respectful attitude expressed by the staff in their interaction with this client group.
This was contrasted with a more typically encountered kind of benevolent
authoritarianism based on a stereotyped evaluation of clients' limited capacity to handle their own lives.

It may be that the earlier research conclusion needs modification as a
result of a more widespread general education regarding "counseling" or
"psychotherapy" broadly defined as a viable approach to personal problem
solving. Low-income clients currently are found to be more receptive to
such help than was previously thought to be the case. Tte current feeling
is that "the research literature concerning social class differences in patient

needs, expectations, and treatment preferences is, at best, mixed. To date, there appears to be no conclusive evidence that lower-class patients need, expect, or want anything different from their middle-class or upper-class counterparts" (Frank et al. 1978:69). In summarizing the research available regarding the possibilities of offering mental health services to low-income groups, Lorian says that "earlier pessimism appears unwarranted" (1978:904).

TWO-WAY EDUCATION

Recognizing that lower-class clients might terminate contact prematurely at a higher rate than middle-income clients, efforts have been made to offer such clients an explicit education regarding casework or counseling or psychotherapy. The supposition is that such clients have little familiarity with, less confidence in, and erroneous expectations of what is involved in such activities.

Clients are given special preparation for entering into treatment interviews through role induction procedures which include didactic instruction, informational interviews, or modeling and role playing. A general overview of the treatment process is given. There is a run-through of what the interviewer is going to be doing and some information is offered on how the process is designed to be helpful for the problem the client brings.

At the same time, greater efforts have been made to help social workers become more aware of their own feelings, attitudes, and expectations in approaching such clients. The worker's anticipation that lower-class interviewees would be more highly resistive and more likely to quit could result in self-fulfilling prophecies. While educating clients regarding counseling, the workers are also educated regarding the life situations, needs, and expectations of low-income clients. This helps to develop a greater receptivity to a wider range of clients beyond the narrowly defined, highly preferred YAVIS client—"young, articulate, verbal, intelligent, successful."

Improvements in interaction between the middle-class interviewer and the low-income client results also from open discussion in supervisory conference of the worker's attitude toward and feelings about lower-class clients.

There is a three-pronged effort involved here—modification of interview arrangements and procedures to more squarely meet the needs of low-income clients, education of clients to the requirements of the role of interviewee in a social agency, and educating the workers to a greater understanding and acceptance of the low-income client.

PROBLEMS WITHIN THE INTERVIEWER

Cross-class interviewing difficulties do not originate exclusively from the interviewee's side of the desk. If the lower-class interviewee is uncomfortable with the middle-class interviewer, the reverse may also be true. The interviewer is understandably more uneasy in those situations in which interviewee's background is significantly different from her own. She cannot fall back on the fund of shared experience to understand what the client is talking about and to guide her judgments. For example, the interview opening may be somewhat more difficult. There is a smaller community of interest on which to base the social small talk which eases transition to the formal interview.

In contact with the unfamiliar, the interviewer is understandably more anxious. But anxiety is not the only feeling likely to be generated. Some of the feelings which may oppress the middle-class interviewer in contact with a lower-class interviewee are detailed by a member of a mental-health interviewing team assigned to a slum area.

> We may experience feelings of guilt because of the realization that we are much better off than they and, in addition, are secretly glad that we are better off. Being faced with the living conditions of the poor and their lack of dignity may also stir up in us fears that "it could happen to me." On the other hand we cannot disregard a second feeling that may be aroused, i.e, the latent wish to be like them. We may envy them their freedom from responsibility, their leisure, and the fact that they are allowed free expression of their drives. We may secretly wish that we ourselves did not have to clean the house or go to work. Since in order to function as members of the middle-class we must reject these wishes, we may in the same way tend to reject the lower-class. (Taylor et al. 1965:328)

The interviewer may feel overwhelmed and depressed at the weight of environmental stresses and deprivation and feel hopeless about her capacity to be of any help.

The more activist-oriented social work interviewer may have another kind of difficulty. Such interviewers may face the overidentification reaction noted by McMahon in medical students who interviewed the poor as part of their training.

> Because of the need to relieve the poor of responsibility and to blame society, they were unable to pay attention to the contribution of intrapsychic factors to their patients' situations. Because they tended to equate diagnosis for character and neurotic problems with criticisms of the poor, they had difficulty in observing and integrating psychological data with the rest of their patients' lives. (McMahon and Shore 1968:565)

The caseworker may feel irritated by the lower-class client who does not afford her the opportunity to practice the more intensive brand of psychotherapy on which social workers still tend to place a high premium. A psychiatrist attached to a public clinic expresses some of the disillusion which might be felt by some social workers in contact with lower-class clients.

> When I first came here I had high hopes of doing something about the neglected people who are sick—the Negroes, Mexicans, Puerto Ricans, the poor in general. But I've become sort of disillusioned. Most of them really can't be reached, because they live in cultures where "acting out" is habitual, where you don't talk much and practically never in intimate terms about yourself. So when I tried to discuss things with them, they just wouldn't discuss. "Look, Doc," they'd say, "forget the horseshit. I know all that. Just give me something to get me through the day so I don't lose my temper so much." Well, what can you do? (Rogow 1970:73)

The quotation reflects one of the principal findings of Hollingshead and Redlich's study of the social class aspects of psychotherapy, namely, that middle-class psychotherapists frequently "dislike patients from a low socioeconomic class, do not understand their values and often have difficulty in understanding them as persons. Reciprocally, lower class patients are less likely to understand what the psychotherapist is attempting to communicate even though they want relief from misery" (1956:397).

REDUCING THE GAP

How can one reduce the gap between interviewer and client, to make the interview more effective? The following suggestions are supported by, and derive from, the writings of workers and researchers who have had experience with lower-class interviewees.

At the start of the interview, use of Mr., Mrs., or Miss rather than just a surname or first names, shaking hands, and introducing oneself need to be observed with seriousness and sincerity. These rituals and forms are not empty gestures to people who have been persistently denied such elementary symbols of civility and courtesy. A clear statement of who the interviewer represents and the purpose of the contact is important. Low-income groups are currently being contacted by a wide variety of people representing a broad range of programs. They have been surfeited with promises. Justifiably cynical to begin with in response to their experience with missionaries from the dominant culture, they assume that everybody has a gimmick. Unless the social work interviewer can clearly communicate who she is, what she represents, and why the interview is being conducted, the interviewee will spend time and psychic energy trying to figure out the worker's gimmick.

The interviewer needs to be more active, take more of the initiative in these interviews than in interviews with middle-class clients. She needs to offer the interviewee a clearly defined and explicit structure; the purpose of the interview needs to be unambiguously stated; greater control and direction need to be exercised over interview interaction to maintain focus. The interviewer should communicate a definite statement of expectations to which she holds the interviewee with polite, kindly firmness. Rather than resenting this, lower-class interviewees may be receptive to direction from professionals whom they perceive as exercising a benign authority in their behalf. Without such direction and activity on the part of the interviewer, the interviewee is faced with responsibility for selecting, organizing, and focusing interview content. He has to have some appreciation and understanding of what material is relevant and the capacity to verbalize without blocking. All of this puts a great burden on the interviewee's skills— a burden that frequently may be beyond the capacity or level of sophistication of the lower-class interviewee.

The tempo of the interview needs to be slower with lower-class respondents. They need more time to accommodate to transitions, more repetition of questions and probes. Such an interview requires more frequent recapitulation and review.

Content selected for the interview and the questions formulated should concern concrete, specific, externally oriented considerations, as against a focus on abstract, symbolic, introspective matters. Concrete examples are better than abstract generalizations, concern with practical tasks preferred to "psychologizing." Questions should be framed in the context of the client's actual life situation.

If the kids don't go to school what do you do? Who talks to them? What does he say? What do you do when Johnny hits the baby?

Where did you go to look for a job? What did you say when he asked what you could do?

The mood that needs to be established is one of informal friendliness and nonpatronizing understanding. Direct, frank, clear, critical statements are preferred over ambiguous subtleties and circumlocutions. The latter are characteristic of social work speech, but with lower-class clients the ambiguous and the indirect tend to be regarded as indicating weakness and also tend to cause confusion.

The class status difference reinforces the role status difference between interviewer and interviewee. The lower-class interviewee thus tends to feel more than ordinarily subordinate. The interviewer therefore has to make a deliberate effort to abandon some of her professional anonymity and come across as a human being. It is necessary to communicate an image of another fallible human being faced with similar problems. Because of the initial social distance, which makes the interviewer more of a stranger than she would be to middle-class people, lower-class interviewees have more of a need to know the interviewer as a person before they can trust her as an interviewer. There is more need for "self-sharing"—mutual problems in child rearing, helplessness in the face of defective appliances, etc.

Social work interviews which have treatment as their objective are oriented toward bringing about changes in attitudes and behavior primarily through use of verbal communication as the means of achieving change. This puts a heavy burden on the interviewee for bringing to the interview a reasonable level of competence in manipulating verbal symbols. "Talking cures" require good talking ability.

As a consequence of the emphasis on verbally explaining and analyzing subjective experiences for the purpose of achieving self-understanding or insight, traditional casework may be less appropriate for those lower-class interviewees with a more limited education and a more limited vocabulary.

The traditional approach is less likely to be effective with clients with limited expressive capacity, who are not psychologically minded and for whom a major component of the problem situation is a highly deprived and constricting environment. Such clients require a modified approach. They require a casework which, in balancing the offer of psychotherapy (changing the client's capacity to cope with the situation) and sociotherapy (changing the situation so that it is easier to handle), includes a heavier emphasis on sociotherapeutic elements. Advice and the sharing of information by the interviewer are very much in line with the expectations of the lower-class interviewee. The working-class clients interviewed by Mayer and Timms on their reaction to their experience with caseworkers "welcomed the idea of receiving suggestions, advice and recommendations from the worker" (1970:88), even though they were not always ready and willing to act on them.

A limited number of both clients and workers from a variety of social agencies were intensively interviewed by Silverman regarding their respective experiences in the social work interviews. The clients, low-income blacks, felt that it was their obligation to inform the worker about their problems. The worker's obligation, in turn, was to "organize this information, explain what it means and tell the client what to do." One client said, "I thought if they found out what was wrong they would explain the situation to me. I thought they would tell me what will work and what is bugging me" (Silverman 1970:627). The workers, however, were oriented to forming a "therapeutic alliance" with the clients so that the interview would be devoted to helping them solve their own problems. "The workers wanted the clients to learn through the interview experience that it is helpful to talk to somebody who understands and cares" (p. 632). The clients, on the other hand, distinguished between talking and helping. They saw talking as an expressive release but one that did not correct or ameliorate the situation for which they were seeking help. The differing conceptions held by worker and client of the way they would work together in the interview made a barrier to communication which was never explicitly discussed.

It might be argued that the social worker is correct in her view of what the interview can accomplish and how she can best help the client deal with his problems. The elementary fact is, however, that she owes the interviewee a clear explanation of her conception of what the interview is all about and also some help in learning to play his part in an interview organized in accordance with such expectations.

With middle-class interviewees the interviewer can assume a preference for "talk" as a mode of problem-solving, a readiness for introspection, and a readiness to talk about feelings. The middle-class interviewer in contact with the lower-class client has the more complex job of socializing the client to the normative demands of the interview as practiced in social agencies. The interviewer has to "teach" the client to focus on feelings, talk about feelings, label feelings. Words and talk are discounted by lower-class interviewees who have been talked into insensibility and cynical skepticism. In establishing a relationship of trust, the worker has to prove her utility to the interviewee on the basis of action. Demonstration of interest and concern by doing something takes clear precedence over verbal expressions of interest and concern.

Actually quieting a crying child, fixing a broken lamp cord, offering a ride when needed, or helping complete a difficult application form, is communicating in a different way what one might have said in the interview. Interview by demonstration is a very appropriate procedure with lower-class clients since they are action-oriented, emphasizing physical and visual communication as against oral communication. Their approach to problem-solving requires adaptations in interviewing technique. The approach is apt to be motoric rather than verbal. Words are used in relation to action. The interview should incorporate opportunities for the lower-class interviewee to act out his situation. Role-playing during some part of the interview may be appropriate.

Male, 32, Puerto Rican, lower class, probation interview.
WORKER: Like, you said you bought this transistor radio and it didn't work from the time you brought it home, and you are out the money but not

sure you want to ask for a refund. Here, let's role-play this—I'll be the store owner, and let's say you're bringing the radio back.

MR. G.: You mean, play it like I was bringing it back?

WORKER: Yeah. Let's suppose it was happening, and you come into my store with the radio. Now what would you do? You go ahead. . . .

In family interviewing with low-income interviewees, games have been used to initiate the usual pattern of family interaction and hypothetical problems have been proposed for family solutions, to get the family to interact—planning a purchase of furniture, or selecting a movie to see.

Many of these possibilities suggest the particular appropriateness of behavior-conditioning interview approaches with lower-class interviewees for those interviews which have a primarily therapeutic purpose. The emphasis in such an approach is on behavior rather than on symptoms, and on direct advice for particular kinds of behavioral problems.

A social worker offering family therapy to low-income families illustrates this partializing task-oriented procedure concerned with specifics in the following excerpt:

THERAPIST: You say you want your husband to take more responsibility in the home; is there anything in particular you would like him to do?

WIFE: Yes, I want him to help more about the house.

THERAPIST: Such as . . . ?

WIFE: Well, just to be more helpful; not leave all the responsibility to me.

THERAPIST: Is there anything specific that he could do between now and our next session that would ease things for you?

WIFE: Well, I suppose there's the door; it's been off its hinges for weeks waiting for him to fix it.

THERAPIST: Okay. Discuss it with him.

HUSBAND: Alright, if you want the door done, I'll do it when we get home. (After a pause)

WIFE: Well, no not really. He's been promising to do that door for weeks now.

THERAPIST: Then I suggest you push him a bit more.

HUSBAND: Look, the door's the least of our problems. We've got much bigger problems than a door.

THERAPIST: I want to find out whether the two of you can solve little problems first. If you can't do that, we stand no chance with the bigger ones. (Pause) Okay. Your wife has asked you to put on the door. Now, what could she do different, in exchange, to make things easier for you?

HUSBAND: Well, she could take more interest in the house.

THERAPIST: Like . . . ?

HUSBAND: She accuses me of being disinterested, but she gives me that impression herself.

THERAPIST: Tell her something in particular you'd like different.

HUSBAND: Well . . . to take more pains over the cooking.
THERAPIST: Talk to her about it. (Cade 1975:142–43)

Action oriented, experientially focused interview procedures which involve task enactment rather than verbal description and which are focused on clearly identified concrete topics have some advantage with this group of clients.

Male–Female

Men and women are members of different sexual subcultures. In many significant ways they differ in their orientations toward social relationships. The differences may result partly from differing socialization experiences. The research literature on public opinion interviewing confirms that the sex of the interviewer affects responses. The general conclusion is supported by studies on the sex of the examiner and responses to projective psychological tests.

In general, females are more accepting of personal counseling interviews than males and likely to be freer about expressing feelings in interviews, whether the interviewer is male or female. Men are more reticent generally, and especially about feelings; boys are less verbally accessible than girls.

Previously there seemed to be some consensus that while most people seeking personal counseling are women, "they seem to prefer men to women as their therapist" (Fabrikant 1978:86). While it is still true that the largest number of clients of social agencies are women, there is less certainty currently about their gender preference for a worker.

A clear answer as to preference is still open. A 1980 review of the relevant research concludes: "Although research on female clients' preference for male and female counselors has been conducted for more than two decades, results have been inconsistent and far from conclusive" (Highlen and Russell 1980:157).

The younger generation of female interviewees are likely to be more sensitive to gender considerations in the interview, reflecting a raised consciousness regarding gender identity. Younger, unmarried women, in particular, are more sensitive and responsive to cross-gender pairings than are older married women. They react more ambivalently and experience less support, less satisfaction in contact with a male interviewer.

Feminists contend that since female interviewees present problems and experiences that are unique to their gender, which are viewed differently by male and by female interviewers, only a woman interviewer can truly understand and empathize with the female interviewee. Some go even further and assert that only a woman who is herself a feminist can truly understand the female client.

The supposition is that the gender of the interviewee is a significant factor in determining how the interviewer will respond. There is the feeling that a female interviewer would be more interested, knowledgeable, and understanding of women's problems and have greater sympathy for such problems than would a male interviewer. Conversely, it is felt that the female interviewee would be readier to disclose to, and easier to ask questions of, a female interviewer.

There is a special rationale, then, for feminist therapist interviewers. However, the difference may not be so much in the process and techniques of interviewing as in the objectives of interviewing. Feminist counselors and therapists are more likely to be identified with clearly defined objectives furthering women's liberation, consciousness raising, and sex role modification. The objectives are achieved not only by the interview interaction, but by the feminist interviewer acting as a role model of a liberated, self-directed assertive woman.

The characteristics associated with the good interviewer—understanding, warmth, acceptance, empathy, affiliative interest, support, nurturance, sympathy—are all characteristics traditionally associated with the female gender. The good male interviewer communicating those attitudes is likely to be perceived as androgynous—combining male and female elements. The good male interviewer is thus not sharply gender differentiated from the good female interviewer.

The demands of the interview situation are thus more congruent with the socialization experiences of the female interviewer and conversely at variance with the socialization experiences of the male interviewer. This would suggest that it is more difficult for a male to achieve the approach required for good interviewing. On the other hand, good interviewing does require control, the imposition of some authority, the acceptance of the dominant states of the interviewer vis-à-vis the interviewee. These requirements are more in line with society's stereotypical expectations of male behavior.

There is considerable discussion of sex role bias and sex role stereotyping in human services interviewing. The frequently made accusation is that male interviewers impose and perpetuate demeaning stereotypes on their female interviewees. A review of the available research suggests that the accusation, as applied to most male interviewers, is "based on questionable data" (Stricker 1977:14) or "weak evidence" (Zeldow 1975:93).

There are assertions that the sex of the interviewer has been a frequent source of bias in perception of adequacy of clients' social functioning, e.g., that behavior acceptable for a man, when manifested by a woman, is regarded as evidence of greater inadequacy by a male interviewer. Four different research studies of social work interviews have come to four different conclusions. A study by Fischer et al. (1976) came to the conclusion that there was a strong anti-male bias among respondents who read a typical social work vignette of a client problem in which the sex of the client was varied. Dailey (1980), replicating Fischer's study, came to the conclusion that there was an anti-female bias. Gingerich and Kirk (1981), replicating both studies but using a videotaped interview as a basis for respondent judgments, failed to find a sex bias in either direction. Jayaratne and Irey, reporting results of a questionnaire completed by 540 graduate social workers, noted that "female workers show a 'positive bias' toward female clients and a 'negative bias' toward male clients" (1981:411).

All of this is further confirmation that there are few unequivocal findings as yet, regarding the effect of gender differences on the interview. Even taken at its face value, the accusation of perceptual bias has less applicability to male social worker interviewers than other clinicians since male social workers, while not as "contemporary in their attitudes toward women's roles as female clinicians," "tend to be more contemporary than traditional males" (Davenport and Reims 1978:308).

There seems to be a growing appreciation that good social work interviewing requires a need for sensitivity to sex role issues and knowledge regarding the psychology and sociology of womens' life situations. Gender orientation has strong value components and the interviewer needs to be aware of the source of her own attitudes regarding gender questions. In this respect female interviewers may have an advantage that they are likely to be more contemporary, less stereotypical, and more knowledgeable about these considerations than their male counterparts.

Even a more androgynously oriented male interviewer may find it hard to understand the changing scene with the same affective intensity that women bring to the situation. While not "sexist," they still may lack a gut-level understanding. Rapid social transition, still in process, increases the probabilities that cross-gender interview participants may hold different pictures in their minds about definitions of "healthy adjustment," "normal behavior," "deviant adaptation," or "problem-solving options."

The male interviewer in contact with female interviewee has to have some clear idea as to how he reacts to the choice of life options which are alternatives to motherhood, some acceptance of the fact that some of the difficulties women face are the result of social bias, and an awareness of the elements of stereotypical thinking regarding sex roles which he may bring to the interview. Now, more than previously, the male interviewer needs to guard against the use of sexist language and terminology which may offend female clients.

However, gender is no guarantee of compatibility in points of view. There is a greater difference in orientation between a committed feminist interviewer and a traditionally oriented "unliberated" woman interviewee than there is between a feminist interviewee and an androgynously oriented male interviewer.

Observed gender is not the same as perceived gender. Male interviewers are more or less masculine in attitude and behavior. Some male interviewers are perceived as more feminine than some female interviewers.

Further complicating the situation is the fact that gender does not stand alone. An interviewer is of a certain sex, a certain race, a certain age, a certain level of experience. A black, older female interviewee may react differently to a white inexperienced female interviewer of a younger age than she would to a black, older, experienced male. It is difficult to delineate what effect gender qua gender contributes to the interaction.

In addition, as in the case of race, the principal problem of concern may effect a preference for compatible pairing. If it is a problem that relates directly to male-female relationship—a question of incest, wife battering, rape, or sexual job discrimination—a female interviewer might be preferred. Younger female clients concerned with clarifying their gender orientation indicate a preference for a female interviewer who is single over a female interviewer who is married.

Some interview content is more directly sex linked than others. It may be easier for women to talk of menstrual difficulties, birth experiences, clothing styles, and discrimination against women with a woman counselor. Men may feel freer to talk about sports, gambling, or impotence with a male interviewer. The differences between "locker room" talk and "beauty parlor" talk reflect the possible barrier in interviews when participants are of opposite sexes.

Theoretically, the reversal in dominance implied in a woman interviewer interviewing a male may make the male interviewee uncomfortable, prompting a negative, hostile attitude in an attempt to redress the balance.

Conversely an insecure male interviewer may feel challenged and made uncomfortable by a woman interviewee who, assertive and self-reliant, rejects traditional dependency in the interview. While theoretically reasonable, there is little empirical or clinical evidence to confirm these suppositions as a general pattern however.

The male interviewer may be overdetermined to prove that he is non-sexist and can be trusted. He may hesitate to use confrontation when necessary or to raise certain painful questions that might be helpful. He may

hesitate to be appropriately supportive since that might suggest harassment. The interviewer may be so on his guard against any possibility that
the interaction could become eroticized that he consequently acts in an
aloof and artificial manner. Despite difficulties, however, a good relationship can, and does, transcend sex differences (Mattson 1970).

It may be easier to be more empathic with a same-sex client as against
an opposite-sex client. Whether this eventuates in more effective service
is, of course, another question. A study of casework services to parents and
children in their own homes concluded that "the sex of the worker had no
significant association with service outcome" (Sherman et al. 1973:111).

A 1978 review of the relevant research came to the conclusion which can
only be repeated here, namely that "few conclusions can be drawn at this
time. . . . There is very little evidence to support any conclusions on the
effects of the same sex versus opposite sex pairs on outcome" (Parloff et al.
1978:262, 264). Intermediate outcome measures such as satisfaction with
the relationship are also equivocal.

The complexity of the question was demonstrated in the results of a nationwide study of family service agency clientele. While male clients assigned to male workers had better outcome scores than those assigned to
female workers, compatable sex matching of female clients with female interviewers did not significantly affect outcome. Male clients assigned to
male interviewers stayed in contact longer, and females assigned to female
interviewers were less likely to terminate prematurely than if assigned to
male interviewers. Female clients treated by female counselors gave higher
ratings to the counselor client relationship than did those assigned to male
counselors. The researchers conclude that

> Though sex considerations in counselor assignments in most instances do not
> produce major difficulties, nevertheless the balance of findings in favor of sex
> matching does lead one to ponder meanings. Perhaps each sex feels more con-
> fident of a sympathetic hearing, understanding of the issues involved, and
> needed support for decision making and action when the counselor is of the
> same sex. Similarly, each may feel reluctant about discussing sexual problems.
> To what extent such findings are increased by the rising awareness of sex roles
> and counterbalanced by cross-sex attraction cannot be ascertained from the
> data. (Beck and Jones 1973:139)

Sexual Preference—Homosexuality

Sexual preference is another consideration which may make for difficulty
between participants in the interview. Homosexuality, as a variation in sexual preference, is currently more openly expressed than ever before. While

there are no valid census figures on this, informed estimates suggest that 10 percent of the population is homosexually oriented, making this group one of the largest minorities in the country. With increasing frequency, interviewers are in contact with clients who acknowledge their gay or lesbian sexual preference. The problems, values, adaptations, life style, and even language of such clients are matters about which most interviewers are ignorant. The heterosexually oriented interviewer has some responsibility to become acquainted with the voluminous literature available on such matters.

Homosexuals identify heterosexism as analagous to racism and sexism. Heterosexism is an attitude which suggests that heterosexuality is an intrinsically superior sexual preference. An affirmative point of view toward homosexuality perceives it as a nonpathological human potential that the interviewer needs to accept, value, and facilitate.

It might be noted that in 1974–75, both the American Psychiatric Association and the American Psychological Association voted that homosexuality no longer be classified as a mental disorder.

While some homosexuals may seek social work help in reorienting their sexual preference, many homosexual clients have accepted their preference and seek help with a variety of general problems in facilitating functioning in accordance with a homosexual orientation. The heterosexually oriented interviewer may have some difficulty in accepting the idea that homosexuality is, for the client, a "normal nonpathological form of human sexual and affectional expression" (Moss and Hawkins 1982:215). The interviewer may be ambivalent about her obligation to help the client in dealing with problems encountered in implementing such an orientation.

The interviewer is likely to be able to conduct a more successful interview if she knows something about the local gay and lesbian community and its resources—the bars and hotels that are open to homosexuals, medical services, homosexual hot-lines, rap groups.

Homophobia, fear and dislike of homosexuals, is pervasive in a heterosexual oriented society. The interviewer may want to examine as objectively as possible his or her own attitudes toward homosexuals. If there is a tendency on the part of the interviewer to see homosexuality as perverted, disquieting, sick, or threatening, it is not likely that the interview will be successful.

The Aged Client

Most social workers are younger than many of their clients. Cultural aspects of age differences may operate as barriers to effective interviewing.

The contact between younger and older people evokes reverberations of the parent-child relationship, but here the positions of helper and helped are reversed; the younger person is in control and directing, however lightly and permissively, the older interviewee. Both participants are apt to be somewhat edgy in response to this "unnatural" situation.

A generation gap is inevitable. The older client was socialized at a time when American problems, values, and mores were quite different. In effect he or she grew up in a different country.

Some older people are living by a value system which has been superseded or modified. To impose on others, to take "charity," to be dependent, to express a concern for self and one's needs was less acceptable in an earlier ethic to which many of the older interviewees subscribe. There is less acceptance of "counseling" and psychotherapy among older people generally.

Educational differences between interviewer and interviewee are likely to compound age differences. By and large, the educational attainment of older citizens is lower than that of the younger population.

Another component of the subcultural age gap derives from the differences in physiology between youth and old age. The abatement of instinctual needs, the greater physical effort required for every activity, the slower tempo, the great susceptibility to physical insult and injury, the immediate awareness of the possibility and inevitability of death suggests that in a thousand major and minor details, the world is a different place for the older person, beyond the easy imagining of a worker living in a 20- or 30-year-old body.

The social derogation of the aged, their foreshortened time perspective, the reversal from adult independence to greater dependency, the lack of a valued, useful social role, tend to differentiate further the aged client from the younger worker and introduce difficulties for empathy and understanding.

The worker, as a member of the younger population and, through the agency, as a representative of the social institutions of society, may be identified with that society and culture which has rejected the aged client. The older client has a more varied potential for transference. Not only can the interviewer represent the older client's parents on whom he is now dependent, she can also represent the client's children.

These factors feed into the interview interaction, increasing the complex ties the interviewer needs to deal with.

More often now people make a distinction between the "young-old" (60s–early 70s) and the "old-old" (75 years of age and older). The decline in capabilities more frequently true of the old-old are often attributed, in agism, to the more adequate young-old.

Agism is the stereotyping of the aged as asexual, impaired in psychological functioning, rigid, and incapable of learning and/or changing. The stereotyping interviewer tends to be deficit-oriented in approaching the aged client.

The aged are more susceptible to confusion in time periods, querulousness which stems from loneliness, and repetitive reminiscing, all of which interfere with efficient, effective interviewing.

Older interviewees frequently tend to blur the focus of the interview by reminiscing. Rather than being random behavior of little purpose, reminiscing may contribute important functions in interview interaction. Pincus points out that reminiscing serves to reduce the age difference between the interviewee and interviewer. Reminiscing has the "effect of bringing the older person mentally back through time to the same age or situation as that of the younger [interviewer], thereby in effect erasing the existing age difference" (1970:51). If age difference is regarded as a threat to status, the older interviewee may meet the threat in this way. Reminiscences about past accomplishments also serve an expressive function. They reassure the interviewee that he was once more competent, more capable, than he is now.

Interviewing in the home rather than the office may be necessary, to spare the client the physical insult of a long, tiring trip to the office, often up and down stairs that are difficult to negotiate. However, because an office interview requires the older person to mobilize himself to move out of his isolation into the world of other people, it could, on occasion, be the desirable choice.

Many of the old-old are living in institutions. Interviewing in such a setting generally involves working in the open where one's behavior can be observed and where one can often be overheard. Observed behaviors in the interview being conducted may affect interviews scheduled with others at a later time. There is a danger, too, that staff and relatives also present during the interview may, protectively, answer for the interviewee.

Nonverbal information (discussed in full in chapter 14) is of particular importance in interviewing the aged. The interviewer needs to be sensitive to the degree of physical and/or mental loss sustained by the interviewee as a result of aging.

Hearing loss is frequent and may be indicated by the forward lean of the interviewee, a tendency to turn his ear toward the speaker, or to gaze intently at his lips. Interviewers should be attentive to whether or not a client is wearing a hearing aid. A facial expression of strained listening and frequent requests to repeat a question suggests hearing difficulties. Interviews with client who have hearing problems may need to be shorter because the strain of listening is exhausting. It may be necessary for the interviewer to speak a little louder, slower, and more distinctly. The interviewer has to be careful to talk directly to the person with her face in a clear light to help lip reading. She should avoid smoking or covering her mouth while speaking.

She should watch for indications that the interview is making excessive demands on the interviewee's limited physical energy. The pace of the interview may need to be slower and the time allotted shorter. Studies of interviewing of aged respondents indicate, however, that large numbers of old people are still capable of engaging in prolonged interviews and do so with zest (Zelan 1969).

The aged client may present a greater difficulty in being understood than a younger client. Some older clients will speak with a foreign accent; others have dental problems which affect the way they talk, or they speak with a slurred diction. Strokes leave some older respondents with impaired speech.

One of the advantages of aging is the freedom to ignore the social niceties. A person may be too old to be concerned with what others think. Such interviewees may be more outspoken, more insistent, more stubborn than the usual interviewee and consequently more difficult for the interviewer to take in stride; a greater measure of patience, understanding, and forebearance may be needed.

The interviewer may have special problems with her own feelings when working with aged interviewees. The problems encountered and the emotional reverberations initiated by contact with the older interviewee may create anxiety for the interviewer. The problems of illness and the constant reminder of the imminence of death haunt such interviews.

The interviewer's own fears of vocational loss, status devaluation and social disenfranchisement, or threats to bodily integrity are intensified in working with the aged. The older client is everyone's parent, and the problem of the young adult in relation to an aging parent is one that many interviewers face in their own lives.

The social worker may feel a sense of futility and despair in response to what she regards as the limited resiliency and adaptability of the interviewee. Certainly there is less of a future available to such a client, and the interviewer may question the expenditure of effort in behalf of this age group. The interviewer may be discouraged by the slow pace of interaction and change exhibited, particularly when these may be compounded by the confusions of incipient senility. She may feel drained and exhausted by the demands made on her as a fellow human being by the interviewee. The world is "filling up with strangers" for many older clients. Faced with growing loneliness and isolation, older interviewees may rank the expressive, social functions of the interview interaction much higher than any possible instrumental rewards.

Some interviewers, wrapped in their own stereotyped views of the aged, tend to "talk down" to the elderly. They approach a client as they would a child incapable of understanding complex ideas, simplifying everything they say.

Because working with the aged frequently requires environmental modification, the interviewer needs to be aware of the network of community resources available for mobilization in the interviewee's behalf.

Children

Interviewing children presents special problems (Rich 1968). The child is still dependent on his parents and still has an intense affective tie with them. It colors his relationships with all adults and may present problems for the interviewer. The possibility of negative association of the adult interviewer with all hurtful, rejecting parental figures is apt to be most intense with disturbed children. Older children, and particularly adolescents, are peer oriented and reticent about communicating with adults. If the interviewer is perceived as a parent surrogate, such resistance is likely to be a major barrier to an effective interview. If perceived more neutrally, however, the interviewer may be able to capitalize on the adolescent's ambivalence regarding adults and tap the component which makes them anxious to share with a friendly adult who has no authority over them. In general, then, the interviewer should clearly dissociate herself from the child's parents and teachers and present herself as a neutral, friendly adult.

A child's fears of collusion between parents and interviewer should be dispelled. Yet the general rules of confidentiality between adult interviewer and interviewee cannot be applied intact to interviews with dependent children. Since the child is dependent on his parents and since they are responsible for him, should all of the child's secrets shared with the interviewer be relayed to the parents? If not, what are the limits of what should be shared? There is currently no clear-cut answer to this difficult question.

When the interviewer meets the child, she can most often assume that he is willing to go with her. Consequently, it is better to say, "The interview room is ahead. Let me show you" than to ask "Do you want to come with me now?" Getting the child away from his mother to go with the stranger into the interview room, however, may present a problem. Moving easily, slowly, with some recognition of the child's anxiety in separating from his mother is a helpful approach.

Boy, 6, middle-class, child guidance clinic.
WORKER: [After introduction made by mother.] Hello, George. Let's go to the playroom together.
GEORGE: [Clings to mother, hides face, speaks in a whisper.] No, no, no.
WORKER: You don't know me, so you don't want to come with me. I can hardly blame you. [George looks shyly at interviewer.] Your mother will be waiting for you when you come back.
MOTHER: You go with the lady, George. I'll be waiting here for you.
WORKER: Yes, if you want to come with me to the playroom, you can look out and see your mother waiting for you.

It may be necessary to permit the parent to accompany the child to the interview room. If the interviewing room is far from the waiting room, the child cannot look out occasionally to see his parent. If it is too close, however, the child might be anxious about the parent hearing what he says.

As simple a gesture as shutting the door to the interview room to ensure privacy and quiet is more complicated in a child's interview. The child may feel frightened now that a way of escape is cut off. It might be well to leave the door open and let the child decide when to close it.

Nonverbal sources of communication provide rich data about mother and child. Their behavior in the agency waiting room is instructive. What seating arrangement have they selected—near each other, at a distance, the child on the mother's lap or standing pressed close against the seated mother? Is the mother reading to the child, talking to him, ignoring him? How does the mother handle the problem of outer clothing for the younger child as he prepares to leave the waiting room for the interview? Does she help with difficult boots and zippers? Does she help even when the child seems capable of managing on his own? What is her tone of voice—affectionate, querulous, guarded? What is the nature of the stream of comments addressed to the child—primarily directive ("Do this," "Do that," "Watch this," "Sit here") or primarily reassuring ("Don't worry," "It will be all right," "I'll be here")? During the interview with the child, nonverbal communication provides a range of information—activity level, resistance to activity, freedom in initiating activity, and its focus, tics, thumb sucking, nail biting, hair stroking, genitalia rubbing, the smell emanating from the enuretic and the soiler.

Usually children do not initiate the contact for an interview. Children are not independent enough to do so, but, more important, the behavior which occasions the request for service is often a problem for others but not, frequently, for the child himself. Since the child almost always is referred and comes at the request or coercion of someone else—his parents, the school, the community—he may not know the reasons for the interview. The interviewer probably should start by asking if the child knows why the meeting was scheduled. Although the child may at least suspect the reason, he may deny having any difficulty. His parents certainly have told him something beforehand, which may only have increased his anxiety and resistance to the interview and interviewer. Clarification of the purpose of the meeting is of primary importance. We often forget that we owe the child an explanation.

Dr. —— asked us to see you because you seem to have a lot of accidents.

Your parents called and said they were worried about your work at school.

Your mother called and said there were constant fights between you and your brother.

The interviewer, recognizing that the appointment with the child was made by others, should indicate that she wants to hear the child's version of the situation.

Just as it is inadvisable for middle-class interviewers to use lower-class speech, or whites to use black ghetto language, the adult interviewer should not affect childish speech nor pat heads, tweak cheeks, or pull ear lobes in effusive intimacy. Some tend to speak in a loud voice, as though children were deaf, or to speak in an unnaturally sweet voice.

Just as there is a tendency to speak down to the child, there is a reluctance to discuss important, possibly painful matters with a child because he might be hurt. This does a disservice to the child in that he is denied the opportunity of dealing with problems that are of concern to him, problems that are neither fleeting nor trivial. The overprotective interviewer who views the child as very fragile tends to seduce the child by overpermissiveness and effusive compliments.

LANGUAGE

Because an interview requires some minimal language facility, there is a lower age limit for productive interviewing. Children younger than age 4 or 5 are in a preverbal stage, in terms of interview language requirements. The child's limited vocabulary requires that the interviewer choose her words carefully so that they are within the child's range. It might be helpful for anyone faced with interviewing children to review some of the studies of normal vocabulary attainments of children at different ages. The child's limited vocabulary also suggests that he may have difficulty in communicating complex feelings. He may not be able to discuss generalized behavior because he lacks the necessary abstract vocabulary. The interviewer in trying to help the child express feelings may list some possible alternatives for choice by the client.

You know, John, you were just telling me how they took your mother in an ambulance to the hospital when she had the accident. How did that make you feel? scared? sad? angry? lonely?

However children have a larger understanding vocabulary than they do a talking vocabulary so that they might grasp more than you give them credit for.

In interviewing children, it helps to conduct the interview at the child's eye level. For the younger child this may mean sitting on the floor.

Interviews with children require more structuring and guidance by the interviewer than do interviews with adults. The child's limited language development and limited conceptualizing capacities make undesirable the funnel approach—initial general, open-ended questions, followed by progressively more limited specification of focus. It is best to start with specifics, although leaving the child considerable choice. Small, understandable questions eliciting a description of his actual behavior and actions are easier for a child to answer than questions asking him to explain his behavior.

What do you do that makes your mother mad?
What did you do yesterday that was fun?

The orientation is toward concrete behavior, not an abstract question like "How do you feel about your teacher?" but rather "What does your teacher do to make you feel good?" "What does she do to make you feel sad or unhappy?" Because a child is highly suggestible, the interviewer has to be careful not to formulate questions so they telegraph an expected or desired answer.

Ambiguous messages are more difficult for children to interpret accurately. The adult, with greater experience in decoding meta-communication signals, discounts a statement made jokingly. The child may take the same message at its face value. The same critical statements made with a smile to soften them are perceived more negatively by a child than by adults. Consequently, in interviewing children it is best to avoid subtlety and indirect or contradictory messages.

Some aspects of childhood offer an advantage for the interviewer. Children have only begun to learn how to control and disguise their behavior and their speech. There is, consequently, a good deal of spontaneity in both, which is very revealing without their being aware of it. Children have less of a tendency to intellectualize and rationalize their situation simply because they have less capacity to do so and less practice at it. There is less concern with and awareness of logic and consistency and what is socially acceptable, hence a great likelihood to "tell it as it is."

Putting thoughts into words is a strain for children, who are new to language use; it is analogous to holding an interview in a foreign language for an adult. Hence children are apt to be tired within a shorter period of time. Since children's thought processes are slower, the interview tempo is slower.

The boundaries between fantasy and reality are more permeable in children, and the interviewer may be puzzled by communication in which the two have to be sorted out. A child's responses are apt to be garbled and redundant, lacking in organization. His sense of time, of past, present and future events, is not so neatly ordered as an adult's. The events that are remembered and are of significance are those which are important to children, not necessarily to adults. A common tendency to word repetition may try the patience of the interviewer. The interviewer faces an additional distraction, particularly with younger children, in poor articulation of words. Understanding a young child's speech may require constant, enervating attention.

The dictum that language often obscures rather than clarifies is even truer for a child than an adult. "What does he mean by that?" needs to be persistently asked in interviews with children. Ginott points to the need for translating the child's latent message. An intelligent child spells playroom "pleyroom" on the interviewing-room blackboard.

He turns to the therapist and says, "Is this the right spelling?" This is not a simple request for information. Johnny, with an IQ of 130, may or may not have known how to spell "playroom." But what he really wants to know is the therapist's attitude toward misspellers. Understanding this, the therapist does not rush to give the "right" spelling. He does not assume the conventional role of a teacher. Instead, he says, "In here you can spell any way you want to". . . .

Johnny learns a great deal from his spelling exercises. He learns that the clinic is a unique place, that the playroom is not a school, and that the therapist is not a teacher.

Next Johnny picks up a splintered plastic car and asks in a righteous tone, "Who broke the car?" What he really wants to know is what happened to the boy who broke the car. Understanding the question, the therapist gives a reassuring answer—"Sometimes toys get broken. It happens."

Johnny gets quite a bit of information with his car question. He learns that this grownup does not get angry easily, even when toys are broken, and that there is no need to be overcautious or to walk a tightrope in the playroom.

Finally Johnny says, "You have so many closets in here. What do you have in them?" The therapist answers, "You want to look and see?" Again Johnny obtains very pertinent information; it is all right to be curious in the playroom without being reminded that curiosity killed the cat. By responding to the hidden meanings of the questions, the therapist not only conveys deep understanding to the child but helps him to get a clearer picture of the therapist and the therapy situation. (Ginott 1961:126)

PLAY

Because children are not as able or as ready to consciously share their thinking and feeling directly with adults, interviews with children employ a variety of adjunctive procedures—doll play, toys and games, thematic apperception pictures that call for a story, picture drawing, puppet play, etc. These materials exploit the child's interest in play and fantasy and permit the active supplementation of limited verbal communication. They are more congruent with a child's usual activities than is the formal interview interaction. Doll play, clay modeling, drawing, and painting permit the child to express himself more freely and with fewer inhibitions than he can in words alone. Not only is the medium of communication more familiar to the child, more in line with his adequacies, but it may also permit him to share indirectly a socially unacceptable response. Absorbed in a game, playing with toys, making up a story, or drawing a picture, he is apt to be less self-conscious and to verbalize some of his related thinking and feeling without being aware that he is doing it.

Games give a child the opportunity of "playing out" his feelings at which he might be more adept than at "talking out."

As the child plays, the interviewer asks questions: "Who is this doll?" "What is he doing now?" "What makes him want to do that?" "What do you think will happen if he does that?" The interview is a combination of nondirective play and interviewer intervention to encourage the child to verbalize about his activities. The danger the interviewer needs to be aware of is that fun and games may become ends in themselves rather than a means for more productive interviewing.

Sometimes the interview cannot get under way until the child has occasion to interact with the interviewer in some nonverbal manner. Playing checkers, dominos, or throwing darts may help the inarticulate child feel comfortable enough to start talking. Game playing is not a waste of time but a necessary preliminary in such instances.

DISCIPLINE

Most children are apt to be restless and full of energy. Probably they will not sit quietly throughout an interview but will sometimes wander about the room while talking. The interviewer needs a tolerance for such distractions and the ability to retain her composure despite constant squirming and fidgeting.

Children also have a limited attention span. Consequently they find it hard to focus for any length of time on one topic. Interviewing a child is, therefore, apt to require more frequent transitions, making such interviews appear erratic and unfocused. It is difficult to adhere to any kind of interview schedule or outline. The interviewer has to be imaginative in using whatever the child offers, in either his activity or verbalization, to tie in topics that need to be discussed. Often questions have to be repeated, sometimes because the child resists answering the question, sometimes because he was distracted and did not listen to it, and sometimes because he did not understand the question and it needs to be reworded.

The problems of restlessness, distractibility, and limited attention span are likely to be greater in interviews with emotionally disturbed children.

Because children have less practice in the social graces and feel less constraint about observing the usual rules of interaction, they can, and do, ignore questions, and feel less of an obligation to contribute to the interview. The sensitive interviewer needs to be aware that children are likely to offend her but primarily because they do not realize they are being offensive.

There is less inhibition to direct physical acting out on the part of the child—kicking, biting, hollering, crying. He is truly "acting his age." Spontaneity and the more limited impulse control of children may require the imposition of behavioral limitations by the interviewer. Kicking, hitting, and biting the interviewer, destruction of toys and office equipment, need to be kindly but firmly stopped. This is done not only in response to concern for self-preservation and the agency budget, but also out of concern for the child. No limits are set on what the child can think, feel, or say, only on what he can do. This acts to protect him from himself. The child depends on adult interviewers to restrain him and help him to control his impulses, to set limits in a way that demonstrates concern and care. It may be advisable to raise the question of limits only when it appears that they will be transcended. As the danger becomes imminent, the interviewer might say firmly:

I can't let you do that.

No hurting people or destroying toys.

You can shoot at the target but not at me.

That's not permitted here.

You can't make so much noise because it will disturb people in the next room.

The prohibition might include a statement of acceptable alternatives and a recognition of the child's feelings that prompted the behavior.

You want to hit me because you're sore at me. Imagine the doll is me and hit him.

On the other hand, actions contraindicated in interviews with adults are sometimes necessary and acceptable with children. Comforting a child during stress by hugging or cradling is good if the child accepts it. Physical contact is useful as a supplement to the more difficult verbal communication channel. Touching of children by adults, patting, holding, arm-on-shoulder is generally acceptable. Feelings that might require a vocabulary beyond the grasp of a young child can be conveyed by nonverbal touching.

Elites

In implementing agency service, the social worker might find it necessary to interview people who have high status in their own setting and are in positions of power and authority. The social worker may need to interview an employer, a housing administrator, a school principal, a bank official, district attorneys, doctors, etc. Social workers interview such collateral interviewees on behalf of the client to get information or give information, to obtain some important resource for the client or induce the collateral interviewee to provide some help to the client, or to enlist the collateral's support in some agency plan for the client.

Interviewing collaterals requires a reorientation of the interviewer's usual situation. Here the interviewer is seeking help rather than offering help. The interviewer wants something from the collateral—something which might be used to help the client. Collateral interviewees are generally in positions of power. They are people who might be difficult to see, who are used to controlling the interaction, who are frequently the dominant status person in any dyadic encounter. Collaterals frequently have little motive for spending time and energy in helping the worker with what she wants to know or do.

The interviewer needs to recognize that collaterals are often resistive to participating in such interviews. They may fear being imposed upon, becoming involved, risking being persuaded to do something that they would rather not do.

In selecting collaterals for interviewing, it might be advisable to find out in advance just who is most likely to have the information that is needed or who actually controls access to the jobs or housing or training that the interviewer wants to request on the client's behalf. Administrators may know less than supervisors about specifics of an agency operation and managers closer to the action may have more control than others over resources.

In scheduling an interview with a collateral, preference needs to be given to his calendar. The time that is "most convenient" for him has priority.

The interviewer is but one of a great variety of people who might be requesting an interview with the high status interviewee. Clear identification of organizational or institutional affiliation is important since the interviewer is a total stranger at first contact. The organizational affiliation further provides legitimation for the request for an interview as well as for the interviewer's mission.

If preparation for every interview is important, preparation for interviews with high status people with an overloaded calendar and limited time is even more important. This might involve some prior study of the interviewee's organization, its services and functions, or review of the interviewee's background available in professional directories and thus would prevent asking irrelevant questions or presenting infeasible requests. Evidence of such preparation in the questions asked or comments made communicates to the interviewee that the interview is a serious matter and that the interviewer has been willing to do some homework in preparation. Any interviewee is likely to respond warmly to this. Some familiarity with the vernacular of the business or professional affiliation of the interviewee is helpful.

For many of the high status interviewees, the most important consideration is time. This is a scarce resource which they need to conserve. They are more likely to respond positively then to the interviewer who makes clear the purpose of the interview and efficiently respects time in focusing the interview.

The interviewer in such interactions may be prompted to seek the approval and approbation of the high status interviewee. Because the etiquette of deference is in favor of the high status interviewee, the interviewer may hesitate to raise some necessary questions or engage in some necessary interventions for fear of offending. The interviewer may find it difficult to be appropriately assertive. At the worst, the interviewer may act ingratiatingly. But if the interviewer has problems with authority and resents differences in status, there may be a tendency to resent the interviewee and act somewhat abrasively.

The high status person is faced with the problem of maintaining appropriate distance without becoming unapproachable. The lower status interviewer has the problem of assuring the interviewee of her competence and expertise in her own area without threatening the interviewee.

The practiced articulateness of high status interviewees may present a problem. They might use their verbal skills as they often do, to be evasive without appearing to be rude. They might take control of the interviewer without the interviewer knowing quite how this happened. In either case, the interview ends without the interviewer's objectives having been achieved.

Elite interviewees have often had long practice in evading questions they do not wish to answer. Elaborate, meaningless circumlocutions are offered without embarrassment. The interviewer has to decide whether pressing for an answer is worth the risk of arousing antagonism. Sometimes the risk must to be taken if the purpose of the interview is to be achieved. Nothing is gained by a pleasant visit during which the interviewer has failed to accomplish what she set out to do.

Elite interviewees are often not as interested in answering the interviewer's questions as they are in stating their own opinions, sharing their own ideas. The interviewer may have to go along with listening to much that is not directly relevant to her interview objectives (Zuckerman 1972).

Because the interviewee who is a professional has some advanced education, we may erroneously presume that he understands the esoteric terms and acronyms used by social workers in talking to each other (support network, generic approach, O.A.S.D.I., etc.). If he does not understand he is less likely to admit his failure because, highly educated, he too thinks he should know.

It is a mistake to presume that because a human is high status and in a position of power that the usual human supports are superfluous. The collateral interviewee, whatever his position, still needs to feel that he is competently performing his role as an interviewee, and that he is being respected and accepted. The high status collateral interviewee may need such assurances less frequently or openly than client interviewees, but his need, however attenuated, is still there.

Interviewing professionals from other disciplines requires recognition that the same problems may be perceived from a different perspective, a different frame of reference, by the interviewee. The social worker and teacher, the social worker and doctor, will come to the same problem situation with different ideas in mind because they are responsible for different aspects of the problem. The lawyer is focused on legal aspects of divorce, the social worker is concerned with the social consequences of divorce. Effective interviewing requires some appreciation of the perspective of the interviewee and the context in which he performs his function—the school, the hospital, the courts.

Should Interviewer and Interviewee Be Matched?

The problems inherent in interviewing across the barriers of class, race, age, and sex lead inevitably to the question of matching. Would it not be desirable to select the interviewer so that she resembles the interviewee in at least some of the crucial characteristics? Would this not reduce social distance, the resistance and constraints in interaction which derive from differences in group affiliation and related experiences and life-style?

Homophily as a factor in human interaction is basic to some agency programs and some agency policies. Homophily suggests that members of some subcultural group prefer to associate with, and feel comfortable with, people of the same subcultural group. The denominational agencies and programs such as Alcoholics Anonymous, Synanon for drug addicts, and Recovery, Inc., for former mental hospital patients, are predicated in part on the factor of homophily. People who have shared the same significant experience are more likely to be "culturally at home" with each other.

In chapter 2 we noted the importance of the interviewer's empathic understanding as a condition for establishing a good relationship. Such responses indicate similarity and compatibility between interview participants and reduce social distance. The worker's responses indicate that the client's life and feelings are not alien and remote. Such empathic understanding is most easily achieved by the interviewer who shares the interviewee's world.

The facilitative conditions for good interviewing would suggest the desirability of pairing the interviewee with an interviewer who is similar in terms of some crucial social characteristics. The ability to empathize, to understand, to feel a sense of trust and mutual liking might be greater under those conditions. The ability to paraphrase and accurately reflect is likely to be greater when there is a knowledge and understanding of where the client is coming from and where there is a shared language and associated pattern of metacommunication. The readiness to disclose requires trust and confidence that disclosures will be understandingly received. It is claimed that more than shared humanity and ability to empathize is required if the interviewer is to be truly understanding. It requires the actual experience of living as a black, or as a woman, or as a gay. Nothing can duplicate the intensity of learning achieved by the living experience. Mutual understanding can be guaranteed only by matching interviewer and interviewee with regard to such crucial factors.

The difficulties of empathic understanding across subcultural barriers can be exaggerated, however, and the disadvantages of matching the interviewer and interviewee can be as easily underestimated. The world's literature is testimony that one can understand and empathize with others despite having a life which is quite different from the life created for the fictional characters. For example, an American Christian, John Hersey, demonstrated empathic understanding of the feelings of the Polish Jew in his novel *The Wall;* a white American Jew, Elliot Liebow, demonstrates his understanding of blacks in the ghetto in *Tally's Corner;* a white South African psychiatrist, Wulf Sachs, shows a sensitive understanding of a Zulu in *Black Hamlet.*

Some of the social and psychological distance is reduced by professional training which enhances a person's ability to empathize with and understand different groups in the community and which provides the knowledge base for such understanding. The gap may be sufficiently reduced so that the interviewer is perceived as "within range," capable of understanding even though he or she is a product of a different life experience.

Waite points out that the interviewer can draw on analogous experiences in helping to bridge the cross-cultural gap. "Empathic resonance with the humiliation experienced by a Negro patient is based primarily upon the white therapist's earlier experiences of threats, insults, restrictions in opportunities and other narcissistic deprivations. . . . This helps fill in the . . . gaps between the therapist's own humiliations and those of his patient which are specific to living in a prejudicial society" (Waite 1968:432).

Not only is it possible to reduce the gap in social distance, but also the effects of matching interviewers and interviewees are not uniformly positive. Some shortcomings of this solution to the problem of social and emotional distance have become more apparent as a result of experience with indigenous paraprofessionals in the human services. As a consequence of the efforts to find new careers for the poor, during the past few years many social agencies have hired people from the areas they serve as case aides of one kind or another. The case aides live alongside the client group in the same neighborhood, generally are of the same ethnic and racial background as the client group, and often are struggling with similar problems. The case aides and the clients share values, life styles, problems, and deprivations. They therefore are in an excellent position to empathize with, and understand, the problems of the poor and the blacks. Some of these expectations are, in fact, achieved, but the problems are also very real.

A study of evaluations of paraprofessional performance by agency executives and supervisors finds that such workers are given high ratings on their ability to establish relationship and rapport with clients. One agency administrator said:

In intake interviewing paraprofessionals are very good at picking up clues and cues from clients. They have a good ear for false leads and "put-ons." Their maturity and accumulated life experience, combined with first-hand knowledge of the client population, assists the agency in establishing communication with clients rapidly. . . . The new client is more comfortable with a paraprofessional because he or she is someone like himself. (Gould 1969:5–6)

Another agency executive observed:

Clients may come in with suspicion based on experience with the white world in the ghetto, where they were dependent on this world for services. Now when they come to the agency, they see people like themselves in a different role, where they are not in a provider-beneficiary relationship, but are in a colleague/partner relationship, providing services to the ghetto or the community and to people like themselves. This serves to increase confidence in the agency. (Gould 1969:6–7)

Despite these advantages, sympathy and understanding do not always automatically result from matching interviewer and interviewee in terms of background. Sobey notes this in a study of nonprofessionals in mental health agencies:

The assumption is often made that nonprofessional status per se ensures greater sympathy to the plight of the client group. However, this is not always so. . . . The fact that the nonprofessional has been hired will often immediately reinforce his social distance from the group being served, and may set off a feeling of superiority, annoyance, or impatience with those he is supposed to help. (Sobey 1970:119–120)

Goldberg (1969) and Grosser (1969) support this statement. Grosser adds that nonprofessional staff "often regard illegitimacy, unemployment, drinking, and even boisterous social behavior as evidence of moral turpitude" (1969:137). Riessman confirms these difficulties. Many paraprofessionals "see themselves as quite different from the other members of the poor community. . . . Moreover nearly all are greatly concerned about their new roles and their relationship to professionals" (1969:154). Too close a matching risks overidentification and activation, or reactivation, of problems faced by the interviewer which are very similar to those which concern the interviewee.

The fact that the worker is of the same sex or class or race as the client does not guarantee that the worker will act differently than a worker of another sex or class or race. (See pp. 310–312 for additional discussion of problem in matching black interviewer and black interviewee.)

Jenkins and Morrison (1978) found the social workers in ethnic agencies, most of whom were members of ethnic or racial minority groups, tended to select traditional responses to a questionnaire designed to test attitudes on ethnic issues in service delivery. There was no sharp difference between the ethnic agency workers' responses and the responses of a national sample of social workers.

Matching for compatibility makes it more difficult for the interviewer to be objective in interaction with the interviewee. This is only partly a result of a tendency toward overidentification. It also results from the fact that the interviewer who shares many of the crucial characteristics with the interviewee may presume to know more about the interviewee, his feelings and attitudes than, in fact, the interviewer does know. There is a risk of not crediting the interviewee with his differences. He is so much like us that we expect him to think and act like us. Being so much alike the participants in the interview may not have much to offer each other in the way of alternative solutions, other points of view, or challenging thinking. Differences can have a catalytic effect for problem solving that is not available with great similarity.

The advantages of difference is that fresh perspectives on the problem might be made available to the interviewee from an interviewer who is able, because of her difference, to see the situation from a different point of view. The value of heterogeneity is expressed in the folk saying: "When two people agree on everything, one of them is unnecessary."

The pull toward personalizing the interview is greater with an interviewee with whom one feels a social affinity because of age, sex, class, or race similarity. The interviewer has to concentrate on maintaining the interaction as an interview rather than having it become a social occasion. The difficulty in keeping the distance necessary for conducting a good interview when the participants are too compatible is described by one interviewer:

Although I tried to maintain the recommended stance with every respondent—not being so friendly as to lose my own objectivity or bias the respondent's views—it was much easier to do so with respondents with whom I had nothing in common. It was much harder with really congenial people. It seemed that the more I sensed similarity between myself and the other person, the harder it was to resist incorporating bits of social conversation. (Converse and Schuman 1974:2)

On the other side of the desk, the interviewee, feeling a deep rapport with the interviewer and anxious to maintain her friendship, might be prompted to give responses that he thinks the interviewer wants to hear or that would make him more acceptable to the interviewer. He does not want to hurt the interviewer's feelings and acts out of obligations of loyalty to the mutually satisfying interaction they have established. High rapport gives the interviewee an investment in the relationship which he would not like to risk by saying or doing anything which might alienate the interviewer.

Research findings on the effects of behavior in the interview when there is similarity between the interviewer and interviewee are complex. While similarity does tend to lead to a greater feeling of closeness and a more positive relationship it does not necessarily lead to greater verbal accessibility and sharing. Polansky and Tessler explain these contradictory findings by noting that people open up more with interviewers who are different from themselves in "the service of the need to reduce discrepencies" and are more secretive with the interviewer who is like themselves because "openness threatens to demonstrate that client and interviewer are not all that similar after all" (1975:362).

If the effects of matching are not invariably positive, equally the effects of difference in cultural background between interviewer and interviewee are not always negative. An interviewer identified with one subculture (of sex, race, age, color, or class) and an interviewee affiliated with another represent one particular aspect of in-group–out-group relations generally. Because she is an outsider, the interviewer does not reflect in-group judgments. For the interviewee who has violated or disagrees with in-group values, this is an advantage. Currently, for instance, a middle-class, white-oriented, accommodative black might find it more difficult to talk to a black worker than to a white.

If the interviewee, in response to aspirations of upward mobility, is looking for sources of identification outside the group, contact with a non-matched interviewer is desirable. The lower-class client anxious to learn middle-class ways would seek such an interviewer.

The very fact that the outsider-interviewer may not initially understand the client may be helpful. In trying to make his situation clear to the interviewer, the interviewee may be forced to look at it more explicitly than before. In explaining it to an outsider, he may explain it better to himself.

In summary, too great a similarity between interview participants risks the danger of overidentification and loss of objectivity; too great a dissimilarity makes for greater difficulty in understanding and empathizing. It is not surprising, then, that the relevant research suggests that effective interviewing is not linearly related to rapport. The relationship appears to be curvilinear. Minimal rapport is undesirable but so is maximum rapport. The best combination for the interview is moderate closeness between interviewer and interviewee. The need for some distance is one of the principal conclusions of Weiss's study of the validity of responses by a group of welfare mothers in a public opinion interview. The answers given in the interview were checked for accuracy against voting records, school records, and welfare department records. In the study, the influence of interviewer-interviewee similarity and rapport were analyzed separately. Both factors operated in the same direction. Increasing the similarity between interviewer and interviewee increased the bias of responses; increasing the level of rapport between participants also increased the bias. Socially desirable rather than valid responses were more likely to result under conditions of high similarity and high rapport. Weiss concludes that:

> Both on factual and attitude items, high similarity between interviewer and respondent . . . particularly when coupled with high rapport, leads to a higher rate of socially desirable responses. On the factual questions, at least, such responses are known to be less valid. . . . The warm personal relationship which the interviewer rates as "confiding" may seem to the low income respondent to be "intrusive." Her reaction is to tell her friendly "confidante" an idealized version of the facts. (1968:69–70).

Hyman, on the basis of his own research, also supports these conclusions.

> Friendliness is important, but a certain degree of businesslike formality may be superior to maximum rapport. At some point on the continuum of increasing rapport, friendliness may pass over into intimacy. Then one is no longer a stranger and the respondent [interviewee] may prefer not to hurt the interviewer's feelings or may be eager to defer to the interviewer's opinion. (1954:214)

Further support comes from Dohrenwend et al., who summarizes her research by stating that "interviewer effects is a curvilinear function of social distance with minimal effects at intermediate social distance" (1964:122).

Perhaps the curvilinear nature of the optimum matching relationship is best described as heterogeneity within a framework of homogeneity.

The research on client preference does not uniformly support the contention that the client would invariably select a professional from his own group. Dubey (1970), a social work researcher, offers empirical support for the contention that blacks do not indicate an overwhelming preference for black workers. He developed an interview questionnaire with the help of black ghetto residents. Employing black interviewers, he asked some 500 residents of the ghetto area such questions as "Would you rather talk with a Negro social worker or with a white social worker?" "Would you rather go to an agency where the director is Negro or to one where the director is white?" Some 77–79 percent of the respondents said it made no difference to them. Only 10–11 percent said they strongly preferred a Negro worker or a Negro agency director.

An interview study with mothers of children in foster care concluded that "There was little support among the respondents that ethnic or religious auspices of the agency made a difference to them. Over 80 percent of the mothers said it did not, and there was almost no ambivalence experienced"; 90 percent of the black mothers in the sample said it made no difference. Many of the mothers stressed the importance of professional competency of the workers. "They made such comments as 'The important thing is if they are professionals'; 'They are trained to do a job'; 'It doesn't matter as long as they do their jobs' " (Jenkins and Norman 1975:88–89).

Another relevant study showed that preference was dependent on certain conditions. Students at a school of social work in Chicago interviewed residents of a black ghetto in 1968 and elicited their racial preferences regarding service personnel. They asked, "If both were equally good, would you prefer that the [doctor, caseworker, teacher, lawyer, parents' group leader] be Negro [black, colored] or white?" Interviewers were both white and black. One relevant result demonstrated the important effects of similarity or dissimilarity in the race of interviewer-interviewee pairs. The white interview had a statistically significant, larger percentage of respondents saying that they had "no preference" as compared with black interviewers, to whom respondents confessed they preferred a black (doctor, caseworker, teacher, etc.). However, of the black respondents interviewed by black interviewers, only 55 percent indicated they would prefer a black caseworker, 45 percent having either no preference or a preference for a white caseworker (Brieland 1969).

The basis for preferring a black caseworker, all other things being equal, was that such an interviewer was more likely to be interested in the problems of the black interviewee, was less likely to talk down to people, was less likely to make people feel that they didn't amount to much, would give them more of a feeling of hope, and would be more likely to know the meaning of poverty.

A second question introduced competence as a factor. The question asked for a statement of preference regarding a white or black worker if the white worker was better qualified. A large percentage of those who preferred "equally good" black caseworkers preferred a white caseworker with better qualifications. Competence, then, proved to be more important than race in determining caseworker preference of this group of black respondents.

These general overall conclusions receive support from reviews of more recent research regarding racial pairings in interviews.

Summarizing ten different studies of interracial interaction in initial interviews, Sattler concludes that the interviewer's "race is, for the most part, not a significant variable in affecting the [interviewer's] performance and reactions . . . However, depth of self-exploration was occasionally more intense in racially similar pairings" (1977:271). In general however, "The contention that Blacks prefer to be counseled only by Blacks or that White therapists cannot be effective in working with Black clients does not receive support from these initial interview-studies" (p. 273).

Second, research regarding the relationship between interviewer and interviewee, while confirming the fact that differences in age or race or class or gender is of some significance for the interview, also confirms, for each group, the more potent significance of the interviewer's skill and competence. If there is any tendency for interviewees to prefer an interviewer who is similar to themselves, there is an even more overriding preference for the competent, effective, facilitative interviewer, despite any dissimiliarity.

Preference for competence is generally given priority over preference for characteristics of social similarity, preference for compatible pairing. If all other considerations are equal, if the level of education experience and competence are the same, interviewees tend to prefer the interviewer who is compatibly matched with them in terms of significant social variables.

Where there is some conflict or ambivalence regarding a person's self-perceived racial identity, there is a greater likelihood of rejection of the non-white interviewer. Greater comfort with and acceptance of one's racial identity tends to make the race of the interviewer less important and the importance of skill given greater priority.

Sattler (1977) additionally summarizes the results of twenty-four different studies concerned with racial preference of interviewees by noting that "other things being equal many Black subjects prefer Black therapists to White therapists. However, a competent White professional is preferred to a less-competent Black professional and the therapist's style and technique are more important factors in affecting Black client's choice than the therapist's race." Many black respondents expressed no racial preference when asked about this by black interviewers. "The overall results indicate that a simple unequivocal answer cannot be given to the question 'Do Black people prefer Black therapists or counselors?' " (1977:267). In the final analysis success in interracial interviewing is dependent on the interviewer's "possession of competence, sensitivity, warmth, understanding, energy, sense of timing, fairness and a hope of interpersonal skills and abilities that can be brought to bear in the therapeutic relationship; being Black or White will not automatically guarantee either success or failure" (p. 284).

However, the interviewer who shares some significant characteristics with the interviewee has a greater probability of being effectively facilitative because of her initial ability to understand, empathize, and inspire trust. So that while an interviewer's competence is more important than an interviewer's race, age, gender, or class, interviewer competence is related to possession of matching characteristics.

A study by Maluccio of clients' reactions to caseworkers showed that compatible pairing made some clients more optimistic about being understood initially. "As the encounter progressed, however, the same clients would not continue to be satisfied unless the worker displayed other qualities such as competence" (1979:135).

Compatibility may have greatest potency at the beginning of contact where such factors of age, sex, race, class are the only kind of information about the interviewer that the interviewee has available. Such factors may be of diminishing importance as the contact continues and other kinds of information about the interviewer, more significant for the help the client wants and needs, becomes available. The effect of matching becomes progressively more attenuated.

The more skillful and competent the interviewer is, the less significant are specific social characteristics in determining interview interaction. As the level of skill and competence decline, the greater the significance of these social factors.

In conclusion, then, while cross-cultural interviewing presents some very real problems, they can be resolved by the sensitive interviewer who takes the time and the trouble to try to understand the interviewee who is different from herself. This is a comforting conclusion, when one considers the administrative nightmare that would follow from a well-validated conclusion that only those who shared the experience of the interviewees could effectively act as their interviewers.

One source of difficulty is that the interviewee does not have a choice of interviewer in coming to a social agency. The client may select his doctor or his lawyer to meet his preferences for race, sex, or age. At the social agency he is assigned an interviewer. Perhaps agencies can offer the interviewee a greater measure of choice if he feels strongly that considerations of matching have considerable importance for him. Experience suggests, however, that these differences are relatively less important in determining the course of the interview than are the psychological climate established by the interviewer and her technical proficiency in conducting the interview. At best, the considerations described in this chapter are general guidelines which might be helpful if flexibly applied, with a listening ear and an understanding heart attuned to detect individual differences.

SUGGESTED READINGS

Richard Dana, ed. *Human Services for Cultural Minorities.* Baltimore, Md:
University Park Press, 1981.
An overview of cultural values that affect utilization of human services by
Native Americans, blacks, Hispanics, and Asian Americans. The appro-
priate kinds of interventions, conditions of service delivery, and unique
characteristics of the four minority groups are discussed.

Wynetta Devore and Elfriede G. Schlesinger. *Ethnic-Sensitive Social Work
Practice.* St. Louis: C. V. Mosby, 1981 (285 pp.).
Calls attention to ethnic factors relating to social work practice. The book's
purpose is to raise the consciousness of social workers to ethnic variables
which have relevance for worker-client interaction and the adaptations
workers need to make to "ethnic reality."

James W. Green. *Cultural Awareness in the Human Services.* Englewood
Cliffs, N.J. Prentice-Hall, 1982 (257 pp.).
Derives from a project in developing a "multiethnic perspective in the
delivery of human services" by a school of social work graduates. While
not directly concerned with interviewing, it provides the kind of background knowledge about minority groups of which a competent interviewer would need to be aware, coming closer to interviewing concerns.
The book makes efforts to relate this background knowledge to the worker-
client interaction.

George Henderson, ed. *Understanding and Counseling Ethnic Minorities.*
Springfield, Ill.: C. C. Thomas, 1979 (535 pp.).
Sections on Afro-Americans, Mexican Americans, Puerto Ricans, Native
Americans, Chinese and Japanese Americans. Each section presents some
background material on the culture of the group and each section ends
with some material on counseling with members of the group.

Shirley Jenkins. *The Ethnic Dilemma in Social Work.* New York: Free Press,
1981 (235 pp.).
Devoted to an examination, based on research, of the extent to which
ethnicity should be an important consideration in the delivery of social
service. The book then sensitizes the reader to the factor of ethnicity in
the interview.

Elaine S. LeVine and Amado M. Padilla. *Crossing Cultures in Therapy:
Pluralistic Counseling for the Hispanic.* Monterey, Calif.: Brooks/Cole,
1980 (303 pp.).
Partly concerned with the culture life styles of and problems encountered
by Hispanics. Based on this information an appropriate approach to counseling Hispanics through personal interviews is suggested.

Anthony Marsella and Paul B. Pederson, eds. *Cross-Cultural Counseling
and Psychotherapy.* New York: Pergamon Press, 1981 (358 pp.).
Includes sections on concepts in cross-cultural counseling and psycho-

therapy and evaluation of attempts at cross-cultural counseling, psychotherapy, and future perspectives. Perhaps the section on "Ethnocultural
Considerations" in interacting with blacks, Hispanics, Japanese Americans, and American Indians contains the material of greater relevance to
the interviewer.

A. Elfin Moses and Robert O. Hawkins. *Counseling Lesbian Women and
Gay Men—A Life Issues Approach.* St. Louis: C. V. Mosby, 1982 (263
pp.).
Written by a social worker and sexologist the book is a good up-to-date
review of the problem faced by homosexuals in a heterosexual society. It
provides a good analysis of what the interviewer might need to know and
be aware of in counseling gay men and lesbian women.

Paul Pederson, Walter Lanner, and Juris G. Draguns, eds. *Counseling
Across Cultures.* Honolulu: University Press of Hawaii, 1976 (228 pp.).
While the focus is on counseling, many of the articles allude to the implications for the interview of differences in cultural background between
interviewers and those interviewed. The objective of the book is to help
the counselor become more sensitive and responsive to culture differences in the interaction.

"The Phoenix from the Flame: The American Indian Today." *Social Casework.* (October 1980), vol. 61, no. 8 (61 pp.).
A special issue devoted to social work with the American Indian. Articles
on various aspects of Indian life as related to social services. The relevance of material to the interview is made explicit.

Andrea Rich. *Interracial Communication.* New York: Harper and Row, 1974
(212 pp.).
A good introduction to the principles of interracial communications. The
emphasis is on perceptions, roles, stereotypes, and attitudes in black-
white communication. There is a special chapter on nonverbal communication in interracial communication that might be of special interest to
the interviewee.

Arthur Smith. *Transracial Communications.* Englewood Cliffs, N.J.: Prentice-Hall, 1973 (148 pp.).
Helps the reader become more aware of the complexities in communication between people of different social groups. In doing so it helps the
reader become more effective in transcending such barriers. The presentation is oriented around communication theory. The concern is primarily
with black-white relationships, but the concepts are applicable to a variety of different cross-cultural relationships.

Gerald W. Sue. *Counseling the Culturally Different: Theory and Practice.*
New York: Wiley, 1981 (291 pp.).
Formulates a general framework that might be applicable to counseling
with any culturally different client. The framework is then loosely applied

in separate sections concerned with counseling Asian Americans, blacks, Hispanics, and Native Americans.

Garry R. Waltz and Libby Benjamin, eds. *Transcultural Counseling: Need, Programs, and Techniques*. New York: Human Sciences Press, 1978 (213 pp.).
Contains articles on counseling Spanish-speaking and black clients and leadership of transcultural groups. The material is of general relevance to transcultural dyadic and group interviews.

Natalie J. Woodman and Harry R. Lenna. *Counseling with Gay Men and Women*. San Francisco: Jossey-Bass, 1980 (144 pp.).
Written by faculty members of a school of social work, the book helps to develop empathy with gay clients through clinical material illustrating counseling.

Joe Yamamoto, Frank Acosta, and Leonard Evans. *Effective Psychotherapy with Low Income and Minority Patients*. New York: Plenum Press, 1982 (164 pp.).
The book contains a series of self-assessment exercises on knowledge and attitudes regarding low income and minority group clients that might be of interest.

CHAPTER 14

Nonverbal Communication

Throughout this book, I have pointed out that verbal content is only one of the channels utilized by interview participants to communicate their messages. In this chapter I will discuss those other channels. "I *see* what you mean" is the nonverbal supplement to "I *hear* you talking."

There always has been an interest in nonverbal communication on the part of those concerned with the personal interview. This is exemplified by Freud's early comment that "He who has eyes to see and ears to hear may convince himself that no mortal can keep a secret. If his lips are silent, he chatters with his fingertips; betrayal oozes out of him at every pore." However, development of systematic study was hampered by lack of technology that would permit "capture" of nonverbal communication for analysis.

Today, the tape recorder, movie camera, and video tape have made possible the preservation of the interview almost intact and the replaying of each moment for repetitive examination by different observers. Technology also permits the electronic analysis of the characteristics of vocal communication—its exact pitch, volume, "roughness," quavering, etc. As a result, the last decade has witnessed the rapid development of interest and research in nonverbal communication of all kinds.

Students of nonverbal language have developed complex systems of notation to increase the objectivity and precision in analyzing such language. The efforts parallel the notations developed by choreographers for the dance—another form of nonverbal language. The degree of interest in and concern with nonverbal communication is indicated by the fact that by the early 1970s an annotated bibliography on body movement could list 900 relevant items (Arno Press 1972). An annotated bibliography of more recent nonverbal behavior studies lists 536 additional entries (Abudho 1979).

Nonverbal communication can be a very expressive channel for those who have a rich gestural vocabulary. The prize fight is a good example of an interview in which all the messages are sent through changes in positioning of arms, legs, body, and head, each fighter carefully watching the other "telegraph" his intentions via body language. A gifted mime, such as Marcel Marceau, can communicate most of what he wants to say without resorting to words. Indian sign language and the sign language of the deaf, which is derived from the communication systems used in monastic orders pledged to silence, indicate the rich possibilities of the powerful language of nonverbal communications. It is important to note, however, that the gestural language of the deaf, like Indian sign language, has a clearly established, standard, consensually accepted lexicon. There is, in effect, a dictionary of definitions of such gestures. This is not true for much of the nonverbal communication that the interviewer will want to decode.

➤ Nonverbal communications are messages about the verbal communication itself. They are signals about signals. They tell us something about the validity of the message, its urgency, whether it is being sent humorously, seriously, sarcastically. A hostile remark is softened if it is accompanied by a laugh, a wink, a slap on the back. It says something about the attitude the person has toward the message he is sending, whether he is concerned or indifferent or upset about what he was saying. Nonverbal communications say something about the speaker's relationship with the listener, whether he feels inferior or superior to the listener, friendly or distant. Nonverbal communications help us interpret the message we are hearing. Verbal communication is concerned with "what" we communicate; nonverbal communication is more concerned with "how" we communicate.

Such communication helps us to interpret more accurately verbal channel communications. What we see enables us to better understand what we are hearing. Think of a situation when you cannot see the person you are talking to—as in telephone conversations. It is hard to make out what the other person really means, what he is feeling about what is being said.

More accurately, communication is neither verbal nor nonverbal; it is a complex integration of both. Nonverbal communication means that we "listen" with our eyes as well as our ears, that we listen to the silent language of gestures as well as the spoken language of voice. It is said that we "speak with our vocal organs and converse with our whole body." "Man is a multisensorial being. Occasionally he verbalizes."

People differ in their capacity for nonverbal communication. Most women have a small but reliable advantage over most men in accurately reading nonverbal communication. This, once again, may be a matter of greater interest in and concern with social relationships as a result of an oppressed status. It has also been suggested that since women are often in contact with the nonverbal, very young child, they get more practice in "reading" nonverbal language.

People who score high on tests of cognitive complexity do better in tests of nonverbal "reading," perhaps because they have a greater aptitude in processing large amounts of data.

Just as some interviewers are better nonverbal "readers," some interviewers are better nonverbal "speakers." They are more fluent, more varied in using gestures and have a greater nonverbal vocabulary.

Sources of Nonverbal Communication

A variety of sources of significant nonverbal communication data have been defined or identified. Each of the following sources will be discussed in turn: chronomic communication; smell and touch; artifactual communication; paralinguistics; proxemics; body language–kinesics.

CHRONOMICS

We have discussed waiting time in chapter 6 as it relates to the client's feelings at the start of an interview. Our discussion here is about time as a general nonverbal message, technically termed "chronomic communication."

The management of time is an act of nonverbal communication. Some of the possible messages communicated are defined by the joke that if you come early for an appointment, you are anxious; if you come on time, you are compulsive; and if you come late, you are resistive. Time does talk.

The client who has to wait for an interviewer who is late for an appointment has lost a measure of control over her own time. Lateness is an expression of the difference in status between the participants of the interview. More often the low status person is kept waiting by the higher status person. The higher status person has more access to the lower status person's time than the reverse. Waiting suggests to the person who is kept waiting that the person for whom she is waiting has something more important to do. Something or someone else is being given preference. Once the interview starts the client's time in the interview may be invaded by interruptions initiated by the interviewer who might take a phone call or speak "for a moment" to a colleague. Invasions of the interviewer's time by interruptions initiated by the interviewee is less likely.

Overscheduling appointments to make certain that the worker's time will be fully utilized shows a greater respect for the worker's time than for the client's time. We tend to be generous with our time in talking to clients we like and enjoy and we (perhaps unwittingly) reduce the time we spend with demanding or unappreciative clients. The power to control the use of and access to one's own time, as well as other people's time, provides the opportunity for making significant nonverbal statements.

Timing is an incremental metacommunication which can give the content of the message increased urgency. If a call is received from a client at 11:00 in the evening, the time of the call suggests some special meaning.

SMELL AND TOUCH

The olfactory channel, a source of considerable communication for lower animals, is rarely, if ever, investigated or discussed as a useful source of communication. Subtle changes in body odor might well signal changes in emotional states. However, the cultural emphasis on cleanliness tends to mask all natural body odors. Also, our noses are not educated to detect changes in body odor, and such messages are rapidly attenuated over even the short distance that separates interview participants. Even if we did detect changes, we would not be able to make psychological sense out of them, because we have not studied them. We are aware of the heavily perfumed or the odoriferous interviewee, the smells of liquor and bad breath, and we draw some general conclusions from such data.

There is the distinctive odor of some settings such as the hospital, and we use our noses in making some assessment of the situation in protective services—sniffing for smells of urine, mildew, garbage, and feces in cases of child neglect. In general, however, we do not use our noses as instruments for information gathering in the interview.

Similarly, tactile sensory communications are rarely employed. This is particularly true for the dyadic interview. There is currently a great burst of interest in tactile communications in group interviewing. The book *Joy* (Schultz 1967) details the "experiences" developed by sensitivity groups, as at Esalen, in the use of tactile communication as a way in which group members get to know each other. *Please Touch*, a book by Jane Howard on the encounter movement, is a further testimonial to the interest in tactile communication.

These exercises have been adopted and employed by some social workers who deal with group therapy. Galper's procedures include (a) exploration of space: "Sit on the floor in a circle fairly close to each other with your eyes closed. Feel the space around you," and (b) pass the person: "Stand in a circle comfortably close to each other. Take turns going into the center, close your eyes, lean back as much as you can and let the group pass you around the circle" (1970:75).

There is the touch which facilitates movement in the interview—the welcoming hand cupping the interviewee's elbow as she is ushered into the room; the open palm on the back speeding the interviewee's departure.

Occasionally, in moments of great stress, interviewers might reach over and briefly touch the interviewee in a gesture of comfort and sympathy, but touching is used very selectively in interviews as an act of nonverbal communication. For the most part the normative cultural proscriptions against touching tend to limit its use. We live in a far from touch-feel culture. Touching is permitted in clearly defined situations between people intimately related and in certain contexts—the medical examination or nursing situation. It is formalized in the handshake which may begin and end the interview, but even there it is clearly more sanctioned between men than between men and women. Even where touching might be acceptable during an interview, the zones of the body that might be touched are prescribed. If the client is crying and distraught, reaching across and touching her hand or holding her hand in a spontaneous gesture of sympathy and support might be acceptable. Putting a hand on the client's knee or upper arm might be less acceptable. Embracing or hugging between a female interviewee and a male interviewer would even be more questionable. The sex of the participants, the nature of the interview context, the zones of the body involved, are factors which enter into the decision to touch or not to touch. Status is involved as well. The interviewer's "entitlement" to touch the interviewee is greater than the interviewee's freedom to touch the interviewer. Once having decided to touch, the nature of the touch gesture itself needs to be considered. One can brush, pat, stroke, squeeze, hold, or embrace. Each communicates a somewhat different message and is differently received by the person touched.

The encounter movement has made an effort to disinhibit the use of touch in therapeutic situations. Such nonverbal communication gestures can be used to good effect in the interview. Pattison (1973) trained counselors to touch clients' hands during periods of clients' self-disclosure, which resulted in greater depth of self-exploration without any negative consequences for the relationship. Clients who were touched in counseling interviews tended to evaluate such interviews more positively than no-touch controls.

The supposition of interviewers holding a humanistic orientation is that some forms of touching facilitate openness and sharing. Touching presumably communicates support, warmth, and caring. The research on the effects of touching does not uniformly support the supposition. Touching is diversely interpreted by interviewees.

Touching may make some people feel anxious. It imposes a greater measure of intimacy than they might be ready to concede. Others may feel that the interviewer is taking advantage of his higher status position. It is differently interpreted when interviewer and interviewee are of the same gender as contrasted with cross-gender pairing.

The available research suggests that the decision to touch needs to be carefully considered by the interviewer for contextual appropriateness and interviewee acceptance. It can be helpful but it has its dangers.

Touching is more socially acceptable when the interviewee is a child but even here the decision to touch needs to be carefully considered. The interviewer's comments in the following vignette notes this.

A seven-year-old child in a residential institution said he didn't like himself, that nobody liked him, not even his mother who had "dumped" him and said he was a shit. He started to cry inconsolably at that point. The worker says:

I felt very tender toward John when I saw him crying so profusely. I wanted to hold him at the time but wasn't sure that my "gut level" response would be appreciated, for many disturbed children react hostilely to physical contact. John seemed ashamed that he was crying. I wanted to assure him that crying was not only acceptable but in this case helpful.

Concern about touching is not wholly unwarranted. Touching does have the effect of physically arousing, is associated with sexual contact, and may be interpreted as sexual harassment. Feminists have campaigned against the "male skin privilege" in touching by men.

Acceptance of touching gestures varies among different ethnic groups. Jourard (1966) observed couples in cafes in a number of different cities and noted how often they touched. This occurred 180 times per hour in Puerto Rico, 110 times per hour in Paris, and close to zero in London.

ARTIFACTUAL COMMUNICATION

Artifactual communication is the language of objects. The channel is the visual channel and the source of artifactual communication is the physical setting and personal adornments—clothes, hair styles, makeup, jewelry, accessories, etc.

Home visits provide a rich source of artifactual nonverbal communcation. People tend to express their interests and taste in the objects they buy and display. In one home the book collection is prominent; in another home the hi-fi and the record collection are given high visibility; in a third home many kinds of plants are everywhere. The type of art on the walls, the magazines on the table, and the style of furniture communicate something about the people. Is the house open or closed to the outside world? Are curtains and shades drawn, or are the windows uncovered so that people can look out and in? Is the decor formal and stiff or loose and familiar, cluttered or uncluttered, bright or dull colored? Is the furniture arranged so that it encourages comfortable conversation? Are there beds enough for everybody, a place for privacy if needed, enough chairs to seat the whole family at one time, a table big enough for a family meal?

Clothing is a source of artifactual communication, similar to home furnishings. Clothing identifies sex, age, socioeconomic status, and nationality. We expect people of different groups to dress differently. At the extremes, the dress of the Bowery drifter and the socialite permit clear identification. In the middle range, drawing inferences may be difficult. It takes a keen eye to distinguish the upper lower-class sales clerk from the upper middle-class minor executive.

We tend to associate certain dress with certain occupations; upon seeing it, we draw inferences about the person. The most obvious examples are, of course, in clothing designated as a uniform, as for the soldier, the policeman, the postman. The priest's collar, the nun's habit, the hospital uniforms distinguishing registered, practical, and student nurses, require a practiced eye for accurate identification. But there is, further, a uniform implied in the designations "white collar worker" and "blue collar worker," and in the stereotype of the tweed-wearing, pipe-smoking professor.

There are uniforms of group identification—the long hair, beard, and headband of the hippie; the studded leather jacket and boots of the Hells Angels motorcyclists; the yarmulka of the Orthodox Jew.

Clothing is an extension of the body and is closely related to body image. It is therefore an expression of self but also conditions our self-image. Choice of clothing designed to make a short man look tall, a plump woman look slender, loose-fitting clothing to disguise corpulence, tight clothing to accentuate voluptuousness, or a scarf worn to conceal neck wrinkles tell us something about the interviewee's body image and response to this image. Clothes permit us to control access to information about ourselves, information which we would rather not share. "As we decorate and clothe ourselves we are in a sense doing a self-portrait" (Fisher 1973).

The reliance on clothing as a nonverbal clue to understanding the client is demonstrated when such information is denied the interviewer. The patient in the hospital, the prisoner in the institution, wears the uniform of the setting. The interviewer is denied the nonverbal individualizing information that might be communicated by the clothing of the interviewee when the interview is conducted in an institutional setting.

In seeking additional nonverbal artifactual information one can observe length of hair, whether the male interviewee is shaved or not, general level of cleanliness, the extent to which eyebrows are plucked and shaped, and level of formality in dress. We can note the age and condition of clothing and how fashionable or how highly individualized it is. These say something about self-concept, concern for self-image projected, level of narcissism, attitude toward the interview, the concern with comfort in clothing or a concern with clothing as a means of decoration and self-expression. Choice of eyeglass style—race driver, granny, steel rim intellectual, sun glasses—communicates a message as does hair style—long, short, crew cut, gamin, piled on top, pony tail.

Jewelry is another unit of artifactual communication. Jewels as artifacts of conspicuous consumption tell something about socioeconomic status. Elks pins, Phi Beta Kappa keys, slogan buttons indicate the subgroups with which the interviewee and interviewer are affiliated and feel identified. Wedding rings, of course, communicate marital status.

With some hesitancy about sounding stuffy and seeming to suggest a restriction of the interviewer's freedom, I tentatively note that it is helpful to the conduct of the interview if the interviewer projects a neutral image. Clear identification of political or ideological affiliation might intensify interviewee resistance and defensiveness. The interviewee who habitually wears a small American flag in his lapel may be initially put off on meeting a worker wearing a large peace symbol necklace or a Gay Pride button.

In *Hamlet* Shakespeare correctly notes that "the apparel oft proclaims the man." The problem lies in accurately deciphering the proclamation. In general, the studies available do not permit easy attribution of personality characteristics from observation of clothing style, choice of colors, etc. The correlation between clothing and tested personality attributes is not generally much greater than chance.

An older person wearing clothing identified with adolescents may suggest problems regarding attitudes toward aging.

There is regional loyalty and an identifiable life-style expressed in Texan, Californian, Hawaiian costuming.

The black client wearing a dashiki may be making a political statement. "Such costumes are not only a reminder or a challenge to the outsider; they can also be a rebuke to other minority group members who are still walking around town in the garb of the majority" (Lurie 1981:93). Afro hairdos and corn-row braids similarly indicate racial consciousness and ethnic pride. Worn by a white middle-class client, a dashiki may indicate an expression of third world sympathy or counter-culture orientation. Similar sentiments may be expressed by peasant costumes worn by clients who are not members of the ethnic group—Moroccan caftans, Mexican serapes, Indonesian Batik shirts.

Wearing clothes that are outmoded may suggest an emotional attachment to the past, but it may also mean that the client has not been able to buy new, more modish clothing.

Subdued colors, restrained cut, heavier fabrics tend to be associated with a conservative life-style.

High interest in dress does seem to suggest some dependence on others for stimulation and approval and more anxiety directed toward the environment of other people. Lower levels of interest in dress indicate less dependence on the environment for stimulation and support. Since one motive that determines clothing choice is a desire to make a good impression on others, to ensure their acceptance and enhance one's self-esteem, a careless disregard for dress suggests a disregard for the reactions of others. If this is not the result of rebelliousness against conventional society and the triviality of concern with dress, it may suggest a depressive withdrawal. Psychiatrists often chart improvements of previously psychotic patients in part by their appearance.

Clothing is worn for protection in addition to serving the cause of modesty and permitting self-expression and pleasure in decorative self-adornment. The social worker in protective service, investigating cases of neglect, observes the child's clothing to determine if it is adequate protection against cold, snow, or rain.

The interviewee also observes the clothing worn by the interviewer. If it is at variance with what is generally expected of a middle-class social worker, the worker communicates a disconcerting message. Of relevance is a study in which manual and white-collar workers were told of a man who was consulting a lawyer for the first time. "The man arrived at the lawyer's office and was surprised to find him casually dressed in a faded sport shirt that hung over an unpressed pair of slacks." They [were asked to indicate] what they would have done in the man's place (Ryan 1966:66). About two-thirds of the respondents indicated a negative evaluation of dress, and a sizable percentage expressed reluctance to use the lawyer's services.

A study of adolescent preferences regarding family planning clinic decor indicated that they did not like "teenage decor, pillows on the floor, rock music, psychedelic posters" and preferred "that clinicians wear white coats" (Shiffer 1976).

Some workers may think they are making egalitarian efforts to establish rapport with lower class clients by deliberate use of informal dress. This may not have the effect intended. Such dress may decrease the credibility for the interviewee in anything the interviewer says and may reduce her feeling of hope that she might be effectively helped. Very casual dress may mean to the worker "I feel comfortable, informal with you." The client might read this as "you don't give a damn and you didn't bother to dress for me."

Whether formally or informally defined, there is a loosely structured dress code to which both interviewee and interviewer respond. Based on such a code the client has some expectations of how a professional such as a social worker is to be dressed for a formal occasion such as an interview. Social workers need then to give some reasonable regard as to how their dress might affect the clients. The fact that people dress differently for different occasions indicates a sensitivity to the contextual appropriateness of dress.

However, it might be noted that experimental attempts to check the effects of interviewer clothing style and interviewer office decor have, up to date, yielded ambiguous results. Therapists dressed more or less casually (open collar sport shirt vs. tie and jacket) and offices decorated with a lesser or greater professional emphasis (pleasant wall rug and sensitivity poster vs. diplomas and dignified photo prints) evoked similar kind of responses from interviewees (Amira and Abramowitz 1979).

PARALINGUISTICS

The principal channel of communication in the interview is, expectedly, the auditory channel, the transmission and reception of "noises" the participants make. There is much more to auditory interaction than the words themselves. A spoken word can be modified in meaning by the accompanying pitch, intensity, speed, stress, intonation, inflection, and articulation. These vocal but nonverbal communications are termed paralinguistic cues. They are the nonsemantic aspects of speech and have been called "nonverbal accoustical signs." These are the noises made which shape the *intonation* and give color to the words being spoken. The flat talk of automatons in space films gives us an idea of what is lost in the absence of paralinguistic cues.

The same verbal communication can carry different messages, depending on the acoustical accompaniment. Vocal nonverbal communication tells us how the person says what he says. These are the oral language sounds which accompany the words but are not a property of the words themselves. The vocal nonverbal accompaniments, the metacommunications, the paralinguistics, are like aerial punctuation marks.

Pitch refers to differences in frequency from low bass to high soprano. The *velocity* of speech refers to movement of the words as they issue from the mouth. Does one word follow another slowly or rapidly? Is the movement jerky or smooth and fluent? Is *articulation* precise to the point of being pedantic or slurred and mumbled? *Intensity* refers to volume of speech—so loud that it beats at you, so soft that you wonder if the person wants to be heard. *Stress* refers to the pattern of increase and decrease in loudness within phrases or applied to different syllables within words. It is concerned with differential emphases given to speech. We can say the same words matter of factly or in a mocking or sarcastic tone of voice.

A frequently cited dramatic illustration of the significance of paralinguistics in giving different meaning to the verbalization of the same words is the following:

Woman without her man would be a savage.
Woman (*pause*). Without her (*voice drop*), man would be a savage.

Voice qualities often affect our perception of the interviewee in response to our preconceived stereotypes. The man with the high pitched voice is perceived as effeminate; the woman with the low-pitched sultry voice is perceived as sexy.

Just as there are postural stereotypes associated with certain occupations—a military bearing, a scholar's stoop—there are occupational voice stereotypes—a clergyman's voice, a teacher's voice, a top-sergeant's voice.

Increased speech rate, vibrant voice, and fluent speech increases persuasiveness and credibility of the message.

A voice can be emotional, so that it breaks, trembles, chokes, is full of sighs, and reflects deep or rapid respiration. It can be flat, neutral, unexpressive, and controlled. A voice can be full of energy or it can be thin. Smooth fluent speech may indicate a lack of conflict or anxiety; it may also indicate a rehearsed speech, designed to deceive.

Emotions are spelled out paralinguistically. Anger tends to be expressed by a relatively fast rate of speech that is more than normally loud, by short durations and short pauses. Grief or sadness is indicated by a high ratio of pauses and by slowness of speech, which are characteristic of contempt as well, although the tone of voice differs; fear is shown by a relatively high pitch. A quavery voice may indicate anxiety; a squeezed voice, depression. Dibner confirmed that repeating words and phrases, leaving sentences unfinished, frequent changes in thought, shifts in volume of voice, and stuttering are related to level of felt anxiety (1956). Rate of speech and productivity increase with anxiety, and the silence quotient is low. Conversely, depression is characterized by a low speech rate and a high silence quotient.

Studies attempting to associate personal characteristics and emotions with speech properties have been reviewed by Kramer (1963) and Starkweather (1961). They suggest that vocal communication tells us something, but exactly what it tells us is not always clear. The length of silent periods, the length of a pause before a response, the length of utterances before a person permits her partner to speak, the frequency and forcefulness with which she interrupts her partner, unnecessary repetitions, the frequency of incomplete sentences, the omission of parts of words, the frequency of "ahs" and "ums" are characteristic speech patterns whose meanings we grasp only in general terms.

The interviewee may speed up her speech and increase the volume in response to a perception that the interviewer wishes to interrupt. Speed and amplitude change are designed to ensure continued control. The interviewee may increase speed when talking about something embarrassing in order to get it over with as fast as possible. She may decrease volume at the same time, as if to hide the words.

Speech disturbance, incomplete sentences, repetitions, stuttering, filled pauses (ah, uh) are more likely when talking about something which is disturbing and makes the speaker uncomfortable and anxious.

Analysis of speech disturbance, body movements, and interview content through movies and tape recordings of interviews leads Boomer to conclude that increases in speech disturbance as well as nonpurposive body movement were related to anxiety and conflict in the interview. He notes that "when the drift of a patient's communication is toward conflictful and difficult areas, his caution increases and there is a greater necessity to choose words carefully. The tension involved in encountering and coping with increasingly frequent and critical syntactic choices is accompanied by rising skeletal muscular tonus" (1963:265).

PROXEMICS

Proxemics, the organization of space relationships between people, is the study of space as nonverbal communication cues. There is a normative distance maintained between people interacting with each other generally in the zone of some 4 to 7 feet. This is a comfortable social distance in American culture. Moving closer in to 3 feet makes us feel as though our personal space had been invaded and the intruder is presuming an intimacy which we may not be ready to grant. Increasing the distance to 9 feet may be regarded as a rejection. Interviewer-interviewee distance is generally in the 5 to 8 foot range, varying somewhat as participants lean forward to engage more fully, leaning backward to disengage.

The interviewer needs to be aware that interaction distance is a nonverbal variable of some significance in determining interview interaction. The interviewer who stays back beyond the normal social distance may be perceived as cold and aloof; if he comes in too close, he may be regarded as inappropriately intimate and pushy.

The use of space is related to status. The interviewer may feel free about invading the personal space of the interviewee by moving closer to her. The interviewee is more likely to be hesitant about moving in on the interviewer.

The fact that the interviewer often has a tilt-chair on coasters while the interviewee generally has a straight-backed chair which is not easily repositioned permits the interviewer greater flexibility in modulating distance. He can tilt forward or back, slide the chair in or away from the interviewee. The interviewee on the other hand has to deliberately and ostentatiously move her chair forward. She can lean forward some but cannot tilt away from the interviewer. The interviewee's leaning forward and back is a significant positive indication of a good relationship, the movements indicating also her more active involvement.

Proxemic shifts and posture changes are very often associated with a change in topic, some transition in the interview. Participants physically change positions as they change topics or direction of the interview. Changing positions acts as a nonverbal steering message that a change in the direction of the interview is about to take place.

There are cultural variations in proxemic preferences. The normative distance for interaction among Mexican-Americans is somewhat closer in than is true for Anglos. Such clients may move closer in to the interviewer without any intention of invading the interviewer's personal space but acting according to their usual behavior.

The usual distance in conversational interaction among blacks is greater than among whites. A white interviewer moving in close may be regarded by a black interviewee as an invader of intimate space.

Men are more sensitive than women to invasion of their personal space and react with more embarrassment and avoidance. An interviewer has to be more careful then in moving in on a male interviewee.

Seating arrangements of interview participants is a proxemic nonverbal cue. Haase and DiMattia studied counselor and client preferences for interview seating arrangement by using four pictures of a male-female dyad talking to each other. In one photograph, the participants' chairs were placed side by side at a 45-degree angle; in the second, the chairs were opposite each other but on the same side of a desk; in the third, the chairs were placed opposite each other with a desk between them; and in the fourth, the chairs were placed at a 45-degree angle with only a corner of the desk between them. A semantic differential scale was used in obtaining a statement of preference. The most preferred position, as indicated by both counselor and client, was the one in which the participants interact over the corner of the desk. Although the counselors also showed a high preference for two chairs facing each other with no desk between them, clients were decidedly more negative toward this arrangement. Apparently the client does not feel sufficiently protected by the open position that might be preferred by counselors because it does encourage openness of interaction. The researchers note that talking over the corner of a desk, as preferred by clients, is somewhat open yet provides a partial barrier. "Conceivably such an arrangement might be preferred by the individual who enters counseling with trepidation about the experience, who is hopeful of help yet threatened by the therapeutic encounter. The 'protected sociopetal space' might serve the purpose of inviting a limited negotiation toward interaction yet offer the necessary security and safety required by most humans in a new and ambiguous situation" (1970:324).

The arrangement least preferred by both counselor and client was two chairs with a desk directly between. This format suggests that the participants are opposed to each other. A face-to-face, opposite position also forces each participant to look directly at the other or deliberately turn her face away, a gesture that hints at rudeness. An arrangement which puts the interviewee sideways to the desk or table and the interviewer across the corner of the desk or table permits the participants to let their gaze wander without seeming to avoid eye contact.

While the across-corner desk position, representing a co-active interaction with interviewer leadership, does result in a greater amount of interaction than the other alternative positions, some interviewers prefer the no-desk, face-to-face arrangement because it represents an orientation of mutuality and colleagueship.

BODY LANGUAGE—KINESICS

Body language, formally known as kinesics, is concerned with movements, gestures, and posture and is an important form of nonverbal communication. As the paralinguistic cues depend on the sense of hearing, kinesics depends on the sense of seeing.

The visual channel is a source of a great deal of information in the interview. Whether he explicitly recognizes it or not, the interviewer is constantly observing the great variety of motions the interviewee makes with various parts of her body. As Hamilton (1946) says, one can observe without interviewing but one cannot interview without observing. Yogi Berra, the ballplayer, often said, "It's amazing how much you can observe by just looking." Good interviewing requires that you be a good "watcher" as well as a good "listener."

Visual sensations, like auditory ones, can be received over longer distances than olfactory or tactile sensations, although here, too, there are limits. Changes in the size of the pupils, tensing of neck muscles, contraction of the pelvic muscles, slight changes in skin coloration (blanching, blushing), and changes in respiration rate all require keen eyesight and are easily lost. At distances of eight or nine feet, distances which sometimes separate interview participants, these messages may not be perceived. Being close to the interviewee may permit detection of subtle movements, but one then may not be able to detect the grosser, more general changes simply because of lost perspective.

The importance of bodily communications is shown by the frequency with which expressions referring to the body are used metaphorically. Schutz has collected a list of expressions in common use that describe behavior and feelings in bodily terms (1967:25–26). Included are the following: chin up, grit your teeth, pain in the neck, sink your teeth into, get off my back, tight-fisted, knuckle under, elbow your way, choke up, shrug it off, itching to do it. We talk of being tight-lipped to indicate secrecy; a stiff upper lip suggests fortitude; and we associate dejection with being down in the mouth. We scan the body for indications of age—wrinkles, sagging, changes in skin color, graying hair, dentures—and for scars, tattoos, tobacco stains, occupational stigmata.

Posture is whole-body communication. It might be the stiff and rigid posture of the military, the bent posture of the book-addicted scholar, the loose, casual, relaxed posture of the *bon vivant*. The posture may be open or closed—open, allowing access to the body; closed, denying access. Arms held crossed across the chest or legs crossed high up, knee placed on knee, are posturally closed conditions.

The body as an object of observation takes on particular importance at the present time, when drugs are a matter of concern. Needle marks on the arms and "tracks" (discoloration along the course of veins in the arms) accompanied by sniffling, flushing, drowsiness, and very contracted pupils may indicate the heroin addict. Shakiness, itching, tension states, profuse perspiration, and body odor all suggest the use of amphetamines (speed). Use of marihuana is not likely to be observable, since the effects wear off quickly and leave no evident signs. If seen very shortly after inhalation of a strong dose, the person may show reddening of the eyes and a cough due to the irritating effects of the smoke on the lungs. If the interviewer knows the characteristic odor of marihuana smoke, he might detect it.

The Face The part of the body which offers the greatest number and variety of gestural cues is the face. The face is naked and so is open to observation. "You should have seen the look on his face" is testimonial to the expressiveness of facial gesturing. Courtesy and custom dictate that we look at a person's face while he talks, so it is legitimate to scrutinize the face for messages. The face is our window on the world. It is said that the most important thing we wear is the expression on our face.

The organs of our sensory input—sights, sound, smell, taste—are located on our face, as well as the entrances to our body for sustenance—air and food and water. It is the site of our output for speech. There are many stereotypes associated with facial features which may suggest—often incorrectly—ideas about the person. There is a tendency to think that people with thick lips are sexy, those with thin lips determined and authoritative. A high forehead and glasses may connote intelligence, and a fat face, jolliness, while protruding eyes suggest an excitable person.

The face is the location of most of the automatic signals of tension—blushing, perspiration on the forehead, the dry mouth and lips. We yawn in boredom and project the glazed look of indifference. We bite our lip in redirected aggression.

The muscles of the face are sufficiently complex that the face is capable of more than a thousand different facial expressions. The forehead wrinkles and furrows, the eyebrows arch and knit, the eyes shift and widen or narrow, eyelids close slowly or flutter rapidly, nostrils flare, the lips curve, curl, tremble, turn up, turn down, open, close, and are moistened and patted by the tongue, jaws clamp, and teeth grind. The head can nod or bob or shake, be raised or lowered; the chin can be thrust forward or drawn in. Anger is expressed by a frown, tensed lips pushed forward, head and chin thrust forward, glowing eyes; pleasant surprise by a broad smile and lifting of the eyebrows.

The facial features are capable of very considerable modulation of gesturing. There is a whole range of possibilities between eyes closed to mere slits and wide-open eyes; between the slight smile and the loud laugh.

We all are experienced in arranging our faces so that they display the emotion that is socially appropriate for the occasion: sadness at a funeral, happiness at a graduation, disgust at an offensive action. We therefore suspect something is amiss when the appropriate facial expression is not displayed. Not only does control over facial expressions consciously permit one to adopt a look "to fit the occasion," it furthers deception and management of the impression one wants to create on others. We control our displays of nonverbal behavior to influence the way others perceive us.

We may "put on" the expression socially called for but not honestly felt. In this case, there is only a partial display of the expression; some element may be missing. The false expression is also apt to be poorly timed—assumed a moment too late, turned off a moment too early.

There are tight smiles and frozen smiles held too long to convey sincerity and there are on-again off-again smiles that belie the words of welcome accompanying them. There are smiles without any depth, reminding us of the Chinese proverb to "beware the man who laughs and his stomach doesn't."

We smile and laugh in happiness and we also smile and laugh in discomfort, confusion, and guilt. We smile in pleasure, in embarrassment, in appeasement, in invitation, in ridicule. Analagously we cry in sadness, we cry for joy, we cry in anger and frustration, we cry in sympathy, in relief, and out of guilt. The same overt behavior results from a variety of different emotions. And just as there are many different kinds of smiles, there are different ways of crying.

Facial expressions of sharply defined and clearly different feelings—fear, happiness, sadness, anger, surprise, disgust—can often be identified by the configuration presented by mouth, eyes, eyebrows, and forehead movements. But most often the expressions are blended so that the emotion being displayed in the facial vocabulary cannot so easily be accurately read.

Facial displays are not only blended, they may be partialized. An expression such as surprise may be displayed only by widening of the eyes rather than widening of the eyes and a raised eyebrow. Only part of the face is activated in expressing the emotion rather than a full display of all of the facial changes associated with the expression. We modulate the same expression so that one can communicate questioning surprise, dazed surprise, puzzled surprise, slight, moderate, or extreme surprise. To complicate matters, there can be a series of these complex expressions, each lasting for a short period of time—micromomentary expressions sometimes lasting as briefly as a fifth of a second.

The face can be hidden behind the hands, as when one shields his eyes or his mouth with his hands. It can also be hidden behind sunglasses, which may block the eyes and part of the face, making them inaccessible. Removing his sunglasses may indicate that the person is ready to make himself more available. In other instances, when a person wears corrective glasses, the gesture of removing them temporarily may indicate withdrawal. Since he sees less with the glasses off, the world is masked from him.

Eyes The familiar comment, "Don't look at me in that tone of voice," is evidence of popular acknowledgment of the importance of the eyes in nonverbal communication. We see "eye to eye" when in agreement and receive an "icy stare" or our "eyes shoot daggers" when in disagreement. There is a "come hither" look and a "fishy look" and a deceptive "shifty eye" look. There is a "sidelong glance." We control others with our eyes as reflected in the expression, "she held him with her eyes," and in the gaze of the hypnotist. The eye is a powerful weapon—"the evil eye."

Looking, unlike listening, needs to be pointed. One can fake listening; looking cannot be faked. Looking is not the same as eye contact. One can look at the other person without necessarily looking into their eyes, which is implied in eye contact. Eye contact is an important component of attending behavior. The interviewer who looks at the interviewee while she is talking is rated as more interested, more sincere, more involved. Eye contact suggests and reinforces mutual affiliation. A message delivered with eye contact has greater credibility. Eye contact affects the nature of the relationship and indicates how the participants feel about each other. An interviewee tends to have more eye contact with an interviewer with whom she has a positive relationship.

Eye contact can indicate liking and attentive listening. Or, it can be taken as a weapon—as a means of competitive dominance. Staring steadily at the interviewee has negative effects. It is a strain and may be embarrassing. Constant efforts to maintain eye contact often end in a power struggle as to who will turn away first. Constant eye contact suggests too great a desire for intimacy and not enough respect for the other person's privacy. Too little contact may suggest disinterest, deception, or dishonesty. A moderate amount of eye contact with intermittent breaks is the most desirable option.

Eye contact is more frequent when the interviewee is discussing content which has a favorable positive associated affect. Actual avoidance of eye contact, sometimes by hiding the eyes with a hand or with dark glasses, may be resorted to when embarrassing material is discussed. Avoidance may indicate shame or a desire to maintain a psychological distance during this time when composure is threatened by the nature of the material being shared. It may also indicate a desire to reduce distraction from introspection, a wish to avoid being threatened by seeing the other person's reaction to the revelations, or a resentful withdrawal from the person who asks personal questions.

It might be wise then to avoid direct eye contact when asking embarrassing or highly personal questions or when the interviewee is sharing such content. Direct eye contact would tend to accentuate feelings of guilt, shame, fear. Staring at this time might be perceived as an invasion of privacy.

The various elements of attending behavior (see also chapter 7) need to be integrated so that the total configuration is not perceived as unduly intimate. The act of leaning closer to the client may call for a corresponding reduction of eye contact. As the nature of what is being said becomes more personal, attending behavior needs to be reduced to maintain an equilibrium of all of the elements contributing to a comfortable level of intimacy.

Eye contact has a clearly regulatory function in controlling the traffic of interviewer-interviewee talk time. The person who is speaking looks at the listener from time to time to see if she is still paying attention and for feedback as to how the message is being received. The speaker then looks away in order not to be distracted. The speaker can avoid being interrupted by avoiding eye contact. A person will attempt eye contact more frequently when listening than when speaking.

Eye and hand gestures and body movements are used as interactional regulators telling the speaker to slow down or hurry up or continue or to finish talking.

When ready to yield the floor the speaker looks directly at the listener and makes more prolonged eye contact with the listener. The speed of presentation slows down and gestures become still or relaxed, hands are lowered, the voice drops lower. All of this communicates, "I am finished talking; I am ready to listen." Eye contact at the end of the comment not only signals "over to you" but it also places an obligation for response on the listener.

Women seek to maintain eye contact more consistently than men, an aspect of their greater orientation toward affectionate and inclusive relationships with others. Feminists have suggested that women use their eyes more consistently because as an oppressed social group they have to be more alert to the signals of others. Thus they have a higher orientation to social stimuli.

Researchers have found ethnic differences in the extent of eye contact usage. Blacks and Hispanics tend to use eye contact less frequently than whites. There is a greater tendency on the part of such interviewees to avoid looking at the face. Native Americans and Asian Americans tend to regard eye contact as disrespectful. Restraint in the use of eye contact is regarded among Native Americans and Asians as a sign of deference and respect. There is greater use of peripheral vision.

Hands and Arms; Feet and Legs   The hands, like the face, are also naked, but are easier to hide. By putting one's hands in pockets or by sitting on them, one can withhold them from view. They can be placed in the lap if the lower part of the body is behind a desk or table.

The fingers can make a fist or be extended, palm upward. An open palm, upward, and extended toward the interviewer, suggests supplication. The fingers of both hands can be interlaced tightly or loosely or fingertips can meet to make a "cathedral." Hands held tightly locked suggest inhibited aggression.

The fingers can be used to scratch or to pull earlobes, or to rub one's nose, knuckle the eyes, adjust one's clothes, nervously arrange and rearrange ashtrays and pencils on the desk, or to pull apart paper clips. A hand touched to the nose may suggest disdain, contempt, or disgust. Scratching may suggest inhibited hostility turned inward. Finger play around the lips may suggest oral gratification. Picking, smoothing, and cleaning gestures may imply obsessive compulsive traits.

The hands can be used to pound the table, rub the desk or arms of the chair, or squeeze a handkerchief. They can be rubbed, clapped, or wrung together, draped over the back of the chair or clasped around the knees. They can rub the temples, slap the thigh or forehead, pat the hair or pass through the hair in a combing motion, or snap a pencil during a stressful moment. When agitated, women make a rapid hand-to-neck movement, disguised as a hair-grooming gesture; men in similar situations may make an open, palm-down sweep of the hair. A palm placed on the back of the neck is associated with a feeling of defensiveness. We pat the stomach to indicate hunger and press our hands to our heart to indicate sincerity. The arms can be crossed at the waist or akimbo at the chest, or be used to swing in an arc.

Some hand gestures are self-comforting. We embrace ourselves in an arm cross. We support our chin, stroke our face, put hand to temple. We tend to gesticulate freely with our hands when we are talking fluently about familiar, comfortable contents. We shrug our shoulders and turn palms up when we have difficulty in verbally expressing what we mean.

We use our hands to point at something, to draw a picture, or to indicate size: "It had a square shape and was about this big"; or as a baton to punctuate or accentuate what we are saying. At points in the interview when difficult questions are voiced and the interviewee is not sure of the answer, there may be a tendency to touch the nose, pull at the ear lobe, and stroke the chin. The nose touch and mouth covering gestures are sometimes associated with nonverbal leakage gestures suggesting guilt.

Fidgeting and fiddling activity suggests anxiety. It is a displacement activity, a substitute for action one might like to take but cannot. Opening paper clips, playing with a pencil, opening and closing a bracelet, adjusting earrings, doodling, ashtray cigarette tapping, straightening desk items, hair twirling, coin jiggling, permit one to engage in some kind of motor activity while still involved in the interview. The activity itself, like cigarette and pipe smoking, has a calming effect. Interviewers as well as interviewees engage in such nonverbal activity.

The feet and legs are less valuable sources of nonverbal communication. Generally the lower part of the body is obscured from view by a desk or table. The feet are hidden in shoes, so that toes curling or the instep arching is difficult to detect. Even if the feet were open to view, it is generally not considered polite to gaze directly at them, particularly if the interviewer is a man and the interviewee a woman.

Feet and legs have a relatively limited repertoire of motions and the rearrangements cannot be rapidly executed. People can tap their feet; they can shuffle them, sliding them back and forth; they can cross their legs in a variety of ways. Women more frequently cross their legs with one knee over the other; men more frequently adopt an "open leg cross," the ankle of one leg over the knee of the other. Women can extend or cross their legs for flirtatious exposure or squeeze them together erotically. Legs can be swung in a circular motion or kicked back and forth.

An open position which permits access to the speaker's body (arms are not crossed, legs are not crossed) is more generally used when in communication with a liked partner.

The following is a summary, a partial list of frequent nonverbal behavior sometimes observable during the course of an interview.

1. Autonomic Messages:
   a. Blushing
   b. Sweating forehead
   c. Dry lips—moisten
   d. Shallow breathing
   e. Damp palms
   f. Paleness
2. Accessibility Messages:
   a. Arms open
   b. Arms folded in lap
   c. Arms crossed
   d. Legs open
   e. Legs crossed
      (at knee, at ankle)
3. Body Movements:
   a. Bending forward
   b. Bending back
   c. Leaning sideways
   d. Rocking
   e. Squirming
   f. Shifting in seat
4. Breathing:
   a. Deep
   b. Rapid
   c. Even
   d. Breathless
   e. Sighing
5. Chin:
   a. Thrust forward
   b. Drawn in
6. Eyebrows:
   a. Raised
   b. Pulled together
   c. Flash
7. Eyelids:
   a. Shut
   b. Widened
   c. Dropped
   d. Fluttering
8. Eyes:
   a. Fixed stare

   b. Intermittent contact
   c. Darting
   d. Cast down
   e. Sidewise glance
9. Feet:
   a. Tapping
   b. Stamping
   c. Kicking
   d. Shuffling
   e. Sliding back and forth
   f. Legs squeezed together
10. Fingers:
    a. Scratching
    b. Fanned over mouth
    c. Touch-rub nose
    d. Rubbing eye
    e. Pulling ear
    f. Drumming on table
    g. Pointing
    h. Squeezing
    i. Picking teeth
    j. Fiddling—clips, pencil,
       keys, etc.
11. Forehead:
    a. Wrinkled
    b. Furrowed
12. Hands:
    a. Clasped in lap
    b. In fist
    c. Rubbing each other
    d. Clasped over knees
    e. On thighs
    f. Sitting on hands
    g. Draped over chair
    h. Palms up
    i. Palms down
    j. Back of neck preening
    k. Hair adjusting
13. Head:
    a. Jerking
    b. Shaking

    c. Bobbing
    d. Nodding
    e. Hanging
    f. Cocking
14. Lips:
    a. Open
    b. Closed
    c. Turned up
    d. Turned down
    e. Trembling
    f. Smiling
    g. Moistened by tongue
    h. Pursed
    i. Biting lips
15. Orientation:
    a. Sits facing directly
    b. Sits at an angle
    c. Turns back to interviewer
16. Posture:
    a. Rigid—stiff
    b. Bent
    c. Loose—relaxed
    d. Slouched
17. Pronunciation:
    a. Clear
    b. Slurred
    c. Affected
18. Shoulders:
    a. Shrugged
    b. Thrust forward
19. Speech disturbances:
    a. Incomplete sentences
    b. Repetitions
    c. Stutter
    d. Stammer
    e. Verbal slips
    f. Filled pauses (ah, uh, umm, er)
    g. Sighs

    h. Inhaling-exhaling
    i. False starts
    j. Superfluous phrases ("you know," "like," "see what I mean")
    k. Omission (part of word left out)
    l. Blockages
    m. Slurs
    n. Hesitations
20. Speech speed:
    a. Slow
    b. Rapid
    c. Jerky
    d. Smooth
21. Voice control:
    a. Smooth
    b. Trembly
    c. Breaking
    d. Quivery
    e. Irregular pauses
    f. Inflection—computer-like; dull flat; monotonic
    g. Tense
    h. Breathy
    i. Gravelly
22. Voice inflection:
    a. Flat, dull monotone
    b. Varied, modulated
23. Voice level:
    a. Inaudible
    b. Whisper
    c. Loud
24. Voice pitch:
    a. High
    b. Low
    c. Frequent changes
    d. Whining

Significance for Interviewing

What importance does nonverbal communication have for the interview? It tells us something about the nature of the relationship between the participants. Body movements toward or away from each other, changes in frequency of eye contact, changes in positioning with reference to each other are indicative of the state of the relationship. The nonverbal messages received by the eye help to confirm the validity of the spoken messages received by the ear. Are the participants comfortable with each other, is there a sense of intimacy and understanding? Body language speaks to these considerations.

Nonverbal information helps to regulate communication. It provides some of the feedback which lets us know if the other person is listening, is anxious to say something, is getting ready to interrupt, is getting bored and restive. It helps to evaluate the emotional response to what is being said. Is the message being received with satisfaction or resentment, with hostility or indifference?

Nonverbal behavior may communicate what the interviewee cannot bring herself to say. The interviewee may not be able to put highly charged material into words, or she may not have sufficient verbal ability to express how she feels. Crying may communicate inexpressible grief; the shame the client may feel but not want to admit may be communicated by hiding her eyes. Emotional expression by nonverbal response was the earliest means of communication available to us as children. In moments of stress we tend to revert to such "language." It substitutes for a verbal message and provides information unavailable otherwise. As Ruesch and Kees (1956) say, "There are certain things which cannot be said; they must be done."

Nonverbal communication provides information about feelings and attitudes of which the interviewee has only dim awareness or of which he is unconscious. Nonverbal behavior "is less susceptible than verbal behavior to either conscious deception or unconscious censoring. . . . [Although people can hear what they are saying], most people do not know what they are doing with their bodies when they are talking and nobody tells them" (Ekman and Friesen 1968:181). Without such feedback, it is difficult to train oneself to control the body so as to transmit the message one would prefer to transmit. Nonverbal behavior tends then to evade and frustrate any efforts of self-censorship. A good deal of it is not only enacted below the level of conscious awareness, but may not be readily available to conscious control. Blushing, twitching, or facial grimaces may "erupt" before the person can gain control.

When speech is difficult or the message if communicated would be too direct and explicit, we tend to code it nonverbally. The message is then

indirect. We did not say it, yet it was said. We are more capable of censoring what we actually say in words so that only when under considerable
stress do we say things we had not intended to share. We have more difficulty controlling and censoring our nonverbal communication. Consequently, it is apt to be more genuine, more spontaneous, less deliberate,
less controlled, and more open to communication leakage, "saying" what
we did not intend to communicate.

Verbal messages are generally concerned with ideas, facts, or recital of
events. Nonverbal messages are more generally concerned with the affective aspects of interpersonal relationships. Nuances of feeling are more easily communicated in nonverbal gestures, particularly of the face. The nonverbal channel then becomes the preferred channel of communication for
feelings.

Nonverbal communication may amplify the verbal message, emphasize
it, contradict it, accent part of it, or anticipate it. In all these ways the
interpretation and understanding of the actual verbal message are aided.

AMPLIFICATION:
She wants me to help with the shopping and watch the kids and clean the
house. Hell, I worked hard enough on the job. I don't want any part of
that crap (gestures with his right forearm, palm out, from his body out-
ward, as though he were pushing it away).

EMPHASIS:
Good, good, that's fine (nodding head vigorously in a yes motion while
smiling).

And every god-damn time she [wife] came to visit, you think she would
stay with me? No (bangs desk), not her! She had to see this doctor, or that
damn doctor (bangs desk) or some damn social worker (bangs desk).

ANTICIPATING:
When Mrs. B. was speaking of her symptoms, with practically no mention
of her husband, she slid her wedding ring back and forth on her finger.
Soon she started to talk about her marital problems which were associa-
tively linked to her symptoms. Her wedding-ring play anticipated her ver-
balizations. (Mahl 1968:322)

ACCENTING:
You just can't make it on welfare. You're always behind. For God's sake,
how the hell would you like to live in this dump? (As she said "you" she
pointed a finger at the social worker; when she said "this dump," she swept
her arm wide to include the room, at the same time turning her head in
half a circle, following her moving arm.)

CONTRADICTION:
I'm not stupid, you know. I know it's wrong. Don't think I don't know
that. I am not proud of it, you know (corners of mouth turned up in what
seemed a self-satisfied smirk).

The interviewee, a bench hand and machinist's helper, deftly manipulated a pencil through a motley of maneuvers extended over most of his interviews. His skill failed him at only one point when he was defensively claiming that his work efficiency was 100%. He lost control over his pencil and dropped it on the floor. (Mahl 1968:320)

The contradiction can be between the verbal content and any single channel of nonverbal communication. Mehrabian (1968) defines sarcasm as a message in which the information transmitted vocally contradicts the message transmitted verbally. One nonverbal message can contradict another. The body posture may be relaxed, but the drumming motion of the fingers on the table indicates tension. When there is possible deception involved in the presentation, the different nonverbal gestures may contradict rather than reinforce each other. If the interviewee is lying, a poker face and eye contact may be contradicted by the feet which are shuffled or crossed and uncrossed and by hand movements.

Because the nonverbal messages are under less conscious deliberate control, the verbal message is often subordinate to the nonverbal message. If there is some discrepancy we tend to accord greater credence and an authenticity to the nonverbal message. A friendly statement in an unfriendly tone of voice is perceived as unfriendly. However, the fact that this is often but not invariably the case suggests the need to check out each instance rather than automatically giving the nonverbal message precedence. The main meaning may lie with the verbal message, the nonverbal message being a subordinate modifier.

Because nonverbal messages are more ambiguous than verbal messages, there is greater need to request feedback for confirmation of what it is we think we "hear" when we "read" nonverbal behavior.

You dropped your voice, you shifted in your seat and clasped your hands in your lap when you said you might have to move to another city. What does that mean?

I noted that you smiled and kind of clapped your hands when you told about that. Am I right in thinking you were glad that it happened?

Although the interviewer is admonished to make a conscientious effort to observe nonverbal communication, it might be noted, in conclusion, that the usual rules of etiquette require that we sometimes avoid noticing such gestures. We "turn away" from ear and nose picking much as we pretend not to hear stomach rumblings, belching, and farting. However, here, as is similarly true for the verbal channel of communication, the courageous interviewer may act on the supposition that the conventional rules of communication etiquette are suspended in the social work interview. Just as the interviewer might "confront" the interviewee with something she has implicitly said but is reluctant to acknowledge, the interviewer might call attention, for instance, to persistent crotch scratching and introduce explicit discussion of the gesture.

The interviewer is communicating nonverbal information as actively as the interviewee. The interviewer's behavior often is deliberate and consciously designed to elicit some kind of interviewee response. Head-nodding, smiles, body movements toward and away from the interviewee, etc., offer encouragement and support, emphasizing the verbal message "go on" or "yes, I understand."

The interviewer, like the interviewee, having less conscious awareness of and control over his nonverbal communication than over his words, runs the risk of "saying" what might best be left unsaid.

A 32-year-old mother on public assistance is talking about her children's vaccinations.
MRS. Y.: And I said, "Bill, when you were little, they put them in your butt."
WORKER: Mm-mmm.

The worker comments:

There was more to this last "mm-mmm" than can be seen in the typescript. I have always had an aversion to the word "butt" and my distaste came out loud and clear in my inflection in this little "mm-mmm." It was clear that Mrs. Y. caught my attitude. A little later I noticed she used the word "thigh" rather than "butt" as we continued the discussion.

A desirable level of interviewer self-awareness involves not only an awareness of what he is thinking and feeling and saying, but also an awareness of the nonverbal behavior he is emitting and communicating.

PROCESS CONSIDERATIONS

Nonverbal behavior at the start and end of the interview is likely to be especially significant. The interviewee's actions communicate her attitude toward the interview, the interviewer, and the agency. Does the interviewee enter aggressively, with quiet confidence, or with apologetic diffidence; does she knock timidly before she enters or does she knock with assurance, asserting her right to the scheduled time; does she interrupt a preceding interview that has run past the time allotted or wait self-effacingly until called; does she keep her coat on after she enters, protecting her withdrawal route, or does she indicate that she is ready to remain? The family therapist is cautioned to observe carefully the manner in which the family enters the room and the seating arrangements they choose—who sits next to whom.

Within the interview itself there is a progression of changes in nonverbal communication. If the interview is going well, the interviewee most likely will feel more relaxed, and the stiff beginning posture should start to loosen, precise diction give way to some slurring, formal speech change to more colloquial speech, the clenched fist open. The interviewee will probably turn more directly toward the interviewer and lean more frequently in his direction. If rapport has developed, one would expect the interviewee to take more initiative in terminating silences.

Interview rapport is associated with the greater likelihood that interviewer and interviewee would mirror congruent postures—that is, if one has his chin in his hand, or is sitting sideways, soon the other will mimic the position without realizing that she is doing so. Not only does interactional synchrony and nonverbal echoing relate to congruous posturing, signs of relaxation and body orientation, it also relates to more specific nonverbal manifestations such as speech rate and foot wagging. A client who is speaking rapidly because she is excited and upset will, as rapport develops, begin to slow down her speech and speak more calmly in synchrony with the interviewer's slower rate and calmer speech.

The tendency toward response matching among participants in a relationship characterized by rapport can be employed by the interviewer in shaping the interview behavior of the interviewee. If the interviewee is upset, the slow, calm related talk of the interviewer may gradually be matched by similar behavior by the interviewee who then might begin to feel less anxious.

At the end of the interview, the participants' behavior again tends to show their attitudes toward each other and toward the interaction. Does the interviewer (or interviewee) keep looking at the clock? Does the interviewee leave hesitantly, trying to prolong the interview by a variety of actions—refusing to rise, put on her coat, move to the door—or does she leave hastily, as though in flight?

PROBLEMS IN INFERRING MEANINGS

In general, the study of nonverbal communication is much farther along in description and codification of behavior than in establishing its "meanings." Detailed studies of nonverbal behavior have identified a very large number of different items of the nonverbal vocabulary. Five thousand distinctly different hand gestures have been identified and one thousand different steady body postures. A detailed and precise observation of nonverbal behavior is important. It is only a first step, however. The interviewer still has to infer some valid meaning from the data. Accurate observation is a necessary but insufficient requisite to understanding the psychological relevance of the gesture.

How valid are the inferences we draw from our observations? Is it true that an uncluttered, neat, clean home implies rigidity and anality? Are most women who use theatrical makeup narcissistic and flirtatious? What valid conclusion can we draw from fluttering eyelids? What exactly is a "long-suffering look," "a mocking smile," "a conspirational glance"? Closing or screwing up the eyes *may* represent an effort to blot out the world; wrinkling up of the nose *may* represent disgust; a swinging foot in short arcs *may* represent annoyance. But how often is this actually the case? What nonverbal manifestations differentiate between the slow, hesitant speech of the timid and the slow, hesitant speech of the uninterested and indifferent? Extreme and frequently encountered emotions are easier to "read"— depression, joy, and anger. But it is difficult to distinguish between anger and impatience or disgust, shame and embarrassment, hate and envy, fear and timidity.

A stiff posture may express a stiffness of character, but it may also result from military training—or rheumatism and arthritis. Crossing and uncrossing legs may be a protective nonverbal maneuver, but it may also be in response to poor circulation or pain in the feet.

We need, and do not have, a dictionary of nonverbal behavior that reliably and validly translates its meanings. The lack of a standard nonverbal vocabulary might be easily tested by the reader. What gestures would *you* use to communicate a moderate level of disgust, an intense feeling of suspicion, a low level of guilt, a moderate level of concern? It might be easier to convey an intense feeling of sadness or of hate but even here there may be differences in what people regard as the appropriate gestural manifestations of such emotional states.

Some gestures, of course, have a commonly accepted meaning for all Americans. There is a general consensus about the meaning of a handshake, a shrug of the shoulders, a fist pounding the table, the "yes" nod or "no" shake of the head, or the eyelid wink of intimacy. These gestures are similar to a sign language "vocabulary" that has general understanding— the extended thumb of the hitchhiker, the thumb forming a circle with the forefinger, and the other fingers then extended, to mean "okay," the undulating, counter-parallel twohanded gesture meaning a curvaceous woman, the waving hand meaning "good-bye," the hand-to-forehead salute of the military, the clenched-fist salute of the militant revolutionary. In the United States we recognize hand clapping as a sign of approval; we raise our hand for attention, point to give direction. It is also easy to interpret nonverbal behavior that is uniform cross-culturally and might be innate—weeping in sorrow, trembling in fear, laughing in joy.

Scheflen rightly warns that attempts to ascribe meaning to nonverbal events should consider the context in which the events occur and the verbal accompaniments. Any interpretation that ignores or slights these considerations is on hazardous ground. He notes, in analogy, that "a letter of the alphabet does not carry meaning until it is part of a word which is part of a sentence which is part of a discourse and a situation" (1964:324). The context gives meaning to the nonverbal communication. But, further, in interpreting the meaning it is necessary not only that we know how to translate the nonverbal communication, but also that we know the ethnic, race, and class setting in which the interviewee learned the gesture. The same nonverbal communication may be differently expressed by a white and a black person, differently expressed by a lower-class Scandinavian and a middle-class Italian. Different "speech communities" assign greater or lesser importance to nonverbal aspects of communication and differ as well on the meaning assigned to specific gestures.

In addition, we have to assess the persistence and repetitiveness of the behavior. A single, fleeting instance in which a father, during a family therapy session, turns his back on the rest of the family is quite different from frequent instances in which the father turns away and maintains this position for some time. It makes a difference, too, if he does this in a furtive, jerky, hesitant manner or if he does it in a deliberate, open manner. The quality of the gesture needs to be taken into consideration.

Interpreting gestures requires the recognition that they have both expressive and communicative functions. The interviewee engages in them because they satisfy some need, not because she consciously or unconsciously wants to communicate a message in every instance. The interviewee is supplying information which she had no intention of communicating, which she is usually unaware of having given.

The interviewer faces yet another problem which is spared us in writing or reading a chapter on nonverbal communication. He has the difficult task of receiving, sorting, understanding, and responding to the great number of messages being transmitted simultaneously and continuously on a variety of channels. And he has to do all of this rapidly, while being bombarded by a continuous stream of these multichannel messages.

In all of this we infer meanings, with least risk, on the basis of deviation. "There is no information in a steady state," so that only by establishing some base line of the way the client talks, moves, etc., can we be aware that at this moment her gesture and/or speech are different. The fact of difference suggests that something is being communicated. Departures from a norm are most significant. If increase in the frequency of motions suggests anxiety, we need to know how much the interviewee tends to move around when at ease. If we say that anger tends to be expressed in a relatively fast rate of speech, we need to know how fast the interviewee tends to speak ordinarily. When she deviates from this base line and speaks at more rapid pace, one might pay close attention to determine whether she is, in fact, responding angrily. Even the base line, however, may have significance. A person whose speech and movements are habitually rapid and jerky—more than the social worker would expect from his acquaintance with a large number of people—may be in a chronic state of nervous tension. Such an inference, should, of course, be checked against the person's response to the content of the interview.

We have learned the nonverbal language as we have learned speech—as a consequence of daily practice, without explicit awareness of how we learned it or what we have learned. Since there is no standard lexicon of nonverbal language, it is not learned as systematically as is speech; responses are apt to be highly individualized. Mahl and Kasl (1965) found that some people uttered more "ahs" as they moved into anxiety-provoking content. Others, however, became more studied in their speech.

The risks in deriving valid inferences from nonverbal communication are to be expected. If, after so many years of talking together, we are still novices in the art of verbal communication, what permits us to presume a facility in the more difficult art of nonverbal communication? In spite of all these necessary qualifications, one must concede the validity of Edward Sapir's cogent summation. In spite of difficulties of conscious analysis, "we respond to gestures with an extreme alertness and, one might almost say, in accordance with an elaborate code that is written nowhere, known by none, and understood by all" (quoted in Birdwhistell 1970:182).

SUGGESTED READINGS

Michael Argyle and Peter Trower. *Person-to-Person Ways of Communicating*. New York: Harper and Row, 1979 (128 pp.).

Some of the essentials in nonverbal communication aptly illustrated by pictures of the nonverbal behavior discussed.

Abne M. Eisenberg and Ralph R. Smith. *Nonverbal Communication*. New York: Bobbs-Merrill, 1971 (133 pp.).

Once again, an overview that pulls together in a succinct way some of the general ideas about nonverbal communication that should be of help to the interviewer.

Robert Harper, Arthur N. Wiens, and Joseph D. Matarazzo. *Nonverbal Communication: The State of the Art*. New York: Wiley, 1978 (353 pp.).
A scholarly written, research-oriented recapitulation of what was known and unknown, about nonverbal communication at the beginning of the 1980s. The book provides bibliographical leads to the essential source material for the reader interested in pursuing the material in greater depth. The book covers research on paralinguistics, kinesics, facial expression, the eyes, and proxemics.

Nancy M. Henley. *Body Politics: Power, Sex, and Nonverbal Communication*. Englewood Cliff, N.J.: Prentice-Hall, 1977 (212 pp.).
Written from a strong feminist point of view, the book spells out the implications of nonverbal communication in male–female interactions in a variety of contexts.

Mark L. Knapp. *Nonverbal Communication in Human Interaction*. New York: Holt, Rinehart, and Winston, 1972 (213 pp.).
A comprehensive and very readable overview of nonverbal communication covering such areas, among others, as environment, space, facial and eye expression, physical appearance, and voice.

Alison Lurie. *The Language of Clothes*. New York: Random House, 1981 (273 pp.).
A witty and perceptive overview of the nonverbal significance of clothing. The book increases the reader's awareness of the meaning of the choices people make in the clothing they select to wear and the messages they seek to transmit through clothing.

Desmond Morris. *Man Watching: A Field Guide to Human Behavior*. New York: Harry U. Abrams, 1977 (320 pp.).
A biologist discusses and shows, with a variety of graphically selected photographs, people engaged in nonverbal behavior in a wide variety of social situations.

Albert E. Scheflen. *How Behavior Means*. New York: Anchor Press/ Doubleday, 1974 (221 pp.).
One of the leading researchers of nonverbal communication in the therapeutic situation summarizes the meanings of nonverbal behavior in dyadic interaction.

L'Envoi——

Its a long journey from the beginning of the book to the end of the book—from the beginning to the end of the course.

Much has been attempted—and we hope much has been achieved. We started by distinguishing an interview from a conversation and the social work interview from other kinds of interviews. Since the interview is a particular kind of communication event, a member of the family of communication events, we then included some discussion of the essentials of the communication process.

And since whenever people communicate in whatever context for whatever reason, a relationship is established, we found it necessary to discuss relationships—the characteristics of a good relationship generally and the social work relationship specifically. Attitudes which have been identified as associated with a positive, facilitative, helping relationship were reviewed—acceptance, empathic understanding, self-determination, authenticity, confidentiality.

We then returned to the social work interview, our principal focus and concern, to introduce the participants—the social work interviewer and the social work interviewee. An effort was made to delineate what each of the participants brings to the interview event, the tasks they each are required to perform in the interview and the problems they encounter.

The largest segment of the book covered by chapters 5 through 10 was concerned with the interview process, the series of sequential steps jointly engaged in by interviewer and interviewee which move the interview toward achievement of its purpose. We discussed the beginning of the process, the routes interviewees take in coming to the agency, their reception and introduction to the interviewer, and the actual beginning of the interview interaction. We explicated the activities the worker performs in ex-

tending the range and depth of the interview—attending, reflecting, paraphrasing, making transitions, summarizing, questioning, and probing. We
followed the interviewer as he/she engaged the interviewee in clarifying,
confronting, and interpreting, in the efforts toward helping the interviewees solve the problems which brought them to the agency. Hopefully the
purpose of the interview was accomplished and the interaction moved toward termination of the interview. The procedure for termination was discussed and the post-interview obligations of the interviewer for evaluation
and recording were noted.

Some significant aspects of interview interaction did not fit neatly into
the discussion of the interview process. These were then reviewed in separate chapters concerned with problems of feedback, self-disclosure, immediacy, and activities such as listening, silence, and humor. The relevance of all of this to the telephone interview was outlined.

We recognized that all general discussions of the interview do an injustice to the individuality of the interviewee. The great variety of interviewees from different cultures and different backgrounds demands that some
attention be paid to the heterogeneity of the interviewees. We, therefore,
presented the material on the adaptation required of the interview in contact with blacks, Native Americans, Hispanics, the poor, children, the aged,
interviewees of the opposite sex, and homosexuals.

And because communication is conducted nonverbally as well as verbally
and sometimes more nonverbally than verbally, we concluded with a chapter on nonverbal communication—proxemics, kinesics, paralinguistics, artifactual communication, touch, and smell.

We warned the reader at the very start of our association together that
ultimately interviewing could only be learned experientially. We still think
this is true. But we are equally confident that much can be taught through
a book that could contribute to the effectiveness of learning from experience; that systematically presented content on interviewing could help illuminate the experience. It was—and is—our feeling that such learning,
such content, helps add competence to commitment. Only the reader knows
whether this is purely a matter of faith and hope or whether this has some
basis in the reality of the reader's experience.

APPENDIX

At various points throughout the text, we have referred to attitudes, skills, and behaviors that distinguish the more competent interviewer from the less competent interviewer. In this appendix, we have recapitulated in tabular fashion the distinction in performance between the two. The listing moves through the interview process from beginning to termination.

MORE COMPETENT	*LESS COMPETENT*
The usual social amenities are observed in a relaxed way. Identity of participants, the purpose of the interview, and the interviewer's agency affiliation are clear.	There is a sense of strain as though there is some difficulty in distinguishing the difference between social and professional interaction. Identification of participants, interviewer affiliation, and purpose of interview is sometimes neglected.
The expressive facilitative conditions of a good interview—respect, caring, warmth, empathic understanding, acceptance, genuineness—are communicated unobstrusively with warmth and assurance. As a consequence interviewee anxiety, defensiveness, resistance are reduced, willingness to share and openness are increased, motivation to participate is intensified.	There is an attempt to communicate the facilitative conditions but the feelings as expressed give the appearance of being mechanical or contrived in response to a deliberate conscious effort. Rather than their being an integral part of the interviewer's smoothly automatic behavioral orientation the interviewer appears to be playing a role. There is then an element of phoniness and an occasional manifestation of moralistic, punitive, rejecting, disrespectful, nonprofessional behavior. As a consequence interviewee resistance and anxiety is increased, motivation to participate reduced.

MORE COMPETENT

The interviewer demonstrates that he has made some preparation for the interview. He knows and makes use of whatever limited information is available on the interviewee, has the interview folder and other necessary materials available, has arranged for privacy, proper lighting, etc.

The interviewer is sensitive to the problems the interviewee has in enacting his role in the interview and seeks to help him with this— clarifying, explaining, deliberately modeling how people act in an interview situation.

The interviewer appears to keep the interviewee as the exclusive focus of his attention, as the focus of his concern, responding to the interviewee's needs and the interviewer's feelings. The needs of the interviewee and the purposes of the interview are given primary priority.

The interviewer controls the progression of the interview but in a flexible adaptable manner. Self-assured in his control he can, when appropriate, share control of interview with interviewee.

Somewhat similarly the interviewer has a clear idea of the purpose of the interview and structures the focus of the interview toward achievement of the purpose. This is, however, accomplished in a flexible adaptable manner. While clear as to purpose, commitment

LESS COMPETENT

The interviewer shares no indication that he has made any preparation for this particular interview.

The interviewer is not aware of the problems or confusions the interviewee may be having in enacting the role of interviewee. There is little effort to help with this.

The interviewer appears to alternate between a focus on the interviewee and on himself, and on the interviewee's frame of reference and his own frame of reference; occasionally the interviewer's needs are given priority over the needs of the interviewee or the needs of the interview.

The interviewer loses control of the interview permitting unproductive, prolonged interviewee digressions or role reversal so that interviewer is being interviewed. When in control he keeps the interview inflexibly on course permitting the interviewee little freedom.

The interviewer is not entirely clear as to the purpose of the interview so that structure is loose and focus wanders. If there is clarity as to purpose, this is rigidly and inflexibly adhered to so that client freedom to modify purpose is given little consideration.

MORE COMPETENT

is lightly held so that purpose can be modified if necessary during the course of the interview.

Because the interviewer knows where he is going and knows how to get there the interviewer appears to the interviewee as well as an observer to have direction, logic, a predictable sequence.

Questions are formulated effectively:
a. They are appropriate and well timed.
b. They are concise, well-phrased, and unambiguous.
c. They are tactfully phrased.
d. They are asked one at a time.
e. They do not suggest an answer.
f. Questions answerable by a "yes" or "no" response are infrequently but appropriately employed.
g. There are more "what" and "how" questions than "why," "when," or "where" questions.
h. There is a preponderance of open-ended questions as compared with close-ended or leading questions, which are used appropriately when asked.

Wording of questions shows sensitivity to vocabulary level of interviewee; appropriate adaptation of communication in response to consideration of age, sex, race, class, ethnic differences between interviewer and interviewee.

The interviewer uses nonverbal be-

LESS COMPETENT

Because the interviewer is uncertain about where he is going and unclear as to how to get there the interview appears to the interviewee as well as to an observer to have no direction, logic, or predictable sequence. It seems somewhat chaotic and confused and confusing.

Questions are often not effectively formulated:
a. They are inappropriate or poorly timed in terms of what the client is saying.
b. They are often wordy, garbled, ambiguous, more apt to include meaningless verbalisms such as "you know," "see what I mean."
c. They are tactlessly phrased.
d. Double questions are asked.
e. Expected answers to the questions are telegraphed by the questions themselves.
f. Many questions require only a "yes," or "no" response.
g. "Why," "when," or "where" questions are more frequently employed than "what" and "how" questions; close-ended and leading questions are more frequent than open-ended questions.

Wording of questions is beyond vocabulary level or habitual usage of interviewee. Inappropriate use of professional language is present. Communication pattern is not varied to accommodate to differences in age, sex, race, ethnicity.

The interviewer's nonverbal behav-

MORE COMPETENT

havior (eye contact, forward lean, distance) to reinforce verbal interventions and to indicate that she is carefully attending to and following the interviewee.

The interviewer's verbal and nonverbal communications are congruent with each other—supplementing, supporting, clarifying so that a clear unambiguous message is communicated.

The interviewer rarely interrupts, or overrides interviewee or finishes his sentences for him. She is sensitive to client's rights to autonomy and has no need to exert power or assert control.

The interviewer conducts the interview so that the ratio of talk time clearly favors the interviewee.

The interviewer uses silence effectively and comfortably, is sensitive to the distinction between different kinds of silences and makes appropriate differential interventions. She knows when to end and when to permit silence to continue.

The interviewer's pace is relaxed, unhurried. There is a longer pause between the client's statement and the worker's response.

The interviewer has the courage to risk being impolite and to interrupt the interviewee and redirect communication if the interviewee has lost his way.

There is comfortable exploration of the client's situation including coverage of relevant intimate de-

LESS COMPETENT

ior sometimes suggests inattentiveness; her verbal interventions are inappropriate to or a digression from what the interviewee has been saying.

The interviewer's verbal and nonverbal behavior are often noncongruent, contradictory, in conflict with each other so that a double or confused message is communicated.

The interviewer frequently interrupts client, overrides him, and ends sentences for him. This is perceived as a violation of interviewee's autonomy and a manifestation of interviewer power and control.

The interviewer conducts the interview so that the interviewer talks more than the interviewee.

The interviewer is apt to be unnerved by silence; is not sensitive to different meanings of silence; her timing in ending or prolonging silence is inappropriate.

The interviewer's pace appears hurried and unrelaxed. There is little response delay, worker response coming almost immediately after client statement.

The interviewer is hesitant about redirecting interviewee even if it is clear that he is engaged in an unproductive digression.

Exploration of the client situation is awkward, hesitant, ineffectual, without assurance. The inter-

MORE COMPETENT

tails. Client self-disclosure is facilitated by the nature of the relationship established and
interviewer's encouragement of
disclosure. Interviewer communicates assurance about her entitlement to the information, conviction of the need for the
information, and willingness and
ability to deal with emotionally
charged material without anxiety.

Exploration of the client's situation
is sharply focused because the interviewer knows clearly what she
needs to know in order to help effectively. This is based on expert
knowledge of the social problem
area and human growth and the
social environment. Most of the
necessary information for understanding the client's situation is efficiently obtained in a short period
of time.

Because of comfort with emotional
contact the interviewer helps the
interviewee explore in depth,
where appropriate, areas of function which have potential significance for achieving the purpose of
the interview. There is then ability to explore both in range and
depth. The interviewer refrains
from too early problem solving and
too early engagement in highly affective content.

Transitions from one topic to another are made smoothly with appropriate explanation. The nature
of the transition selected indicates
the interviewer has been attentive
to what the client has been saying;

LESS COMPETENT

viewer is made embarrassed or
anxious by emotionally charged
content, does not feel entitled to
intimate personal information
about client, nor does she communicate conviction in the need
for the information.

Exploration of the client's situation
is diffuse and protracted. The interviewer is not clear as to what
data is most significant for a valid
understanding of the client's situation because of limited knowledge of the social problem and human growth and the social
environment. Despite a greater
expenditure of time and effort, less
significant useful information is
obtained.

Because of discomfort with emotional intimate personal details,
interviewer tends not to explore in
depth. There is then rapid movement over a range of topics of
potential significance but little
exploration in depth. The
interviewer has a tendency to
move too quickly toward problem
solving and becomes involved too
early in heavy feeling content.

Transitions are abrupt, not explained, often irrelevant and unrelated to what the client has been
talking about. There is a sense that
the interview is fragmented and
discontinuous.

MORE COMPETENT   *LESS COMPETENT*

there is, consequently, continuity in content and mood.

The interviewer tends to hold conclusions and inferences lightly and tentatively, seeking feedback in confirmation or validation of tentatively held hypothesis.

The interviewer tends to come to closure on conclusions too early assuming he knows more than he does know; he does not seek confirmation or disconfirmation of his conclusions.

Interventions seem to suggest that the interviewer is open-minded, attempting to individualize interviewee rather than fitting her into some predetermined catagories.

Interventions seem to suggest stereotypical thinking and catagorization of the interviewee in terms of predetermined assumptions.

Intervention such as reflection, interrelation confrontation, and summarization are appropriately made as to timing, dosage, formulation, and phrasing.

Intervention such as reflection, interpretation, confrontation, and summarization are often not relevant to the objective of the interview, are poorly timed or inappropriate in view of the manifest and latent content of the client's preceding statements, and are phrased so as to heighten, rather than dissipate, resistance.

The interviewer uses a variety of interventions flexibly and selectively or in combination, rather than tending to use one kind of intervention repetitively. The interviewer is equally competent and confident in the implementation of a variety of procedures.

The interviewer tends not to be selective in his use of a variety of intervention procedures.

Interviewer tends to be minimally directive in problem solving, in offering advice and solutions. She maximizes interviewee self-involvement in problem solution.

Interviewer tends to be more active and directive in offering advice and proposing solutions. She tends to do for the client in implementing problem solutions.

Interventions such as reassurance are made only when there seems a basis in fact for the validity of assurances.

Reassurance is offered despite the fact that there may be little basis for reassuring statements.

If notes are taken during the inter-

The manner of note-taking tended to

MORE COMPETENT

view this was done unobtrusively without breaking continuity of the interviewing or intruding on the progress of the interview.

The interviewer's behavior is always role appropriate, making a clear distinction between social and professional relationships.

In line with this, in exploring the situation or in making change interventions the approach of the interviewer is to be uniformly helpful rather than consistently popular.

The ending of interview is consciously and deliberately planned in line with achievement of interview objectives. The interviewer prepares clients for interview termination, controlling level of affect. She summarizes, recapitulates and ties interview to next contact.

LESS COMPETENT

interfere with the continuity of the interview and interfered with the primary purposes of the interview.

The interviewer inappropriately makes highly personal references or unprofessional, irrelevant interventions or permits prolonged small talk.

In line with an interviewer's focus on her own needs, her choice of action is determined by a desire to be consistently popular rather than invariably helpful, to please the client or at least not to offend the interviewee, rather than to do what is needed to help the client.

The ending is ragged, often sudden, abrupt, and not in line with where participants are in the interview at that point. Interviewee is not prepared for ending; summarization, recapitulation and tie to next contact neglected.

The difference between the expert and the inexpert interviewer, as described by counseling interviewers, is similarly recapitulated by Schmidt and Strong:

The *expert* shakes the student's hand, aligning the student with himself, and greets him with his first name. He seems interested and relaxed. He has a neat appearance but is not stuffy. . . . He talks at the student's level and is not arrogant toward him. The expert assumes a comfortable but attentive sitting position. He focuses his attention on the student and carefully listens to him. He has a warm facile expression and is reactive to the student. His voice is inflective and lively, he changes his facial expressions, and uses hand gestures. He speaks fluently with confidence and sureness. The expert has prepared for the interview. He is informed as to why the student is there and is familiar with the student's test scores, grades, and background. . . . He asks direct and to-the-point questions. His questions are thought-provoking and follow an apparently logical progression. They seem spontaneous and conversational. The expert is willing to help determine if the student's decisions are right, but does not try to change the student's ideas forcefully. He lets the student do most of the talking and does not interrupt him. The expert moves quickly to the root of the problem. He points out contradictions in reasoning, and restates the student's statements as they bear on the problem. . . . He makes recommendations and suggests possible solutions.

The *inexpert* is awkward, tense, and uneasy. He seems to be afraid of the student. He does not greet the student by name to put him at ease. . . . He is not quite sure of himself or of some of his remarks. He seems too cold, strict, and dominating and too moral in attitude and action. His gestures are stiff and overdone. . . . The inexpert slouches in his chair. He is too casual and relaxed. . . . His voice is flat and without inflection, appearing to show disinterest and boredom. . . . The inexpert comes to the interview cold. He has not cared enough about the student to acquaint himself with the student's records. The inexpert asks vague questions which are trivial and irrelevant and have no common thread or aim. His questioning is abrupt and tactless with poor transitions. He asks too many questions like a quiz session, giving the student the third degree. . . . The inexpert is slow in getting his point across and is confusing in his discussion of what the student should do. . . . The inexpert does not get to the core of the problem. . . . He just doesn't seem to be getting anywhere. (1970:117)

REFERENCES

Abel, Charles M. and H. Wayne Johnson. 1978. "Clients' Access to Records: Policy and Attitudes." *Social Work* (January), 23:42–46.

Abudho, Constance. 1979. *Nonverbal Behavior: An Annotated Bibliography.* Westport, Connecticut: Greenwood Press.

Amira, Stephan and Stephan I. Abramowitz. 1979. "Therapeutic Attraction as a Function of Therapist Attire and Office Furnishings." *Journal of Consulting and Clinical Psychology,* 47:198–200.

Atkinson, Donald, Mervin Maruyama, and Sandi Matsui. 1978. "Effects of Counselor Race and Counseling Approach on Asian Americans Perceptions of Counselor Credulity and Utility." *Journal of Counseling Psychology,* 25:76–83.

Baldock, John and David Prior. 1981. "Social Workers Talking to Clients: A Study of Verbal Behavior." *British Journal of Social Work,* 11:19–38.

Bandura, Albert, David Lipsher, and Paula Miller. 1960. "Psychotherapists' Approach: Avoidance Reactions to Patient's Expression of Hostility." *Journal of Consulting Psychology,* 24:1–8.

Banks, George P. 1971. "The Effects of Race on One-to-One Helping Interviews." *Social Science Review,* 45:137–46.

Barnlund, Dean C. 1974. "Communication, the Context of Change." In B. R. Patton and K. Giffin, eds., *Interpersonal Communication.* New York: Harper & Row.

Beck, Dorothy F. and Mary A. Jones. 1973. *Progress on Family Problems: A Nationwide Study of Clients' and Counselors' Views on Family Agency Services.* New York: FSAA.

Bergin, Allen E. and Sol L. Garfield. 1978. *Handbook of Psychotherapy and Behavior Change: An Empirical Analysis.* New York: Wiley.

Bernstein, Basil. 1964. "Social Class, Speech Systems, and Psychotherapy." *British Journal of Sociology,* 15:54–64.

Biestek, Felix P. 1956. *The Principle of Client Self-Determination in Social Casework.* Washington, D.C.: Catholic University of America Press.

Biestek, Felix P. 1957. *The Casework Relationship.* Chicago: Loyola University Press.

Biestek, Felix P. and Clyde C. Gehrig. 1978. *Client Self-Determination in Social Work: A Fifty-Year History.* Chicago: Loyola University Press.

Billingsly, Andrew. 1964. *The Role of the Social Worker in a Child Protective Agency: A Comparative Analysis.* Boston: Massachusetts Society for the Prevention of Cruelty to Children.

Birdwhistell, Ray L. 1970. *Kenesics and Context: Essays on Body Motion Communication.* Philadelphia: University of Pennsylvania Press.

Bloom, A. A. 1980. "Social Work and the English Language." *Social Casework,* 61:332–38.

Boehm, Werner. 1959. *Objectives of the Social Work Curriculum of the Future.* New York: Council on Social Work Education.

Boomer, D. C. 1963. "Speech Disturbances and Body Movement in Interviews." *Journal of Nervous and Mental Disease,* 136:263–66.

Borenzweig, Herman. 1981. "The Self-Disclosure of Clinical Social Workers." *Journal of Sociology and Social Welfare* (July), 7:432–58.

Bradburn, Norman and Seymoure Sudman. 1979. *Improving Interview Methods and Questionnaire Design.* San Francisco: Jossey-Bass.

Bradmiller, Linda. 1978. "Self-Disclosure in the Helping Relationship." *Social Work Research and Abstracts* (Summer), 14:28–35.

Braginsky, B. M. and D. D. Braginsky. 1967. "Schizophrenic Patients in the Psychiatric Interview: An Experimental Study of Their Effectiveness at Manipulation." *Journal of Consulting Psychology,* 31:543–47.

Brieland, Donald. 1969. "Black Identity and the Helping Person." *Children,* 16:170–76.

Brown, Luna B. 1950. "Race as a Factor in Establishing a Casework Relationship." *Social Casework,* 31:91–97.

Bruneau, Thomas J. 1973. "Communicative Silences: Forms and Functions." *Journal of Communication* (March), 23:17–46.

Bundza, Kenneth and N. R. Simonson. 1973. "Therapist Self-Disclosure: Its Effect on Impressions of Therapist and Willingness to Disclose." *Psychotherapy: Theory, Research, and Practice* (Fall), 10:215–17.

Burns, Crawford E. 1971. "White Staff, Black Children: Is There a Problem?" *Child Welfare,* 50:90–96.

Burrill, George C. 1976. "The Problem-Oriented Log in Social Casework." *Social Work* (January), 21:67–68.

Cade, Brian. 1975. "Therapy with Low Socio-Economic Families." *Social Work Today* (May 29), 6(5):142–45.

Calnek, Maynard. 1970. "Racial Factors in the Counter-Transference: The Black Therapist and the Black Client." *American Journal of Orthopsychiatry,* 40:39–46.

Cannell, Charles F., Floyd J. Fowler, and Kent H. Marquis. 1968. *The Influence of Interviewer and Respondent: Psychological and Behavioral Variables on the Reporting in Household Interviews.* Public Health Service Publication, series 2, no. 26. Washington, D.C.: GPO.

Cantril, H. 1956. "Perception and Interpersonal Relations." *American Journal of Psychiatry,* 114:119–26.

Carkhuff, Robert R. 1969. *Helping and Human Relations Practice and Research,* vols. 1 and 2. New York: Holt, Rinehart, and Winston.

Carkhuff, Robert R. and Charles Truax. 1967. *Toward Effective Counseling and Psychotherapy: Training and Practice.* Chicago: Aldine-Atherton.

Chelune, Gordon J. and Associates. 1979. *Self-Disclosure: Origins, Patterns, and Implications of Openness in Interpersonal Relationships.* San Francisco: Jossey-Bass.

Clemes, S. R. 1965. "Patients' Anxiety as a Function of Expectation and Degree of Initial Interview Anxiety." *Journal of Consulting Psychology,* 29:397–401.

Cohen, Pauline and Merton S. Krause. 1971. *Casework with Wives of Alcoholics.* New York: Family Service Association of America.

Converse, Jean M. and Howard Schuman. 1974. *Conversations at Random: Survey Research as Interviewers See It.* New York: Wiley.

Cormican, John D. 1978. "Linguistic Issues in Interviewing." *Social Casework* (March), 59:145–51.

Cormier, William H. and L. Sherilyn Cormier. 1979. *Interview Strategies for Helpers: A Guide to Assessment, Treatment, and Evaluation.* Monterey, Calif.: Brooks/Cole.

Cox, A., D. Holbrook, and M. Rutter. 1981. Psychiatric Interview Techniques. VI. "Experimental Study: Eliciting Feelings." *British Journal of Psychiatry,* 139:144–52.

Dailey, Dennis M. 1980. "Are Social Workers Sexist? A Replication." *Social Work* (January), 26:46–50.

Danish, Steven J. and Allen L. Hauer. 1973. *Helping Skills: A Basic Training Program.* New York: Behavioral Publications.

Davenport, Judith and Nancy Reims. 1978. "Theoretical Orientation and Attitudes Toward Women." *Social Work* (July), 23:306–9.

Davis, Inger P. 1975. "Advice-Giving in Parent Counseling." *Social Casework* (June), 56:343–47.

Davis, John D. 1971. *The Interview as Arena: Strategies in Standardized Interviews and Psychotherapy.* Stanford, Calif.: Stanford University Press.

Davis, Martha. 1972. *Understanding Body Movement: An Annotated Bibliography.* New York: Arno Press.

Dewane, Claudia. 1978. "Humor in Therapy." *Social Work* (November), 23(6):508–10.

Dexter, Lewis A. 1970. *Elite and Specialized Interviewing.* Evanston, Ill.: Northwestern University Press.

Dibner, Andrew. 1956. "Cue Counting: A Measure of Anxiety in Interviews." *Journal of Consulting Psychology,* 20:475–78.

Dilley, J., J. L. Lee, and E. L. Verill. 1971. "Is Empathy Ear-to-Ear or Face-to-Face?" *Personnel and Guidance Journal,* 50:188–91.

Dillon, Carolyn. 1969. "The Professional Name Game." *Social Casework* (June), 50:337–40.

Dohrenwend, Barbara S. 1965. "Some Effects of Open and Closed Questions." *Human Organization,* 24:175–84.

Dohrenwend, Barbara S. 1970. "An Experimental Study of Directive Interviewing." *Public Opinion Quarterly,* 34:117–25.

Dohrenwend, Barbara S., J. Colombotos, and B. P. Dohrenwend. 1968. "Social Distance and Interviewer Effects." *Public Opinion Quarterly,* 32:410–22.

Dohrenwend, Barbara S. and Stephen A. Richardson. 1963. "Directiveness in Research Interviewing: A Reformulation of the Problem." *Psychological Bulletin*, 60:475–85.

Dohrenwend, Barbara S., J. A. Williams, and C. H. Weiss. 1969. "Interviewer Biasing Effects: Toward a Reconciliation of Findings." *Public Opinion Quarterly*, 33:121–29.

Dubey, Sumati. 1970. "Blacks' Preference for Black Professionals, Businessmen, and Religious Leaders." *Public Opinion Quarterly*, 34:113–16.

Egan, Gerard. 1975. *The Skilled Helper: A Model for Systematic Helping and Interpersonal Relating*. Monterey, Calif.: Brooks/Cole.

Ekman, Paul and Wallace V. Friesen. 1968. "Nonverbal Behavior in Psychotherapy Research." In John M. Shlien, ed., *Research in Psychotherapy: Proceedings of the Third Conference*. Washington, D.C.: Psychological Association.

Erickson, Frederick and Jeffery Schultz. 1982. *The Counselor as Gatekeeper: Social Interaction in Interviews*. New York: Academic Press.

Ewalt, Patricia and Janice Kutz. 1976. "An Examination of Advice Giving as a Therapeutic Intervention." *Smith College Studies in Social Work* (November), 47:3–19.

Fabrikant, Benjamin. 1978. "The Psychotherapist and the Female Patient: Perceptions, Misperceptions, and Change." In Violet Franks and Vasanti Burtle, eds., *Women in Therapy*. New York: Brunner-Mazel.

Fanshel, David and William Labov. 1977. *Therapeutic Discourse: Psychotherapy as Conversation*. New York: Academic Press.

Fischer, Joel. 1975. "Training for Effective Therapeutic Practice." *Psychotherapy: Theory, Research, and Practice* (Spring), 12(1):118–23.

Fischer, Joel. 1978. *Effective Casework Practice: An Eclectic Approach*. New York: McGraw Hill.

Fischer, J. and H. Miller. 1973. "The Effect of Client Race and Social Class on Clinical Judgement." *Clinical Social Work*, 1:100–109.

Fischer, Joel et al. 1976. "Are Social Worker Sexists?" *Social Work* (November), 21:428–33.

Fischer, Seymour. 1973. *Body Consciousness*. Englewood, N.J.: Prentice-Hall.

Foran, Robert and Royston Bailey. 1968. *Authority in Social Casework*. London: Pergamon Press.

Fortune, Anne E. 1979. "Communication in Task-Centered Treatment." *Social Work* (September), 24:390–96.

Fortune, Anne E. 1981. "Communication Processes in Social Work Practice." *Social Services Review* (March), 55:93–128.

Frank, Arlene, Sherman Eisenthal, and Aaron Lazare. 1978. "Are There Social Class Differences in Patients' Treatment Conceptions?" *Archives of General Psychiatry* (January), 35:61–69.

Freed, Anne O. 1978. "Client's Rights and Casework Records." *Social Casework* (October), 59:458–63.

Freud, Sigmund. 1958. "On the Beginnings of Treatment." In *Complete Works*, vol. 12, J. Strachy, ed. London: Hogarth Press.

Galper, Jeffrey. 1970. "Nonverbal Communication Exercises in Groups." *Social Work*, 15:71–78.

Germain, Carel B. 1976. "Time, an Ecological Variable in Social Work Practice." *Social Casework* (July), 57:419–26.

Gill, Merton, Richard Newman, and Frederick Redlich. 1954. *The Initial Interview in Psychiatric Practice*. New York: International Universities Press.

Gingerich, Wallace and Stuart Kirk. 1981. "Sex Bias in Assessment: A Case of Premature Exaggeration." *Social Work Research and Abstracts*, 17:38–43.

Ginott, Haim G. 1961. *Group Psychotherapy with Children: The Theory and Practice of Play Therapy*. New York: McGraw-Hill.

Gitterman, Alex and Alice Schaeffer. 1972. "The White Professional and the Black Client." *Social Casework* (May), 53:280–91.

Gladstein, Gerald. 1977. "Empathy and Counseling Outcome: An Empirical and Conceptual Review." *The Counseling Psychologist*, 6(4):70–78.

Golan, Naomi. 1969. "How Caseworkers Decide: A Study of the Association of Selected Applicant Factors with Workers' Decisions in Admission Services." *Social Service Review*, 43:286–96.

Goldberg, Gertrude. 1969. "Non-Professionals in Human Services." In Charles Grosser, William Henry, and James Kelly, eds., *Non-Professionals in the Human Services*. San Francisco: Jossey-Bass.

Goldenberg, G. M. and Frank Auld. 1964. "Equivalence of Silence to Resistance." *Journal of Consulting Psychology*, 28:476–79.

Goldman-Eisler, Frieda. 1952. "Individual Differences Between Interviewers and Their Effect on Interviewees' Conversational Behavior." *Journal of Mental Science*, 98:660–71.

Goldman-Eisler, Frieda. 1954. "A Study of Individual Differences and of Interaction in the Behavior of Some Aspect of Language in Interviews." *Journal of Mental Science*, 100:177–97.

Gould, Carolyn. 1969. *Where Do We Go from Here: A Study of the Roads and Roadblocks to Career Mobility for Paraprofessionals Working in Human Service Agencies*. New York: National Committee on Employment of Youth.

Grater, Harry A. 1964. "Client Preferences for Affective or Cognitive Counselor Characteristics and First Interview Behavior." *Journal of Counseling Psychology*, 11:248–50.

Greene, M. 1976. "Ring-A-Day: A Telephone Reassurance Service." *Health and Social Work*, 1:177–81.

Grinnel, Richard and Nancy S. Kyle. 1975. "Environmental Modification." *Social Work* (July), 20:313–16.

Grosser, Charles. 1969. "Manpower Development Programs." In Charles Grosser, William Henry, and James Kelly, eds., *Non-Professionals in the Human Services*. San Francisco: Jossey-Bass.

Grumet, Gerald W. 1979. "Telephone Therapy: A Review and Case Report." *American Journal of Orthopsychiatry* (October), 49:574–84.

Gurman, Alan S. 1977. "The Patient's Perception of the Therapeutic Relationship." In A. S. Gurman and A. M. Razin, eds., *Effective Psychotherapy: A Handbook of Research*. New York: Pergamon.

Haase, Richard F. and Dominic J. DiMattia. 1970. "Proxemic Behavior: Counselor, Administrator, and Client Preference for Seating Arrangement in Dyadic Interaction." *Journal of Counseling Psychology*, 17:319–25.

Hackney, Harold L., Allen E. Ivey, and Eugene R. Oetting. 1970. "Attending Island and Hiatus Behavior: A Process Conception of Counselor and Client Interaction." *Journal of Counseling Psychology*, 17:342–436.

Hahn, Irving. *The Case of Ricky*. American Academy of Psychotherapists Tape Library, vol. 19. Camden, N.J.: American Academy of Psychotherapists, n.d.

Hall, Anthony. 1974. *The Point of Entry: A Study of Client Reception in the Social Services*. London: Allen & Unwin.

Halmos, Paul. 1966. *The Faith of the Counselors*. New York: Schocken Books.

Hamilton, Gordon. 1946. *Principles of Social Case Recording*. New York: Columbia University Press.

Hammond, D. Corydon, Dean H. Hepworth, and Jean G. Smith. 1977. *Improving Therapeutic Communication*. San Francisco: Jossey-Bass.

Hardman, Dale G. 1975. "Not With My Daughter, You Don't!" *Social Work* (July), 20:278–85.

Hart, John. 1979. *Social Work and Sexual Conduct*. London: Rutledge & Kegan Paul.

Hartman, Barbara L. and Jane M. Wickey. 1978. "The Person-Oriented Record in Treatment." *Social Work* (July), 23:296–99.

Hein, Eleanor, C. 1973. *Communication in Nursing Practice*. Boston: Little Brown.

Heine, R. W. 1950. "The Negro Patient in Psychotherapy." *Journal of Clinical Psychology*, 6:373–76.

Henry, Charlotte S. 1958. "Motivation in Non-Voluntary Clients." *Social Casework*, 39:130–36.

Highlen, Pamela and Bettina Russell. 1980. "Effects of Counselor Gender and Counselor and Client Sex Roles on Females' Counselor Preference." *Journal of Counseling Psychology*, 27:157–65.

Hogan, Robert. 1975. "Empathy: A Conceptual and Psychometric Analysis." *The Counseling Psychologist*, 5:14–17.

Hollingshead, A. and F. Redlich. 1956. *Social Class and Mental Illness*. New York: Wiley.

Hollis, Florence. 1967. "Explorations in the Development of a Typology of Casework Treatment." *Social Casework* (June), 48:338–49.

Hopkinson, K., A. Cox, and M. Rutter. 1981. Psychiatric Interviewing Technique. III. "Naturalistic Study: Eliciting Feelings." *British Journal of Psychiatry* (May), 138:406–15.

Houghkirk, Ellen. 1977. "Everything You Have Always Wanted Your Clients to Know but Have Been Afraid to Tell Them." *Journal of Marriage and Family Counseling* (April), 3:27–33.

Hyman, Herbert H. 1954. *Interviewing in Social Research*. Chicago: University of Chicago Press.

Isaac, Jean R. 1965. *Adopting a Child Today*. New York: Harper & Row.

Ivey, Allen E. and Jerry Authier. 1978. *Microcounseling: Innovations in Interviewing, Counseling Psychotherapy, and Psychoeducation*. 2d ed. Springfield, Ill.: C. C. Thomas.

Jacobs, Jerry. 1969. "Symbolic Bureaucracy: A Case Study of a Social Welfare Agency." *Social Forces,* 47:413–22.

Jayaratne, Srinika and Karen V. Irey. 1981. "Gender Difference in the Perception of Social Workers." *Social Casework* (September), 62:405–12.

Jenkins, Shirley and Barbara Morrison. 1978. "Ethnicity and Service Delivery." *American Journal of Orthopsychiatry* (January), 48:160–65.

Jenkins, Shirley and Elaine Norman. 1975. *Beyond Placement: Mothers' View of Foster Care.* New York: Columbia University Press.

Johnston, Norman. 1956. "Sources of Distortion and Deception in Prison Interviewing." *Federal Probation,* 20:43–48.

Jourard, Sidney M. 1966. "An Exploratory Study of Body Accessibility." *British Journal of Social and Clinical Psychology,* 5:221–31.

Jourard, Sidney M. and Peggy E. Jaffe. 1970. "Influence of an Interviewer's Disclosure on the Self-Disclosing Behavior of Interviewees." *Journal of Counseling Psychology,* 17:252–57.

Kagan, Norman and David R. Krathwohl. 1967. *Studies in Human Interaction: Interpersonal Process Recall Stimulated by Videotape.* East Lansing, Michigan State University.

Kahn, Alfred J. et al. 1966. *Neighborhood Information Centers: A Study and Some Proposals.* New York: Columbia University School of Social Work.

Kassell, Suzanne D. and Rosalie A. Kane. 1986. "Self-Determination Dissected." *Clinical Social Work,* 8:161–78.

Katz, David. 1979. "Laboratory Training to Enhance Interviewing Skills." In Frank W. Clark, Morton L. Arkava and Associates, *The Pursuit of Competence in Social Work.* San Francisco: Jossey-Bass.

Kiesler, D. G. 1969. "A Scale for Rating Congruence." In Carl R. Rogers et al., eds., *The Therapeutic Relationship and Its Impact.* Madison: University of Wisconsin Press.

Kincaid, Marylou. 1969. "Identity and Therapy in the Black Community." *Personnel and Guidance Journal,* 47:884–90.

Kinnon, R. and R. Michels. 1970. "The Role of the Telephone in the Psychiatric Interview." *Psychiatry,* 33:82–93.

Kinsey, Alfred, Wardell Pomeroy, and Clyde Martin. 1948. *Sexual Behavior in the Human Male.* Philadelphia: Saunders.

Knapp, Mark. 1973. "The Rhetoric of Goodby: Verbal and Nonverbal Correlates of Human Leave Taking." *Speech Monographs* (August), 40:182–98.

Komarovsky, Mirra. 1967. *Blue Collar Marriage.* New York: Random House, Vintage Books.

Korsch, Barbara M., Ethel K. Gozzi, and Vida Frances. 1968. "Gaps in Doctor-Patient Communication." *Pediatrics,* 42:855–71.

Kramer, Ernest. 1963. "Judgment of Personal Characteristics and Emotions from Nonverbal Properties of Speech." *Psychological Bulletin,* 60:408–20.

Kubie, Lawrence. 1971. "The Destructive Potential of Humor in Psychotherapy." *American Journal of Psychiatry,* 127:181–86.

Lambert, Michael and Steven S. DeJulio. 1977. "Outcome Research in Carkhuff's Human Resource Development Programs: Where Is the Donut?" *The Counseling Psychologist,* 6:79–86.

Lennard, Henry L. and Arnold Bernstein. 1960. *The Anatomy of Psychotherapy: Systems of Communication and Expectation.* New York: Columbia University Press.

Lerner, Barbara. 1972. *Therapy in the Ghetto.* Baltimore: Johns Hopkins University Press.

Lester, David and Gene W. Brockopp. 1973. *Crisis Intervention and Counseling by Telephone.* Springfield, Ill.: C. C. Thomas.

Levine, Jacob. 1977. "Humor as a Form of Therapy." In Anthony J. Chapman and Hugh C. Foot, eds., *It's a Funny Thing, Humor: International Conference on Humor and Laughter.* New York: Pergamon Press.

Lorian, Raymond P. 1978. "Research on Psychotherapy and Behavior Change with the Disadvantaged: Past, Present and Future Directions." In Sol Garfield and Alan Bergin, eds., *Handbook of Psychotherapy and Behavior Change.* New York: Wiley.

Luborsky, Lester, Barton Singer, and Lise Luborsky. 1975. "Comparative Studies of Psychotherapies: Is It True That Everybody Has Won and All Must Have Prizes?" In Robert L. Spitzer and Donald F. Klein, eds., *Evaluation of Psychological Therapies.* Baltimore: Johns Hopkins University Press.

Lurie, Alison. 1981. *The Language of Clothes.* New York: Random House.

Macarov, David. 1978. "Empathy: The Charismatic Chimera." *Journal of Education for Social Work* (Fall), 14:86–92.

McIsaac, Hugh and Harold Wilkinson. 1965. "Clients Talk About Their Caseworkers." *Public Welfare,* 23:147–54.

McKay, Ann, E. Matilda Goldberg, and David J. Fruin. 1973. "Consumers and a Social Services Department." *Social Work Today* (November), 4(16):486–91.

McMahon, Arthur W. and Miles F. Shore. 1968. "Some Psychological Reactions to Working with the Poor." *Archives of General Psychiatry,* 18:562–68.

Mahl, George F. 1968. "Gestures and Body Movements in Interviews." In John M. Shlien, ed., *Research in Psychotherapy: Proceedings of the Third Conference.* Washington, D.C.: American Psychological Association.

Mahl, George F. and S. V. Kasl. 1965. "The Relationship of Disturbances and Insitations in Spontaneous Speech to Anxiety." *Journal of Personality and Social Psychology,* 1:425–33.

Maluccio, Anthony N. 1979. *Learning from Clients: Interpersonal Helping As Viewed by Clients and Social Workers.* New York: Free Press.

Margolis, Marvin, Henry Krystal, and S. Siegel. 1964. "Psychotherapy with Alcoholic Offenders." *Quarterly Journal of Studies on Alcoholism,* 25:85–99.

Mattinson, Janet. 1975. *The Reflection Process in Casework Supervision.* London: Tavistock Institute of Human Relations.

Mattson, Ake. 1970. "The Male Therapist and the Female Adolescent Patient." *Journal of the American Academy of Child Psychiatry,* 9:707–21.

Mayadas, Nazeen S. and Donald E. O'Brien. 1976. "Teaching Casework Skills in the Laboratory: Methods and Techniques." In *Teaching for Competence in the Delivery of Direct Services.* New York: Council on Social Work Education.

Mayadas, Nazeen and W. D. Duehn. 1977. "The Effects of Training Formats and Interpersonal Discrimination in the Education for Clinical Social Work Practice." *Journal of Social Service Research,* 1:147–61.

Mayer, John E. and Noel Timms. 1969. "Clash in Perspective Between Worker and Client." *Social Casework*, 50:32–40.

Mayer, John E. and Noel Timms. 1970. *The Client Speaks: Working-Class Impressions of Casework*. London: Routledge & Kegan Paul.

Mayfield, E. C. 1964. "The Selection Interview: A Reevaluation of Published Research." *Personnel Psychology*, 17:239–60.

Mehrabian, Albert. 1968. "Communication Without Words." *Psychology Today*, 2(4):52–55.

Meitz, Mary J. 1980. "Humor, Hierarchy, and the Changing Status of Women." *Psychiatry* (August), 43:211–23.

Merton, Robert K., Marjorie Fiske, and Patricia Kendall. 1956. *The Focused Interview*. Glencoe, Ill.: Free Press.

Meyers, Jerome K. and Bertram H. Roberts. 1959. *Family and Class Dynamics in Mental Illness*. New York: Wiley.

Miles, Arthur. 1965. "The Utility of Case Recording in Probation and Parole." *Journal of Criminal Law, Criminology, and Police Science*, 56:285–93.

Miller, Roger. 1970. "Student Research Perspectives on Race." *Smith College Studies in Social Work*, 41:1–23.

Miller, Warren. 1973. "The Telephone in Outpatient Psychotherapy." *American Journal of Psychotherapy* (January), 27:15–26.

Mintz, N. L. 1956. "Effects of Esthetic Surroundings: Prolonged and Repeated Experience in a Beautiful and Ugly Room." *Journal of Psychology*, 41:459–66.

Mitchell, Kevin M., Jerold D. Bozarth, and Conrad C. Krauft. 1977. "A Reappraisal of the Therapeutic Effectiveness of Accurate Empathy, Non-Possessive Warmth, and Genuineness." In A. S. Gurman and A. M. Razin, eds., *Effective Psychotherapy: A Handbook of Research*. New York: Pergamon Press.

Morris, Richard J. and Kenneth R. Suckerman. 1974. "The Importance of the Therapeutic Relationship in Systematic Desensitization." *Journal of Consulting and Clinical Psychology*, 42:148–152.

Mullen, Edward S. 1969. "Differences in Worker Style in Casework." *Social Casework*, 50:347–53.

Murphy, K. C. and S. R. Strong. 1972. "Some Effects of Similarity Self-Disclosure." *Journal of Counseling Psychology*, 19:121–24.

National Association of Social Workers. 1967. "Model Statute Social Workers' Licensing Act." *N.A.S.W. News*.

Nelsen, Judith. 1975. "Dealing with Resistance in Social Work Practice." *Social Casework* (December), 56:587–92.

Nelson, Judith C. 1980. "Support a Necessary Condition for Change." *Social Work* (September), 25:388–92.

Oldfield, R. C. 1951. *The Psychology of the Interview*. London: Methuen.

Orfanidis, Monica. 1972. "Children's Use of Humor in Psychotherapy." *Social Casework*, 53:147–55.

Orlinsky, David E. and Kenneth I. Howard. 1967. "The Good Therapy Hour: Experimental Correlates of Patients' and Therapists' Evaluation of Therapy Session." *Archives of General Psychology*, 16:621–32.

Orlinsky, David E. and Kenneth I. Howard. 1978. "The Relation of Process to Outcome in Psychotherapy." In Sol L. Garfield and Allen E. Bergen, eds.,

Handbook of Psychotherapy and Behavior Change: An Empirical Analysis. New York: Wiley.

Ornston, Patricia S., Domenic Cicchetti, and Alan P. Towbin. 1970. "Reliable Changes in Psychotherapy Behavior Among First-Year Psychiatric Residents." *Journal of Abnormal Psychology*, 75:7–11.

Overton, Alice. 1959. *Clients' Observations of Social Work*. Mimeo. St. Paul, Minnesota, Greater St. Paul Community Chest and Councils, Inc., Family Centered Project.

Overton, Alice and Katherine Tinker. 1959. *Casework Notebook*. Mimeo. St. Paul, Minnesota, Greater St. Paul Community Chest and Councils, Inc., Family Centered Project.

Parloff, Morris, Irene E. Weskow, and Barney E. Wolte. 1978. "Research on Therapist Variables in Relation to Process and Outcome." In Sol L. Garfield and Allen E. Bergen, eds., *Handbook of Psychotherapy and Behavior Change: An Empirical Analysis*. New York: Wiley.

Pattison, J. F. 1973. "Effects of Touch on Self-Exploration and the Therapeutic Relationship." *Journal of Consulting and Clinical Psychology*, 40:170–75.

Pei, M. 1965. *The Story of Language*. New York: Lippincott.

Perlman, Helen H. 1979. *Relationship: The Art of Helping People*. Chicago: University of Chicago Press.

Pfeiffer, William S. and John E. Jones. "Openness, Collusion, and Feedback." In *1972 Handbook for Group Facilitators*, pp. 197–201. San Diego: University Associates, 1972.

Pfouts, Jane H. and Gordon E. Rader. 1962. "The Influence of Interviewer Characteristics on the Initial Interview." *Social Casework*, 43:548–52.

Pilsecker, Carleton. 1978. "Values: A Problem for Every One." *Social Work* (January), 23:54–57.

Pincus, Allen. 1970. "Reminiscence in Aging and Its Implications for Social Work Practice." *Social Work*, 15:47–53.

Pittinger, R. E., C. F. Hockett, and J. S. Daneby. 1960. *The First Five Minutes: An Example of Miscroscopic Interview Analysis*. Ithaca, N.Y.: Martineau.

Pohlman, Edward and Francis Robinson. 1960. "Client Reaction to Some Aspects of the Counseling Situation." *Personnel and Guidance Journal*, 38:546–51.

Polansky, Norman and Richard C. Tessler. 1975. "Perceived Similarity: A Paradox in Interviewing." *Social Work* (September), 20:359–63.

Rees, Stuart. 1978. *Social Work Face to Face*. London: Edward Arnold.

Reid, A. A. 1981. "Comparing Telephone with Face-to-Face Contact." In Ithiel de Sola Pool, ed., *The Social Impact of the Telephone*, pp. 386–414. Cambridge: MIT Press.

Reid, William S. 1978. *The Task-Centered System*. New York: Columbia University Press.

Reid, William S. and Barbara Shapiro. 1969. "Client Reaction to Advice." *Social Service Review*, 43:165–73.

Reid, William S. and Ann Shyne. 1969. *Brief and Extended Casework*. New York: Columbia University Press.

Rhodes, Sonya L. 1978. "Communication and Interaction in the Worker-Client Dyad." *Social Service Review* (March), 52:112–31.

Rich, John. 1968. *Interviewing Children and Adolescents*. London: Macmillan.

Riessman, Frank. 1969. "Strategies and Suggestions for Training Non-Professionals." In Bernard Guerney, ed., *Psychotherapeutic Agents: New Roles for Nonprofessionals, Parents and Teachers*. New York: Holt, Rinehart, and Winston.

Rogers, T. F. 1976. "Interview by Telephone and In Person: Quality of Responses and Field Performance." *Public Opinion Quarterly* (Spring), 39:51–65.

Rogow, Arnold A. 1970. *The Psychiatrists*. New York: Putnam.

Rose, Sheldon D., Jay J. Cayner, and Jeffrey L. Edleson. 1977. "Measuring Interpersonal Competence." *Social Work* (March), 22:125–29.

Rosen, Aaron and Elizabeth Mutschler. 1982. "Correspondence Between the Planned and Subsequent Use of Interventions in Treatment." *Social Work Research and Abstracts*, 18:28–34.

Rosenthal, Robert. 1966. *Experimenter Effects in Behavioral Research*. New York: Appleton-Century-Crofts.

Ruesch, Jurgen and Weldon Kees. 1956. *Nonverbal Communication: Notes on the Visual Perception of Human Relations*. Berkeley: University of California Press.

Rutter, M. et al. 1981. Psychiatric Interview Techniques. IV. "Experimental Study: Four Contrasting Styles." *British Journal of Psychiatry*, 138:456–65.

Ryan, Mary S. 1966. *Clothing: A Study in Human Behavior*. New York: Holt, Rinehart, and Winston.

Sager, Clifford J., Thomas L. Brayboy, and Barbara R. Waxenberg. 1970. *Black Ghetto Family in Therapy: A Laboratory Experience*. New York: Grove Press.

Sainsbury, Eric. 1975. *Social Work with Families*. London: Routledge & Kegan Paul.

Sainsbury, P. 1955. "Gestural Movement During Psychiatric Interviews." *Psychosomatic Medicine*, 17:458–69.

Sattler, Jerome. 1977. "The Effects of Therapist-Client Racial Similarity." In Allens Gurman and Andrew M. Razin, eds., *Effective Psychotherapy: A Handbook of Research*. New York: Pergamon Press.

Schatzman, Leonard and Anselm Strauss. 1955. "Social Class and Mode of Communication." *American Journal of Sociology*, 60:329–38.

Scheflen, Albert F. 1964. "The Significance of Posture in Communication Systems." *Psychiatry*, 27:316–31.

Schmidt, Julianna. 1969. "The Use of Purpose in Casework Practice." *Social Work*, 14:77–84.

Schmidt, L. D. and S. R. Strong. 1970. "Expert and Inexpert Counselors." *Journal of Counseling Psychology*, 17:115–25.

Schulman, Eveline D. 1974. *Intervention in Human Services*. St. Louis: C. V. Mosby.

Schutz, William C. 1967. *Joy*. New York: Grove Press.

Schwartz, Arthur and Israel Goldiamond. 1975. *Social Casework: A Behavioral Approach*. New York: Columbia University Press.

Seaburg, Brett. 1980. "Communication Problems in Social Work Practice." *Social Work* (January), 25:40–45.

Shepard, Martin and Margerie Lee. 1970. *Games Analysts Play*. New York: Putman.

Sherman, Edmund, Michael Phillips, Barbara Haring, and Ann W. Shyne. 1973.

Services to Children in Their Own Home: Its Nature and Outcome. New York: Child Welfare League of America.

Shiffer, Clara. 1976. "Teens want Confidentiality." *Family Planning Perspectives,* 8(6):276–78.

Shinke, Steven P., Thomas Smith, Lewayne Gilchrist, and Stephan Wong. 1978. "Interviewing-Skills Training: An Empirical Evaluation." *Journal of Social Service Research* (Summer), 1:391–401.

Shinke, Steven P. et al. 1980. "Developing Intake-Interviewing Skills." *Social Work Research and Abstracts,* 16:29–34.

Shulman, Lawrence. 1977. *A Study of the Helping Process.* Vancouver: University of British Columbia.

Shulman, Rena. 1954. "Treatment of the Disturbed Child in Placement." *Jewish Social Service Quarterly,* 30:315–22.

Shyne, Ann W. 1954. "The Telephone Interview in Casework." *Journal of Social Casework,* 35:342–47.

Silverman, Phyllis R. 1970. "A Re-Examination of the Intake Procedure." *Social Casework,* 51:625–34.

Simon, R. et al. 1974. "Two Methods of Psychiatric Interviewing: Telephone and Face to Face." *Journal of Psychology,* 88:141–46.

Sloan, R. Bruce et al. 1975. *Psychotherapy Versus Behavior Therapy.* Cambridge, Mass.: Harvard University Press.

Sobey, Francine. 1970. *The Nonprofessional Revolution in Mental Health.* New York: Columbia University Press.

Starkweather, J. A. 1961. "Vocal Communication of Personality and Human Feelings." *Journal of Communication,* 11:63–72.

Stone, George C. 1979. "Patient Compliance and the Role of the Expert." *Journal of Social Issues,* 35:34–59.

Street, David, George Martin, and Laura K. Gordon. 1979. *The Welfare Industry: Functionaries and Recipients in Public Aid.* Beverly Hills, Calif.: Sage Publications.

Stricker, George. 1977. "Implications of Research for Psychotherapeutic Treatment of Women." *American Psychologist* (January), 32:14–22.

Strupp, Hans H., Ronald Fox, and Ken Lessler. 1969. *Patients View Their Psychotherapy.* Baltimore: Johns Hopkins University Press.

Sturges, J. C. 1975. "Ability of Social Work Students to Identify and Formulate Helpful Referral Statements." *Journal of Social Welfare,* 2:27–39.

Sullivan, Harry Stack. 1954. *The Psychiatric Interview.* New York: Norton.

Svarstad, Bonnie L. and Helene L. Lipton. 1977. "Informing Parents About Mental Retardation: A Study of Professional Communication and Parent Acceptance." *Social Science and Medicine,* 11:645–51.

Taylor, James B., Phyllis Levy, and Ronald Filippi. 1965. "Psychological Problems in Low-Income Families: A Research Project." *Bulletin of the Menninger Clinic,* 29:312–39.

Toseland, Ron and Gil Spielberg (1982). "The Development of Helping Skills in Undergraduate Social Work Education." *Journal of Education for Social Work* (Winter), 18:66–73.

U.N. 1963. United Nations Department of Economic and Social Affairs. *1963 Report on the World Social Situation*. New York: United Nations.
U.S. Department of Health, Education, and Welfare. Office of the Undersecretary. 1965. *Closing the Gap in Social Work Manpower*. Washington, D.C.: GPO.
Van der Veen, Ferdinand. 1965. "Effects of the Therapist and Patient on Each Other's Therapeutic Behavior." *Journal of Consulting Psychology*, 29:19–26.
Volsky, T. et al. 1965. *The Outcomes of Counseling and Psychotherapy*. Minneapolis: University of Minnesota Press.
Vontross, Clemmont. 1970. "Counseling Blacks." *Personnel and Guidance Journal*, 48:713–19.
Waite, Richard R. 1968. "The Negro Patient and Clinical Therapy." *Journal of Consulting and Clinical Psychology*, 32:427–33.
Walden, Theodore, Greta Singer, and Winifred Thomat. 1974. "Students as Clients: The Other Side of the Desk." *Clinical Social Work Journal* (Winter), 2:279–96.
Wasserman, Harry. 1970. "Early Careers of Professional Social Workers in a Public Child Welfare Agency." *Social Work*, 15:93–101.
Webb, Allen P. and Patrick V. Riley. 1970. "Effectiveness of Casework with Young Female Probationers." *Social Casework*, 51:566–72.
Weiner, Morton and Albert Mehrabian. 1968. *Language Within Language: Immediacy, A Channel in Verbal Communication*. New York: Appleton-Century-Crofts.
Weiner, Myron F. 1978. *Therapist Disclosure: The Use of Self in Psychotherapy*. Boston: Butterworths.
Weiss, Carol H. 1968. *Validity of Interview Responses of Welfare Mothers: Final Report*. Bureau of Applied Social Research, Columbia University.
Weller, Leonard and Elmer Luchterhand. 1968. "Comparing Interviews and Observations on Family Functioning." *Journal of Marriage and the Family*, 31:115–22.
Whyte, William F. 1955. *Street Corner Society*. Rev. ed. Chicago: University of Chicago Press.
Wikler, Lynn. 1979. "Consumer Involvement in the Training of Social Work Students." *Social Casework* (March), 60:145–49.
Wile, Marcia et al. 1979. "Physician-Patient Communication: Interpretations of Non-Technical Phrases." Mimeo.
Wilkie, H. Charlotte. 1963. "A Study of Distortions in Recorded Interviews." *Social Work*, 8:32–36.
Williams, Frederick and Rita C. Naremore. 1969. "On the Functional Analysis of Social Class Differences in Modes of Speech." *Speech Monographs*, 36:78–102.
Wolberg, Lewis. 1954. *Techniques of Psychotherapy*. New York: Grune & Stratton.
Yarrow, Marian R., John D. Campbell, and Roger V. Burton. 1964. "Reliability of Maternal Retrospection: A Preliminary Report." *Family Process*, 13:207–18.
Zelan, Joseph. 1969. "Interviewing the Aged." *Public Opinion Quarterly*, 33:420–24.
Zeldow, Peter B. 1975. "Sex Differences, Evaluation, and Treatment: An Empirical Review." *Archives of General Psychiatry* (January), 35:89–93.
Zimmerman, Don. 1969. "Tasks and Troubles: The Practical Basis of Work Activi-

ties in a Public Assistance Organization." In Donald Hansen, ed., *Explorations in Sociology and Counseling*. Boston: Houghton Mifflin.

Zuckerman, Harriet. 1972. "Interviewing an Ultra-Elite." *Public Opinion Quarterly*, 36:159–75.

Zurcher, Louis. 1910. *Poverty Warriors*. Austin: University of Texas Press.

Index